A loss of innocence?

MANCHESTER
1824

Manchester University Press

For Robin, Molly, Nicholas and Shane

A loss of innocence?
Television and Irish society 1960–72

Robert J. Savage

Manchester University Press

Published by Manchester University Press
Altrincham Street, Manchester M1 7JA, UK
www.manchesteruniversitypress.co.uk

British Library Cataloguing-in-Publication Data is available

Library of Congress Cataloging-in-Publication Data is available

ISBN 978 1 7849 9112 8 *paperback*

First published by Manchester University Press in hardback 2010

This edition first published 2015

Printed by Lightning Source

Contents

List of figures

Acknowledgements

This book would not have been possible without the support of many friends and colleagues. The Boston College Irish Studies Program, founded over thirty years ago by Kevin O'Neill and the late Adele Dalsimer, has provided an ideal environment for teaching, research and writing and I am very fortunate to be part of a vibrant and supportive community of scholars. Thanks to colleagues Seamus Connolly, Mike Cronin, Tom Hachey, Ruth-Ann Harris, Marjorie Howes, Kevin Kenny, Vera Kreilkamp, Phil O'Leary, Kevin O'Neill, Joe Nugent, Jim Smith and Ann Spinney. I also wish to acknowledge the support of Deans David Quigley and Joseph Quinn of the College of Arts and Sciences and the Office of the University Provost.

The lion's share of the research for this project was completed while I was at the National University of Ireland, Galway as Irish American Cultural Institute-NUIG, Visiting Professor in Irish Studies. In Galway I was made a welcome member of the Centre for Irish Studies, directed by Louis de Paor. The centre proved a stimulating interdisciplinary environment and an ideal base from which to work. I appreciate all those at the centre who patiently listened to presentations and offered advice while this work was in a very primitive form and to Gearóid Ó Tuathaigh, Nicholas Canny, Mary Harris, Nollaig Mac Congáil, Donncha O'Connell and Tadhg Foley.

Much of the work on RTÉ was carried out in the RTÉ Written

Archives where Brian Lynch once again provided invaluable help. His relentless desire to answer challenges, remarkable ability to find material, and understated sense of humour were critical to the project. The long-time Secretary of the RTÉ Authority, Tom Quinn, helped me navigate the RTÉ Authority Archive and this greatly enhanced this study. The National Archives of Ireland, Public Record Office of Northern Ireland, National Library of Ireland, Diocesan Archives in Dublin, Galway and Cashel, the Representative Church Body Archive, and the archives of Trinity College, Dublin, University College Dublin and the University of Notre Dame were also important to the project. The BBC Written Archives in Caversham, the Public Record Office at Kew and the O'Neill Library at Boston College were also tremendously helpful and I am indebted to all the archivists and librarians at these institutions for their patience and professionalism.

I was able to complete most of the manuscript while a Leverhulme Fellow at the Institute for Advanced Studies, University of Edinburgh. Susan Manning enjoys a well-deserved reputation for directing a world-class humanities institute and being part of that community was an enriching experience. At the University of Edinburgh I found friendship and support from a diverse body of scholars at IASH and from other members of the university community. In the Department of History, Tom Devine, Alvin Jackson, Owen Dudley-Edwards and Enda Delaney were kind enough to listen to presentations of draft chapters and offer sound advice, while Christopher Ivic also proved an engaging colleague. The Leverhulme Trust made possible the extended stay in Scotland and supported lectures at a number of UK institutions including the University of London, Liverpool University, Warwick University and Hertford College, Oxford. Special thanks to Maria Luddy at Warwick and Ian McBride at the University of London for arranging seminars and lectures. I'd also like to acknowledge the generosity and support that Roy Foster, Marianne Elliott and Alvin Jackson provided for this project. All encouraged me to apply for the Leverhulme Professorship and the IASH Fellowship and the time spent in Edinburgh proved invaluable.

Many colleagues read draft chapters and offered constructive criticism. In Galway Gearóid Ó Tuathaigh and Louis de Paor were tremendously helpful. A former colleague at Boston College, now based at the University of Notre Dame, Brian Ó Conchubhair, deserves special mention for patiently reading parts of the manuscript as it evolved. At Boston College, Burns Scholar in Irish Studies, Tom Garvin of University College, Dublin, Joe Nugent, Philip O'Leary and Mike Cronin were also kind enough to read excerpts and offer advice as this work progressed. Special thanks to Morgan Adams, Kelly Sullivan and Ian Delahanty, graduate students in Irish Studies, who helped proofread the manuscript. Jim Leonard, a graduate of the programme proved a consummate professional in reading an earlier version of the project. Gary Murphy at Dublin City University was helpful in addressing the politics of the 1960s. Also in Ireland, Eunan O'Halpin and the Seminar for Contemporary History at Trinity College offered a supportive venue to present parts of this work. Thanks also to Perry Curtis, Professor Emeritus at Brown University, Joe Lee at New York University, Mary Daly at University College Dublin, Peter Dunn of the Radharc Trust, Peter Kelly of Esras Films, Sunniva O'Flynn at the Irish Film Institute, Margaret Kelleher at NUI, Maynooth, Thea Gillen at Boston College-Ireland, Bert Hogenkamp at the Netherlands Institute for Sound and Vision, Lance Pettitt at Leeds Metropolitan University and friends Vincent Doherty, Pearse Kearney, William B. Neenan SJ and Tony Blackwell. Special thanks to Press Ombudsman John Horgan.

My first monograph, published by Cork University Press in 1996, considered the political, economic and cultural debates that preceded the establishment of Telefís Éireann in 1960. While conducting research for that project I interviewed many people who were involved in broadcasting and all provided invaluable information for my earlier book and this one. Some of those have passed away, others have retired from broadcasting, the civil service or politics but all were very helpful when I was a graduate student many years ago. Those that helped in 1990 include John Irvine, Thomas Hardiman, Dónall Ó Móráin, Pádraig Ó Raghallaigh, Paul Warren, Meave Conway-Piskorsky, the Most Reverend Dr Henry Robert McAdoo, Áine Ní Chanainn, Cathleen Roth, Emir Ó Broin and Eilish MacCurtain Pearce. More recently Dr Garret FitzGerald, Ruairí Brugha, Seán Mac Réamoinn, Aindrias

Ó Gallchóir, Eoghan Harris, Owen Dudley Edwards, Janet Moody, Lelia Doolan, Bill O'Herlihy, Dermod McCarthy, Kevin B. Nowlan, Alan Whicker and Muiris MacConghail were kind enough to grant interviews.

Most importantly I would like to thank my wife Robin for her patience, love and support and Molly, Nicholas and Shane for enriching our lives and making life so meaningful.

Chestnut Hill

Introduction

Telefís Éireann made its debut on a cold, wintry New Year's Eve in 1961, helping to erode a sense of isolation that characterised Ireland in the post-war period. In doing so it opened wide an exciting yet often unsettling window on the world. This book considers how television helped to undermine the conservative consensus that dominated Ireland into the 1960s. It traces the evolution of the national television service during a critical period in contemporary Irish history by exploring its uneven development during a decade of unprecedented change. It also considers the development of television in Northern Ireland, addressing how its presence became a disconcerting feature in the life of the province.

By enabling Irish society to have direct access to news, information and popular culture and bypassing traditional intermediaries, including the Church and the local and national press, television helped quicken the pace of modernisation that began when Seán Lemass became Taoiseach. Coming to power in 1959, Lemass initiated a number of critical reforms that profoundly affected Ireland's moribund economy, thereby initiating a period of economic, political and cultural transformation that significantly changed Irish society. His economic schemes were, in an Irish context, a radical shift from previous government policies as they reduced tariffs, encouraged foreign investment and recognised the need for the government to take risks in order to realise economic growth. Conservative, even protectionist policies that had held sway were discarded and the country began a lengthy process of fully engaging with the global economy. The turnaround of the economy was uneven but, given the dire state of the economy in the post-war period, remarkable.

During the 1960s, Ireland became a more modern consumer society as the economy expanded, emigration slowed, and a modest prosperity developed. In this new environment suburbs grew, and cars, extended holidays, and new forms of entertainment such as rock and roll became features of Irish life. External reforms added to a genuine sense of progress that was palpable at the time. For example, the reforms initiated by Vatican II contributed to an easing of the authoritarian nature of Irish Catholicism despite the best efforts of Dublin's archbishop to deny that substantial reforms had been implemented. Ireland was not immune to the vibrant youth culture that embraced a questioning of authority resulting in widespread unrest in university campuses across Europe, America and much of the world. Opposition to the war in Vietnam and support for civil rights and equal rights for women resonated in Ireland among a generation of men and women determined to confront issues of social justice both at home and abroad.

Although the sexual revolution of the 1960s may have been slowed by the strength of the Irish Catholic Church, traditional attitudes towards sexual conduct were evolving. Later in the decade the publication of the papal encyclical, *Humanae Vitae*, reaffirming the Church's prohibition on birth control, proved a watershed in Catholic Ireland. For many it appeared the Vatican was returning to an authoritarian past where rigid rules were applied with absolute certainty. This stimulated public debate and helped provoke a major challenge to the Catholic Church from Irish women. It also helped to usher in a period of activism that witnessed the opening of the first family planning clinic in the capital in 1969, highly publicised protests and the founding of the Irish Women's Liberation Movement in 1970. Writing about this period the political historian Tom Garvin observes that these changes were 'foreseen with nervousness, anger and foreboding by some of the older generation of leaders and very obviously, by many traditionalists'.[1]

Throughout this period governments and institutions struggled to adapt to changing circumstances brought on by the arrival of indigenous television. Political, religious and cultural elites in the Irish Republic and Northern Ireland were especially upset with what they viewed as the medium's pronounced lack of deference. The first reaction of many politicians and senior civil servants to aggressive reporting by news and current affairs programmes was to try to control, discipline, or censor broadcasters, insisting that they serve the state rather than broadcast programmes critical of it. In the Irish Republic politicians came to realise that the Broadcasting Act of 1960 was a genuinely liberal document offering a considerable amount of protection to broadcasters. After a series of awkward interventions, the government found that it could act to silence the national broadcasting service only as a last resort and in the most extraordinary circumstances. Such silencing occurred in 1972 when the government of Jack Lynch summarily dismissed the Radio Telefís Éireann Authority for broadcasting material it considered seditious.

As the 1960s unfolded, governments in the Irish Republic, Northern Ireland and the United Kingdom increasingly considered television a threat to their interests and to the security of their respective states. This was especially true as political unrest in Northern Ireland extended into years of civil strife. These governments became increasingly ambivalent about the degree of freedom and independence television enjoyed, fearing its ability to undermine national security and state policy. When threatened they struck back by imposing draconian legislation that curtailed basic press freedoms, or by instituting elaborate systems of checks and balances that introduced a level of self-censorship into broadcasting.

The economic, social and cultural transformation Ireland experienced in the 1960s was a gradual one. Although great strides were made in improving the quality of life for many citizens, there were still serious social problems that plagued the country throughout the decade. Many less fortunate citizens continued to live in poverty and in sub-standard housing in both rural and urban areas, where employment and educational opportunities were lacking. Oftentimes stark comparisons are made between the stagnation that characterised 'de Valera's Ireland' and the more dynamic and modern Lemass era. However, care needs to be taken in making these comparisons, as the expansion of the Irish economy was gradual and in many respects uneven. In spite of profound changes taking place in the 1960s Irish society remained a conservative one where the Catholic Church continued to be a powerful force.

Indeed, Ireland's 'great moderniser' Seán Lemass shared many of the concerns of his mentor Eamon de Valera, including an innate social conservatism and an unyielding conviction that Fianna Fáil was the only party fit for government. Like de Valera, Lemass did not have much patience for the political opposition and because Fianna Fáil dominated the decade he and many of his colleagues regarded criticism by broadcasters as proof that those operating Irish television were political opponents intent on undermining government policy. Lemass in particular became a vociferous critic of Irish television, lashing out both publicly and privately at perceived slights from the station. As the decade unfolded, however, some of television's most determined critics learned it was counter-productive to react to programmes with outrage and harsh criticism. Over time, many politicians, church leaders and a number of cultural groups came to terms with the medium, learning how to use it proactively and innovatively for their own purposes.

Writing contemporary history can be risky business, and trying to cover a period of twelve years forces one to make difficult choices in addressing the many issues associated with television. Although I have a healthy respect for media studies, film studies, post-colonial studies and other theory-based disciplines, it is important to make it clear that I regard myself as a historian. This project is the product of research conducted in written archives, enhanced I hope, by oral history and a close review of secondary sources. In researching and writing this book I sense that much more work needs to be done. John Horgan, Lance Pettitt, the late Rex Cathcart and others have contributed much to our understanding of the role of television in Irish society. I hope this volume will encourage others to undertake research in a field of history that deserves greater attention and scholarly study. Areas within Irish media history that cry out for research include the role of women in shaping television as well as their representation on the screen. Education, drama, music, health, sport, labour relations, children's programming, audience and advertising also require more scholarly investigation. With more archival material coming into the public domain in Ireland, Northern Ireland and Great Britain, there is tremendous potential to address this void and to enhance our understanding of the recent past.

Notes

1 Tom Garvin, *Preventing the Future: Why was Ireland so Poor for so Long?* (Gill and Macmillan, Dublin, 2004), 203.

1

A compromise with commerce?
The origins of Irish television

Ireland in the 1950s witnessed seemingly endless debates about television and how a native service should be structured and introduced to the nation. Throughout the decade both Coalition and Fianna Fáil governments maintained that, given the costs involved, television simply was not a priority for the state. As early as 1950 the Department of Finance dismissed a request from the Department of Posts and Telegraphs for funding to initiate research into the establishment of an Irish television service as 'extraordinary' and 'ridiculous', arguing that television was a 'luxury service' that the state could not afford.[1] For Ireland the 1950s was a difficult decade that witnessed seemingly relentless emigration, high levels of unemployment and stubborn economic stagnation. In this depressing economic and social environment establishing a television service was simply not a priority for the ineffective governments that held power during the decade.

Despite such reluctance, many levels of society understood that television was inevitable and basic questions had to be confronted. Much of the discussion in the press and in government during this period revolved around the question of who would control Irish television and the programmes it would transmit. Therefore the issue of what structure or form television would take became increasingly critical. From the outset, looking to Britain and the United States, the government saw two models from which to choose. The first would be to set up a state-owned and financed public service modelled on the BBC. This was an attractive though costly option, popular among those who advocated using the medium to provide high-quality educational material that would explore the complexities of Irish history and literature, support the Irish language, and generally reinforce what many regarded as a frail Gaelic culture.

The alternative model would follow the example of the Independent Television Authority in the United Kingdom and the commercial networks in the United States by granting a licence to an entrepreneur as a commercial venture. This option would not require government financing as television would be owned and operated by investors interested in generating profits by selling airtime to advertisers. As a market-driven enterprise, it would seek the widest possible audience for its underwriters and therefore feature predominantly imported American and British programmes. As a popular commercial endeavour, television would be designed primarily to entertain its audience. For those who advocated using television to inform and educate viewers, this was the antithesis of public service broadcasting and was regarded as a threat to the integrity of Irish culture.

This notion of two diametrically opposed models should not be taken too far. Commercial television was also expected to feature serious material and not simply be a source of entertainment. In the United Kingdom the charter of the Independent Television Authority (ITA) required the regionally-based constituent companies to transmit material that would include a public service component. In the United States the Federal Communications Commission (FCC) required licensees to dedicate a portion of broadcasts to serve the public interest. During this period independent television companies in Britain and commercial networks in the United States developed remarkable documentaries and innovative current affairs programmes that were highly influential and remarkably popular. Throughout the 1950s and 1960s American networks such as CBS developed an international reputation for excellence in television news broadcasting, and some of the regional companies of the ITA such as Granada were known for developing innovative current affairs programmes. These commercial concerns also dedicated airtime for religious broadcasts to satisfy their public service obligations.

As the department responsible for broadcasting matters, the

Department of Posts and Telegraphs attracted many proposals and queries concerning television. During this period the secretary of the department León Ó Broin was well placed to influence government policy and keenly interested in trying to shape the structure and form of Irish television. Ó Broin was a highly cultured and deeply conservative man, a linguist who wrote history in his spare time, including *Parnell* (1937); *The Unfortunate Mr Emmet* (1958); *Dublin Castle and the Rising: The Story of Sir Matthew Nathan* (1966); *Charles Gavan Duffy, Patriot and Statesman* (1967); *The Chief Secretary, Augustine Birrell in Ireland* (1969); *Fenian Fever: The American Dilemma* (1971) and *Michael Collins* (1980). He also translated books from English into Irish for *An Gúm*, a state-funded Irish language publisher.

His contemporaries understood him as a committed Catholic who served as editor of *Maria Legionis*, the organ of Frank Duff's Legion of Mary, but also as a man interested in encouraging dialogue among religious, cultural and political groups. While a member of the Legion of Mary in the early 1940s, Ó Broin helped establish the short-lived Pillar of Fire Society, an organisation designed to bring Christians and Jews together to discuss religious and social issues. After two brief meetings the society was closed down on the orders of authoritarian John Charles McQuaid, Archbishop of Dublin. Ó Broin was also an active member of the Mercier Society, established to encourage dialogue between Catholics and Protestants, but it too was suppressed by a suspicious hierarchy. Ó Broin was a Catholic intellectual who empathised with outspoken critics of the government and the censorship regime it put in place, including Sean O'Faolain, Frank O'Connor and Peadar O'Donnell. He was able to bring these writers together with Frank Duff, who many considered to be partly responsible for promoting the oppressive environment of anti-intellectualism that alienated dissident writers. This interest led to the formation of Common Ground, yet another short-lived society intended to promote dialogue, which included O'Faolain, the poet Paddy Kavanagh, former minister Desmond FitzGerald and the founder of the Legion of Mary, Frank Duff.[2]

Ó Broin was also a formidable civil servant who began his career in the Cumann na nGaedheal Government working in the

1   Writer, historian and Secretary of the Department of Posts and Telegraphs León Ó Broin.

Department of Education in 1925 before moving on to Finance and finally settling at Posts and Telegraphs in 1940. Throughout his career he demonstrated a very strong interest in the media, especially television. Regarding the programmes broadcast by commercial television networks in Britain and America with deep suspicion, Ó Broin considered the BBC as the best model for Irish television to emulate. He fully embraced the Reithian philosophy of broadcasting, which maintained that both radio and television should inspire, educate, and 'uplift' the nation, not simply provide popular entertainment for the masses.[3] Throughout the 1950s and into the 1960s he consulted with the BBC on a regular basis, enjoying a strong professional relationship with Directors-General Sir Ian Jacob and Hugh Carlton-Green. These men were quiet, though important, allies of the secretary, and broadly sympathetic to his effort to see Irish television established as a public service.[4] In the late 1950s, Sir Ian Jacob was acting out of his own institutional self-interest in helping Ó Broin undermine commercial schemes submitted to the Irish government by American and continental entrepreneurs. Two of these applicants proposed establishing commercial radio stations in Ireland that would target British audiences with popular programmes, thereby challenging the hegemony of the BBC. It is not surprising that the BBC quietly intervened to help Ó Broin weaken and ultimately defeat these proposals.[5]

For much of the 1950s Ó Broin waged a protracted battle with the Department of Finance over how an indigenous service should be structured and financed. Given Ireland's dire economic situation it is not surprising that the department did not regard television as a priority. As early as 1950 Ó Broin found that Finance was not interested in offering any help to investigate options available to the state. That year a request from Posts and Telegraphs for £180 to purchase a television receiver and aerial for monitoring broadcasts from the United Kingdom was rejected. Finance dismissed the request, confidently maintaining that the Irish people simply had no interest in television. Finance understood that Ó Broin was looking to follow the public service model in the United Kingdom and was adamantly opposed to underwriting an Irish public television service.[6]

One reason that the issue remained in the public domain was due to television broadcasts making their way into Ireland from Britain and later from Northern Ireland. Signals from British transmitters could be picked up along Ireland's east coast in the 1950s as viewers erected aerials to capture British programmes. In 1953 the BBC built a temporary transmitter in Belfast, enabling citizens to witness the coronation of Queen Elizabeth II. The range of these broadcasts increased when the Divis Mountain transmitter became operational in 1955. This enabled approximately 80 per cent of the people of Northern Ireland and many people south of the border to view BBC programmes. A study conducted by engineers in the Department of Posts and Telegraphs in 1957 determined that broadcasts from Northern Ireland could be received by approximately 40 per cent of the population of the Irish Republic.[7] These broadcasts from Britain and Northern Ireland created discomfort for political, religious and cultural elites who grew increasingly concerned at the content of programmes, which they regarded as objectionable.[8] In 1958, when it was estimated that there were between 20,000 and 22,000 sets in the Irish Republic, the government established a Television Commission to consider how an indigenous television service should be established.[9] This commission heard evidence from a wide range of cultural and political organisations, and sorted through proposals from domestic and foreign companies interested in gaining an exclusive licence to operate a television station in Ireland. Many of the proposals were from foreign companies, some with subsidiaries in Ireland, though the Irish-language organisation Gael-Linn submitted one of the more comprehensive applications. The Gael-Linn application made it clear that it viewed television primarily as a didactic tool to revive the Irish language.

One of the American firms, the Texas-based McLendon Corporation, offered what amounted to a free television service for the country if it was granted permission to set up a high-power commercial radio service that could broadcast directly into Britain. Gordon McLendon, outfitted in cowboy boots and a ten-gallon hat, appeared before the commission to make the case that his company's proposal was an opportunity that was simply too good to be turned down.[10] His offer was similar to that of a Paris-based company owned and operated by Charles Michelson, a Romanian exile and another media entrepreneur interested in international broadcasting. Michelson spent weeks in Ireland meeting with politicians and businessmen, lining up support for his scheme. Initially his lobbying paid off, as his proposal received support from a number of semi-state companies and a good deal of interest from Taoiseach Seán Lemass. One of the most intriguing sources of support for his project came from the Vatican. Representatives of the Roman Catholic Church secretly visited Dublin and lobbied for the scheme, arguing that the proposal put forward by Michelson would enable Ireland to be at the forefront of the titanic struggle against communism, 'irreligion and materialism'.[11] Although the Vatican endorsed this proposal, the Irish Catholic Church, and especially the powerful archbishop of Dublin, John Charles McQuaid, was not impressed.[12]

Ó Broin testified before the Commission, fortified with technical and legal advice from colleagues at the BBC who were appalled at the notion of American commercial radio invading the airwaves of the United Kingdom. Underscoring the fact that the McLendon and Michelson proposals required Ireland to withdraw from an international treaty governing wavelength allocation, Ó Broin succeeded in convincing the Commission that these and other commercial proposals were not viable. Given the small size of the Irish population and the relative poverty of the country, Ó Broin understood that for financial reasons the public service model he cherished would not be accepted. He therefore reluctantly proposed an alternative, a state-owned service that combined the two seemingly incompatible models. This proposal was much more palatable to the Department of Finance, which in the end offered reluctant support.[13]

In 1959 the Lemass Government decided to create a state-owned, commercial public service that would be financed by both advertising revenue and licence fees and would be overseen by a public authority. Under Ó Broin's supervision, Posts and Telegraphs drafted a broadcasting bill with the assistance of senior civil servants in the British Post Office and staff and lawyers at the BBC. This followed a well-established tradition whereby the Irish Civil Service looked to their counterparts in London for advice and guidance, a convention that León Ó Broin understood and exploited. Although the bill provided the new service with a significant degree of autonomy, there were sections of the act that allowed the government to intervene directly in important matters that later proved highly contentious. Ó Broin was personally involved in drafting the legislation and clearly understood that these sections of the bill would prove controversial. As the bill was being drafted he worked closely with John Irvine, a senior civil servant who later became Head of Administration when the new television service was established and later still became Deputy Director-General.[14]

Ó Broin knew that the bill might provoke controversy and made sure that his minister was prepared to answer critics of the legislation when the Broadcasting Bill was introduced into the Irish Senate. The minister, Michael Hilliard, was given an 'unofficial explanatory memo', which defended the legislation, including a document awkwardly but accurately titled *General lines of reply to possible charges that the Minister for Posts and Telegraphs is reserving too much power to himself in the bill.*[15] The document provided the minister with a broad outline of the bill and carefully thought-out advice on how he could answer critics of the proposed legislation. It is clear that Ó Broin expected objections from senators concerned with the level of influence that the government, through the minister, would wield over the new entity.

The argument put forward by Ó Broin acknowledged that although there were many references to the minister in the bill these were necessary to protect the government, comparing the bill to a household lease and the minister to a landlord, a rather peculiar comparison for an Irish historian. Both Ó Broin and Hilliard were sensitive to any charges of censorship that might arise during the debate, especially concerning Section 31 of the bill, which stipulated:

> (1) The Minister may direct the Authority in writing to refrain from broadcasting any particular matter or matter of any particular class, and the Authority shall comply with the direction. (2) The Minister may direct the Authority in writing to allocate broadcasting time for any announcements by or on behalf of any Minister of State in connection with the functions of that Minister of State, and the Authority shall comply with that direction.[16]

Hilliard was told to argue, 'The only power reserved by me to which I think there may be some ground – I do not say good ground – for objection is the veto power.' This power to veto material was defended by arguing that the government hoped that the new Broadcasting Authority would

> always act reasonably and circumspectly but its judgement – like all human judgements – will not be infallible. It is inevitable that despite any system of censorship objection on various grounds will be taken to some programmes and it will be a matter of the Authority in the vast majority of cases to decide whether the objection is reasonable or not, and to frame its future policy accordingly. Cases may occasionally arise, however, where the Authority may propose to broadcast a programme or series of programmes that may be objectionable in a way or ways that may not be fully apparent to the Authority at the time.[17]

Although Hilliard was advised to admit that the powers reserved for the government under Section 31 might be cause for concern, he was told that assurance should be given that the powers would not be used unless broadcasts were defined by the government as 'detrimental to the public interest'.[18] Other powers defended in the document included the exclusive power of the minister to appoint and dismiss the director-general, a position that Ó Broin defined as a 'key post – hence the need to be sure that the best man is appointed. He will be exposed to criticism to an extent that does not, or is not likely to, apply to the occupant of a similar post in any semi-state organisation.'[19] Importantly, the legislation provided the minister with the authority to decide the amount of advertising that was appropriate for both radio and television, arguing that this was needed to 'ensure that an excessive amount of time will not be devoted to advertising'.[20] This provision enabled the government to exert tremendous financial leverage on the new broadcasting service and illustrates Ó Broin's unease with the hybrid structure that he helped negotiate.

Ó Broin kept in regular contact with senior officials in the BBC, many of whom proved critical allies in his battle to keep Irish television from becoming a purely commercial enterprise. He continued this dialogue with Hugh Carlton Greene who, after assuring the BBC Board of Governors that he was not a Catholic, succeeded Ian Jacob as director-general in 1959.[21] When the Broadcasting Bill was being drafted, Ó Broin sought the advice of Greene, sending a complete copy of the draft legislation to London for comment and advice. The director-general consulted with colleagues and lawyers within the corporation and wrote back to Ó Broin stating quite forcefully that the BBC believed the Irish government should not exert as much control as proposed in the Broadcasting Bill. BBC officials had serious reservations about the very aspects of the Irish legislation that Ó Broin had identified as potentially controversial. Greene explained these reservations unequivocally to Ó Broin:

> We feel that everything possible should be avoided which gives the Minister or the Government any detailed control over the actions of the Authority. It seems to us that the provision ... that the Director-General of the Authority can only be appointed and dismissed with

the consent of the Minister could place the Authority in an impossible position with their own Director-General tied to a Minister and able to flout the Authority.[22]

Greene reported that in the United Kingdom a Board of Governors appointed the director-general of the BBC without government consultation. Ó Broin's British allies clearly believed that the new Irish service and the authority that would oversee it should have greater autonomy than the government was willing to concede. Ó Broin was also advised that the Irish government should avoid getting involved in deciding the distribution and amount of advertising: 'With a Minister in charge there would be an endless source of argument and the Minister would be brought too much into detailed control of output.'[23] After reading the draft of the Broadcasting Bill, BBC executives made clear they were concerned with what they defined as 'the degree of Ministerial control of finances, staff, and output which would be considered right and proper'.[24] On these points the advice of the most senior members of the BBC and the British Post Office was simply ignored by Ó Broin and his minister, who believed that the government should have a strong voice in determining how the Irish service would function. Both men wanted to retain a large degree of control over the service, displaying a paternalism that later created tremendous headaches for broadcasting authorities and directors-general. During his tenure as Minister for Posts and Telegraphs, Michael Hilliard followed the lead of his influential secretary whom he trusted and admired.

Hilliard introduced the Broadcasting Authority Bill in the Irish Senate on December 16, 1959. The legislation created the corporate structure governing both radio and television and defined the relationship between the national broadcaster and the government. The bill called for the establishment of a government-appointed authority of up to nine people responsible for overseeing both television and radio. The new service was named Radio Éireann, and later the television component was defined as Telefís Éireann before the entire radio and television service was renamed Radio Telefís Éireann (RTÉ) in 1965. The Radio Éireann Authority was given the power to appoint staff, originate programmes, acquire and dispose of land and generally be responsible for overseeing both radio and television. Although there was debate about sections of the bill that some senators found objectionable, supporters of the government prevailed. For instance Fianna Fáil opponents wanted the legislation altered to allow a bipartisan process to appoint members to the authority in an effort to ensure political balance in its composition. Given significant Fianna Fáil opposition, the effort to amend the legislation failed. One concession made by the government stipulated that any ministerial order or decision to censor a broadcast under Section 31 of the Act could be made public at the discretion of the Broadcasting Authority. In the Senate Professor Michael Hayes, a veteran of the 1916 Easter Rising, pointed out that this concession on the part of the government was an improvement as it provided a welcome degree of transparency that was lacking in the original draft.[25] Section 31 of the Broadcasting Act later proved tremendously controversial as it enabled the state to prohibit journalists from broadcasting interviews of members of proscribed organisations during 'the troubles' in Northern Ireland.[26]

The 1960 Broadcasting Act created a service that was given two contradictory objectives. It was required to 'serve the nation' by providing educational and cultural programmes, and it was responsible for providing popular entertainment that would find a large audience and attract rate-paying advertisers. Thus Irish television was established as an awkward amalgam, a commercial public service charged with generating popular programmes that would produce enough revenue to sustain itself while also offering educational and cultural programmes that would inform and educate viewers. Unsurprisingly, Posts and Telegraphs was designated the department responsible for working with the new public authority, and in the formative years the secretary León Ó Broin adopted a proactive posture in trying to shape the new service. Even though Ó Broin had been one of the key architects of Irish television, he quickly became troubled by the requisite compromise with commerce. Ó Broin grew increasingly uncomfortable with the emphasis on entertainment in programming and tried to steer television towards fulfilling the public service remit stipulated in the act. His efforts to influence the direction of television, after the establishment of the Broadcasting Authority, were supported by his minister and complicated relations between the Fianna Fáil Government and the new service.

In April 1960 the new Broadcasting Authority Act became law, and a short time later the first Authority was appointed. Eamonn Andrews was named Chairman and was joined by Earnest Blythe, Managing Director of the Abbey Theatre and a former Cumann na nGaedheal Minister for Finance; Fintan Kennedy, General Secretary of the Irish Trade and General Workers Union and member of the national executive of the Irish Congress of Trade Unions; businessman Charles Brennan, Chairman of Brennan Insurance Ltd.; Theodore W. Moody, Professor of Modern Irish History at Trinity College Dublin; Áine Ní Cheanainn, a school-teacher, native Irish speaker and founding member of the Irish Youth Cinema who had broadcast experience in Radio Éireann; James I. Fanning, editor of the *Midland Tribune* and founder of the Little Theatre Group in Birr; George Crosbie, publisher of the *Cork Examiner*; and Edward McManus, identified in the press as a publicity executive but also known to be a strong supporter of Fianna Fáil. Both McManus and Crosbie had served on the Television Commission. Moody and Brennan had been on the Comhairle Radio Éireann.[27] Moody was a distinguished Irish historian and an important public intellectual who demonstrated a keen interest in broadcasting. He was intimately involved in radio and television for twenty years and was responsible for encouraging the development of innovative educational programmes including the Thomas Davis Lecture Series, broadcast on Radio Éireann, a series that brought many of Ireland's best-known academics to a national audience.

Although the selection of Eamonn Andrews as Chairman of the Radio Éireann Authority made sense to the Lemass Government, he was hardly the Reithian intellectual Ó Broin would have preferred. Andrews was born in Dublin and educated at the Christian Brothers' School in Synge Street. A handsome, charismatic and hard-working entrepreneur, he was also an Irish junior boxing champion. He later studied acting, took part in plays broadcast on Radio Éireann, and published a play, *The Moon is Black*, in 1941. He became known in Dublin as the host of the popular *Double or Nothing* show at the Theatre Royal in the late 1940s and broadcast a number of boxing matches for Radio Éireann before making his way to London where he enjoyed tremendous success in British radio and television. He became the BBC's 'voice of boxing' and presenter of the popular flagship programme, *Sports Report*.[28] He hosted popular entertainment programmes for the BBC including such classics as the panel guessing game *What's My Line?* and the celebrity celebration show *This is Your Life*. Admired by men for his macho boxing background and knowledge of sports, he was also an attractive, telegenic young man with whom many women were enamoured. He became an icon of British popular culture in the 1960s and one of the best-known Irish figures in the United Kingdom.

Andrews was initially approached about becoming the director-general of the new service but declined, owing to commitments at the BBC. After meeting with Seán Lemass in September 1959 he agreed to chair an advisory committee with the understanding that he would be appointed Chairman of the Broadcasting Authority when it was formally established. He was consulted about the make-up of the first Radio Éireann Authority by a government keen for advice from a veteran in the field of television. An advisory committee was set up to help decide important technical issues that needed immediate attention, including the type of equipment to be purchased and the location for studios and transmitters. Andrews's contacts within the BBC quickly proved useful, and the British Postmaster General and the director-general shared technical advice with Lemass and staff at Posts and Telegraphs.[29]

Although the work of this committee was concerned with technical issues, Andrews quickly learned that this would not prevent criticism from one interest group, the Irish language lobby, which would prove to be his nemesis throughout his tenure with the Authority. In the autumn of 1959 letters to the Taoiseach and the Minister for Posts and Telegraphs from the Gaelic League expressed dismay at the composition of the advisory committee after it became clear that members would be offered positions on the new Broadcasting Authority. The language lobby proved to be one of the most vociferous pressure groups challenging Irish television throughout the 1960s. The term 'language lobby' needs to be used with care because there was not a unified group or organisation with a clear agenda and set of goals. Advocates for the Irish language ranged from groups and individuals who supported efforts to nurture and encourage the use of Irish to more zealous activists who believed that the government was obligated to restore Irish as the primary language of the people. For organisations such as the Gaelic League, television could be a critical tool in the restoration of the Irish language. To that end, Secretary of the Gaelic League Donncha Ó Laoire wrote to Lemass in the autumn of 1959 complaining that no advocate of the language had been consulted or appointed to the advisory committee: 'We have always felt that the success or failure of the Irish Language Revival may well be determined by the impact of our own television, and for this reason we have consistently advocated that the service should have from its inception a strong bias in favour of the language.'[30] The role of the Irish language in television broadcasting would be a contentious one that would challenge the television service and governments for years to come. The pressure exerted by the language lobby would be the primary reason Eamonn Andrews resigned as Chairman of the Broadcasting Authority in April 1966.[31]

Although the new service was not scheduled to go 'on the air' until 1961, the Taoiseach was concerned with the impact the new medium would have on Irish society.[32] Although he had reluctantly supported the creation of a state-run service, he was apprehensive about the new medium. Much like his predecessor, Eamon de Valera, Lemass was uncomfortable with the advent of Irish television. Both men believed that the state should have a strong voice in determining what should and should not be broadcast on an Irish service. Lemass and de Valera argued that it was essential that the government protect the Irish people from what both considered the potentially insidious influence an unsupervised service might impart.[33] The concern of Lemass is evident in the strict instructions he wrote for the television authority his government had recently appointed. The Taoiseach was clearly interested in trying to influence the authority, as can be seen by his decision to issue what he termed 'policy directives'. Lemass drafted these instructions a few months before the television authority was scheduled to convene for its inaugural session. In a detailed memorandum to Maurice Moynihan, secretary of his department, Lemass stated that he felt it was imperative the authority understand that 'stage-Irishisms [and] playboyisms' should be avoided. In language that captured his vision of a native service he argued that the station should produce an 'image of a vigorous progressive nation, seeking efficiency'.[34] In regard to social and economic problems that challenged the country, he emphasised that television should 'encourage objective presentation of facts and constructive comment. The "God-help-us" approach should be ruled out'.[35]

Although Lemass believed television could be used in an intelligent manner, he cautioned: 'objectivity should not be allowed to excuse the undue representation of our faults. What you should aim to present is a picture of Ireland and the Irish as we would like to have it, although our hopes and aims may well be helped by the objective presentation of facts in association with constructive comment.'[36] He made it clear that Irish television needed to avoid coverage or comment about Northern Ireland that might upset the Stormont government and maintained that the issue of partition should be addressed only with the greatest of care. According to the Taoiseach, the new authority had to act with prudence when dealing with other sensitive topics such as sex, religion and education.

Lemass's memo met with resistance from the secretary of his department, who argued that the 'policy directives' were unnecessarily severe and would ultimately prove counterproductive. In a courageous memorandum, Maurice Moynihan tried to dissuade the Taoiseach from issuing orders he considered draconian. Moynihan, who belonged to an anti-Treaty family from Tralee, was a veteran civil servant who worked as Eamon de Valera's personal secretary before becoming secretary to the Department of the Taoiseach in 1937, remaining in the post until 1960. He argued that the recently passed Broadcasting Act made provision for the Taoiseach's concerns by establishing a strong, government-appointed, public authority charged with overseeing Irish television. Moynihan argued that dictating terms to this new organisation would be seen, 'both at home and abroad, as an illiberal action, calculated to hamper unduly the freedom of the Broadcasting Authority'.[37] The secretary also pointed out that the proposed directives ran counter to the spirit of Article 40 of the Irish Constitution that 'guarantees liberty of expression for organs of public opinion'.[38]

Despite Moynihan's best efforts, Lemass insisted that these directions or 'policy directives' be issued, as he believed they would provide important guidelines for the authority. To underscore this concern he ordered that the written directives be incorporated into a formal speech that would be delivered by the Minister for Posts and Telegraphs at the inaugural meeting of the board. He also insisted that printed copies of the directives be distributed to each member of the authority in order to ensure that all were aware of the government's position. Lemass rejected Moynihan's assertion that through the appointed authority the government would have the final word on television, declaring, 'On these matters it is not enough to have the last word, if we do not have the first.'[39] A few years later Lemass would claim that Irish television was 'an instrument of public policy'. One could make the case that this, perhaps his most famous statement about Irish television, had its roots in these policy directives.[40]

Notes

1 Robert J. Savage, *Irish Television: The Political and Social Origins* (Cork University Press, Cork, 1996), 8–10.

2 See León Ó Broin, *Just Like Yesterday* (Gill and Macmillan, Dublin, 1985) 147–56, and Maurice Harmon, *Sean O'Faolain, a Life* (Constable, London, 1994), 157.

3 The term derives from John Reith, the first Director-General of the BBC who advocated using radio not simply to entertain listeners, but to inform and educate and therefore 'uplift' the audience.

4 See Savage, *Irish Television*.

5 Ibid., see Chapter 6, 'British Influence in the Development of Irish Television', 117–29.

6 Ibid.

7 Ibid., 146, n. 12.

8 Ibid., 136.

9 Ibid.

10   McLendon was a true American media magnate, at one time owning over four hundred radio stations. In the United States he is credited with bringing major league baseball to national audiences and refining the successful top forty format for popular music in the 1950s.

11   Savage, *Irish Television*, 154.

12   Archbishop of Dublin John Charles McQuaid dismissed the proposal believing it would require the Irish government to be complicit in an act of 'piracy'. (Dublin Diocesan Archives, McQuaid Papers, marginal note of McQuaid on a Statement of Monsignor Georges Roche, July 18, 1958).

13   In his seminal white paper *Economic Development*, Secretary of the Department of Finance T. K. Whitaker explained that the department first considered how the advent of television might help the country's overall development. However, that thinking changed significantly as the department considered how the advent of television in Ireland could contribute to the economic growth that characterised the 1960s. Finance understood that a commercial service could play an important role in supporting its plans. T. K. Whittaker underscored this point: 'In Economic Development our interests focussed on the potential manufacture of sets and parts, we regarded TV as primarily for entertainment rather than education.' (Correspondence with the author, December 1990.)

14   A native of Belfast, Irvine served with great distinction in Telefís Éireann and was described by one former director-general as the 'backbone' of the service. He was in many ways unseen and underappreciated but was a gifted manager who proved fiercely protective of the station's independence.

15   National Archives of Ireland, 2001/78/97 (January 13, 1960).

16   Ibid.

17   Ibid.

18   Ibid.

19   Ibid.

20   Ibid.

21   See Savage, *Irish Television*, 128, n. 6. Greene's brother, the writer Graham Greene, was a convert to Catholicism.

22   BBC Written Archives, Caversham. Greene to Ó Broin, October 5, 1959.

23   Ibid.

24   Ibid.

25   Seanad Éireann (Vol. 52), April 6, 1960 Broadcasting Authority Bill, 1959 (Seanad Bill Amended by Dáil).

26   For a consideration of Section 31 and censorship, see *Political Censorship and the Democratic State: The Irish Broadcasting Ban* (eds) Mary Corcoran and Mark O'Brien (Four Courts Press, Dublin, 2005).

27 Minister for Posts and Telegraphs Erskine Childers established the Comhairle Radio Éireann in 1951 to offer advice on broadcasting matters. See Maurice Gorham, *Forty Years of Irish Broadcasting* (Talbot Press, Dublin, 1967), 210–12.

28 Michael O'Hehir, *My Life and Times* (Blackwater Press, Dublin, 1996), 84.

29 The other members of the Committee included Fianna Fáil supporter E. B. McManus, who had served on the Television Commission; Commander George Crosbie, director of the *Cork Examiner* and a solicitor from Naas; P. P. Wilkinson who had served on a number of semi-state boards.

30 National Archive of Ireland [hereafter, NAI], S16726, Letter from Donncha Ó Loire to Lemass, October 5, 1959.

31 See Chapter 6.

32 See also Brian Girvin and Gary Murphy, *Seán Lemass and the Making of Modern Ireland* (University College Dublin Press, Dublin, 2006) and Robert Savage, *Ireland in the New Century* (Four Courts Press, Dublin, 2003).

33 See Savage, *Irish Television*, for discussion of de Valera's speech made at the opening of the television service on New Year's Eve 1961.

34 NAI DT, S14996D, Lemass to Moynihan, March 30, 1960.

35 Ibid.

36 Ibid. According to John Irvine, a senior civil servant familiar with the 'policy directives', the speech that Lemass had been so obsessed with was never read out at the Television Authority's inaugural meeting, although the text was distributed to members. Instead, it appears to have been given by Lemass himself at a dinner celebrating the first meeting of the authority in 1960. (Author's interview with John Irvine, December 1990.)

37 NAI DT, S14996D, Moynihan to Lemass, April 4, 1960.

38 Ibid.

39 Ibid., Lemass to Moynihan, April 1960.

40 Lemass later insisted that these 'policy directives' be shared with the producer of American television series, *The Twentieth Century*. The documentary *Ireland, the Tear and the Smile*, broadcast in the United States in 1961, upset the Lemass Government. The Taoiseach was convinced the programme acted in bad faith and damaged the image of the country. See Robert Savage, 'Introducing Television in the Age of Seán Lemass', in *The Lemass Era: Politics and Society in the Ireland of Seán Lemass* (eds) Brian Girvin and Gary Murphy (University College Dublin Press, Dublin, 2005) and Robert Savage, 'Constructing/deconstructing the image of Sean Lemass's Ireland', in *Ireland in the New Century: Politics, Culture and Identity* (ed.) Robert Savage (Four Courts Press, Dublin, 2003).

2

'A stranger among us': Edward Roth and the establishment of Telefís Éireann

At the first meeting of the Radio Éireann Authority in June 1960, Michael Hilliard, the government minister responsible for overseeing the new service, delivered a sharply worded address, much of which had been written, reviewed and edited by Seán Lemass.[1] Hilliard made it clear that there were important matters that he wanted to share privately and off the record with the new Radio Éireann Authority. The minister declared that the government expected the new service to become financially stable as quickly as possible, relating the achievement of this goal to the degree of independence television would enjoy. There was no mistaking the threat of state intervention in his remarks. Here the fiscal concerns of the new service far outweighed any 'public service' expectation. He gave an unequivocal warning that this was 'a fundamental matter so far as the well being of your organization is concerned. Genuine independence may be a matter of outlook but it is, unfortunately, as often a matter of finances.'[2]

Hilliard promised the Authority that the government intended to give the new organisation 'the greatest possible freedom from direct State control' but warned that as long as state funding was involved, 'there will remain a temptation – and I will put it no stronger – for the state to interfere in matters which will be properly your concern'.[3] The Lemass Government effectively placed the new Authority on notice that the financial stability of the new service was paramount and that any serious difficulty in this regard would place the independence of Telefís Éireann in jeopardy.[4]

One month later the Chairman of the Radio Éireann Authority, Eamonn Andrews, met with the newly appointed board to discuss filling perhaps the most critical position in Telefís Éireann, that of director-general. This appointment was key, as the director-general would be charged with the complex task of getting Irish television off the ground and on the air. Many viewers along the east coast and on or near the border had become familiar with the programmes of the BBC and ITA, two networks that transmitted high-quality programming, effectively establishing a standard that would challenge the new Irish service. This was clearly understood by the British government, which had recently renegotiated an agreement with Dublin allowing both the BBC and ITA stations in Northern Ireland to boost the power of their transmitters. Confidential correspondence between London and Belfast made reference to the risks this agreement posed to the finances of a new Irish television service.[5]

Eamonn Andrews and the Authority understood that the director-general would be quickly confronted with a wide array of important decisions about programmes and priorities and would be under intense pressure from the government, myriad interest groups, and of course the general public to establish an entertaining and informative service. The Catholic Church and the Irish language lobby had already made it quite clear that they would be watching Telefís Éireann closely, monitoring decisions and policies that were developing as the service was being established.

Douglas Gageby, editor of the *Irish Times*, made this point in a letter to his friend Ernest Blythe, a former Cumann na nGaedheal Minister for Finance. At the time Blythe was the Artistic Director at the Abbey Theatre and had recently been appointed to the Radio Éireann Authority. Gageby warned his friend, 'No matter what sort of an Archangel you put in as Director-General you will have buckets of complaints every day about the corrupting influence of the stuff you are putting into Irish homes.'[6] Under Gageby the *Irish Times* slowly began making a recovery after a period of retrenchment and decline. During his tenure as editor the newspaper became a critical component in the transformation Ireland experienced in the 1960s and provided an editorial voice that supported an often-time beleaguered television service. Gageby proved an able and courageous editor, telling Blythe, 'I am growing a very thick skin but think I'm moving things slowly in the way I want.'[7] He understood that television would be tremendously controversial and knew that the position of director-general would require an individual with a 'thick skin' like his own. From the start members of the Radio Éireann Authority realised that filling this position with an Irish person possessing the requisite technical and managerial skills would be a difficult, if not impossible, task. In the autumn of 1959 Maurice Gorham, Director of Broadcasting at Radio Éireann, decided not to complete his contract, which ran until June 1961. Although there was speculation that he might be appointed director-general of the new service he decided that it would be best if he resigned 'to leave both the Minister and himself free in the matter when the time comes'.[8] Although he did not take himself out of the running for the position, he had no interest in remaining a 'lame duck' at Radio Éireann. He was short-listed for the position of director-general but his application was not one that convinced the Radio Éireann Authority and its most important member, Eamonn Andrews. Gorham was championed by León Ó Broin who regarded Gorham as a natural for the position; but his efforts to have Gorham appointed director-general were unsuccessful.

By the summer of 1960, over seventy applications were received for the post, but none were considered qualified for the position. Although members of the Radio Éireann Authority were reluctant to even consider hiring a non-national, the simple reality became clear quickly: there were no Irish candidates qualified for the position.[9] In fact, the first round of applications was so disappointing that a decision was reluctantly made to extend the search. Just as things began to look bleak, an application arrived from Guadalajara, Mexico, that stood out above the rest. This came from an American, Edward Roth, who made a strong impression.

Andrews wrote to Seán Lemass and Michael Hilliard in August 1960 explaining that the Authority was 'coming up against some thorny problems but progress is most encouraging … we are seeing the American Roth … and please God will be in a position … to make you a recommendation for the post of Director-General. I took up one of his references through the Consul General in

New York with excellent results.'[10] In fact, Roth's references were impressive and his referees included the Vice President of the American broadcasting giant National Broadcasting Corporation (NBC), the Directors of the Mexican and Peruvian television stations Roth had organised, the Archbishop of Peru, and the Vice President of the station at the University of Notre Dame in Indiana where Roth had worked.[11]

One can see why Roth's application impressed an authority under considerable pressure to find a candidate not only with very specific technical and managerial expertise but also one who understood the commercial component of television broadcasting. Roth's résumé appealed to Eamonn Andrews and fitted Lemass's vision of Ireland as a 'vigorous progressive nation, seeking efficiency' precisely because he was regarded as a person who could deliver effectively what they understood was a key component to a more modern Ireland, a dynamic commercial television station.[12] Andrews and the authority knew that appointing a foreigner to the highly sensitive position of director-general could be problematic. However, as an Irish-American Catholic, Roth possessed the ethnic and religious background that provided a certain level of comfort and cover for the Radio Éireann Authority.

Roth was born in Boston, Massachusetts; both his maternal and paternal grandparents had emigrated from Ireland at the turn of the last century. His father tended bar at one of Boston's oldest establishments, Jacob Wirth's, and was a minor celebrity in the city, known for having an encyclopaedic knowledge of baseball. When he applied for the position in July 1960 Roth identified himself as a Catholic from an Irish background, pointing out that his grandparents had emigrated from Cork and Mayo around 1900 and that his wife's grandparents also emigrated from Ireland at the turn of the century. Growing up in an Irish-American home in Boston and being part of that community made him aware of his heritage and provided a sense of identity that he was keen to emphasise.

> I suppose there must have been times in my younger years when I believed myself in Ireland … rather than in Boston … so great is the Irish influence in that city … Although it is perhaps true that as the years passed by the Irish in Boston did become increasingly

'Americanised', it would be equally true that my twenty seven years in Boston did give me the opportunity to acquire a considerable depth of insight to the Irish people, their likes and dislikes, their history and their culture … through my personal family inheritance, my experience and my independent study. [13]

During the Second World War Edward Roth served for four years in a Marine Corps intelligence unit in the South Pacific. During the conflict he developed an interest in broadcasting from listening to American radio while stationed in the jungles of the Solomon Islands. He explained to one interviewer that while stationed in the Pacific 'he discovered first hand, how valuable the radio was as a link to the outside world'. [14] When he returned home he was determined to find a career in broadcasting and earned a Bachelor of Science degree from Boston University. He enrolled in additional communications courses at Harvard University and the Massachusetts Institute of Technology before attending Columbia University in New York, where he earned a Master of Arts degree. Roth later won a scholarship from *Encyclopaedia Britannica* to study communications and public relations and spent a semester at the University of Notre Dame teaching, later returning to South Bend, Indiana, to help organise the university's television station. [15] He intended to finish a doctorate at Columbia but soon found himself married with a growing family to care for. [16]

Roth joined the American network NBC in 1951 before moving to Paramount News where he produced educational films that were commissioned by CBS and the Carnegie Trust. He produced material with a strong social justice component, including a programme about prison life filmed inside the Massachusetts State Penitentiary. He was later credited with being one of the original writers for the iconic American children's programme, *The Howdy Doody Show*. The influential programme ran on NBC from 1947 to 1960 and was a pioneer in children's programming, subsequently setting the pattern for many similar shows. Before returning to NBC, he spent two years working as Program Manager for WGN in Chicago. Roth proved an able and adventurous manager and technician and, in 1959, the network sent him to set up television stations first in Lima, Peru, and then in Monterrey and Guadalajara, Mexico. He was finishing his work in Guadalajara when he saw the position of director-general advertised in the June 1960 issue of the television trade journal *Broadcasting*.[17]

His professional skills were detailed in his letter of application in which he explained he had 'large scale experience in nearly all aspects of television including station design, purchase of equipment, staff organisation, sales, accounting, personnel and union contracts, film purchasing, programming, staff training (and) experience in dealing with political and monopoly problems in Peru and Mexico'.[18] When his application arrived in Dublin, Eamonn Andrews quickly saw to it that each of the references he listed was contacted. John Irvine, who was Head of Administration in the new service, wrote to each of the referees explaining that Roth had applied for the job of director-general and outlining what the position entailed. He asked referees for their views on the young American executive, seeking candid opinions about his suitability for the position. Alejandro Diaz, Chairman of the Board of Directors, Television Tapatie in Guadalajara, wrote to Irvine and explained in some detail the difficult conditions that confronted Roth while he worked to set up a television service in Mexico:

> We had the equipment but no one here to start our station. Mr. Roth was forced to work under undesirable conditions since we had no suitable personnel available. However, through Mr. Roth's hard work we now have a successful operation. … He is gifted with a clear and sound mind, has exceptional ability to grasp difficulties … we are certain that he will establish your Irish National Television Service in a short period, no matter what difficulties he might encounter in a foreign country.[19]

Similar letters praising Roth's technical and managerial expertise arrived from Gustavo de la Garza, Director-General of XET-TV in Monterrey, Mexico; Alfred R. Stern, President of NBC International in New York; and Robert F. Stolfi, Director of Sales Development at CBS in New York.

Testimonials from Mother Maria Trinita, IHM in Lima, Peru, and Revd William R. McCarthy, also from Lima, praised Roth as an honest family man. And Juan Landázuri Ricketts, Archbishop of Lima and Primate of Peru, testified to his reputation as an honest and capable man, describing him as a good Catholic who was deeply respected and admired while living and working in Peru.[20] As noted previously, Andrews asked his friend John M. Conway, Consul General in New York, for help in researching Roth's background. Conway knew the Vice President of the University of Notre Dame and asked him for a full and frank evaluation of Roth. Edmund P. Joyce CSC then Executive Vice President of the University of Notre Dame and later President of the University, replied praising Roth's tenure at Notre Dame and stating he had 'proved to be very industrious and hard working while at the same time possessing a serene and pleasing personality … Mr. Roth is to my knowledge, a fine practising Catholic, a good family man, and a man of integrity and high ideals.'[21]

One can see why Roth made such a remarkable impression. He was interviewed by the Radio Éireann Authority in August 1960 and did not disappoint. Chairman Eamonn Andrews wrote a detailed report to Michael Hilliard explaining that the members were 'unanimous in their opinion' that Roth should be hired. Significantly, Andrews understood that Roth was a product of American commercial television. Given the government's warnings about the need for the new service to be financially viable, he understood that this was a critical component of Roth's make-up. In his report Andrews emphasised that Roth did not come from a 'public service' background, maintaining that this was an asset that would bring what he described as 'an American viewpoint to balance our inevitably close association with … the BBC'.[22] Another dimension favouring Roth was defined as his diplomatic skill, as Andrews pointed out he was 'impressed by his negotiations on delicate subjects with the Catholic hierarchy when he was with the Notre Dame station'.[23] The Chairman of the Radio Éireann Authority understood that the Archbishop of Dublin, John Charles McQuaid, was a formidable cleric with a penchant for involving himself in the political and cultural life of the country. He knew McQuaid could complicate the work of the new television service and appreciated Roth's experience in working with powerful religious leaders in Peru, Mexico and the United States. Andrews even dared to address his one glaring problem: 'His weakness is, of course, his lack of first hand knowledge of Ireland … Balanced against this are such factors as his proven ability to adapt himself to other countries, his academic qualifications, his Catholicity, and his Irish ancestry.' He concluded his report stating, 'In short, his defects seem to be considerably outweighed ... by his capacity to get the station on the air in the most economic and sensible way.'[24] The strategy Andrews developed for selling Edward Roth to the Irish people was straightforward. He explained to the government that the appointment would 'surely be ... popular ... if we presented him as he is – a Catholic of Irish ancestry, a young man, a married family man, a go-getter with international experience and no strings attached'.[25] A short time later the government informed Andrews that it would not object to the hiring of the American as director-general.[26]

Edward Roth arrived in Dublin in November 1960, signed a contract, and had his first formal meeting with the Radio Éireann Authority where he was given a document it had drafted titled simply *A Statement of Policy*. This document was an attempt to educate the American about the peculiarities of an Irish television service that had not yet gone on the air. It was in many respects a contradictory report that highlighted the tension that remains part and parcel of Irish television. This *Statement of Policy* first mandated that the service should have a 'distinctly Irish quality [which] will reflect traditional values, and will recognise ... [its] responsibilities as a public service concerned with cultural interests'.[27] However, it continued by emphasising 'there should be a very high popular entertainment content in the [initial] programmes for audience building purposes'. The document argued for the 'maximum possible amount of home material' then, in some contradiction, recognised 'the necessity to import a great deal of programme material'.[28] Roth was told that he was expected to deliver both popular material that would draw large audience numbers and quality cultural programmes to educate and inform viewers. Throughout his tenure as director-general, Roth struggled to navigate the tension inherent in this hybrid entity, and many of his critics argued vociferously that he ignored the public service remit of Telefís Éireann.

Shortly after meeting the Radio Éireann Authority the new director-general and Eamonn Andrews held a highly publicised press conference that made headlines in all the Irish newspapers.

Roth said all the right things and promised to deliver 'in a year, or maybe less, a service we can be proud of'.[29] Editorials in the Irish press expressed satisfaction that Roth had made 'a promising opening to his career' and 'allayed many fears as to the direction the programmes would take'.[30] Other writers were impressed by the sense of confidence this 'handsome six-foot-four Bostonian' exuded and appreciated 'his general views on what an Irish service should be'.[31] Pictures of Edward Roth and his family appeared on the front page of all the major newspapers, which featured biographies and interviews with the new director-general.

However, as Edward Kenny pointed out in the *Sunday Independent*, there were sceptics. Kenny met with Roth for an extended interview, reporting '[a]lready ... he has been at the centre of some controversy. There are those who have said he is overpaid, over publicised, and – as a man who has visited Ireland only once – unsuitable for the job at hand.'[32] Press reports pointed out that Roth would draw a salary larger than that of the Taoiseach Seán Lemass, one that would match that of President Eamon de Valera.[33] More importantly, concern was expressed regarding what was described as Roth's American approach to programming. Moreover, questions were raised about 'the intellectual level of the ... shows he ... specifically named as desirable acquisitions – [which were] "The Life of Riley", "Perry Mason", "Gunsmoke", and "Bugs Bunny"'.[34]

From the outset Roth made it clear that he had specific ideas about television and the types of programmes that should be broadcast. He clearly understood the government's position, articulated quite forcefully on a number of occasions, that the service should not become a financial liability and had to generate substantial income as quickly as possible. In interviews with the press Roth's desire to feature 'popular' programmes that would appeal to the widest possible audience become obvious. In these interviews Roth stressed his firm conviction that television was primarily a medium of entertainment. He often mentioned his fondness for 'Westerns' and cautioned that at the outset the service would have to rely on a steady diet of programmes produced outside Ireland.

Journalist Peter Black, writing for the English newspaper the *Daily Mail*, visited the station's offices in Clarendon Street a month before it was to begin broadcasting, finding a mood of 'dedicated excitement, overwork, confusion and foreboding which at once affected me'.[35] He found Edward Roth and Michael Barry, the controller of programmes, 'both hollow-eyed from overwork' and reported that Roth explained, '[e]veryone's been working night and day to get as much live stuff as possible. But it will be a miracle if we can start off with twelve hours a week. We must reckon in the beginning on an overwhelming preponderance of American film.'[36] In the first few months of broadcasting the amount of home-produced material broadcast was impressive but this was labour-intensive, expensive, and took its toll on a relatively inexperienced staff. In spring 1962 home-produced programmes occupied an average of nineteen hours per week, but this proved unsustainable.[37] As controller of programmes, Barry decided to cut back on indigenous material in the summer of 1962 in an effort to give staff a break and concentrate on stockpiling home-produced programmes for the autumn.[38] The result was a marked increase in foreign programmes that were relatively cheap, averaging £24 per hour as opposed to the cost of home-produced material, which averaged £214 per hour.[39]

In its early days Telefís Éireann featured countless American Westerns; thus 'cowboys and Indians' became regular visitors in Irish homes, as the station cultivated a following that succeeded in delivering revenue to the fledgling service. John Doyle, in his memoir, *A Great Feast of Light: Growing Up Irish in the Television Age*, recalls the excitement in his home when his father brought home a television in May 1963. For a six-year-old growing up in Nenagh, Tipperary the arrival of television and especially *Bat Masterson* was a special event. Although he had seen older Westerns in a crowded, noisy local cinema, television delivered a special hero from the American West into the intimacy of his home. 'This man Bat Masterson was different. He was a rebel, you could tell by the cut of him, and he was in my own house where I could watch everything he was doing, without the bother of screaming children and the fear of somebody pulling my hair.'[40]

Much to the chagrin of many of the urban middle-class intelligentsia, some of these American programmes became tremendously popular. We can only speculate how much the tastes of this American director-general – who took it upon himself to negotiate and purchase many of these programmes during his tenure – moulded popular tastes in 1960s Ireland.[41] American Westerns had already become popular in cheap fiction, comic books and cinema; the Westerns that now made their way into Irish homes reinforced a penchant for this American genre. Purchasing 'canned' American and British material was cheaper than developing indigenous programmes, and given the financial constraints of Telefís Éireann, the 'public service' component of Irish television languished.

When Roth arrived he inherited a staff that included John Irvine, Head of Management, and Riobeard Ó Farachain, Controller of Programmes in sound broadcasting. The position of controller of programmes in television remained vacant until Michael Barry was hired, just as the service was about to go on the air. The position was a critical one, requiring a skilled manager capable of working with a diverse group of producers. The controller was responsible for all programming with the exception of the news, which was handled by the head of news. Michael Barry came to Telefís Éireann from the BBC where he had been Head of Drama. His public service background made him sceptical of the emphasis on entertainment and inevitably soured his relationship with the American director-general. According to the then assistant controller of programmes, Pádraig Ó Raghallaigh, Roth and Barry had very different philosophies about broadcasting and tension developed in their relationship. Although the two men worked together closely during the critical first few months of broadcasting, Barry became disillusioned with the direction of the television service and resigned in 1962.[42] Gunner Rugheimer replaced him in June 1963.

The delay in hiring a controller of programmes was an issue that created some tension within the ranks of the new service and may have been intentional.[43] It enabled Roth to make important decisions about programming himself in the critical first year as he purchased much of the non-Irish programming on his own. While it is true that Roth had the experience to negotiate the purchase of many of these programmes, he also understood what had worked in Peru and Mexico and hoped that these programmes would build an Irish audience.[44] The continued broadcast of older American programmes energised many of his critics in Telefís Éireann's first year but Roth succeeded in building an audience.

By the spring of 1961, months before the initial broadcast, Roth ran into problems on a number of fronts, especially with Secretary of the Department of Posts and Telegraphs, León Ó Broin. The department was responsible for overseeing the new broadcasting service, though its powers to influence it were limited by the 1960 Broadcasting Act. The secretary of the department was a formidable character and was deeply disturbed at the emphasis that Roth placed on television as primarily a source of entertainment. Much to the consternation of Roth and Eamonn Andrews, Ó Broin challenged the Authority on a number of policy issues, even making direct enquiries into the content of programmes that were being scheduled for transmission. Eamonn Andrews and Edward Roth regarded these interventions as unwarranted and tried to protect the independence of the new station.

In the early years León Ó Broin was one of the station's most difficult critics. He believed that the conception of a hybrid television service, which he had played a critical role in shaping, should do more than pay lip-service to educating and enlightening citizens. Before the service went on the air he watched Edward Roth and Eamonn Andrews closely and became bitterly disappointed by the programmes scheduled for broadcast. For him the Chairman of the Radio Éireann Authority, Eamonn Andrews, and particularly the American Director-General Roth were truly Visigoths, 'barbarians at the gate' threatening to corrupt the nation by transmitting 'crude' Anglo-American material. León Ó Broin had wanted Maurice Gorham appointed director-general and later complained that there were members of the Authority that did not appreciate the former director of Radio Éireann, 'otherwise they would have appointed this most cultivated Irishman who had unequalled experience of all forms of broadcasting to be their director-general instead of an unknown and relatively inexperienced American'.[45] Ó Broin examined the programme schedule being developed and was mortified at the list of what he believed were mind-numbing game shows, insipid cartoons, and the many programmes featuring 'cowboys and Indians' or 'cops and robbers'. He was so alarmed with Roth's programming decisions that he consulted lawyers for advice to determine how much power he had under the Broadcasting Act to intervene in policy decisions.

Though he no doubt had the best of intentions in trying to push Telefís Éireann closer towards being a true 'public service', this proved an impossible task. The reality was that the 1960 Broadcasting Act had not created television as a true public service; instead, it formed a commercial hybrid that depended on licence fees and advertising revenue to survive. Despite Ó Broin's best efforts, the service enjoyed a significant degree of independence. Ó Broin's heavy-handed interventions only served to alienate the chairman, director-general, and members of the Radio Éireann Authority. Even after Roth's departure there was a consensus within the Authority that resented his tendency to 'seek excessively information of a day-to-day nature which was the responsibility of the Authority alone'.[46] The objections of the Authority would not have received much sympathy from the Taoiseach Seán Lemass, who wanted to see television prove itself as a successful commercial enterprise, caring little for these concerns or the ideology of public service television that Ó Broin cherished. One member of the first Authority clearly believed that Ó Broin was overly interventionist: Áine Ní Channainn maintained that the minister, Michael Hilliard, though a 'nice man', was unable to stand up to his civil servants, especially León Ó Broin, and therefore simply followed his lead. Though Roth impressed her, she cautioned, 'I thought he was being codded up to his eyes by civil servants from the Department of Posts and Telegraphs.'[47]

Ní Channain made it clear that members of the Authority and the director-general were greatly annoyed with what they regarded as overt government interference and that Roth complained to her about being 'dictated to' by the secretary of Posts and Telegraphs. She was upset with what she regarded as 'orders' that were issued by civil servants who, she claimed, treated members of the Authority like 'dummies', pointing out that in Posts and Telegraphs those 'at the top [thought] they were the bosses'.[48] During this time both Eamonn Andrews and Edward Roth had to deal with almost

2 (Left to right) Canon Cathal McCarthy, Edward Roth, Eamon de Valera and Eamonn Andrews at the opening ceremonies for Telefís Éireann, New Year's Eve 1961.

constant pressure emanating from Hilliard and Ó Broin. When the Authority needed authorisation from the minister to adjust hours or advertising fees the department exploited what it saw as an opening and made demands for information that the Authority regarded as being inappropriate. Eamonn Andrews grew so frustrated with these difficulties that he later wrote to Minister Michael Hilliard complaining, without naming Ó Broin explicitly, about the interference of senior staff at Posts and Telegraphs. It is an ironic measure of Hilliard's faith in Ó Broin that the secretary drafted the response to Andrews, arguing that there had been no interference at all and that the minister and staff at Posts and Telegraphs were 'of the same mind' on all of these issues.

Tension between the government and the Authority intensified when the Radio Éireann Authority requested permission to extend broadcasting hours to enable programmes to be transmitted on Sunday afternoons. Under the Broadcasting Act this could only be done with the formal approval of the Minister of Posts and Telegraphs. Following the advice of Ó Broin, Michael Hilliard used his power under the Broadcasting Act to block an increasingly frustrated television service in December 1963. In explaining why the government could not accept Sunday afternoon television, Ó Broin argued that additional programming might cost as much as £7,000 per year. In these circumstances, he argued, '[t]here has been considerable criticism of the quality of television programmes but I am not aware of any strong public demand for an increase in weekly programme hours. Accordingly, it seems to me that any revenue which can be spared from developing the television service should be devoted to improving programme standards rather than to extending broadcasting hours.'[49]

In the end the minister's letter was toned down, and the reference to 'considerable criticism' was deleted. However, Eamonn Andrews, the Authority and staff at Telefís Éireann were becoming exasperated with what they considered government obstruction, represented by Michael Hilliard as the Minister for Posts and Telegraphs and engineered by León Ó Broin. An angry Eamonn Andrews replied, dismissing the argument made by Hilliard as 'fallacious' and arguing that there was demand for Sunday afternoon television and pointing out that Irish viewers were turning to both the BBC and Independent Television Authority:

> Since more than 40% of television viewers in the [R]epublic can receive these services, it is disappointing to many of them and to the viewers outside of their range that our national service is not also available on Sunday afternoons. It is, I may add, as disappointing to me, that you cannot permit us to cover viewers with access to BBC and UTV. The technique of audience building is an elementary factor in the planning of any single day's programme and the beneficial effect of commercial revenue in the later hours from securing viewers' loyalty in the earlier ones will, I imagine, be obvious … I want to go on record as saying that I do not believe your ruling to be in the best interest of national broadcasting, nor as making a contribution to our overall relations with the public or to the image of the service.[50]

Later that year Andrews once again requested permission for an increase in broadcasting hours. This time he was told that broadcasting hours could be extended to allow for Sunday afternoon broadcasts with one condition. The Radio Éireann Authority was told that the government expected television would follow the 'tradition' of radio and not broadcast any advertisements. Ó Broin and his minister continued to cause problems for the Authority, and this clearly angered Eamonn Andrews who grew increasingly frustrated with the interference that characterised the relationship between the television service and the civil service. The Radio Éireann Authority and the director-general believed that the progress of both radio and television was being thwarted by the government and most certainly would have identified León Ó Broin as the culprit in trying to micromanage the national broadcaster. The refusal of the department to allow Telefís Éireann to make its own decisions concerning extended hours on Sundays and the role of advertising in both radio and television was a source of tremendous aggravation. An exasperated Andrews complained to Hilliard about the government trying to force an archaic 'tradition' upon a new and exciting medium. In a forceful letter to Hilliard he argued:

> the Authority have never been able to escape the impression that the Department regards the former Radio Éireann sound broadcasting service as a model in its traditional standards for the television service to follow. We were, as you know, refused permission to incorporate what would have been an excellent sponsored serial play in evening radio time because this was against tradition; we have had no reply to our request for a small amount of advertising time at tea-time to carry notices and advertisements of a commercial character; we have been refused permission to have advertising on Sunday afternoon on television because it was contrary to traditional policy of sound broadcasting to have advertising.[51]

The old Radio Éireann was not a model that impressed Eamonn Andrews, Edward Roth (his successor as director-general), Kevin McCourt, or members of the Authority. There was obvious resentment that the government should try to impose the 'tradition' on Telefís Éireann. Andrews told Hilliard that the radio service the Authority inherited was in crisis and desperately required a major overhaul. He explained that audience numbers were declining and 'if we were to allow the service to continue indefinitely in its traditional way, we would have a situation of more and more money being spent on producing and transmitting programmes to a smaller and smaller audience'.[52] Andrews made the position of the Authority quite clear: 'We have no doubt, however, that if the television service had to be modelled on the sound broadcasting service, it would be a public failure.'[53] Andrews had grown tired of the obstructionism that he believed had stymied his efforts to build a dynamic television and radio service, upset that the views and recommendations the Authority had made were quickly dismissed without serious discussion.

Once again Ó Broin drafted the Minister's reply to the Chairman of the Authority. It was both dismissive and defensive, arguing that no directive or statement had ever been delivered concerning the need for the Authority to follow the tradition and the standard of the old Radio Éireann. It also clearly illustrated that the government would not refrain from trying to micromanage the affairs of the Authority. Again one can hear the voice of Ó Broin in the Minister's reply:

> What I have laid down – and what I would expect the Authority to never lose sight of – is that sheer necessity only should drive the sound service further into commercial broadcasting than it had gone at the time of the change-over; and that on the television side the necessarily large element of commercial advertising and worse features of it should be subject to close control and any step involving a further departure from the desirable ideal of a public broadcasting service solely dependent on licence revenue should be examined with a particularly critical eye.[54]

Irish television may have won a small, hollow victory in extending the hours it was able to broadcast, but it failed to gain sanction to run advertisements on Sunday afternoons. In fact this battle would continue for years. As late as January 1972 the government was still refusing to allow advertisements on Sunday afternoons. By the time this wrangling was taking place Kevin McCourt, a successful businessman, had replaced Roth as director-general.

In May 1962 Eamonn Andrews met with Seán Lemass to discuss the tenure of the American director-general whose two-year contract was due to expire that autumn. Andrews told the Taoiseach that there was nobody within the Radio Éireann organisation capable of replacing Roth and that the Authority wanted to try and convince him to stay, believing 'it was essential to keep Mr. Roth for another year at least'.[55] Andrews wanted the Taoiseach to help make this possible but reported that Roth was 'shocked' at the heavy taxes on his salary, pointing out that he had not paid taxes on his previous appointments in Mexico and Peru. He told Lemass that the Authority wanted to try and offer Roth a bonus for his work to offset the heavy income tax he was subject to. At the time Roth was also being courted to take over the troubled government-owned Ardmore Studios. Lemass wrote to León Ó Broin and the Secretary of the Department of Finance, T. K. Whitaker, for advice on retaining Roth and on how he might be compensated.

Ó Broin responded that he had discussed the status of the director-general with Eamonn Andrews and believed that Roth would be a good fit at Ardmore Studios, noting that there was speculation that Ardmore might be purchased by Warwick Film. If that was the case he advised 'it might be all to the good to let Mr. Roth go there. I gather that the State's interests in Ardmore are such that any development that would effect an improvement in the financial prospects of those Studios would be most welcome.'[56] He told Lemass: 'The real question is – how important is Mr. Roth to R.E.? Mr. Andrews is satisfied that, while there are deficiencies in his make-up, Mr. Roth has done a good job. I think we would all agree with this. At the same time, his deficiencies are such that I believe that it would be well not to hold him for too long.'[57] Ó Broin saw two alternatives, keeping Roth for another year or trying to find a successor and asking Roth to continue as a consultant. In the end both Ó Broin and T. K. Whitaker suggested that the government make an effort to retain Roth's services for another year, allowing time for the Authority to find a replacement and time for Roth 'to make up his mind about Ardmore'.[58] Lemass agreed with the advice, telling Eamonn Andrews that the government would approve of a one-year extension of Roth's contract and suggesting that he be retained as a paid consultant if he was not prepared to stay. However, Lemass made it clear to Andrews that the Ministers of Finance and Posts and Telegraphs would not approve of an increase in the director-general's compensation.[59]

Roth had hinted from early on that he would 'move on' once the service was operational and, in September 1962, he announced that he would be leaving to take a position as deputy managing director of Associated Television Ltd in London. Although financial considerations may have influenced his decision to leave, he also understood that it was time to go. He survived his two-year contract at Telefís Éireann and succeeded in the daunting task of getting the service 'on the air'. His entanglements with the language lobby, outraged cultural organisations, angry unions and myriad critics inside and outside government were numerous. He denied rumours that his departure was due to conflict with the government, the Radio Éireann Authority, or within Telefís Éireann itself. However, he was not above lashing out at critics, remarking '[i]t sometimes appears that television criticism has replaced hurling as the national game. I feel bound to say that much of what has passed for criticism of Telefís Éireann has been neither honest, nor well informed, and a great deal of the spoken and printed comment has been entirely wide of the mark.'[60]

Later he argued quite forcefully that the government should make substantial changes in the Broadcasting Act if Irish television was to prosper: 'The dilemma of Irish television is that it combines two objectives; one is to establish and maintain a service which will further national culture and aims and have regard to the prestige of the nation and, secondly that the service must be a paying commercial enterprise.'[61] His experience convinced him that the tension inherent in trying to run a commercial, 'public' service was debilitating, concluding that the government should admit that public service broadcasting was simply antithetical to commercial TV.

When Roth first arrived in Dublin he wrote to Sean O'Casey asking if he could visit him in Devon. He wanted to gain the playwright's permission to produce his plays for television and to try to get him to appear on a Telefís Éireann programme called *Self Portrait*.[62] Initially O'Casey refused to allow any of his work to be featured on Telefís Éireann and refused Roth's request that he write a play for television. He also declined to be featured in the *Self Portrait* programme 'on the channel called Telefís Eireann. What a name! Sounds as if it were a kinda coelecanth, a prehistoric fish hooked up out of the deeper oceans off the coasts of Cork or Kerry'.[63]

The two men met on a number of occasions in England and kept up an often amusing correspondence. When the playwright received a copy of the Telefís Éireann guide he told Roth that he did not care for the symbol of the station, explaining the 'St. Bridget's Cross – looks like a fading starfish dissolving out its last days on a lonely seashore; but it will serve, for oddly enough, it also has a faint look of modern abstract design about it'.[64] Roth's persistence paid off; the play *The Moon Shines on Kylenamoe* was broadcast in the week of September 14, 1962. The Authority agreed to take the play 'even if it was a slight one ... in the hope it would persuade O'Casey to release the rest of his more important work for television'.[65]

O'Casey wrote to Roth when he heard he was leaving and made reference to some of the battles that had challenged the American director-general during his tenure. O'Casey complained about his failing eyesight, explaining that he could no longer see to read but that his wife Eileen read to him an *Irish Times* article titled 'Donnybrook Fair'. No doubt referring to Roth's difficulties with Irish language supporters in general and Ernest Blythe in particular he wrote that he understood

> that you had handed in your gun – without using it on a few in general, and one fat, fatious, fool ... of a pinchback Buddha having power enough (because those around are on their knees) to order many more intellegent Irish to plod along roads they should never travel. As for me and my thoughts Ed, – now that you have definitely resigned – I think you will be well out of this mass morass of men and women crowding round the studios, with their various voices shouting 'for a job, for a job!' 'What can we give to Ireland' has changed to a fever of feeling of 'What can we get out of her'! The watchword of Ireland now is 'Put Money in Thy Purse'. Even God himself would be unable to help in that crowd at 'Donnybrook Fair' ... Still, I'm sorry that you're going. You fixed things up, straight & steady; and set all going; I now wonder what will happen when you say 'Inishfallen, Fare Thee Well!' I can well guess – they will look to the captains and the kings.[66]

Roth responded by thanking him for his 'most interesting letter' and confirmed that he was leaving Telefís Éireann at the end of 1962.[67] The following summer he wrote to O'Casey from Green Harbor, Massachusetts, a seaside community south of Boston where he was spending time with his family. He had just moved his wife and children from their home in Dublin and was making arrangements for them to join him later in London. Roth explained that his time in Ireland had been bittersweet. 'It is not an experience we would want to repeat … yet we are all much better for having had it … and we wouldn't have missed it for the world. Perhaps it is a sad admission on my part … but I confess I don't understand the Irish anymore than I did when I left the sunny shores of Mexico. So be it.'[68] This prompted a sympathetic reply from the cantankerous O'Casey:

> My dear Ed, you would be at least a demi-god if you understood the Irish, for they aren't able to understand themselves, and worse still, they never try. Your advent was something of an invasion, reminding them of the Normans; you were Chief of Radio and Television … and they resented it. Your presence gave them a hint of the memory o[f] what had been said so often by the English – 'the Irish aren't yet fit to govern themselves'. God damned insolence, of course, and wrong when applied to you. We knew nothing about Television, and had to be taught. The Irish middle class don't like this, especially by a Yank; they don't think they need to be taught anything…. We are a muddled and a puzzled people, envious of one another, so how can a stranger be at peace among us?[69]

Edward Roth never considered himself an agent of Anglo-American cultural imperialism but simply as a director-general and manager with a very difficult task to perform. He freely admitted that mistakes had been made during his two years at Telefís Éireann. He also argued that the 1960 Broadcasting Act was highly problematic as it limited the options for the men and women who were responsible for Irish television. Many of his critics failed to appreciate the tension between public service and economic viability and the challenges that confronted the director-general and his staff. Understanding that this 'hybrid' structure restricted Irish television is critical to understanding the success and failures of Edward Roth and Irish television in general, not only in these early formative years, but also in succeeding decades. Although not Irish-born, Roth was one of Ireland's modernisers, a man who was able to withstand a great deal of criticism from a wide array of interest groups with poise and dignity. He also possessed a sense of humour as is clear from the papers he held onto after his departure from Telefís Éireann. An oversized scrapbook kept by the Roth family chronicles a remarkable career that stretched from the gritty Mission Hill neighbourhood of Boston through the jungles of the South Pacific, to New York City, Chicago, South Bend, Indiana, and on to Lima, Guadalajara, Monterey, Dublin and London. Pasted into this book are press clippings from American, Peruvian, Mexican, Irish and British newspapers; correspondence with professional acquaintances and two anonymous poems that poked fun at the American director-general and those working with him in Telefís Éireann in its formative years.

TELEFÍS ÉIREANN

For two months they hid behind St. Bridgid's Cross,
    And behind Edward Roth, the big yankeee boss:
But now they've emerged for all to see
    Do you wonder the nickname they've got is 'Tee-Hee'?
They were deep in the red from the very word 'go'
    They were staffed by the boys who were all in the know;
Their 'talents' are such they can't run a live show,
    So with old westerns films they sit back and they crow ...
Now I hear they're on strike and just won't work at all
    And with Roth and with Andrews refuse to play ball:
And indeed it doesn't surprise me at all,
    For we all have expected to see its downfall.
Still, I can't write much more for I've not seen it yet,
    For where *I* live the Telefísh we cannot get:
But if rumours are true and the ... jobbery
    Has made Televish Eirann even worse than R.E.
Then Ed Roth must be wishing he never crossed the sea
    To lay claim to his Irish Grannie,
Or to sign any contract ...
    For the one to be blamed ... will be he.
    (wait and see)

RADIO ÉIREANN

This is the Station that gives us the 'Pips'
    That's run by the yahoos with tight eyes and lips:

With American accents from hamlet … and bog,
  Which come over the ether through some sort of smog;
Not a word understood – could be all Irish or Greek,
  It's 'controlled' by the boys whom are all in the clique,
Who know something we don't about Easter Week,
  And who can't be uprooted for fear they might speak!
(With apologies to Mr. Roth, the stranger in our midst)[70]

At the end of 1962 Edward Roth left Ireland for a new position at Associated Television in London. While working in Ireland he met Eamon de Valera on a number of occasions, and the two men established a cordial relationship. Roth was invited to a reception held for President Kennedy at the residence of the President of Ireland, but he was on holiday at that time in Massachusetts and unable to attend.[71] Nevertheless he corresponded with the elderly President de Valera in the spring of 1963 and sent a 16 mm copy of the film *Rebellion*. De Valera told Roth he was looking forward to watching the film with 'a few old cronies and hear(ing) their comments'.[72] Roth also tried to assist de Valera in finding a publisher to issue a new American edition of Dorothy Macardle's iconic book *The Irish Republic*. De Valera explained to the former director-general that the book

> … should be in public libraries in the United States where there are so many communities with origins in Ireland who need a book of this kind. It ought, I think, likewise have considerable sale in Canada, Australia, India and in Universities and amongst the leaders of the new independent African states … It is an excellent well written book that has been exposed to historical criticism and to the antagonists of Irish Republicans for decades, and it has not been found wanting … If you succeed in getting this book republished, either in paper or hard back, you will not merely put me under a deep debt of gratitude but will deserve well of historians and the Irish people everywhere …[73]

Roth was unable to deliver a publisher for de Valera's favourite history book but he remained interested in Ireland. In September 1971, he offered testimony to a United States Senate Committee chaired by Senator Hubert H. Humphrey of Minnesota. The Senate Committee was investigating the outbreak of violence in Northern Ireland and considered how the United States government should respond to the growing unrest. Roth predicted continuing violence in the province and criticised the British government for not putting more pressure on Stormont to initiate substantial reforms that would fully enfranchise the Catholic community. He predicted that the failure of London to act in this regard would result in the suspension of the Stormont Parliament and the imposition of direct rule. He also criticised the controversial policy of internment as biased, pointing out that the government had not apprehended loyalist paramilitaries. He argued that the Irish government should do more to 'curb and ultimately eliminate IRA activities within its borders' and clearly had no sympathy for the IRA and its activities in Northern Ireland. [74] Given the often distorted views Americans held at the time concerning 'the Troubles' and their causes, Roth's analysis was impressive.

Roth returned to visit Ireland a few years after moving to London but found that there was little interest among his old colleagues in seeing him and he was, for the most part, shunned. Perhaps he embarrassed his former associates who were uncomfortable at being reminded they needed the technical and managerial expertise of foreigners to help establish a television station. John Irvine, who served under Roth as Head of Management before being named Deputy Director-General, recalls meeting his former boss at the Dublin airport, taking him for a long drive into the Wicklow hills, and spending a somewhat bittersweet day with him. Irvine may not have always agreed with Roth but felt obligated to extend a degree of hospitality to him. The two men worked closely together in the hectic formative years of Telefís Éireann and Irvine's gesture must have been deeply appreciated by the American visitor.[75]

Irish historians who tend to dismiss or simply ignore Roth's brief tenure as insignificant have ignored his legacy. This is a mistake. Roth worked in difficult circumstances and succeeded with the help of others in the arduous task of getting the television service on the air. He proved himself an able diplomat in dealing with the often maddening pressures of the government, Catholic Church and the Irish language lobby. Roth was a technocrat who succeeded in completing the task that was assigned to him when he first came to Dublin. He focused on getting the service established on a firm foundation, and succeeded in this assignment.[76] It is true that under his direction the service developed little 'quality' indigenous programming, but that failure was hardly his fault. Given the daunting task that confronted Roth when he was appointed, he served the government quite well. When he left, a viable television service was up and running, one that had serious programming issues to confront, but a television service that had developed a foothold that others would try to expand, improve and develop. Roth's critique of the structure of Irish television and the 1960 Broadcasting Act proved prophetic, and illustrated that he was keenly aware of the problems that inhibited Irish television. His calls for reform were largely ignored, and his successors struggled within that structure throughout the decade under consideration in this study.

Notes

1   It should be noted here that, confusingly, under the 1960 Broadcasting Act, Radio Éireann was the official name of the combined radio and television service. An amendment to the Act changed the name of the combined service to Radio Telefís Éireann or RTÉ in 1965.

2   RTÉ Authority Archive, Minutes of the Television Authority, June 2, 1960.

3   Ibid. Throughout the tenure of Seán Lemass there were a number of suggestions that the 1960 Broadcasting Act might be amended to make television and radio more accountable to the government. Short of invoking Section 31 of the Act there was little the government could do except pressure the Radio Éireann Authority or senior officials in Telefís Éireann through indirect and direct communications.

4   Ibid.

5   See Chapter 9 on television and Northern Ireland. London understood that the increased range of the stations in Northern Ireland threatened the finances of an Irish television station.

6   University College Dublin Archives, Blythe Papers P/24/1174, Gageby to Blythe, May 9, 1960.

7   Ibid.

8   NAI, S16726, Department of the Taoiseach memorandum, August 25, 1959.

9   The first round of applications the Authority considered included 7 Irish applicants, 21 Americans, 13 Britons, 2 Scots, 1 Australian and 1 Canadian. Archives Department, University College Dublin, Blythe Papers, P24/957.

10 NAI, Department of Communications TW 8990, cover letter and

memorandum dated August 13, 1960, from Andrews to Hilliard.

11   Ibid.

12   NAI DT, S14996D.

13   RTÉ Written Archives, Irvine Papers, Roth to Administration Officer, July 9, 1960.

14   Profile of Roth, Michael George, *The Irish Tatler and Sketch*, June 1961.

15   The appointment of Roth as Program Director of WNDU-TV was announced in the *Evansville Indiana Courier* and the *Anderson Indiana Bulletin* on June 10, 1950. For details concerning the history of the station see the pamphlet, *For the Record, A History of the WNDU Stations, by W. T. Hamilton,* University of Notre Dame Archives, South Bend Indiana (record no. PNDP 40-Wn-1).

16   Author's interview with Mrs Cathleen Roth, Cohasset, Massachusetts, May 1992.

17   *Broadcasting*, June 27, 1960, 87. Roth kept the original advertisement in the family scrapbook, Roth Papers, Boston, MA.

18   RTÉ Written Archives, Roth file. Information is from Roth's application. He explained that in Mexico he was helping to organise two independent television stations which was problematic because 'Television in Mexico is 100% owned by one man, Don Emilio Azcarraga who, like most Latins, dislikes competition.' See also RTÉ Written Archives, Irvine Papers, Roth to Administration Officer, July 9, 1960.

19   Ibid., letter from Alejandro Diaz to John Irvine, September 6, 1960.

20   Ibid., letters from each are in the file in the RTÉ Written Archives.

21   Ibid., letter from Edmund P. Joyce CSC to John M. Conway, Consul General of Ireland, New York, August 5, 1960.

22   RTÉ Minutes of the Radio Éireann Authority, June 2, 1960.

23   Ibid.

24   Ibid.

25   Ibid.

26   RTÉ Written Archives, John Irvine papers, memorandum recording a meeting with the Minister for Posts and Telegraphs and John Irvine, Head of Management, August 23, 1960.

27   RTÉ Authority Archives, Minutes of the Radio Éireann Authority, Statement of Policy, November 9, 1960.

28   Ibid.

29   *Irish Press*, November 17, 1960.

30   *Irish Independent*, November 17, 1960.

31   *Evening Herald*, November 17, 1960.

32   *Sunday Independent*, November 20, 1960.

33   Roth's hiring was reported in the Boston press; Brendan Malin reported that Roth would make the equivalent of $14,000 per year, which is $2,800 more than Seán Lemass made as Prime Minister.

34 *Sunday Independent*, November 20, 1960.

35 *Daily Mail*, November 30, 1961.

36 Ibid.

37 *RTÉ Chronology*, Vol. I, 1960–1966 (RTÉ Library, issued February 1974).

38 Ibid. Home-produced material was reduced to 15 hours a week in the summer of 1962 before increasing to 18 in the autumn.

39 Lelia Doolan, Jack Dowling and Bob Quinn, *Sit Down and Be Counted: The Cultural Evolution of a Television Station* (Wellington Publishers, Dublin, 1969),

40 John Doyle, *A Great Feast of Light: Growing Up Irish in the Television Age* (Aurum Press, London, 2005), 15.

41 Author's interview with John Irvine, December 1990.

42 Author's interview with Pádraig Ó Raghallaigh, December 14, 1990, Dublin. He believed that if Barry knew Roth was leaving at the end of 1962 he would not have resigned. John Irvine made this same point in an interview with the author in Dublin, December 1990.

43 Ibid. John Irvine explained that he believed Roth waited too long to hire a Controller of Programmes and that the delay created problems for the service during its inaugural year.

44 Ibid.

45 León Ó Broin, *Just Like Yesterday, an Autobiography* (Dublin, Gill and Macmillan, 1985).

46 RTÉ Authority Archive, Minutes of the Authority, October 31, 1963.

47 Author interview with Áine Ní Chanainn, Dublin, December 7, 1990. Áine Ní Chanainn is a schoolteacher, native Irish speaker and founding member of the Irish Youth Cinema.

48 Ibid.

49 NAI, Department of Communications, 2001/78/12 draft memorandum, Hilliard to Andrews, January 1964.

50 Ibid., letter from Andrews to Hilliard, January 13, 1964.

51 NAI, Department of Communications, 2001/78/35, Andrews to Hilliard, September 25, 1964.

52 Ibid.

53 Ibid.

54 Ibid., Hilliard to Andrews, October 23, 1964.

55 NAI, Department of the Taoiseach, S.16922B, memorandum of Seán Lemass, May 18, 1962.

56 Ibid., Ó Broin to N. Ó Nualláin, Department of the Taoiseach, June 13, 1962.

57 Ibid., 2.

58 Ibid., Whitaker to Ó Nualláin, June 13, 1962.

59 Ibid., Ó Nualláin to Whitaker and Ó Broin, June 16, 1962.

60 *Television Mail*, January 18, 1963, 5.

61 *Irish Times*, January 3, 1963.

62 National Library of Ireland, Department of Manuscripts [hereafter NLI], O'Casey papers, MS 38092, letter from Roth to O'Casey, May 15, 1962.

63 Ibid., O'Casey to Roth, May 21, 1962.

64 Ibid., O'Casey to Roth, undated letter. In the same letter he asked about Roth's wife Cathleen: 'I hope Mrs Roth finds weather and people more kindly to her feelings than B. Shaw did, who told me he never went to Ireland now because the people and weather drove him mad.'

65 RTÉ Authority Archive, Minutes of the Authority, June 13, 1962, 3. See *RTV Guide*, September 14, 1962.

66 Roth Papers, Boston, MA. O'Casey to Roth, October 3, 1962.

67 NLI, Department of Manuscripts, Roth Papers, MS 38092, Roth to O'Casey, October 19, 1962.

68 Ibid., Roth to O'Casey, June 26, 1963.

69 Roth Papers, Boston, MA, O'Casey to Roth, July 2, 1963,

70 Ibid., anonymous.

71 See Kenneth P. O'Donnell and David Powers with Joe McCarthy, *'Johnny, We Hardly Knew Ye'* (Little, Brown & Company, Boston, MA, 1970), 358–71. These pages, written by aides to Kennedy who accompanied him on the trip, provide a colourful account of Kennedy's visit to Ireland, indicating just how much the President enjoyed the June 1963 visit. The authors point out that his speech to the combined Dáil and Senate was the first event ever broadcast from the chamber on Irish television. See also Harvey O'Brien's essay, '"We are proud of you": Screening Kennedy in Ireland', in *Screening Irish-America: Representing Irish-America in Film and Television* (ed.) Ruth Barton (Irish Academic Press, Dublin, 2009).

72 Roth Papers, Boston, MA, de Valera to Roth, May 4, 1963.

73 Ibid.

74 Ibid., memorandum from Roth to Senator Hubert H. Humphrey, September 5, 1971.

75 Author's interview with John Irvine, December 1990.

76 Roth was determined that the new service should not run a deficit. When the accounts were in for the twelve months ending March 31, 1962, there was a surplus of £29,560. A short time after his departure, in March 1963, the total number of combined television and radio licences had reached 150,000. This figure would grow to 221,874 in March 1964 when the Authority reported that 39 per cent of all homes were capable of receiving television programmes and that the number of rural homes capable of receiving programmes had grown from 62,000 to 113,000. *RTÉ Chronology*, Vol. I (RTÉ Library, issued February 1974).

3

An instrument of public policy? Political culture and television in Lemass's Ireland

The inaugural broadcast of Telefís Éireann on New Year's Eve 1961 opened with an address by an elderly President Eamon de Valera uneasily peering at the camera and expressing a remarkable degree of anxiety:

> I must admit that sometimes when I think of television and radio and their immense power I feel somewhat afraid. Like atomic energy it can be used for incalculable good but it can also do irreparable harm. Never before was there in the hands of men an instrument so powerful to influence the thoughts and actions of the multitude. The persistent policy pursued over radio and television, apart from imparting knowledge, can build up the character of the whole people, inducing a sturdiness and vigour and confidence. On the other hand, it can lead to decadence and disillusion.[1]

Although de Valera's comments illustrate the concern of an ageing politician who had dominated independent Ireland before retiring from active politics, his successor Seán Lemass shared many of his concerns.[2] Much has rightly been made of the dramatic shift that took place once de Valera stepped aside and Seán Lemass became Taoiseach.[3] Lemass was interested in breaking away from the narrow constraints of the protectionist Sinn Féin economic policy that characterised the long tenure of Eamon de Valera. As Taoiseach Lemass encouraged foreign investment and dismantled the very tariff walls he had helped erect decades earlier, he looked forward to an Ireland that was fully involved with the global economy and understood that engagement with Europe was critical for Ireland's future. Lemass was not interested in the cultural ideology that energised his predecessor, having little time for notions of rural homesteads or the revival of the Irish language. Throughout his tenure as Taoiseach, Lemass focused his energy on economic development and trying to end the scourge of emigration.

Nevertheless, it is often overlooked that he shared many of the concerns that animated his elderly predecessor, and television was certainly one such issue. This has been illustrated in the draconian and surprisingly unrealistic 'policy directives' he drafted for the first meeting of the Broadcasting Authority. When it came to television and radio, Lemass was an interventionist, comfortable with personally contacting chairmen, directors-general, ministers and other government officials to offer scathing criticism of programmes. Anxiety, suspicion and awkward intervention marked his relationship with television throughout his tenure as Taoiseach.

Lemass was never fully at ease with the independence that the Broadcasting Act provided Telefís Éireann and, throughout the 1960s, Fianna Fáil governments viewed the new and increasingly aggressive form of electronic media with apprehension. During the formative years of television, this unease can be seen in the efforts of ministers, deputies, and civil servants to influence television programming. Political elites were used to working with a complacent Radio Éireann and had long enjoyed an unwritten protocol of quiet cooperation with the government, which ensured that there was rarely any friction between the national radio service and the state. Politicians were not prepared for the challenges television provoked, and many – especially those of the older post-revolutionary generation – were slow to realise that in a democratic society television was inherently subversive. As the 1960s unfolded a sense of anti-authoritarianism took root in young university-educated men and women in many parts of the Western world, including Ireland. This scepticism and questioning of institutions and elites was amplified by a television service that grew increasingly antagonistic as the decade progressed.

Close to a year after the launch of the television service, the Taoiseach addressed the inaugural Telefís Éireann Critics Award banquet sponsored by the Jacob Biscuit Company. He congratulated recipients of the awards chosen by the television writers of the national newspapers, wryly joking that 'everybody is a television critic'.[4] Importantly, he used the occasion to publicly explain his own views on the medium and explain his government's thinking on a television service that had experienced considerable growing pains in its short life. While his comments highlighted his belief that the public service remit of Telefís Éireann was secondary to that of entertainment, he nevertheless had very strong ideas about this aspect of broadcasting. The remarks underscored his conviction that the government should be vigilant and carefully monitor television and, if necessary, take steps to ensure that it would operate in what he defined as the national interest:

It is always necessary to stress that television is primarily a medium of entertainment, and that its function in informing the public about events at home and abroad, of promoting the love of our country, its language and its culture, and understanding the aims to which all our people, irrespective of party or creed … is in a sense secondary to the entertainment function, because viewing television is essentially a voluntary act by every citizen and, unless he switches on his set, no message can reach him. However, this secondary function is very important all the same, and is, of course, the aspect of the television service in which the government are most keenly interested.[5]

Lemass carefully articulated his concept of how the television service should function and contribute to society. He noted that it would not be long before Telefís Éireann reached the entire country and that in rural areas particularly it would be a positive development. He argued it would provide

… a sense of belonging to a larger community, which is the Irish nation … the television service must not only be free of any suspicion of bias, but so organised as to be in complete harmony with all the elements which compromise the national character, and so directed as to offer effective means by which the national effort can be organised for worthy purposes. The government have, by the legislation enacted, given responsibility in this matter to the Radio Éireann Authority, but do not, of course, regard themselves as released from their own over-riding responsibility. The television and radio services of Radio Éireann belong to the nation, not to the Authority, or the staffs whom they employ, and understanding of the responsibilities arising from its national character must penetrate every section of its organisation if the purpose in view of its establishment is to be fully realised.[6]

3   Seán Lemass during the filming of an interview with correspondent Patrick Gallagher broadcast on RTÉ Television on December 4, 1967.

Lemass's conviction that the service belonged to the nation and was established to support what he defined as the 'national effort' is imperative to understanding how he believed television should function in society. For Lemass, improving the economy, creating jobs, and curtailing emigration were critical issues that required a commitment from all citizens and he expected Telefís Éireann would do its part to help. He admitted that the Broadcasting Act had given the Authority responsibility for the service but argued forcefully that the government retained 'over-riding responsibility'. He expected television and radio to serve the national interest as *he* defined it, believing every endeavour should be made to ensure the service would work in complete harmony to enhance the 'national effort'.[7]

What exactly did this mean? Even at this early stage in the life of Irish television, Lemass continued to express anxiety about the power it possessed to undermine government policy or what he termed the 'national effort'. Much like his mentor Eamon de Valera, Lemass defined the national interest as synonymous with his government's interest and believed that Fianna Fáil was the

propaganda medium?

personification of the nation. When not entertaining viewers he expected television to play a positive role in Irish society by supporting his government and its policies. When programmes featured what he considered ill-founded or unhelpful criticism of projects undertaken by his government, he felt justified in complaining that Telefís Éireann was betraying its obligation to serve the national interest. The tension that developed between his government and the national radio and television service originated in this partisan definition of what constituted the national interest, a definition that was problematic for those who disagreed with Lemass or Fianna Fáil. Not surprisingly, the 'complete harmony' he sought proved elusive throughout his tenure as Taoiseach.

A series of clashes marked the progress of the television service throughout the Lemass era. These controversies illustrate that an increasingly aggressive television service unnerved political elites and upset a stagnant political culture that had grown comfortable governing without being held immediately accountable to a growing and more demanding form of media.

A short time after his arrival as the first director-general, Edward Roth learned just how sensitive Lemass could be about broadcasting. In the summer of 1961, months before television went on the air, the Taoiseach contacted Roth directly to complain about a bulletin issued by Radio Éireann. The particular news report addressed negotiations leading up to a settlement of a strike by electricians and suggested that a deal to end the strike was imminent. It concluded by reporting that the most recent proposal would increase the hourly wage by one penny, a comment Lemass regarded as objectionable. An embarrassed Irish Congress of Trade Unions protested to the government claiming that the bulletin was 'mischievous reporting'. Lemass wasted no time in telling Roth that the news bulletin was 'most unfortunate' and blamed it for undermining a tentative agreement.[8] A chagrined director-general apologised to the Taoiseach explaining that he was convinced there was no malice intended. He assured Lemass, 'we are giving the closest possible attention to the need for absolute accuracy and impartiality in the news bulletins put out by Radio Éireann'.[9] Under the new Broadcasting Act the director-general was responsible for both Radio Éireann and the television service that, at the time, had yet to begin broadcasting. Roth was troubled by the radio service he inherited, regarding it as an unwieldy civil service creation that was an unpopular, unresponsive and expensive burden.[10] The fact that Lemass contacted Roth directly to criticise the report served as an early lesson for the American director-general. On a number of occasions during his stormy two-year tenure Roth heard complaints from elected officials, senior civil servants, and from Lemass himself.

Roth ran into additional difficulties a short time later when Radio Éireann botched another news report, this time neglecting to accurately report on the nomination of Lemass as Taoiseach. The News Bulletin announced that James Dillon, the leader of Fine Gael had been elected Taoiseach, when in fact Lemass had been elected. Edward McManus, a member of the Radio Éireann Authority known to be a key supporter of Fianna Fáil, complained bitterly to his colleagues that he was 'particularly perturbed' by the report, calling for 'serious disciplinary action' against personnel responsible.[11] Roth accepted that a mistake had been made but took exception to any member of the Authority becoming involved with staffing issues. He argued that any disciplinary action would be solely his responsibility, making it clear that he was not willing to see a precedent set where the Authority or individual members interfered in staffing issues. Roth explained that he would settle the matter and any action taken would be 'merely reported back to the Authority as an accomplished fact'.[12] The Authority accepted his point of view but asked to be informed about any disciplinary action taken against staff.

An irritated director-general wrote to the Taoiseach acknowledging that Radio Éireann had indeed, 'misreported the vote in the Dáil for your nomination as Taoiseach. I would like to assure you that we do appreciate the great distress and embarrassment which this must have caused you and I apologise sincerely for the most regrettable error and for the public misunderstanding which it caused.' In the same correspondence Roth also took the opportunity to apologise for Radio Éireann's failure to mention his attendance 'at the Marist celebrations in Dundalk … This was due to inadequate reporting from Dundalk which also causes us concern'.[13]

These early difficulties with Radio Éireann reinforced Roth's low opinion of the national radio service. He knew that it would take a massive effort to overhaul Radio Éireann but did not want this to distract him from the formidable task of getting the television service operational. He explained to Lemass that once the television service was established there would be a new structure for both radio and television and that the head of the news department would report directly to him as director-general. In his correspondence with Lemass, Roth referred to the difficulties he and Eamonn Andrews were experiencing with the Department of Posts and Telegraphs. He carefully signalled that there was a degree of tension that was creating problems for the new service. In what was most certainly a reference to the meddlesome tactics of León Ó Broin he informed Lemass, '[t]he position here is not, however, an altogether straightforward one'.[14] In attempting to 'clear the air', Roth and Eamonn Andrews asked for and were granted an appointment to meet the Taoiseach. Although Lemass was willing to hear out the complaints of Andrews and Roth and would have been sympathetic to some of their concerns, he did not intervene and was comfortable with Hilliard's department keeping close tabs on the emerging service.

A few months after these incidents, Lemass wrote to Michael Hilliard complaining of advertisements that were running on Radio Éireann promoting jobs for women in London. This hit a raw nerve for the Taoiseach who believed the ads encouraged emigration, declaring 'I do not think that Radio Éireann should accept advertisements of this kind, and you should write to the Authority and express this view'.[15] Hilliard responded by stating that he contacted the Radio Éireann Authority and had a meeting scheduled to discuss the issue. He suggested that it would not make sense to 'introduce piece-meal restrictions' but believed it would be more productive to informally discuss, address and define what 'type of advertisements are inappropriate for inclusion in the Irish sound broadcasting and television services'.[16] According to one long-serving official in Telefís Éireann, Hilliard was not interested in confrontation and worked to defuse any controversy by addressing governmental concerns in a quiet and confidential manner.[17]

This was not the style of Padraig O'Hanrahan, director of the Government Information Bureau and one of Lemass's intermediaries in broadcasting matters. A veteran civil servant from County Mayo, O'Hanrahan regarded both the international and domestic media as potentially hostile forces that could not be trusted and required careful handling. He had worked as a private secretary for Eamon de Valera and earned a reputation for being fiercely protective of the elderly Taoiseach and President. Lemass wrote to O'Hanrahan in September 1962 to complain about *Broadsheet*, a current affairs television programme that greatly annoyed him. He told O'Hanrahan that he did not have an opportunity to see the programme very often but, when he did, had not been impressed:

> I received the impression that it is becoming increasingly a medium for the uncritical presentation of the views of persons associated with various ramps and crank projects. I do not necessarily object to such ideas getting publicity on the programme but they should then be subject to critical questionings instead of being treated by the Comperes with respectful deference as reputable and established; and in subsequent programmes the alternative viewpoints should get at least equal publicity.[18]

Lemass told O'Hanrahan that he had no trouble taking up the matter at a 'higher level – which I will do if necessary', but first wanted him to try to address the problem directly with the programme-makers.[19] 'I think you should talk with the editors of the programmes to express these views. A list of the "controversial" topics of this nature recently dealt with should be requested, and the editors requested to state their intentions regarding the correction of the misleading ideas given publicity.'[20] The Taoiseach wanted Telefís Éireann to produce programmes that would correct those he believed were misleading; broadcasts that challenged or criticised government policy.

O'Hanrahan dutifully met with Roth and with the Head of Public Affairs, Jack White, and eventually reported back to the Taoiseach. He informed Lemass that both men were in broad agreement with his concerns and that Roth remarked that 'he couldn't agree more' with the Taoiseach's critique. Roth and White blamed the problem on the lack of highly skilled professionals that could ensure high-quality current affairs programming. Both men claimed that one of the challenges confronting the new television service was finding first-rate presenters that could conduct informed and intelligent interviews. O'Hanrahan reported that 'Roth certainly gave me the impression that he would gladly dispense with most – if not all – of the present interviewers on T.E. – male and female – if he could find better but this … he has failed to do.'[21] At this juncture Roth and his staff were able to mollify O'Hanrahan and Lemass by attributing any perceived shortcomings to the growing pains of the new service. They promised every effort would be made to improve programmes that addressed current affairs.

Although he did not secure an agreement to broadcast corrective programmes, O'Hanrahan took the opportunity to write at length to Lemass about pressuring Telefís Éireann to produce what he defined as more appropriate material. One might argue that the director of the Government Information Bureau was simply telling Lemass what he wanted to hear, but the correspondence highlights the sense of anxiety felt by many senior civil servants and political leaders of their generation. O'Hanrahan's memo to Lemass and the Taoiseach's reply also illustrate the unrealistic expectations these men held concerning the new broadcasting service. O'Hanrahan argued that it was not simply rude or ill-informed correspondents that were causing the government embarrassment. Instead he was convinced the problem lay in the failure of Telefís Éireann to accept its responsibility to Irish society. Some of the rhetoric from the exchange made its way into Lemass's speech at the first annual Jacob's Award ceremony cited earlier. 'There is … an obligation on the Authority to harmonise with broad National policy and to see to it that none of their programmes on television or sound run contrary to it … I do think that the Authority needs to have this impressed on them very forcefully.'[22] O'Hanrahan also believed it imperative for reporters, presenters and programme-makers to defer to the government. He complained to Lemass about what 'can only be described as the Authority's appalling failure to see to it that T.E. shows proper sense of values and priorities, and respect for the organs and institutions of government and holders of high office'.[23]

Lemass agreed emphatically and believed one solution would be the establishment of a formal Advisory Committee, arguing that such a body could serve as a watchdog to monitor television, ensuring that it supported national policy. He noted that the 1960 Broadcasting Act allowed for the establishment of such an organisation and expressed a willingness to intervene directly with the Radio Éireann Authority. He too was upset with what he considered the failure of Telefís Éireann to serve the government and the policies it was pursuing, arguing:

> The importance of getting understanding throughout the Radio Éireann organisation of their role in relation to national policy in the widest sense is becoming increasingly obvious. I think this is, principally, the responsibility of the Authority itself. I have mentioned this on occasions to the Chairman, and have also discussed with the Minister for Posts and Telegraphs the selection of the Advisory Committees for which the Act provides. We decided, however, not to move at this stage in view of the change now pending in the top direction of T.E.[24]

The change the Taoiseach referred to concerned the director-general, Edward Roth, who had given notice that he was would leave when his contract expired at the end of 1962. Lemass understood that the Broadcasting Act allowed his government the exclusive right to choose Roth's replacement, and no doubt hoped for a more sympathetic executive. Kevin McCourt became the second director-general in January 1963 and, although sympathetic to Fianna Fáil, tension between the government and the national broadcaster continued throughout Lemass's tenure as Taoiseach.[25] The review committee Lemass mentioned was anathema to the Radio Éireann Authority that had no interest in having a government-appointed board looking over its shoulders and questioning its decisions.[26] Nevertheless, Lemass told O'Hanrahan he wanted to develop a list of 'informed persons' that could put forward the official point of view and challenge the 'cranks' that were appearing on *Broadsheet*.

A short time after McCourt took up his position as director-general he was quickly confronted with labour unrest as members of the National Union of Journalists went on strike.[27] This kept all news programmes off the air for nine months but Telefís Éireann still managed to upset the Taoiseach who remained especially sensitive to the issue of emigration, regarding it as profoundly embarrassing. John Horgan's landmark biography of Lemass makes this point convincingly, emphasising that the Taoiseach viewed emigration as an indictment of failed government policy.[28] In January 1963 a television programme that addressed emigration prompted another angry letter to O'Hanrahan, ordering that a strong protest be delivered to Telefís Éireann. The Taoiseach described the objectionable programme as 'the usual non-critical "somebody should do something" kind, directed mainly against the government, with exaggerated statements allowed to pass unquestioned ... The general effect was to leave the impression "nobody cares a damn about emigration or the emigrants." It was thoroughly bad and depressing, and represented exactly the approach to serious national problems that Telefís Éireann should not adopt.'[29] Lemass argued that it was essential that informed persons who studied the problems associated with emigration be included in such a programme, persons 'capable of presenting ... [emigration] in an objective way, and that the aim in all such programmes should be to encourage a positive and constructive approach to them'.[30] He noted that he was soon to meet with the new director-general of Telefís Éireann, Kevin McCourt, and intended to emphasise this view. In the meantime, Lemass insisted that the Radio Éireann Authority be informed of his concern and criticism.

The Taoiseach made it clear that he was unhappy with seeing television programmes about emigration that 'represented it as some sort of injury done to the nation by someone, a grievance to be met by bemoaning it, rather than as evidence of the existence of a challenging economic and social problem'.[31] Lemass outlined to O'Hanrahan the kind of programme that he wanted Telefís Éireann to develop, a programme that would be structured around a series of questions that would challenge citizens to contribute to the type of economic development that would end the curse of emigration. The programme he envisioned provides both an opportunity to understand Lemass's priorities as Taoiseach and explains what he meant by arguing Telefís Éireann could do more to contribute to the realisation of national priorities. He outlined a series of questions that would challenge citizens and, in his mind, truly serve the nation:

> To the taxpayers: Are they prepared to accept the financial implications of a more aggressive development policy which would involve appropriating through taxation a much higher proportion of the national income? ...
>
> To the trade unions: As full employment is always possible at some level of living standards, are the trade unions prepared to agree that, at this point in our history, the raising of the level of employment to reduce emigration is more important than raising wage rates?
>
> To the farmers: Are they prepared to agree to a more ruthless pursuit of a policy transferring ownership of farms from old and incompetent farmers to younger and more active men and to accept cooperation as a means of intensifying activity on the land?
>
> To the shopkeepers: Are they prepared to press the sales of Irish products in an aggressive way to expand employment opportunities in Ireland?
>
> To banks and investors: [Are they prepared] to take risks in financing Irish development instead of seeking security of profit by investing elsewhere? It is the notion that emigration is always 'somebody else's business' that needs to be killed. This is the task to which T.E. should be devoting itself. Tell them to take the whine out of their voices when doing it.[32]

The correspondence encapsulates the Taoiseach's thinking on economic development in the characteristic brusque language he was famous for. He made it clear that sacrifices would have to be made by all citizens for the good of the nation. The document also suggests how he thought current affairs programming should mobilise the nation by producing constructive programmes that would support and enhance government policy.

There were other members of the government who did not hesitate to meddle in Telefís Éireann affairs. Many were used to the passivity of Radio Éireann, which had been operated by the civil service and functioned as a government enterprise from 1926 until the passage of the Broadcasting Act in 1960. This is noteworthy as, prior to 1960, the government expected the national radio service to feature basic informational news reports and issue ministerial statements, effectively serving the government of the day. Although limited autonomy was granted to the nation's radio service in 1952 when Erskine Childers, Minister for Posts and Telegraphs, established Comhairle Radio Éireann, an advisory committee to help guide Radio Éireann, the service was still part of government bureaucracy. A small amount of current affairs broadcasting was developed in the 1950s but radio functioned as a conservative civil service undertaking until 1960.[33] To that point, Radio Éireann had seldom been a source of controversy, as it enjoyed little actual independence. At the time many political figures were accustomed to a conservative national press that served party interests. The *Irish Independent* was piously Catholic and deferential to the church, the *Irish Press* was a Fianna Fáil daily, and the *Irish Times* was considered a newspaper that represented the views of Protestant Ireland. These national newspapers did not have a history of innovative investigative journalism or display an interest in consistently challenging the status quo. The national press slowly emerged as agents of modernisation, tackling complex economic, social and political issues and adding a critical voice to a society undergoing significant change. This was especially true of the *Irish Times* under the editorship of Douglas Gageby.

One of the most strident and persistent critics of Telefís Éireann was Charles J. Haughey who, in 1963, was Fianna Fáil Minister for Justice. That summer he contacted his cabinet colleague Michael Hilliard to complain vociferously about the manner in which television was conducting political reporting. The minister was not shy about expressing his concerns, informing Hilliard that in the past when he had complaints about broadcasts he had 'always taken the matter up directly with the Authority, either through the Government Information Bureau, or personally'.[34] At this juncture, Haughey explained that he had reached an impasse with the new director-general Kevin McCourt. Haughey was upset with newsroom staff in Telefís Éireann editing statements he issued as Minister for Justice. He insisted that 'in a case where I or my Department issue a prepared statement of special importance, or where I reply to a Parliamentary Question of particular importance, the statement or answer should be reported verbatim or not at all'.[35]

4   Charles Haughey when he was Fianna Fáil Minister for Finance, poses
     with his ministerial bag, 22 April 1968.

McCourt had rejected the assertion, explaining that Telefís
Éireann had every right to edit statements and pronouncements
issued by the government and its ministers. A frustrated Haughey
found the director-general's position intolerable and wanted
Hilliard to intervene directly as minister. On receiving Haughey's
complaint Hilliard passed it on to McCourt knowing that he
would not accept Haughey's demands. Unsurprisingly McCourt
once again politely rejected Haughey's request as 'not feasible' but
was at pains to state that Telefís Éireann would work closely with
any minister of state – even suggesting that on special occasions
ministers might prepare a summary that would assist staff in the

newsroom in writing their reports.[36]

The tenacious young Minister for Justice was not satisfied and refused to let the issue go. He wrote back to Hilliard insisting that his view be accepted, arguing once again that he was referring only to what he described as 'specially prepared statements of particular importance issued by Ministers or their Departments'.[37] The tone of his letter to Hilliard suggests Haughey expected Telefís Éireann to continue to act as an instrument of the government:

> I think it is an appalling state of affairs that the Director General is not prepared to give these [statements] the recognition to which they are entitled. They can be of the most fundamental importance and as you know yourself they are prepared with the utmost care and every word is weighed and considered. They should not be edited by anybody because, I submit, nobody outside the Department concerned is in a position to edit them … To my mind this is arrant nonsense and is an arrogant assumption of the right by Radio Éireann to which they could not possibly be entitled.[38]

Haughey and many politicians were uncomfortable with the power of the new television service and upset that they could not exert more control over it. Haughey dismissed McCourt's argument that there had been very few complaints from ministers as evidence of the impartiality, arguing crossly: '[t]his I can only regard as naive when I think of the numerous occasions on which different Ministers have been enraged by the manner in which Radio Éireann dealt with various political manners and the business of their different Departments'.[39] Although Haughey's angry complaint might be dismissed as the misguided intervention of an imperious young minister, the historical context of these remarks are noteworthy. Ministers and their civil servants had become used to working with an acquiescent national radio service that accepted government policy and pronouncements. The 1960 Broadcasting Act granted broadcasters significant independence, upsetting and disorienting political elites. McCourt's effort to keep the television and radio service free of direct ministerial interference infuriated Haughey and many of his colleagues. But short of getting Hilliard to issue a directive under Section 31 of the Broadcasting Act, Haughey could do little.

Haughey was not alone in finding difficulties with the new

television service. A few weeks later both the Fine Gael and Labour parties were incensed by comments made by the Professor of Modern History at University College Dublin, Desmond Williams. Williams was interviewed live on Telefís Éireann, commenting on how the Fianna Fáil government had won an important vote on a controversial turnover tax. The government survived narrowly a vote of no confidence, which impressed Williams who praised the political skill of Seán Lemass. He was not so kind in describing the work of the leaders of the opposition, however, referring to the head of the Labour Party, Brendan Corish, as 'an incompetent and incapable man, a man who had blundered badly' and the Fine Gael leader James Dillon as a man 'of no importance'.[40] As the programme was covered extensively in the press, it sparked uproar in the Dáil; consequently, Labour and Fine Gael deputies denounced what they considered the partisanship of Telefís Éireann. Deputy Gerard Sweetman of Fine Gael complained directly to the director-general, admitting that although he had not seen the programme he had been inundated with complaints. He protested 'it is clear to me that the programme was disgracefully partisan and lacking in moderation [and had] exceeded bounds of reasonable controversy and comment'.[41] The leader of Fine Gael, James Dillon, also complained to McCourt, arguing that the observations of Professor Williams were 'so remote from objectivity as to constitute a grave misuse of this powerful medium of news'.[42]

The director-general rejected the criticism and denied a bias against either of the two opposition parties. He responded to both Dillon and Sweetman, arguing that theirs were the only complaints received about the programme. He denied that the broadcast was one-sided, stating 'I am satisfied that it gave a factual picture of what occurred and that the comments included in the programme were fair and relevant to the happenings of that day in the Dáil.'[43] Later in the month when Hilliard prepared a speech about broadcasting complaints he admitted, '[s]ince the Authority was established I have received criticisms from all parties in the House about various programmes but no programme gave rise to anything like the volume of criticism from Deputies as the televised interview with Professor Williams'.[44] This line was later deleted from the speech that the minister gave in the Dáil, indicating that he did not want to exacerbate an already difficult situation.

A short time after the Professor Williams interview, an award-winning Irish language programme, *An Fear Agus A Sceal*, was cancelled, provoking charges of censorship from members of the Labour Party and the national press. When interviewed by the press the surprised producer, Proinsias Mac Aonghua, complained that he was at home with friends waiting for the programme to come on the air and was perplexed when it did not. Kevin McCourt issued a statement indicating that he cancelled the programme due to an interview with Con Lehane, a former Clan na Poblachta Dáil Deputy. McCourt's statement maintained that 'certain answers given by the interviewee were lacking in moderation and exceeded the bounds of reasonable controversy and comment'.[45]

Sensing the firestorm the cancellation of the broadcast would provoke McCourt called León Ó Broin and explained why he had ordered the programme withdrawn. He listed three reasons that compelled him to act:

> (1) A reference to Dr. Noel Browne not being 'honest' with his Clan na Poblachta colleagues on the Mother and Child controversy (2) A reference to the 'Murder' of George Plant. The government, Lehane had said, had not been able to get at Plant under the existing law; and had brought in special legislation to have him executed. (3) – and most importantly – on being asked for his opinion on Partition, had expressed the view that so long as a British soldier remained on Northern Ireland territory it was the right, and indeed the duty of young Irishmen to use force to put them out.[46]

McCourt's specific reasons for cancelling the broadcast were not shared with the press and this led to speculation that the Fianna Fáil government had stepped in and censored the programme. The government denied that it had anything to do with the broadcast being cancelled and referred reporters to the statement issued by the director-general. The *Irish Times* was not convinced that the government had not pressured McCourt to cancel the programme: 'Whether the word was whispered in Mr. McCourt's ear … or the question was resolved by Mr. McCourt alone, controversy has been silenced and a comment still-born on T.E. – a sad happening in a country with a tolerable good democratic record.'[47] In an atmosphere increasingly marked by suspicion of political bias and fear of censorship, the decision to cancel *An Fear Agus A Sceal* alarmed opponents of the Fianna Fáil government.

Labour and Fine Gael deputies believed Telefís Éireann was protecting the government by censoring programmes critical of its policies and employing analysts who supported its performance. These two episodes led to intense wrangling a short time later in the Dáil when Fine Gael Deputy Richie Ryan asked Hilliard if he was aware 'of the widespread public uneasiness regarding the growing political bias of Telefís Éireann'.[48] During the ensuing debate Hilliard denied that there was any such unease or bias and defended the comments of Professor Williams and the decision of the director-general to censor the Lehane interview. But his opponents were not convinced. Labour deputies remained furious with the remarks about their party leader and launched into a ferocious attack on both Fianna Fáil and Professor Williams. Sean Treacy, a Labour Deputy from Tipperary, told Hilliard he was 'creating a very dangerous precedent by allowing T.E. and R.E. to be used as a propaganda device for the government party by permitting insults to be hurled at members of the Opposition'.[49] He demanded assurances from Hilliard that 'guttersnipe tactics' would no longer be used by Telefís Éireann, describing Professor Williams's comments as 'insidious propaganda delivered by a party hack that was put there for the purpose of insulting the Leader of the Labour party'.[50]

An unsuccessful motion was brought forward by Labour condemning the government for not being more forthcoming in answering complaints about television in the Dáil. Brendan Corish, Labour Party leader, denounced the government for failing to answer queries about broadcasting, arguing this was 'contrary to the assurances given by the Minister during the debate on the Broadcasting Authority Bill'.[51] Hilliard defended the government, pointing out that since the Authority had been established, he had been asked 147 questions concerning broadcasting and in only 21 cases had he referred a deputy to the Radio Éireann Authority. He reminded the Dáil that an independent authority that enjoyed a substantial degree of autonomy operated broadcasting. Hilliard argued that the Dáil had accepted, with some misgiving, that the

Radio Éireann Authority should have a substantial degree of independence and be free from direct ministerial control of day-to-day matters.

He also made it clear that Fianna Fáil too had experienced problems with Telefís Éireann, maintaining that he thought there were programmes that 'could have given the government a fairer crack of the whip'.[52] He recalled that the decision to place radio and television 'under an independent authority was taken by the government with very considerable hesitation and doubt', pointing out that the 'view was strongly expressed at the time that direct ministerial responsibility for the control of the authority, and for its television and sound programmes, was the preferable arrangement'.[53] At this point Hilliard defined the 1960 Broadcasting Act as 'experimental', stating that if his government thought it was not working, changes would be made in the Act to make the service directly accountable to him as minister. He cautioned the Dáil that '[i]t is not yet clear on which side the balance of advantage lies, but if we should decide to restore the principle of direct responsibility by the Minister, it will involve legislation so that the Dáil will have full opportunity of debating it'.[54] Although it was improbable that drastic legislation to rewrite the 1960 Broadcasting Act and overhaul the service was imminent, the minister's remarks underscore the vulnerability of the new service. His comments also highlight the continuing unease television caused within the ranks of the Fianna Fáil government and politicians in general.

With the loss of a by-election in March 1965, it became clear that Seán Lemass would call for a general election, hoping that Fianna Fáil could gain a majority in the Dáil. The Taoiseach did not want the new television service to complicate his efforts, and wrote directly to Hilliard stating he wanted radio and television to steer clear of politics. Although he understood that formal party broadcasts would be featured, he told his minister, 'you should have a direction given to the Radio Éireann Authority that, during the course of the General Election, programmes with a political content (other than party broadcasts) or which might be considered to have political implications, including discussion programmes which might turn to political subjects, should be discontinued'.[55] Fianna Fáil won exactly half the seats in the Dáil and Lemass was able to form a government with the support of independent deputies.[56]

After the 1965 election there was a sustained effort to try to develop informed political programming that would bring spokesmen for the various political parties into the world of television. John Horgan's survey of public affairs broadcasting has traced the difficulties experienced by a number of earlier programmes including *Strictly Politics, Headlines and Deadlines* and *The Hurler in the Ditch.* For the most part these early programmes featured political correspondents addressing current events; the appearance by members of the Dáil or Senate was rare.[57] These were not the type of current affairs programmes that many in Telefís Éireann wanted to produce, and a renewed effort to develop more effective current affairs programming that would formally engage the major political parties began in earnest in the summer of 1966. This was done under the direction of Gunner Rugheimer who replaced Michael Barry as Controller of Programmes in June 1963.[58]

Rugheimer proved a controversial figure within Telefís Éireann, upsetting many staff members who were alienated by an abrupt personality that did not suffer fools. He was determined to change the culture within Telefís Éireann, pushing the service to establish an identity and develop a voice as a confident and independent player in modern Ireland. He quickly earned the respect and admiration of many of his colleagues who shared his desire to challenge and modernise the country's political culture by using television to force political elites to be more accountable to the public they served. Later he alienated a number of producers who believed more emphasis should be given to Irish cultural production and believed an Irish-born controller of programmes should be appointed.

A native of Sweden, Rugheimer joined Telefís Éireann from the Canadian Broadcasting Corporation in June 1963. He has been described as an adventurous man who was 'bold and courageous', enjoying a truly remarkable varied life.[59] Like Seán Lemass he was the son of a hat maker, but was born in Sweden in 1923 and studied at the University of Stockholm. During the Second World War he assisted victims of the Nazis who had been used as slave labour in northern Finland and Norway. He was in Helsinki when the Finns made an uncomfortable peace with the Soviets and helped large numbers of Belgian and Dutch citizens quietly slip out of the country. Later posing as a journalist from Chicago while working for American intelligence, he helped smuggle more than 400 Polish officers out of the country by 'drinking with the Russians by day and aiding the escapers at night', saving the Poles from being handed over to the Red Army.[60] Rugheimer later worked for the United Nations Relief and Rehabilitation Agency before emigrating to Canada where he worked in shipping before joining the Canadian Broadcasting Corporation, working in radio. When the CBC started a television service he became head of the news division. As his résumé suggests, Rugheimer was a man of remarkable courage and not easily intimidated. He quickly proved a force to be reckoned with inside of the Donnybrook station.

When he arrived in Ireland he immersed himself in Irish politics and culture, befriending a number of like-minded intellectuals. He realised that Ireland was undergoing significant political, social and economic change and was interested in using television to facilitate the transformation. He was anxious to immerse himself in the study of Irish history and hired the veteran political correspondent for the *Irish Times*, John Healy, to act as a tutor in an effort to come to grips with the complexities of Irish culture.[61] Rugheimer's efforts to develop and support professional, hard-hitting current affairs programming to address difficult issues created tremendous discomfort for a generation of politicians accustomed to a significant degree of deference from the press. Rugheimer proved an enormous influence and inspiration to Muiris MacConghail, regarded as the most innovative current affairs producer in Irish television in the 1960s. MacConghail produced compelling programmes that challenged a complacent political culture and became a thorn in the side of Fianna Fáil, the political party that dominated the decade.

In the early summer of 1966, Rugheimer approached the Fianna Fáil Whip, Michael Carty, telling him that he wanted to develop a current affairs programme for that autumn that would enable each political party to participate. The terms he proposed were simple, though in an Irish context ambitious. The programme would be

5   Gunnar Rugheimer, Controller of Programmes (1963–66) at the 13th
Golden Harp Festival in Galway, May 1979.

developed as a political magazine to run Friday evenings and be
overseen by a chairman. Political correspondents would be invited
to participate and rotate through the programme, which would
begin with a report on the business that had been conducted in
the Dáil during the week. Rugheimer explained to Carty that
deputies and senators would be invited by producers to be interviewed by professional political correspondents. Balance would be
maintained by working closely with the various parties to ensure
each was fairly represented. In the fourth week of each month the
format would change to allow for a live studio debate between
representatives of the three largest parties, Fianna Fáil, Fine Gael
and Labour. Rugheimer believed that the plans would 'promise to
bring a new interest and depth to the television coverage of political life'.[62] He was clearly influenced by current affairs programmes
broadcast on the BBC and interested in making politics and politicians accessible to the viewing public.

After meeting Rugheimer, the Fianna Fáil Chief Whip forwarded the proposal to Seán Lemass for advice. The Taoiseach read Rugheimer's proposal carefully and replied in detail, spelling out the conditions that would have to be met if Fianna Fáil deputies were to cooperate. He made it clear to Carty that Fianna Fáil would only participate in the proposed programme if five conditions were met. He first stipulated that Fianna Fáil would not take part unless it first approved of the moderator who would host the programme. The Taoiseach also insisted that the government, not the producer, should select deputies to appear in any of the proposed programmes. Additionally he told Carty that broadcasts described as 'constituent surveys' and features that profiled Fianna Fáil deputies would require pre-approval by his government. Lemass also insisted that any programme featuring debates would require even representation of government and opposition. He did not want a situation to arise whereby a single Fianna Fáil deputy would have to answer to more than one opponent, concerned that Fine Gael and Labour might gang up on a member of his party. 'Make it clear that we will not agree to participate in any programme on the basis of two opposition party spokesmen for one Fianna Fáil spokesman.'[63] Lastly, Lemass wanted it made clear that if the government thought the programme was in any way biased against Fianna Fáil it would immediately withdraw.

Rugheimer rejected many of these demands, maintaining he would not surrender editorial control of the programme to Fianna Fáil. Although he agreed that the chairman of the programme should be a person acceptable to all parties, he argued, 'we consider it the responsibility of Radio Telefís Éireann to pick an impartial Chairman for the programmes, and we would not feel entitled to transfer this responsibility to any outside body'.[64] He assured Carty that the programme would be fair and balanced. In any segment of the programme that would feature debate, RTÉ wanted to have one representative from each of the major parties. However, in an effort to allay the fears of Lemass Rugheimer offered a compromise that would allow a total of four deputies to participate in debates; two from Fianna Fáil, one from Fine Gael and another from Labour. Rugheimer accepted that it would be the responsibility of each party to choose participants for debates.

While Rugheimer wanted to feature these debates roughly once every month, the other three broadcasts would have a magazine format, described as 'a new concept, coming closer to the treatment of politics which has now become familiar to much of our audience from viewing of British television services'.[65] In programmes with a magazine format, Rugheimer insisted that the producer be able to select the deputies and constituencies that would be featured. He explained that a producer could not be answerable to the government: 'it is essential therefore that he should have the editorial responsibility of choosing the person, whether Minister or Deputy, to be invited for interview'.[66]

As negotiations dragged on Seán Lemass remained deeply involved, reviewing each of Rugheimer's lengthy letters and outlining the response to be pursued by the Fianna Fáil Whip. He was blunt in explaining his political interest, stating 'it is of course necessary to emphasise that our concern is not so much to produce attractive programmes from RTÉ's viewpoint but to *protect our party's interest*'.[67] After a number of meetings Lemass was told 'negotiations became deadlocked on the issue that Telefís Éireann would wish to have the right to invite ... Fianna Fáil deputies of their own choice to participate in the programme'.[68] Lemass's efforts to set the parameters for these programmes illustrate that his primary concern was to protect his government and Fianna Fáil. After a long and difficult process, a Code of Practice for political programmes was finally hammered out with all the political parties. Jack White, Assistant Controller, formally outlined programmes that RTÉ wanted to begin broadcasting. These developed into two separate current affairs programmes, a news magazine titled *Division* and a second programme to feature political debates, *The Politicians*. A third programme, *Seven Days*, produced by Lelia Doolan – destined to develop as an iconic and tremendously controversial addition to current affairs broadcasting – was also organised. These new programmes made their debut in the autumn of 1966 and were an important new departure for RTÉ.

Muiris MacConghail recalls the negotiations and meeting he attended with Rugheimer and the party whips, which included Carty for Fianna Fáil, Gerry L'Estrange for Fine Gael, and Frank

Clusky for Labour. He was convinced the party whips 'collectively tried to create a framework as they saw it where politicians would not embarrass themselves'.[69] Party whips were concerned with how individual deputies might appear on television, knowing that many of their fellow deputies were not particularly articulate. For party leaders and ministers, the notion of a backbench deputy being asked difficult questions about important government or party policy was unnerving. Many politicians were profoundly uncomfortable being exposed to the probing eye of the camera and not used to taking part in detailed, free-flowing conversations about complex political issues. The prospect of a programme profiling a day in the life of a deputy chosen by producers of current affairs programmes also created much discomfort. Lemass, already suspicious of the agenda of programme-makers, did not want Telefís Éireann broadcasting unflattering portraits of Fianna Fáil deputies to a national audience.

MacConghail, who produced *Division* and went on to produce *Seven Days,* argues convincingly that although many of the experienced lawyers and younger deputies took to television like 'ducks to water' many older members:

> were dead weight, incapable of expressing themselves, including Liam Cosgrave who used monosyllabic form. The brightest people were those in the small Labour Party and many young men who came to politics after the 1965 election. But for the most part we were dealing with a dull, colourless group. These were older men most of whom were not used to speaking freely and debating back and forth, they had no real skill in this regard, the Dail was too tame, ordered and structured.'[70]

The long and difficult negotiations that produced the Code of Practice spelled out the terms and conditions under which the parties would engage with one another and with RTÉ. While producers would choose subjects for discussion and debate, the code stipulated that this would be done in accordance with Section 18 (1) of the Broadcasting Act, which maintained that the service had a duty to ensure strict impartiality in programming.[71] RTÉ promised to consult with party whips before invitations to participate in programmes were extended to members of the Dáil or Senate and committed to accepting the advice of the party whips, 'unless RTÉ believes that the acceptance of it would be calculated to lead to a breach of Section 18 (1) of the Act'.[72] Importantly all parties agreed that the balance of representation between the political parties 'will be maintained over a reasonable period, not necessarily in any individual programme'.[73]

It was understood that *The Politicians* could develop into a contentious programme and therefore RTÉ explained that it would be regarded by the Authority as a Party Political Broadcast as defined by Section 18 (2) of the Broadcasting Act. RTÉ agreed that party whips would nominate participants and, to satisfy the concerns of Fianna Fáil, set a ratio of participants to include three Fianna Fáil deputies, two from Fine Gael and one from Labour. The Code of Practice maintained that an impartial chairman would be nominated by RTÉ and would provide a short introduction and conclusion. Initial topics scheduled for debate included education, labour relations, health care, the Common Market and agriculture.[74] The programme was at best uneven, plagued by contentious, sometimes ugly arguments by its guests who ignored the moderator and embarrassed all concerned. It was not popular but somehow managed to stagger on until eventually ending in February 1968.[75]

Muiris MacConghail became a critical presence in RTÉ, working as a producer in current affairs and enjoying the support and encouragement of Gunnar Rugheimer. As a young man MacConghail had a great interest in film and was intrigued with the possibilities television had to offer once Telefís Éireann went on the air. While a student of Celtic Studies at University College Dublin, he applied for a position in the new service as producer-director and much to his surprise was hired. At the time Telefís Éireann did not have facilities to instruct new members of staff and he ended up training with the BBC where he worked in current affairs with *Panorama,* a pioneering documentary programme that influenced his thinking when he began working in RTÉ. While training in England, MacConghail found himself assigned fascinating projects including coverage of Winston Churchill's funeral. Struck by the challenges and demands that current affairs broadcasting presented, he returned to Dublin committed to breaking with the staid traditions that characterised print and electronic journalism of the period.

MacConghail believed that the conservative culture of print journalism influenced the News Division in RTÉ making it passive and unresponsive. Working with *Panorama* he learned that an agile, energetic team of reporters could develop cutting-edge current affairs broadcasting that could address the exciting changes taking place in Irish society. In developing innovative current affairs broadcasting he assembled a team of dynamic young men and women who were willing to respond quickly to developing stories. For MacConghail, innovation required the ability to recognise thought-provoking stories that often upset a complacent political culture. This required accepting a frenetic pace in order to take advantage of the opportunities that developed. It also required having the institutional backing of a strong, like-minded controller of programmes willing to defend and protect programmes and producers from pressures both within RTÉ and outside it. In joining Radio Telefís Éireann while Rugheimer was establishing new programmes, MacConghail was in the right place at the right time. He was asked to develop a current affairs programme along with David Thornley, a dynamic young lecturer in politics at Trinity College Dublin. Thornley was an emerging star in current affairs, a quick-witted presenter who became a familiar face in the emerging current affairs programming. He left broadcasting for politics in 1969 and was elected to the Dáil as a Labour deputy in Dublin West and for a number of years was regarded as an intellectual force in the party.

The programme they developed, *Division,* went on the air in the autumn of 1966. It did not take long for the new enterprise to upset the political establishment. Once again, Charles J. Haughey, now Minister for Agriculture, was at the centre of the controversy. During a highly contentious dispute with the National Farmers' Association, Haughey objected to a *Division* programme that intended to interview him and his nemesis, Rickard Deasy, President of the National Farmers' Association.

Division was shown on Fridays and MacConghail understood that there was a very good programme that could be made about the dispute. A disruptive and well-publicised march had begun earlier that week in Bantry and was scheduled to arrive in Dublin on the Friday *Division* was scheduled for broadcast. MacConghail began planning for the Friday broadcast early in the week, arranging coverage of the march as it made its way across the country toward the capital. The march itself was covered extensively in the press, and during the week MacConghail made arrangements with Haughey's department for the minister to be interviewed when the march arrived in Dublin. He also arranged for Rickard Deasy to appear along with Haughey; as the march approached Dublin, the 'story of the week' became the much-anticipated encounter between the two men.[76]

As tension built and Friday approached, Haughey contacted RTÉ claiming he never agreed to participate in the programme and arguing he had no intention of appearing with the President of the National Farmers' Association. It was clear that he did not want to appear next to an unelected figure, believing the interview would suggest parity between him and the President of the NFA, a parity Haughey did not accept. MacConghail points out that Haughey was in fact being quite clever in trying to control the programme by withdrawing and testing the objectivity of the television service. If the minister thought programme-makers would cancel the appearance of Deasy they were mistaken. Confronted with Haughey's refusal to appear, Rugheimer and MacConghail decided that a journalist could put the government's case forward.[77] When *Division* was broadcast that Friday, David Thornley, the chair, introduced journalist Ted Nealon who presented an overview of the dispute putting forward the government's case and providing an 'appraisal of the conflict between the NFA and the Minister'.[78]

Prior to the broadcast, Haughey got wind of these plans and was outraged. He made public a letter he sent to Gunner Rugheimer denouncing RTÉ, stating 'I must emphatically reject the right of any person not authorised by me to do so to purport to outline the policy of this Department. Mr. Nealon is not authorised and to convey any other impression is an attempt to mislead the public.... It is grossly irresponsible to make these serious matters the subject of the type of programme you have in mind and whose main purpose would seem to be to entertain rather than to inform.'[79] Fianna Fáil Whip Michael Carty wrote to Rugheimer denouncing the *Division* programme as 'a flagrant breach of [the] Code' and announced that Fianna Fáil was formally withdrawing from the programme and threatening to lodge a formal objection under Section 18 (1) of the Broadcasting Act.[80]

A review of the Code of Practice supports the decision that had been made by Rugheimer and MacConghail. There is nothing in it that prohibits members of the public from appearing with elected officials or journalists presenting the government's position. Rugheimer steadfastly defended the programme and issued a statement denying the agreement had been breeched, dismissing Haughey's critique by replying to the minister, '[a]s you know, we would have wished for your participation: we respect your wishes about that; but are not thereby relieved of our obligation to provide information to the public on a subject of grave significance to our economic well being'.[81] This dispute was reported widely in the national press, which quoted the letters and statements of Cary, Haughey and Rugheimer extensively. The episode illustrates the 'thin skin' of Fianna Fáil and especially the beleaguered minister, Charles Haughey, who was locked in a fierce battle with the farming community over unpopular Fianna Fáil agricultural policies.

A short time later another decision by RTÉ concerning coverage of the dispute between the government and the farmers infuriated Haughey. When the News Division broadcast a story juxtaposing an interview he had given with one by Rickard Deasy, an enraged Haughey called the newsroom directly to complain. This resulted in a change to the programme that had gone out at 6 p.m.; in the subsequent 9 p.m. broadcasts the interview with Deasy was dropped.[82] Reports of ministerial censorship and interference in the affairs of RTÉ provoked a storm of protest in the print media. During the ensuing controversy the *Irish Independent* featured an article that included an excited accusation by Deasy that the government had 'threatened to take over the station … that the government intended to sack the Authority of RTÉ … they had in mind to set up their own news service'.[83]

Director-General Kevin McCourt, speaking a short time later at a Dublin Chamber of Commerce function, defended the decision of the Head of News, Pearse Kelly, who had made the change after Haughey's call to the station. McCourt maintained that the original news bulletin was made in error, telling his audience 'there is neither mystery nor intrigue involved in this. We made an error in editorial judgement'.[84] McCourt argued that a mistake had been made by Telefís Éireann and that the head of news had the courage to correct it, noting that he 'fully supported the action he took'.[85] The National Union of Journalists was not impressed by McCourt's explanation and made this clear by issuing a strongly worded statement after holding an emergency meeting. The union argued that the news item including the statements made by both Haughey and Deasy would have continued in subsequent broadcasts 'but for the complaint of Mr. Haughey. The item was omitted on the order of the Head of News, and in our view, this was the only error of judgment involved.'[86] The union noted that in February 1965 it had presented McCourt with a memorandum detailing instances of what it defined as outside interference, which it claimed had affected the content and presentation of news programmes. At the time McCourt was said to have rejected the allegations as being based on misconceptions. 'We were assured that outside pressures had never been, and never would be successful. Now it appears that the action after outside intervention can be excused by the phrase "error of editorial judgement".'[87]

An *Irish Times* editorial chastised the director-general, stating that it was absurd to argue that outside pressures did not have an effect on RTÉ: 'One would like to feel that there was a bit more steel in the members of the Authority and their senior servants in Montrose.'[88] The editorial commended television for 'opening up Irish life … Its discussions go deep into some matters though they tend to shy away from the most controversial. The director-general would be more in line with current thinking if he asserted that it was his intention to press on with the further opening up, with providing not only more controversy but perhaps even satire.'[89] The paper praised the critique offered by the National Union of Journalists, concluding 'Mr McCourt could not over-estimate the value of word being passed from mouth-to-mouth at Montrose that on the occasion of the next imperious telephone call the answer had been "Tell the Minister to go to hell."'[90] As one might expect, the National Farmers' Association was not pleased with what it regarded as outright censorship and the muzzling of its president, and exploited the episode to lash out at the government and especially Haughey. To that end the NFA issued a statement lambasting Haughey for 'his most recent efforts in trying to control criticism of himself on our national radio and television network'.[91]

These controversial events created ample headlines and certainly caught the attention of the Taoiseach. Again it should be stressed that in many respects RTÉ had a captive audience that was fascinated with the political theatre playing out on television, which was covered extensively in the national press. In these circumstances the tension building between the national broadcaster and the government was tremendous. All the while, Lemass's son-in-law, Charles Haughey, remained defiant, maintaining that he had done nothing wrong or improper. The Fianna Fáil government defended Haughey and firmly backed his position as appropriate. When the issue was raised in the Dáil a week later Seán Lemass made his much quoted statement concerning RTÉ being an 'instrument of public policy'. This was not an off-the-cuff remark thrown out by an angry and frustrated Taoiseach; Lemass wrote the speech himself and thought long and hard about the language he used. Lemass had at first included a more threatening line that argued the government 'could, in grave circumstances, require either changing the membership of the Authority or the law under which it operates'.[92]

This early draft, warning that changes might be made in the composition of the Radio Éireann Authority or that broadcasting legislation might be changed was written to reply to a question put forward by the leader of the Labour Party, Brendan Corish, who once again was questioning government interference in Radio Telefís Éireann. While drafting the reply, Lemass ordered his secretary to make sure that each member of his cabinet was fully aware of his answer. Furthermore, he instructed the cabinet that if asked questions concerning the role of the government in broadcasting they should refer to 'this reply by me to the same question'.[93]

Joseph Brennan, who had replaced Michael Hilliard as Minister for Posts and Telegraphs in April 1965, reviewed the Lemass speech and was clearly concerned that it was too severe. He advised the Taoiseach to de-escalate the controversy, hoping he would tone down his remarks:

> I agree generally with the line you propose. I think, however, that it might be better not to make any reference now to changing the members of the Authority, or to the law under which it operates, particularly in view of the recent statement by Mr. Rickard Deasy. Moreover, the draft reply is rather strongly worded and would make it difficult for me to resist pressure to intervene in programme matters and matters of day-to-day administration. There is, I know, a subtle difference between representations and intervention.[94]

Brennan was referring to Deasy's excited remarks in the press about an impending Fianna Fáil takeover of Radio Telefís Éireann. Reluctantly Lemass rewrote the speech, adding language defining RTÉ as an 'instrument of public policy' but dropping the more threatening language that referred to removing members of the Authority or revising the Broadcasting Act. The critical point here is that Seán Lemass carefully crafted the draconian language used and if not for the intervention of Joseph Brennan the language would have been even more menacing. The exchange in the Dáil is worth considering as Lemass exclaimed:

> Radio Telefís Éireann was set up by legislation as an instrument of public policy and as such is responsible to the government. The government have overall responsibility for its conduct and especially the obligation to ensure that its programmes do not offend against the public interest or conflict with national policy as defined in legislation. To this extent the government reject the view that Radio Telefís Éireann should be, either generally or in regard to its current affairs and news programmes, completely independent of Government supervision. As a public institution supported by public funds and operating under statute, it has the duty, while maintaining impartiality between political Parties, to present programmes which inform the public regarding current affairs, to sustain public respect for the institutions of Government and, where appropriate, to assist public understanding of the policies enshrined in legislation enacted by the Oireachtas. The government will take such action by way of making representations or otherwise as may be necessary to ensure that Radio Telefís Éireann does not deviate from the due performance of this duty ...

Mr. Dillon: Has any individual member of the government a right of censorship as opposed to a right of reply on Radio Telefís Éireann? Has any individual member a right to say: 'Take that item off'?

The Taoiseach: Yes. The Minister for Posts and Telegraphs has that power … When Telefís Éireann was being established we had very considerable hesitation in adopting this device of entrusting it to an independent authority instead of retaining it as a service under the control of the Minister responsible to the House, as was the radio service before the Act of 1960. There is, I think, a very special obligation on the government to ensure that the decision to entrust this responsibility to an independent authority does not conflict with the public interest.[95]

Lemass's statements underscore that he was rearticulating his long-held conviction that television and radio should serve the nation as he defined it and not descend into fractious party politics. These ideas had been expressed years earlier when he drafted policy directives for the first meeting of the Broadcasting Authority and while preparing remarks at the inaugural Jacobs Awards ceremony. Lemass's pronouncement has often been quoted as proof of the government's ambivalence to the freedom of the press, but the remarks were not a new departure for the Taoiseach. The declaration is indeed extraordinary but it also illustrates that Lemass was consistent in seeing how television could become a threat to the national interest, as he defined it. The fact that he was prepared to be much more aggressive in his remarks to the Dáil illustrates quite clearly that he had strong reservations about the degree of autonomy that RTÉ enjoyed.

A short time after this controversy, Lemass announced that he was stepping down as Taoiseach. The term the 'great Irish moderniser' is accurate in describing Lemass, as he displayed remarkable courage and determination in reorienting the Irish economy, encouraging increased support for education, and initiating a dialogue with the Government of Northern Ireland. However, when dealing with the emerging electronic media, Lemass's attitude towards modernisation proved quite ambivalent; the accelerating modernity he did so much to encourage proved a two-edged sword.

Television changed the political culture of the country, becoming a popular and tenacious critic of the status quo.[96] The government thus found itself in the uncomfortable position of being on the defensive, answerable to an increasingly aggressive and often 'inconsistent' press. These changes were rapid and for many disorienting, proving that television was a critical agent of Ireland's transformation during the 1960s.

Notes

1   See Savage, *Irish Television* (Cork University Press, 1996), xi.
2   See Brian Girvin, *From Union to Union: Nationalism, Democracy and Religion in Ireland* (Gill and Macmillan, Dublin, 2002), 203–5.
3   See, for instance, John Horgan, *Seán Lemass: The Enigmatic Patriot* (Gill and Macmillan, Dublin, 1997); Paul Bew and Henry Patterson, *Seán Lemass and the Making of Modern Ireland* (Gill and Macmillan, Dublin, 1982); Brian Girvin and Gary Murphy (eds), *The Lemass Era: Politics and Society in the Ireland of Seán Lemass* (University College Dublin Press, Dublin, 2005) and Robert Savage, *Seán Lemass* (Historical Association of Ireland, Dublin, 1999).
4   NAI, AGH&I 2001/78/18, speech by Lemass, December 4, 1962.
5   Ibid.
6   Ibid.
7   Ibid.
8   NAI, Department of the Taoiseach, S3532 C/63, Lemass to Roth, September 2, 1961.
9   Ibid., Roth to Lemass, September 1, 1961.
10 Author's interview with John Irvine, December 1990.
11 RTÉ Authority Archive, Minutes of the Authority, October 25, 1961, 3.
12 Ibid., 4.
13 NAI, Department of the Taoiseach, S3532 C/63 Roth to Lemass, October 21, 1961.
14 Ibid.
15 Ibid., Lemass to Hilliard, February 2, 1962.
16 Ibid., Hilliard to Lemass, the exact day is unclear; either February 7 or 8, 1962.
17 Author's interview with John Irvine, December 1990.
18 Quoted in John Horgan, *Broadcasting and Public Life* (Four Courts Press, Dublin, 2004), 29.
19 NAI, Department of the Taoiseach, S3532 C/63, Lemass to O'Hanrahan, September 9, 1962.
20 Ibid.
21 Ibid., O'Hanrahan to Lemass, September 26, 1962.

22 Ibid.

23 Ibid.

24 Ibid., Lemass to O'Hanrahan, October 1, 1962.

25 McCourt was given a five-year contract with an annual salary of £5,500 from January 1, 1963.

26 The Broadcasting Review Group was established in the early 1970s in an effort to monitor and provide feedback to the RTÉ Authority.

27 The Radio Éireann Authority announced the strike on February 28, 1963, indicating members were seeking BBC pay rates for its members. (RTÉ Written Archives, Irvine Papers.)

28 Horgan, *Seán Lemass*; see also Enda Delaney, 'Emigration, political culture, and post-war Irish Society', in *The Lemass Era* (eds) Girvin and Murphy. On this correspondence see Horgan, *Seán Lemass*, 316–17.

29 NAI, Department of the Taoiseach, S3532 C/63, Lemass to O'Hanrahan, January 4, 1963.

30 Ibid. See also Horgan, *Seán Lemass*, 317.

31 NAI, Department of the Taoiseach, S3532 C/63, Lemass to Hilliard, March 7, 1963. Instead, Lemass insisted emigration be addressed as a 'practical problem capable of being solved provided there is a general national will to do it, involving acceptance of all the requirements of a comprehensive policy for a solution'.

32 Ibid. See also Horgan, *Seán Lemass*, 317.

33 One of the earliest current affairs programmes, *Roundtable and World Affairs* featured senior journalists addressing contemporary issues. One long-time producer in both radio and television, Aindrias Ó Gallchóir, recalls the programmes being recorded and having to be cleared for broadcast by León Ó Broin. (Interview with Aindrias Ó Gallchóir, Dun Laoghaire, June 2007.)

34 NAI, 2001/78/35, Haughey to Hilliard, July 17, 1963.

35 Ibid.

36 Ibid., McCourt to Ó Broin, September 11, 1963.

37 Ibid., Haughey to Hilliard, October 19, 1963.

38 Ibid. Again, under the Broadcasting Act, Radio Éireann was the official name of the combined radio and television service.

39 Ibid.

40 *Sunday Independent*, editorial, November 3, 1963.

41 NAI, 2001/78/33, Sweetman to McCourt, November 1, 1963.

42 Ibid., Dillon to McCourt, November 1, 1963.

43 Ibid., McCourt to Dillon, November 6, 1963.

44 Ibid., speech prepared for the Minister for Posts and Telegraphs and delivered November 20, 1963, in Dáil Éireann.

45 *Evening Herald*, October 29, 1963. Lehane was a Dublin solicitor who in the 1930s had been a member of the IRA Army Council. The Fianna

Fáil Government jailed him for eighteen months in 1935 then interned him briefly at the start of the Second World War, although he had left the IRA when it embarked on a bombing campaign in England in 1938. He was a founding member of Clan na Poblachta, representing Dublin South Central from 1948 to 1951, and throughout his career defended several generations of republican activists, earning tremendous respect from republicans.

46 NAI, 2001/78/33, memorandum by León Ó Broin, October 29, 1963. The Mother and Child controversy had helped undermine the first Coalition Government in 1951 when the government refused to support health legislation when confronted with opposition from the Catholic Church. George Plant was an IRA member who was charged with the murder of an informer during the Second World War. After his prosecution by a civilian court failed, he was charged once again, tried by a military tribunal, found guilty, and executed. Eunan O'Halpin makes the point that '[h]is fate provided an echo of the executions policy which the Cosgrave government had operated during the civil war'. *Defending Ireland* (Oxford University Press, Oxford, 1999), 202.

47 Ibid., *Irish Times*, October 31, 1963.

48 Dáil Debates, Vol. 205, November 7, 1963.

49 Ibid.

50 Ibid. Senior staff at Telefís Éireann advised Hilliard it stood by the programme. Desmond Williams was defended as simply maintaining that 'a power situation was resolved in a certain way that ... resulted in a victory of generalship for An Taoiseach. While he made personal comments on the tactics employed, he waved no flags and neither applauded nor disapproved of the result.' ((RTÉ Written Archives, Irvine Papers, Hardiman to Ingoldsby, November 5, 1963).

51 Ibid.

52 Ibid.

53 Ibid.

54 Dáil Debates, Vol. 205, November 20, 1963.

55 NAI, 98/6/83, Lemass to Hilliard, March 15, 1965.

56 Fianna Fáil won 72 seats, Fine Gael 47, Labour 22 and independents 3 seats in the election.

57 See John Horgan, *Broadcasting and Public Life* (Four Courts Press, Dublin, 2004), 36–7.

58 NAI, 98/6/83 Rugheimer to the Chief Whip of Fianna Fáil Michael Carty, June 3, 1966. The controller explained, 'there remains room for a more detailed treatment, on an adult level, of the political affairs of the nation'.

59 *Daily Telegraph*, obituary, March 3, 2003.

60 Ibid. The fate of 4,500 Polish officers massacred by the Soviets in the Katyn Forrest at the time suggests that his efforts may have saved the lives of these men.

61 Author's interview with Muiris MacConghail, April 18, 2007.

62 NAI, 98/6/83, Rugheimer to Carty, June 3, 1966.

63 Ibid., Lemass to his Parliamentary Secretary, June 10, 1966.

64 Ibid., Rugheimer to Carty, July 1, 1966.

65 Ibid.

66 Ibid.

67 Ibid., Lemass to Parliamentary Secretary, July 12, 1966 (added emphasis).

68 Ibid., Parliamentary Secretary to Lemass, July 28, 1966.

69 Author's interview with Muiris MacConghail, April 18, 2007.

70 Ibid., Later in the decade when he became Minister for Posts and Telegraphs, Erskine Childers recognised this and convinced the Lynch Government to train deputies in the use of television.

71 Section 18 required that, when broadcasting matters of public controversy, the Authority ensure 'that information, news or feature is presented objectively and impartially without any expression of the Authority's own view'. Section 18 (1) provided the Authority the power to feature political party broadcasts. *Broadcasting Authority Act*, Section 18 (Stationery Office, Dublin, 1960).

72 NAI, 98/6/83, Jack White to James Gibbons, T.D., August 17, 1966.

73 Ibid.

74 Ibid.

75 See Horgan, *Broadcasting*, 37–9.

76 Author's interview with Muiris MacConghail, April 18, 2007.

77 See Horgan, *Broadcasting*, 40–1.

78 *Irish Press*, October 8, 1966.

79 Ibid., Haughey to Rugheimer, published in the *Irish Press*, October 8, 1966.

80 NAI, 98/6/83, Carty to Rugheimer, October 5, 1966.

81 Rugheimer to Haughey, published in the *Irish Press*, October 8, 1966,

82 Horgan, *Broadcasting*, 41.

83 *Irish Independent*, October 11, 1966.

84 *Irish Press*, October 4, 1966.

85 Ibid.

86 Ibid.

87 Ibid.

88 *Irish Times*, October 5, 1966.

89 Ibid.

90 Ibid.

91 Ibid.

92 NAI, 98/6/19, Taoiseach's draft, October 7, 1966.
93 Ibid.
94 Ibid. Brennan to Lemass, October 1966.
95 Dáil Debates, Vol. 224, October 12, 1966.
96 By March 1965 it was estimated that 48 per cent of all homes in the
    state were receiving Telefís Éireann programmes and that 54 per cent
    of these programmes were home-produced. The number of homes
    increased steadily. One year later 53 per cent of all homes in the state
    were reported to have licensed televisions. *RTÉ Chronology*, Vol. I,
    1960–66 (RTÉ Library, issued February 1974).

4

Transition

For a variety of reasons, 1966 was a transitional year in Ireland's history. The year witnessed the departure of Ireland's great moderniser, Seán Lemass, who stepped aside as Taoiseach and rather awkwardly handed over the reins of power to Jack Lynch. There were also significant changes in broadcasting as a number of individuals assumed critical roles in RTÉ. Prior to leaving, Lemass appointed C. S. (Todd) Andrews Chairman of the RTÉ Authority after Eamonn Andrews resigned in frustration with the newly appointed Authority. A lifelong supporter of Fianna Fáil, Andrews had fought in the War of Independence and Civil War opposing the 1921 Treaty that established the Irish Free State. Arrested by the Free State government and interned until the spring of 1924, Andrews decided against a career in politics, instead studying commerce at University College Dublin. After graduation he began a long and distinguished public service career beginning with the Irish Tourist Association in 1926 and moving to the Electricity Supply Board in 1930. He proved remarkably capable, quickly rising through the ranks, and was named managing director of the Turf Development Board before becoming chair of the national transportation organisation, Córas Iompair Éireann. According to Kevin McCourt, Todd Andrews used his connections within Fianna Fáil to secure the position of Chairman of the Authority. McCourt recalled, 'when Eamonn Andrews resigned, Todd went to "Dev" and said he wanted the job. That's how he got it.'[1]

When Andrews met him to talk about the position he recalled

the Taoiseach expressing little interest in RTÉ, although he was told by Lemass that 'some of the staff seemed to be "losing the run of themselves" in thinking that the government had no function in relation to the National Broadcasting Authority, a point of view no government could accept'.[2] Andrews fully supported Lemass's position that RTÉ was set up as an 'instrument of public policy', believing the service should be accountable to the government. Unlike Eamonn Andrews, he had no familiarity with broadcasting, but a career's worth of experience working in and running semi-state organisations. He tended to view RTÉ much like the organisations he directed, despite it being a truly unique institution. As a veteran republican of the revolutionary period, Todd Andrews was sympathetic to the politics of Lemass and Fianna Fáil and grew increasingly uncomfortable with what he referred to derisively as the 'creative people' in Irish television.[3] In naming Andrews chairman of the RTÉ Authority Lemass was appointing a senior figure with a proven track record as an effective and energetic manager. Lemass hoped that Andrews's managerial strengths could be harnessed to ensure that RTÉ would operate in what the Taoiseach defined as the national interest.

Todd Andrews became chairman of the RTÉ Authority as the Irish television service was becoming more comfortable addressing societal changes that were having a profound effect on the country. During his tenure political, cultural and religious elites grew increasingly uncomfortable with programming that challenged the conservative consensus that had defined the country since independence. Programmes broadcast by RTÉ became more aggressive in challenging both the domestic and foreign policies of the Fianna Fáil governments that were in power throughout the 1960s. Andrews was chairman of the Authority from 1966 to 1970, years that saw widespread popular unrest across Europe and North America, supporting civil rights and opposing the Vietnam War. Ireland was not immune to these movements and the student activism that contributed to a wider counter-culture that took on a decidedly anti-establishment hue. Protesters took to the streets in Irish cities, addressing a range of social justice issues. Protests demanded affordable housing and an end to the destruction of Georgian Dublin by property developers; supported women's rights; advocated for economic development of the Gaeltacht; supported the Irish language; and opposed the war in Vietnam. This period also witnessed the development of a civil rights campaign in Northern Ireland and the outbreak of 'the Troubles'.

Andrews understood that many RTÉ employees were young, university-educated men and women who regarded themselves as political activists and were critical of a powerful, socially conservative Fianna Fáil party that dominated the decade. They did not impress him and he regarded many as possessing a sense of entitlement he found unnerving. He believed they

> claimed to be 'concerned', which was the vogue word of the time. They were a difficult group for a director general to cope with ... 'Concerned' citizens seemed to me to be divided into different categories. Some were idealists prepared to go to the scaffold to eliminate the injustices of society. Some were dissatisfied because their jobs did not give them the power and influence they felt capable of exercising on contemporary events. Some were parlour pinks enjoying the social cachet attached to radical chic in pubs and suburban drawing rooms. Many of them were convinced that they were living and working in a society which was rotten to the core; they believed that they had a mission to change it through the use of television.[4]

Andrews was the product of a generation that had fought and won independence for Ireland, experiencing first-hand the violence, deprivation and loss of war. He regarded many of the critics who took to the airwaves to assail the conservative nature of Irish society and the dominance of Fianna Fáil with a mixture of amusement and contempt.

His predecessor Eamonn Andrews stepped down as Chairman of the RTÉ Authority in April 1966, publicly stating he was leaving because he was opposed to increasing Irish language programming. However, this was only part of a more fundamental problem that created tremendous frustration – leading to his alienation and eventual resignation. There were sharp ideological differences within the recently appointed Authority that came to a head when some members began to insist on replacing the controller of programmes. The controller of programmes was one of the most demanding positions within RTÉ, requiring a strong and effective leader to oversee the work of producers, writers and technicians. As the name implies, the controller, who reported directly to the director-general, was also responsible for almost all of the programmes the station broadcast.[5]

The issue of replacing the controller touched on the tremendously sensitive question of non-nationals working in important positions within Irish television. The Swedish-born Gunnar Rugheimer replaced Michael Barry as Controller of Programmes in the autumn of 1962 and proved an energetic force within the station. Rugheimer was admired by many within Telefís Éireann for his commitment and professionalism and enjoyed the full support of Eamonn Andrews and Kevin McCourt. However, for some members of the recently appointed Authority who were committed to a greater emphasis on Irish culture, and the language in particular, Rugheimer's biggest failing was that he was not Irish. There had been an undercurrent of mild xenophobia in the service since Telefís Éireann was first established, as many key members of staff were foreign-born.[6] This led, perhaps inevitably, to a degree of friction among staff. The head of children's programming remembered that there was resentment towards the British and American presence within the television service, recalling that taking instructions particularly from British managers became problematic for some.[7] This resentment of foreigners within the station came to a head in 1966 as the expiration of Rugheimer's contract approached.

The question of renewing Rugheimer's contract first became an issue in the autumn of 1965 after a new RTÉ Authority was appointed. Unlike the first Authority which was appointed to a five-year term, the second Authority was given a one-year term. It included existing members Eamonn Andrews as Chair, Professor T. W. Moody, James Fanning, Edward McManus and Fintan Kennedy. Charles Brennan, Ernest Blythe, Commander George Crosbie and Áine Ní Chanainn were not reappointed. The new members were the founding director of Gael-Linn, Dónall Ó Móráin; the widow of President Seán T. Ó Cheallaigh, Phyllis Bean Uí Cheallaigh; Fianna Fáil supporter Michael Noonan, who later was elected to the Dáil; and Ruairí Brugha, whose father Cathal had been killed in the civil war. Ruairí Brugha was elected to the Dáil in 1973 as a Fianna Fáil deputy and later served two terms in the Senate.

Ó Móráin, Uí Cheallaigh, and Brugha all shared a desire to see RTÉ feature more Irish language programming. The question of Rugheimer's status provided an opening for critics within the new Authority who were upset that the controller had not provided more opportunity for them to become actively involved in programme policy. This was not a new complaint: as early as 1962 the first Authority complained to Edward Roth about his perceived failure to involve members more closely in decisions concerning programming. Although both Edward Roth and Kevin McCourt subsequently tried to work more closely with the board, the members of the recently reconstituted Authority demanded meaningful input into decisions affecting programme policy.

Some members of the new Authority were passionate cultural nationalists, convinced that RTÉ had to do more to promote the language, history and traditions of a Gaelic Ireland. They believed Rugheimer did not understand or appreciate Irish culture and pushed for the drafting of a detailed statement of policy that would be presented to him. Professor Moody was charged with drafting a document that would emphasise the need for a greater appreciation of cultural programmes and call for greater consultation between the board and the controller of programmes. Moody pragmatically proposed a simple and direct statement: 'Radio Éireann is a national service and its aim is a programme that will have a distinctive Irish quality and will reflect and cherish traditional Irish values.'[8] Dónall Ó Móráin, one of the new members of the Authority and a passionate advocate of the language, rejected Moody's draft outright, believing that specific reference should be made to the need to support the Irish language.

Ó Móráin proposed five amendments but could not gain enough support to prevail, and each was defeated. Even though he had the support and sympathy of a number of members this was not enough to get a majority of the Authority as most thought his versions were too extreme. In the end, all members accepted the statement drafted by Moody with the notable exception of Ó Móráin, who insisted that his dissent be formally recorded. The minutes of the Authority therefore state, 'In the context of the minimal amount of Irish used in TV programmes since the establishment of the service, he regarded the statement as inadequate and could not subscribe to it.'[9] The statement of policy drafted by Moody was delivered to Rugheimer, signalling the Authority's newfound desire to promote Irish culture and become involved in decisions regarding what types of programmes should be broadcast. When the document was delivered, Rugheimer was already deeply involved in overseeing a number of documentaries and feature projects to commemorate the fiftieth anniversary of the 1916 Easter Rising.[10]

Eamonn Andrews resented the belief held by some members of the Authority that Rugheimer's contract should not be renewed, not because of any uneasiness with his performance, but simply because he was a foreigner. He was disturbed by demands by members that an Irish national be appointed, even if it meant that the person hired was less qualified than Rugheimer. When the contract actually came up for renewal Andrews wanted to award him a five-year extension. This was a tactical error, as some members who considered the terms too generous may have supported a shorter contract. During these discussions some members believed advertising the position was essential because, if Rugheimer were re-hired, it would be under a clause in the Broadcasting Act that allowed certain positions to be declared specialised, enabling the hiring of a non-national. Although no decision was made at this juncture, the director-general was asked to informally approach Rugheimer to ask about his interest in remaining in his position. Kevin McCourt reported back to the Authority that Rugheimer wanted to stay and pointed out that he accepted the statement of policy that had recently been delivered to him and understood there was a need to improve the quality of Irish language broadcasts.

A short time later the Authority once again debated whether or not the position of controller of programmes should be advertised. Eamonn Andrews reiterated his conviction that this would be a mistake, maintaining that in his professional opinion there were simply no qualified Irish applicants available. He was concerned that by advertising the position the Authority would risk alienating Rugheimer, who might leave, forcing the hiring of another non-national without his depth of experience. Again, Moody looked to find a compromise, suggesting the Authority offer Rugheimer a three-year contract. Although Andrews, Moody, Kennedy and Noonan supported the proposal, opposition from more nationally minded members, Ó Móráin, Brugha, McManus, Fanning and Ui Cheallaigh narrowly defeated it, exposing a rift in the Authority that thwarted the efforts of Eamonn Andrews, his allies on the board, and Kevin McCourt. Each of those who opposed Rugheimer insisted that every conceivable effort should be made to hire an Irish person. McCourt was given the unpleasant task of informing Rugheimer that a search would be conducted in the hope that a qualified Irish-born candidate would emerge to take his position, although he was also encouraged to apply. McCourt reported back to the Authority that the meeting was awkward and upset Rugheimer. 'I explained carefully to Mr. Rugheimer the reason for the Authority's decision. I told him the Authority felt it had a responsibility to ensure that there was not some place in the world an Irishman who could fill this position.'[11]

In the months leading up to these discussions there had been some rumbling within Telefís Éireann regarding Rugheimer's management style; a resulting complaint submitted to the Authority by the Trade Union Group represented a number of senior producers and department heads including James Plunkett Kelly, Meav Conway, Aindreas Ó Gallchóir, Jim Fitzgerald and Pádraig Ó Raghallaigh. They understood that Rugheimer's contract was due to expire and hoped to influence a decision against renewal. A copy of their complaint was leaked to and reproduced in the *Irish Times,* causing the controller of programmes considerable embarrassment.[12] Lelia Doolan, who supported Rugheimer and held a number of high-level positions in Telefís Éireann during her tenure, remembers the 'Gaelic mafia' inside of the station 'disliked Rugheimer and would have asked: "Why do we have to have a foreigner here?"'[13]

Although these producers complained about working conditions inside the station, they specifically targeted Rugheimer for his management style. According to Doolan he could be brusque and a bit of a 'tyrant, but he knew what he wanted and knew broadcasting'.[14] Another senior producer maintained a 'green element' within the station that was increasingly upset with foreigners holding positions of power and wanted an Irish national appointed to the position of controller.[15] Irish Actors Equity also weighed in, arguing that it was 'incongruous' that a 'non-national should be trying to evolve a philosophy of Irish consciousness'.[16] Not to be outdone, the Gaelic League stepped up to protest that an Irish national should be controller of programmes, arguing Rugheimer 'did not understand the Irish way of life'.[17]

When McCourt met with Rugheimer he assured him that these complaints had not influenced the Authority's decision to advertise his job. However, the majority of the Authority were clearly uncomfortable with a foreigner as controller of programmes and shared the concerns articulated by a number of producers, the union and the Gaelic League. McCourt told Rugheimer that although he hoped he would apply for the position, Rugheimer should not assume that he would be hired. He was blunt in explaining to the controller the position of the Authority. 'The purpose of advertising would be to seek an Irishman – it might be that someone with Irish connections would come close enough to the Authority's specifications – and the great sensitivities attaching to the influence of a Programme Controller in television programmes would require the Authority to make a wide and conscientious search.'[18] Rugheimer advised McCourt that although he would like to stay he would not apply for the position 'as it was quite clear that he would only be a second choice in the mind of the Authority, he could not take the risk of applying and, thereby, wasting three or four valuable months were he not successful'.[19]

Rugheimer was disappointed in the Authority's decision and anxious that it be handled carefully. He was worried about the implications that advertising his job might create and that he would be regarded internationally as a professional failure. McCourt understood this and tried to protect him as best he could. He told the Authority that the matter had to be handled with a great care to ensure that Rugheimer's professional reputation would not be harmed. McCourt regarded Rugheimer as a true professional and remarkable controller general and was upset with the Authority's decision. He wanted Rugheimer to stay and tried unsuccessfully to convince him to apply for the position. Referring to the representation made by the Trade Union Group,

McCourt told the Authority that he was worried that the decision to advertise Rugheimer's job would imply that he was being dismissed because of these protests. He maintained that a small number of staff within the Telefís Éireann unhappy with Rugheimer's management style had manipulated the representatives from the Trade Unions Group and did not want the union or these staff members to think they had succeeded in getting the controller fired.[20] McCourt noted that the Authority had not even discussed the representation from the union, implying that it was never taken seriously. The director-general understood that advertising the post shortly after the complaint had been made public could undermine not only his power (and that of any future controller) but that of the RTÉ Authority itself.

Rugheimer asked that he be able to make an announcement simply indicating that he would not stay in his position or in Ireland once his contract expired. McCourt asked the Authority to consider a short-term solution, extending his contract by several months, which provided time for a full and extensive search to be conducted while allowing Rugheimer to avoid public embarrassment. He had run this past the controller who had said he would accept a seven-month extension 'on the grounds that he really has no alternative but to accept any practical suggestion that would give lie to the implication that he was being "fired" by non-renewal of contract'.[21]

A search committee was established to identify suitable candidates for the position that included Eamonn Andrews, Kevin McCourt and Ruairi Brugha, a recently appointed member of the RTÉ Authority. Brugha was part of the more nationally minded faction in the Authority and tended to support Ó Móráin on the language issue. He proved outspoken in arguing the importance of hiring an Irish national into the position – even if the person appointed was less qualified than a non-national. By the spring of 1966 the committee reported to the Authority that efforts to identify a qualified candidate for the position had run into serious difficulties. Brugha reported to the board that his priority remained hiring an Irish person. The experienced professionals in broadcasting, Eamonn Andrews and Kevin McCourt, strongly disagreed. Brugha was supported by Ó Móráin, Ui Cheallaigh, Fanning and

McManus, all of whom argued that the position should be offered 'to a candidate whose love for and knowledge of Ireland was not necessarily matched by the technical and managerial qualities of other candidates from outside of the country. It was an insult to Ireland and the Authority's staff to suggest that an Irish Controller could not be found.'[22]

Andrews was convinced this was a mistake, emphasising that it was critical that the person appointed have the expertise to take on a challenging leadership position that required a high degree of managerial, administrative and technical expertise. He explained that it was his opinion that none of the Irish applicants had the requisite skills. Professor Moody once again suggested a compromise, arguing that Rugheimer should be retained indefinitely until a qualified Irish candidate could be identified. He praised the incumbent, maintaining that Rugheimer had worked diligently to gain an impressive knowledge and understanding of Ireland. He was convinced that the 'Authority should not risk a second-class appointment to this key position for the sake of nationality'.[23] Andrews, McCourt and Noonan supported Moody but once again opposition from Brugha, Ó Móráin, Fanning, McManus and Ui Cheallaigh undermined his effort to reach a compromise. A critical impasse had been reached, and tension within the Authority grew palpable.

For Andrews, the aggressive tactics of Ó Móráin, Brugha, and their allies on the Irish language issue, combined with the strident cultural nationalism that emerged in these discussions, threatened to undermine the effectiveness of Radio Telefís Éireann. He believed that a board of political appointees, many of whom knew little of the complexities of television, were treating Rugheimer disgracefully. This, combined with written statements circulated to staff at the insistence of Ó Móráin and his allies, troubled Andrews and complicated his efforts to run what he believed was a successful service. These statements emphasised the need for staff to use Irish and informed personnel that one's ability to speak Irish would be considered in staff promotions and hinted darkly at past conspiracies to ridicule and undermine the language.[24] In these circumstances and knowing that the Lemass Government was about to reappoint the same Authority, Andrews felt he had no other option but to resign.

The resignation of Eamonn Andrews was a shock to many within RTÉ and, according to the director-general, lowered morale throughout the service. At a meeting of the Authority on May 11, 1966, Andrews read out a statement to a stunned Authority explaining his decision. He made it clear that he was frustrated with the new emphasis on the need to bring the Irish language into the service and was especially upset with the group's treatment of Rugheimer. Though he claimed to both support efforts to revive the Irish language and the need for Irish language programming, Andrews maintained, 'I do not believe we have the right to cut off in any major way from communication with us the majority of our viewers and listeners, i.e. those who do not as yet understand Irish.'[25] He told the Authority that he thought the efforts to replace Rugheimer were a critical mistake, complaining

> when the expensive and arduous search for an Irish Programme Controller outside the organisation failed to reveal a suitable candidate, I felt the refusal to make a last minute effort to retain Rugheimer was tantamount to saying we would accept second best ... We were also choosing to overlook the fact that the present Programme Controller, although not Irish, had succeeded in understanding our needs so well that he had organised and launched among many others our successful and indigenous Education, History, and Farming programmes, not to mention our 1916 celebration features.[26]

Andrews informed the members of the Authority that he could not in good conscience continue to 'help implement policies in which I do not believe and which I feel will have sad effects on both the television service in particular and on the country in general'.[27] He rejected appeals to reconsider his resignation, alarming his allies on the board, with Fintan Kennedy going so far as arguing that the entire Authority should resign if they could not convince Andrews to stay. Ó Móráin was not impressed, stating that the chairman was resigning because he could not have his way, maintaining he 'was unhappy that the Chairman of all people would take such drastic action'.[28]

When Andrews's resignation was made public the controversy surrounding the departure of Rugheimer was not addressed out of respect to a man who had made a remarkable contribution to Irish television. Instead, Andrews's opposition to the renewed emphasis on the language was highlighted. The Authority debated issuing a statement challenging Andrews's criticism, but Professor Moody cautioned against this, pointing out that it was clear that Andrews was always uncomfortable with the push to do 'too much too quickly of the language'. He told the Authority that the most significant factor in the resignation of the chairman was the decision to advertise the position of controller of programmes and the treatment of Rugheimer. Moody's mention of Rugheimer provoked a response from Uí Cheallaigh that put in a nutshell why the Swedish-born controller of programmes was not retained. She pointed out that 'Mr. Rugheimer's engagement was being terminated by the Authority not merely on the basis of his Irish language qualifications but because of his diminished capacity, as a non-national, to have an appropriate national feeling for programming.'[29]

There was also genuine concern that any press release challenging the Chairman's statement to the press would inevitably involve disclosures about the divisions within the Authority following the debates over the controller of programmes position. It was therefore decided that a simple statement be issued thanking Andrews for his service and dedication. Rugheimer left Telefís Éireann at the end of November 1966. He was in many respects an outstanding pioneer who contributed tremendously to upgrading the television service during his tenure. His 'misfortune' at RTÉ was simply that he had not been born in Ireland.

Rugheimer's departure had serious consequences for Irish television. By all accounts he was an incredibly energetic professional and a leader who helped shape the culture of television broadcasting in Ireland. His emphasis on developing hard-hitting current affairs programming unsettled many political, cultural and religious elites and was an important part of the transition Ireland experienced throughout the 1960s. As controller of programmes he supported and protected a generation of current affairs producers and writers who tested the limits of public service broadcasting. He held a key position at a critical time, and his departure created a void that proved impossible to fill. This became obvious as his replacement struggled to withstand the many pressures that Rugheimer had withstood and indeed thrived on.

A number of influential producers were supportive of the controller of programmes arguing 'Gunnar Rugheimer had more insight into the "Irish mind" than many a native, and had done more to reflect it than those that employed him ... His great defect was not that he did not know the Irish mind: rather he had an uncanny gift for exposing it to its own gaze.'[30] They believed his departure ruptured a sense of community within RTÉ. The producers and department heads who called for Rugheimer's resignation found themselves isolated and cut off from the main body of producers, many of whom supported Rugheimer. They were described as a 'valuable group of colleagues who remained in virtual "exile", though they continued to carry on'.[31] It would take a major confrontation with the government in 1969 to bring the majority of programme staff back together and reignite a sense of solidarity within RTÉ.[32]

Michael Garvey, an Irish-speaking intellectual who came from Radio Éireann, replaced Gunnar Rugheimer as controller of programmes. His contemporaries saw him as a kind and cultured man who was primarily interested in drama, not in the highly stressful and confrontational world of current affairs broadcasting. In his new role Garvey hoped to forge a productive relationship with the Fianna Fáil Government. Unlike his predecessor, he had little stomach for controversy and was fully aware of the discord and clashes that had characterised the relationship between the government and RTÉ. He was keen to avoid similar troubles.

Garvey encountered a different Fianna Fáil Government as controller because another transition occurred in November of 1966. After a long and distinguished career, Seán Lemass stepped down as Taoiseach and was replaced by Jack Lynch. The new Taoiseach made an effort to repair the fractured relations between Fianna Fáil and RTÉ by appearing for an interview on *Division*, effectively ending his party's boycott of the programme that had begun the previous October. However, RTÉ continued to create problems for the new Taoiseach and tension between the national broadcaster and the government was never far from the surface.

When Lynch became Taoiseach, Erskine Childers retained his portfolio of Minister for Transport and Power but also became Minister for Posts and Telegraphs, replacing Joseph Brennan. This appointment initiated a new round of ministerial interest in broadcasting as Childers returned to a department he had overseen in the 1950s, when he had been responsible for providing radio with a degree of autonomy by setting up Comhairle Radio Éireann. He proved to be much more the activist than either of his predecessors, Michael Hilliard or Joseph Brennan, taking the initiative on a number of occasions to influence broadcasting. He was especially anxious to improve the image of Fianna Fáil politicians in front of television cameras.

León Ó Broin recounts Childers's return to Posts and Telegraphs as being a challenge for him and the department as he once again proved overly assertive, sending a flood of minutes which Ó Broin 'did not like one bit'.[33] Ó Broin was close to retiring and held on until August 1967, stepping down after a long and distinguished career in the civil service including twenty years as Secretary of the Department of Posts and Telegraphs.[34] During his tenure as Minister Childers wrote a series of memoranda that outlined the state of Irish broadcasting and made countless recommendations to the Taoiseach. He had a reputation for frequently sending memoranda and press clippings to colleagues and civil servants, a habit that recipients found annoying. As minister, many of his interventions created headaches for colleagues in the cabinet, civil servants in Post and Telegraphs, and for the new Chairman of the Authority, Todd Andrews. Later Childers proved to be an important ally to Lynch in a controversy that threatened to undermine the Fianna Fáil Government at the end of the decade. At that time allegations of ministerial misconduct and collusion involving smuggling of arms to the IRA led to the forced resignations from the Cabinet of Charles J. Haughey and Neil Blaney, and Lynch's dismissal of Minister for Justice Michael Ó Móráin.

When he became minister, Childers urged the government to appreciate the power of television and encouraged members of the cabinet and deputies to learn how to use the medium for the benefit of the government and party. Looking back to Haughey's confrontation with the National Farmers' Association and Rickard

Deasy, he told Jack Lynch that no minister should ever contact RTÉ directly to complain about any aspect of programming. Instead he insisted they should first contact him directly or contact Paddy Lalor, his parliamentary secretary. He believed Haughey's intervention had been an embarrassing mistake; arguing that if neither he nor Lalor could be reached only the director-general Kevin McCourt or the assistant director-general John Irvine should be contacted. He insisted that procedures be put in place that would prevent future embarrassment for the government, telling Lynch 'I know far more about broadcasting than my colleagues and will not accept the idea that a Minister should protest to anyone in an inferior position.'[35] Childers's tone was often arrogant and condescending but he understood the importance of being proactive and engaging with the media better than many of his colleagues.

As minister he made an effort to meet regularly with both Todd Andrews and Kevin McCourt to keep lines of communication open in the hope of avoiding controversy. He counselled Lynch that it was only natural for RTÉ to be in conflict with the government and that there would always be a degree of tension in Fianna Fáil's relationship with the television and radio service. Childers argued that there were many friends of Fianna Fáil in positions of power in broadcasting that were sympathetic to the government and its policies. After meeting with the new Chairman Todd Andrews and Kevin McCourt, he told Lynch that both were aware of the validity of much of the government's criticism but blamed the problem on 'an absolute dearth of talent in regard to features of various kinds'.[36] This was an argument that Eamonn Andrews and Edward Roth had used to mollify Lemass and his staff years earlier. Childers reported that in his conversations with Todd Andrews the chairman had emphasised that Fianna Fáil had plenty of support inside the Authority and on the staff at RTÉ, concluding 'the idea that there is not sufficient Fianna Fáil support is ludicrous'.[37]

Childers was a realist; he understood that RTÉ was not going to be a source of propaganda for any one political party, especially Fianna Fáil. He wanted others to accept this reality, and believed all government ministers should understand that television could be used proactively for positive publicity. He first mentioned the need for Fianna Fáil members to train in the use of television in November 1966, explaining that media-savvy politicians could use the power of the medium for their own political benefit, assuming they were smart enough to exploit it. On Lynch's request Childers presented a formal *Memorandum for the Government* that was addressed by the Cabinet in January 1967. Childers laid out the state of government-RTÉ relations, arguing once again that his Cabinet colleagues were wrong to think RTÉ was overly critical of Fianna Fáil. The formal report was in many respects enlightened as Childers explained that criticism of the government and its policies was inevitable and was not going to cease, just as criticism of RTÉ by political parties would not end. He once again decried the inexperience of politicians in handling television, advocating that all three parties send one representative abroad for 'indoctrination and experience'. He understood that becoming comfortable with the medium was critical for Fianna Fáil's political prospects, asking 'How soon will T.D.s have to be reasonably articulate and good TV personalities? The whole problem is linked to the future organisation of the party.'[38]

However the minister delivered, in the end, a seventeen-part memorandum that simply was too much for the cabinet to digest. When the cabinet met to discuss broadcasting it was decided that the code of practice that had been negotiated with RTÉ in August 1966 should be renegotiated with the hope that *Division*, the programme that had been so contentious and divisive, would be replaced with one 'limited to members of the Houses of Oireachtas, the staff of Radio Telefís Éireann and political correspondents of the newspapers'.[39] After another long and difficult series of negotiations an agreement was arranged between the new controller of programmes and representatives of Fianna Fáil, Fine Gael and Labour.[40]

Fianna Fáil Whip Michael Carty reported to the Taoiseach that RTÉ would not be willing to allow any of the political parties to veto the appearance of guests 'and that experts in particular fields e.g., economists, town planners etc. should be treated in the same way as political correspondents and be acceptable to the Parties'.[41] However, Carty had received assurance from Garvey that there would be no pre-arranged confrontations featured in the series and that if any of the parties refused to appear on a particular programme, RTÉ would 'not comment on the non-appearance of the party in question nor draw attention to that fact in any way'.[42] Michael Garvey hoped that by developing current affairs programmes in collaboration with party whips and offering assurances about their tone and structure he could avoid a return to the contentious programmes of the past.

The arrangement had its detractors, especially Arthur Noonan who covered politics and the media for the *Irish Independent*. He criticised the agreement, arguing that politicians and broadcasters had secretly conspired to create a non-confrontational programme, thus shirking their responsibility to the public. Fine Gael Party Whip Gerry L'Estrange defended the agreement arguing that it was not secret, concluding 'we neither desire, nor have we sought, for control over political broadcasting on RTÉ'.[43] L'Estrange maintained that the agreement between the party whips had been 'a freely agreed arrangement between all political parties and the Controller of Programmes at RTÉ'.[44] Noonan retorted, 'that of course is the point. All three political parties, covering 141 members of the Dáil and most of the Seanad, made a "free" agreement between themselves and the officials of a semi-state body, providing the framework or cocoon within which political television would be permitted ... There is no escaping the fact that representatives of nearly all the members of our sovereign parliament made a private arrangement with the servants of a State-controlled mass publicity outlet.'[45]

Although progress had been made in sorting out the details of participating in political programmes, Childers remained unhappy that the government had not accepted all of his recommendations. Childers understood that the Cabinet was divided about how to deal with RTÉ and mentioned this to Lynch, arguing that 'it would be quite impossible to get any agreed statement through the government because everybody has a different point of view'.[46] He prepared another exhaustive memorandum, 'General RTÉ Policy', and asked the Taoiseach to simply endorse it. Childers wanted Lynch to review the document and approve it as official policy, thereby bypassing his colleagues in the cabinet, telling the Taoiseach, 'you would have the rightful authority to examine this and tell me that it is in accordance with your general views'.[47]

In a covering letter to Lynch, Childers was unusually concise, telling the Taoiseach that relations between RTÉ and the government would improve but that ministers should accept that television could not be controlled by the government. No doubt with an eye towards Haughey, he underscored the point that any complaints about political broadcasts had to be reasonable and transmitted through his office, or, in an emergency, to the director-general or assistant director-general, explaining, 'I cannot have scripts read to me by the D.G. save in a situation of crisis ... RTÉ must be able to debate social economic issues where the government will be on the defensive – here and elsewhere ... offensive statements against the government cannot be automatically attacked as biased.'[48]

Childers also insisted that RTÉ treat fairly any formal statement issued by the government: 'Ministers should not be confronted with sharp-shooting critics when announcing policy.'[49] He assured Lynch that Fianna Fáil had good friends in RTÉ and on the RTÉ Authority who were sympathetic to the government including the chairman of the Authority.[50] Childers argued that the government was being treated well by the television service, referring to the recent Fianna Fáil Ard-Fheis as proof. He pointed out that the extensive coverage allowed Fianna Fáil to dominate current affairs and news programming for weeks as RTÉ provided 'overwhelming majority coverage to FF during the period, followed by comment on the by elections and this would be the judgement in Europe'.[51]

Although his advice to Lynch and fellow cabinet members illustrates a progressive streak in the minister's attitude towards RTÉ, the events of 1967 changed his outlook as relations between RTÉ and the government deteriorated rapidly. Responding to the growing hostility that characterised the relationship between the government and the television service, Childers gave a remarkably hostile speech to the Trinity Historical Society later in the year. Although he claimed to welcome positive criticism and defended RTÉ – stating it was doing a good job, and improving – he launched into a blistering attack that received widespread coverage in the press. This underscored his party's discomfort with news and current affairs programming. 'There was a cynical, anti-everything, angry-young-man, nihilistic approach to human life and destiny everywhere. This attitude was negative and in his view entirely unsuited for broadcasting ... Hustling, rude, impatient interviewing was completely wrong in RTÉ.'[52] The *Irish Times* saw in Childers's speech the government's unhappiness with the Television Authority, pointing out that Childers had insisted that the Authority had to have his confidence as minister. What had transpired in the course of 1967 to provoke such angry remarks from Childers?

The hostility of the minister was due to a number of controversies throughout the year that deeply embarrassed the Lynch Government. One of the most sensational occurred when Lynch stopped an RTÉ crew from travelling to Vietnam to report on a war that was creating tremendous political and social unrest throughout the United States and Europe. In March 1967 a short article appeared in the *Sunday Independent* entitled 'Sending Irish Civilians to War Zone'.[53] The piece complained RTÉ was sending a crew to report a conflict that had already taken up too much of the attention of the national broadcaster, complaining, 'if there is one thing that the screens of Montrose do not lack, it is coverage of the Vietnam war'.[54] The article maintained that the war had been extensively covered by international agencies and that the Irish public had grown 'jaded of this long drawn out struggle, which is not likely to be clarified by the arrival of an Irish television team'.[55] This article was brief and buried inside the paper, but it caught the attention of Frank Aiken, Minister for Foreign Affairs. Alarmed that a trip to North Vietnam would offend the United States, he tried to reach Childers to demand he intervene to halt the trip. Unable to reach Childers, Aikens contacted the Taoiseach directly, requesting that Lynch intervene to stop the project. Aiken was upset that such a trip could be planned without his department's sanction and quickly intervened to quash the project; meeting with the Taoiseach to make sure his concerns were understood.[56] Lynch responded by quickly telephoning Todd Andrews, ordering him to cancel the project. Andrews, in turn, ordered Director-General Kevin McCourt to abandon plans for the programme.

Understanding that the government's intervention would provoke controversy, RTÉ quickly issued a statement that was drafted by Todd Andrews and Jack Lynch. According to Andrews, this was done at his insistence, as he wanted it to be made clear that the decision to cancel the Vietnam undertaking had been made by the government. Andrews knew trouble would follow and wanted it clearly understood that he was responding to a direct intervention from the Taoiseach. The statement he released was concise but clear. 'The Taoiseach has informed me that in the opinion of the government the best interests of the nation would not be served by sending a team to Vietnam; it would be an embarrassment to the government in relation to their foreign policy. In the circumstances the project must be dropped.'[57] In his remarkable memoir, *Man of No Property*, Andrews maintains he initially supported the idea of an RTÉ news team travelling to Vietnam, and was sympathetic to complaints from members of staff that the coverage of the conflict in South East Asia was overly reliant on American reports that carried an inevitable bias. He wrestled with the dilemma, unsure if he should stand by the decision to send a crew to Vietnam and insist that the first ministerial directive under Section 31 of the Broadcasting Act be issued, or acquiesce and accept the demands of the government. In the end, he decided to compromise after speaking with Lynch who agreed that a statement could be issued explaining that the cancellation was due to the Taoiseach's intervention. He later regretted not having forced the Taoiseach to issue a formal order under Section 31 of the Broadcasting Act compelling RTÉ to cancel the programme. As was expected, reaction to government intervention in the Dáil and in the national press was hostile.

In the Dáil, Labour Deputy Frank Cluskey grilled the Minister for Foreign Affairs about the sequence of events that led to the cancellation of the project, and accusations of Fianna Fáil censorship of RTÉ once again provoked heated debate. Aiken defended the government's action, admitting that he had contacted Lynch who intervened to insist that the project be cancelled.[58] Pressed for a reason for the cancellation of the trip and an explanation as to why a news team travelling to Vietnam was not in the best interests of the state, Aiken responded by arguing that the Irish people had seen and heard enough about Vietnam. He had no problem arguing that the government knew what was best for its citizens. 'They have been deluged with pictures from Vietnam and they have been deluged with newspaper stories. They can read about it in periodicals; they can read about it in books and those who are interested in it have followed it very closely.'[59] His paternalistic response illustrates that although there had been a change in the office of the Taoiseach, the Lemass line remained firmly in place. Aiken was one of the last members of his generation to remain in a position of power and shared Lemass's unease with television and the perceived agendas of those making programmes. His comments illustrate how difficult it was for many in Fianna Fáil to accept television as a legitimate source of news and information. He told the Dáil that because RTÉ was a semi-state organisation the government had to be cautious because some might conclude RTÉ was travelling 'at the request, or with the approval, or at the instance of the government. If they went to Vietnam, I would be asked why the government do not use their influence to send them to many of the other troubled spots all over the world.'[60]

Although his own view of television may have been shared by many politicians of his generation, this outlook was becoming increasingly anachronistic. His remarks in the Dáil were ridiculed in the print media that covered the controversy extensively. He told the Dáil,

> I think, on the whole, if these were private individuals who were going, it would be all right. We would have no responsibility for it. If we want any more information; if anybody in this country does not know the issues in Vietnam, somebody could go at his own expense, or a group could go at the expense of people who send them out. They would be able to go out there, learn the language, live there for a couple of years and describe it fully with their pens rather than try to describe it with a few odd pictures which have to be selective and which could give a wrong impression.[61]

Aiken was particularly upset that RTÉ had failed to consult his department 'before they decided to send a team of this magnitude to the other ends of the earth. I do not know whether the team would even know the language spoken there'.[62] The expectation that his department would be consulted about the project illustrates that television ruptured the sense of deference the government had become accustomed to. The fact that Aiken had effectively quashed the project enabled the opponents of Fianna Fáil inside and outside the Dáil to complain bitterly once again about censorship and heavy-handed government tactics. The telephone call to the Chairman of the Authority by the Taoiseach and the Authority's decision not to challenge the government called into question the independence and freedom of RTÉ to 'serve' the public.

Headlines in the *Sunday Independent* exclaimed, 'Hold it, Big Brother's on the phone', capturing the sense that the Fianna Fáil Government was once again dictating policy to RTÉ.[63] Another excerpt read, 'Where does Government control begin, where does it end? Here is the great, overriding question for the people to decide if they are not to have a national television service that is merely the plaything of the politicians.'[64] Not all press reports were hostile to the government's intervention and the episode under-lined Ireland's ill-defined sense of neutrality. Some press reports reminded readers of the statement Seán Lemass had made three years earlier to the effect that 'the Irish did not belong to NATO for the simple reason that they had never been asked to join, but Irish sympathy was unmistakably on the side of the free western democracies and opposed to communism'.[65] Other observers pointed out proudly that Ireland was alone among western nations in not having diplomatic ties with communist nations. Sean Dunne, a Labour TD, wrote to the director-general to ask for clarification about the reports, later stating, 'There is a feeling among some people in Ireland that this was government interference. My view is that they were right to interfere. We in Ireland should keep out of Vietnam. By sending a camera team to Hanoi we would appear to be lining up with the Communists in the eyes of many nations throughout the world.'[66]

Nevertheless, the intervention was an awkward one that embarrassed the government and provided fodder for critics. The National Civil Liberties League joined many in condemning 'the apparent ease with which the "hot line to Montrose"' was used while Senator Sheehy-Skeffington argued that the news team may have reported the truth and 'the truth might have been embarrassing to a great and friendly power. So the government thought it was better not to know.'[67] RTÉ responded to the state's intervention with a defiant gesture by showing a Polish film on the controversial war. Press reports indicated that the cabinet met to discuss the controversy and was upset by the station's decision to screen the Polish documentary considering it 'a gesture of independence and perhaps even a "nose thumbing" at the government'.[68] The controversy led to a review of government policy regarding the war by External Affairs which outlined the government's position by referring to statements that had been issued by Frank Aiken in the Dáil in 1965 and 1966 that 'all the smaller members of the UN can do is to hope that all the States involved will be wise enough to negotiate a settlement which will bring peace to the sorely afflicted people of Vietnam and prevent a disastrous extension of the conflict'.[69]

This controversy highlights the tension that could erupt into a real crisis for the Fianna Fáil government. Arthur Noonan, the political correspondent for the *Irish Independent,* predicted that there was no escape from 'permanent war between the government and State television'.[70] A letter to the Taoiseach signed by one hundred employees of RTÉ protesting the government's cancellation of the Vietnam project underscored the sense of outrage within RTÉ. The letter was criticised by the director-general who 'deplored' the action of staff.[71] These events induced a sense of anxiety within Fianna Fáil provoking the government to closely watch RTÉ. It decided to keep a tight leash on its ministers and deputies by carefully monitoring their appearances on Irish television. Throughout 1967 the Taoiseach was kept informed about all requests made by the national broadcasting service to interview or feature Fianna Fáil politicians.[72]

Undaunted by these problems Michael Garvey contacted Fianna Fáil Whip Michael Carty a short time later to inform the government of plans for the autumn 1967 programming, including *The Politicians.* Garvey maintained that the format employed in the past would be used again for the new season, stating that it had produced 'the most effective form of continuous Party Political broadcasting that we have so far devised. Reaction from viewers appears to bear out this judgement.'[73] Garvey also informed Carty that the two current affairs programmes, *Division* and *Seven Days*, would be amalgamated into one programme, *Seven Days*, to be broadcast twice a week. Carty was told that the Assistant Controller of Programmes, Jack White, would oversee all current affairs programming and that the producer of *Seven Days* would be Muiris MacConghail, who had produced *Division*.

The Taoiseach sent his Minister for Finance, Charles J. Haughey, to meet with Michael Garvey to review the proposal for the autumn current affairs programming. Haughey's meeting with Garvey was uneventful, the minister agreeing to the format laid out by RTÉ, which allowed the three political parties to be represented in a discussion moderated by RTÉ. Garvey explained that the subjects scheduled for debate would be presented to the three party whips well enough in advance for each to choose a suitable deputy or senator to prepare and participate.[74] The controller assured Haughey that he was committed to avoiding controversy and improving relations with the government. In the new *Seven Days* programme Garvey promised that if political subjects required the involvement of deputies or senators, the producer would contact the party whips to arrange for their participation. Garvey promised Haughey that in programmes that did not require the participation of politicians 'Telefís Éireann would always endeavour to see that both points of views were fairly put.'[75] Haughey was pleased with his encounter with Garvey and sensed the controller of programmes would work to improve the troubled relationship between the television service and the government. He told Lynch that the new controller was sincere in wanting to improve relations and that Garvey 'felt that a great deal of unnecessary heat had been generated about the independence [of RTÉ] and interference and that he personally felt that there was no need for these attitudes and he hoped they would not arise in the future'.[76]

Garvey's hopes were not so easily realised. The programme *The Politicians* quickly led to trouble as televised debates descended into acrimonious spectacle with politicians shouting at one another while a bewildered chair appealed for calm. After one particularly troublesome episode Erskine Childers wanted the programme suspended.[77] In an effort to save the remainder of the season all of the party whips met with producers to salvage the programme. The meeting produced an agreement that the series should continue but '[m]ore rigid control would be exercised by the interviewing Chairman'.[78] Efforts were made to keep participants from digressing as RTÉ circulated main headings of topics to be discussed and insisted 'speakers would be confined to these headings, and no irrelevant matter would be introduced by the Chairman or would any speaker be allowed to digress irrelevantly'.[79] In an attempt to restore order and provide more structure, it was agreed that each programme would feature a four-minute opening statement by the government spokesman, which would be followed by a three-minute response by the other speakers. It was also agreed that *The Politicians* would cease during general elections, local elections, or by-elections.

While producers at the station implored politicians to act in a dignified manner, the party whips took exception to politicians becoming fodder for the entertainment side of television broadcasting. Carty reported that 'All three Whips took grave exception to the introduction of politics as such on other RTÉ Programmes, and asked that their views on this matter should be conveyed officially to RTÉ. In particular it was stressed that we deplored the fact that RTÉ should vilify and ridicule politics and politicians in shows like "Late Late Show", "Seven Days" etc'.[80] The Authority did not issue a ban on political satire and deputies grew increasingly anxious with a medium that failed to exhibit the deference they expected.

Earlier that same month, Gay Byrne had telephoned the office of the Taoiseach in an effort to schedule a meeting with Lynch to discuss bringing Fianna Fáil ministers on to his popular variety programme, *The Late Late Show*. Lynch was told that Byrne wanted to move away from light entertainment and address serious matters of public interest. 'He has already approached a number of Ministers (Messrs. Haughey, Colley and O'Malley were mentioned) and said that at least one of them (Mr. O'Malley) would be willing to participate if he had the Taoiseach's approval'.[81] Lynch was not impressed, ordering his staff 'to tell Gay Byrne that he didn't approve of Ministers going on *The Late Late Show* and that there was already provision for political discussions: there wasn't therefore any need for Gay Byrne to call on him'.[82] In a cabinet meeting that addressed broadcasting, Childers reported that Byrne had been dealt with. 'With regard to the approach made by Gay Byrne to the Taoiseach, he has been severely censured for this breach of instructions.'[83] In his study of public affairs broadcasting, John Horgan suggests that any censure of Byrne by the director-general would have been a mild one given McCourt's 'track record'.[84]

Controversy continued to follow RTÉ and friction with the government became a constant in Irish life. The national press delighted in providing detailed coverage of its troubles and reporting extensively on the trials and tribulations of the national broadcaster. While these events were taking place Eamonn Andrews, who had resigned from his position as Chairman of the RTÉ Authority, gave a hard-hitting speech to the Cork Literary and Scientific Society that was covered extensively in the national press and was highly critical of the state of Irish broadcasting. He singled out for criticism the influence of the BBC in the department responsible for overseeing television and radio, Posts and Telegraphs. No doubt remembering his many battles with León Ó Broin and his minister he argued that Irish broadcasting was in crisis because it 'had so slavishly followed the pattern of British broadcasting ... and given us the benevolent but incomprehensive dictatorship that produced one of the worst but best-meaning radio services in the world, and then let television escape to nibble the grass of freedom but still to find a long rope around its neck and a tight string on its fetlock'.[85]

He complained that Posts and Telegraphs, situated strategically between the government and RTÉ, inhibited both radio and television. 'This to me is one of the most unbelievable situations in the world. Great men of a previous generation fought to give us some element of freedom in the shaping of our destiny. They overlooked the Civil Service machine, the magnificent but antiquated system of administration bequeathed to us by our former masters'.[86] Although he insisted that he was not interested in bashing the Irish Civil Service he complained about the endless efforts of Posts and Telegraphs to micromanage RTÉ. Decrying the overreaching paternalism of the department, Andrews argued that it was impossible for Ireland to protect itself from the outside world, maintaining that it was wrong to 'insulate with ignorance':

> Somewhere someone believes that too many hours of broadcasting would be bad for us; that we must sleep or we must eat or we must pray or we must do something other than listen or watch, and that we are not capable of making the choice ourselves. I cannot and have never gotten over the fact that some grown and highly paid man has a stop watch which if it shows one minute, two minutes, five minutes over a certain arbitrary figure of time will chase up by telephone or by memo the broadcasting authority responsible for this heinous crime and demand an explanation. I'm not saying we need more broadcasting hours or fewer. But for Heaven's sake, let us decide for our selves. We're grown people.... I do most sincerely wish that the Department of Posts and Telegraphs (or the Minister) could hand over totally and irrevocably the whole business of broadcasting to the RTÉ Authority.[87]

When the director-general's Programme Policy Committee met a short time later McCourt complained that statements by the former chairman of the RTÉ Authority had done 'more harm than good'. He told his colleagues that much had changed since the departure of Eamonn Andrews, noting that the relationship between the Department of Posts and Telegraphs had improved dramatically. He claimed that it was understandable that in the early years the department would have 'difficulties when faced with the beginning of an independent situation on Donnybrook'.[88]

This was the political climate in which Childers made his remark about RTÉ embracing a 'cynical, anti-everything, angry-young-man, nihilistic approach to human life and destiny' cited above. His efforts to encourage a less aggressive methodology by broadcasters in current affairs proved futile. A short time after Childers made these hostile remarks the government was blindsided by a television programme that undermined a critical Fianna Fáil initiative, convincing many in the party that RTÉ and current affairs in particular had to be reined in.

In December 1967 Fianna Fáil decided once again to try to eliminate proportional representation (PR), the election process that its leaders knew undermined its efforts to gain strong majorities in

Dáil elections. The producer of *Seven Days* got wind of the government's plans, which were strategically scheduled for release to the press on the quiet Saturday before the Christmas holiday. Fianna Fáil operatives understood that releasing news about the controversial decision to introduce a referendum to eradicate PR would be less sensational if it was announced on the weekend before the busiest holiday season of the year. The all-party committee released its report with a press embargo for Saturday December 23, 1967, understanding that the report would not be closely scrutinised in the press until the new year. Muiris MacConghail, producer of *Seven Days,* understood this and quickly gathered his staff and put together a programme broadcast on Friday, December 22, 1967. He understood that the weekend newspapers would already have been written and were not in a position to react to the news and believed the News Division of RTÉ was 'asleep'.

With the energy and drive that had helped *Seven Days* become the most popular and respected current affairs programme on Irish television, David Thornley, Basil Chubb and Ted Nealon prepared a programme to forecast what elections would look like if PR were abolished. Basil Chubb, one of the country's leading political scientists and David Thornley, a lecturer at Trinity College, worked with the Politics Department of Trinity College and produced research that illustrated quite convincingly that if PR were scrapped, Fianna Fáil would win overwhelming majorities in national elections. Although Chubb was unable to participate in the programme, veteran journalist Ted Nealon joined Thornley and presented the research live from the Donnybrook studios. By today's standards the presentation was quite primitive, with projections written in chalk on studio blackboards. But the actual research was sophisticated and convincing, demonstrating what would have happened in past elections without PR and suggesting what could happen in the future if voting patterns remained largely the same. The programme predicted that if PR were abolished Fianna Fáil could expect to win close to one hundred of the one hundred and forty-four seats in the Dáil. When RTÉ's Assistant Director-General John Irvine read the research before the broadcast, he was startled and understood that it would not be well received by the Lynch Government. However, the programme was produced by a team

6   David Thornley, broadcaster and politician (left) with producer Muiris MacConghail, on the set of *Division* circa 1966. The current affairs programme ran from 1966 to 1967 with MacConghail producing and Thornley presenting.

of highly qualified experts who were able to explain in clear terms the consequences of a Yes vote on any constitutional referendum to eliminate proportional representation.

Although the actual referendum was not until the autumn of 1968, the results of that one broadcast were devastating to Fianna Fáil. Any hope of a constitutional amendment being supported in a national referendum evaporated overnight. One observer reported that nevertheless 'the party blundered on like a big, wounded animal to a crushing defeat'.[89] The referendum on the abolition of proportional representation failed with over 60 per cent of the electorate voting against it. MacConghail remembers meeting Jack Lynch afterwards and being told 'you are to blame for all this!'[90] *Seven Days* succeeded in infuriating many within the Fianna Fáil establishment who believed that people inside RTÉ had an anti-Fianna Fáil agenda. Although MacConghail enjoyed a friendly and professional relationship with Jack Lynch, there were many in the party who were outraged with the broadcast, and with RTÉ in general, and determined to find a means of striking back. The incident illustrates that current affairs at RTÉ was positioned to address a critical void that neither the News Division nor the national press were able to fill. According to MacConghail, the modest architect of the programme, 'three guys killed [PR], Chubb, Thornley and Nealon, but at the time *Seven Days* was the only show in town'.[91]

As 1968 unfolded, conflict with the government continued to create problems for current affairs, and *Seven Days* in particular. A programme planned on the Nigerian Civil War, which proposed a visit to Biafra became the next crisis that pitted RTÉ against the government. In February 1968 Todd Andrews learned from Kevin McCourt that a crew from RTÉ was en route to Biafra, provoking McCourt to order the recall of the crew, who were in Lisbon waiting to travel on to Africa. Andrews claims in his autobiography that when he learned about the trip he advised Kevin McCourt to cancel it. The director-general ordered the crew to return, denying that the government played any role in the decision. However, the archive indicates that there had been extensive contact between Andrews, McCourt and officials in the Department of Foreign Affairs who did not want the *Seven Days* team to travel to Africa. The fact that neither the controller of programmes nor the director-general was aware of the programme nor the crew travelling to Biafra embarrassed Kevin McCourt and undermined Michael Garvey, the controller of programmes.

Notes from the director-general's programme policy meeting indicate that McCourt told those in attendance that he had cancelled the project as 'soon as he found out about it'.[92] He argued that there were many Irish missionaries in Nigeria who would be vulnerable to attack if the Nigerian government believed the Irish national television service was involved in the making of propaganda. McCourt was alarmed that the *Seven Days* crew had already made their way to Lisbon and anxious that his actions 'would not be misinterpreted as government intervention on the same lines as appeared in the Vietnam issue'.[93] In an effort to salvage something from the journey to Lisbon, Brian Cleeve was contacted in Portugal and instructed to 'try to rescue something out of the operation by covering a local story or stories in the area'.[94]

The director-general's decision to recall the film crew once again led to complaints about government interference and censorship in the press and in the Dáil. Within RTÉ disquiet grew and, unbeknownst to the director-general, a programme about Biafra made by the British production company Granada, with a soundtrack narrated by RTÉ, was broadcast.[95]

A short time after the *Seven Days* programme on Biafra had been cancelled another programme made without the knowledge of the director-general or the controller of programmes proved to be the last straw for an increasingly frustrated director-general. A feature made about the Garda Special Branch came to the attention of the Chairman of the Broadcasting Authority who asked to see it and determined it to be 'trivial and lightweight in content and unsuitable for transmission'.[96] Andrews had no real sympathy for the Special Branch but still defined the programme as the product of the 'injudicious if not irresponsible' 'creative people' that he scorned. Todd Andrews arranged for the programme to be screened for the entire Authority who agreed with his assessment, and the programme was withdrawn.[97]

It was in these circumstances that Kevin McCourt took drastic action and moved *Seven Days* to the News Division where it would report directly to the Head of News. The decision was announced to staff in a terse note posted in the RTÉ Newsletter in February 1968.[98] *Seven Days* was creating ongoing headaches for the government and for Todd Andrews and Kevin McCourt. The Biafra controversy and the programme on the Special Branch proved to the director-general that the controller of programmes could not control the aggressiveness of *Seven Days* and its producer Muiris MacConghail. According to MacConghail, Michael Garvey did not like the constant friction inherent in overseeing current affairs programming and was much more interested in developing quality cultural programmes. It is clear that the director-general and the RTÉ Authority had lost confidence in Garvey. McCourt was especially upset that he had not been informed of the broadcast of the Granada programme on Biafra featuring an Irish soundtrack, regarding it as an insolent gesture. The RTÉ Authority fully supported McCourt's decision and decided to formally reprimand the controller of programmes.[99]

Moving *Seven Days* to the News Division enabled McCourt to placate Todd Andrews, who wanted *Seven Days* held accountable under the supervision of an experienced journalist – the Head of News, James McGuinness. McGuinness, a close confidant of Andrews, had replaced Pearse Kelly as head of news a short time after Haughey's infamous call to the newsroom in 1966. The transfer of the programme was designed to demonstrate to producers exactly who was in charge; it was a calculated decision to exert decisive executive power in order to restore a degree of control that McCourt, Andrews and the Authority believed had been lost under an ineffective controller of programmes.

Director of Personnel Hugh MacNeill warned McCourt that his decision would provoke a 'very violent reaction' from staff in RTÉ for a number of reasons. Moreover, MacNeill argued the move would lead to allegations of 'muzzling and political pressure', placing management on the defensive. He told McCourt that staff believed they had every right to be consulted in advance of significant organisational changes that would affect them, suggesting that the announcement state that the changes would take place within two weeks instead of immediately. McCourt believed that management had every right to make decisions concerning organisation and structure and insisted that the transfer take place immediately, noting 'the Authority would not tolerate further delay'.[100]

As predicted, moving *Seven Days* into the News Division was tremendously controversial, provoking a short-lived strike. The unions representing staff working on the *Seven Days* programme passed a resolution stating that members would not work on the programme 'until such time as the implications of management's decision on working conditions are discussed to the satisfaction of the Trade Unions'.[101] The unions were careful to indicate that they were not challenging the power of the Authority to make the changes but were within their right to dispute the manner with which the issue had been handled. Confronted with the challenge from union staff McCourt and senior managers in RTÉ initially decided not to suspend union members who were refusing to work 'principally to permit an opportunity for further negotiations and to avoid bad publicity'.[102] The director-general was wary of how these events would be portrayed in the national press and wanted to be sure the 'sequence of events not be in any way distorted'. When an impasse was reached, Muiris MacConghail, producer of *Seven Days*, was ordered to inform any and all staff that stood by their resolution that they were suspended and that once he had done this he should then consider himself suspended.

With RTÉ roiled by labour unrest, raucous debates about censorship once again took place in the Dáil. Labour Deputies Frank Cluskey and Sean Dunne were keen to exploit these difficulties and both attacked the Fianna Fáil Government for suppressing programmes they did not like by 'amalgamating the *Seven Days* programme with the news'. Amid shouts and catcalls from deputies, Sean Dunne accused the government of appointing 'stooges' to do the bidding of Fianna Fáil, maintaining the Taoiseach was afraid of the programme. Jack Lynch dismissed the accusations as 'fabrications'.[103]

In the midst of this turmoil Kevin McCourt quietly contacted MacConghail to ask if he and David Thornley would meet with him privately at the Shelbourne Hotel on St Stephen's Green. McCourt explained to both men that he had given notice to the RTÉ Authority that he would be retiring in April 1968 and asked if his leaving earlier would help restore calm to the national broadcaster. MacConghail recalls 'McCourt made it plain to both David and me that the chairman of the Authority, Todd Andrews, had developed strong editorial views in the matter of news and current affairs, and that this was making life difficult for everybody'.[104] MacConghail and Thornley were convinced that if McCourt stayed 'RTÉ might fall asunder in a sort of civil war fuelled by ideology, ambition and personal dislike. Goaded by a frenzy which had occupied the place, the government might then assume the editorial direction of the national broadcaster'.[105]

A conciliation tribunal ended the dispute and the suspended staff members were reinstated; the strike notice was withdrawn while the order moving *Seven Days* to the News Division stood.

In spite of the fact that MacConghail had to report directly to McGuinness, the two men developed a strong professional relationship. *Seven Days* retained a degree of autonomy even though MacConghail was required to report to McGuinness every morning at 9 a.m. to discuss programming. If Todd Andrews, Kevin McCourt and the RTÉ Authority thought that the transfer would draw the teeth of the programme they were sorely mistaken. MacConghail maintains, 'At the end of the day if *Seven Days* was supposed to go away it didn't.'[106]

A short time after these controversies Kevin McCourt resigned as director-general. Later, in an interview with the *Irish Press*, he maintained there had been very little government interference in the affairs of RTÉ during his tenure: 'Reports of alleged interference by the Minister and other officials of the government in the internal workings of RTÉ during his term of office had been grossly exaggerated.'[107] McCourt left office on March 31, 1968 and was replaced by Thomas Hardiman.[108]

Although the Chairman of the RTÉ Authority was a lifelong supporter of Fianna Fáil, Todd Andrews often fought with Fianna Fáil governments when he believed they were encroaching upon the duties or responsibilities of the Authority. When McCourt announced his resignation, a committee was established to find a replacement; that committee was chaired by Andrews and included three members of the Broadcasting Authority, Professor T. W. Moody; Fintan Kennedy, president of the Irish Trade and General Workers union; and Dónall Ó Móráin, director of Gael-Linn. In addition, two outsiders, the former director of Radio Éireann, Maurice Gorham and a senior civil servant John Garvin were asked to join the committee. From the start of the confidential process, Minister for Posts and Telegraphs Erskine Childers began to pressure Andrews for the names of those applying for the position. The minister was upset that Andrews would not disclose the identity of the applicants and continued to push for the names of those applying for the highly sensitive position. After being rebuffed a second time, Childers informed Andrews that he was under specific orders from the Taoiseach to identify all of the applicants. Andrews again refused, telling Childers that he was prepared to tell the Taoiseach himself that the promise of confidentiality extended to all applicants in the interviewing process could not be broken.[109]

During much of Andrews's tenure as Chairman of the Authority Childers was Minister for Posts and Telegraphs and it is clear that Andrews grew increasingly annoyed with Childers's incessant nervousness and complaining. Andrews believed that most of the criticism he heard from the minister originated in cabinet meetings, resulting in the minister coming to see him 'in great distress'. The exasperated chairman eventually advised the minister to 'tell his most persistently critical colleagues to go to hell, and if this did not put a stop to their silly complaints I proposed that he and I should go to see the Taoiseach and ask him to exercise a restraining influence'.[110]

When Thomas Hardiman was named Kevin McCourt's replacement, Andrews hosted a dinner to introduce him to Erskine Childers. At the dinner the minister produced a secret list of undesirables who were associated with RTÉ, claiming they were '"lefties" if not card-carrying communists, and should be treated as suspect subversives'.[111] Andrews maintains that both he and Hardiman knew most as respectable socialists and neither were concerned that these alleged 'subversives' would undermine RTÉ. On challenging Childers to identify the source of the list, the minister refused. Andrews professed 'I had no hesitation in asserting that it had been compiled by the Special Branch under the inspiration of the paranoid Department of Justice. I assured Erskine that no attention would be paid to the allegations nor would I give the list to Hardiman for the record.'[112] As a young man and anti-treaty republican Andrews had been harassed by the Special Branch and was determined that nobody in RTÉ would 'suffer economically or otherwise for their political opinions'.[113] He sent what he described as a 'rather violent' letter of protest to Childers asking him to share it with the Taoiseach.

Andrews later defended a controversial *Seven Days* programme on illegal money-lenders that infuriated the government and resulted in the establishment of a formal tribunal. Not long after the controversy surrounding the broadcast of this programme on 'loan sharking' Andrews resigned his position as Chairman of the Broadcasting Authority. At the time his son David had been appointed chief whip of Fianna Fáil and Andrews did not want to risk a conflict of interest. He recalls that he sent a letter of 'resignation to the Taoiseach, without much regret. I had the feeling it was accepted with even less.'[114]

The tenure of Todd Andrews as Chairman of the Broadcasting Authority was a turbulent one and his account of the four-year term in his memoir *Man of No Property* provides valuable insight into how he tried to navigate the difficult straits of broadcasting during a tumultuous period in contemporary Irish history. Although he was certainly not a Fianna Fáil 'hack', he fully accepted Seán Lemass's argument that RTÉ was 'an instrument of public policy and [as] such was responsible to the government' and makes this clear in his autobiography.[115] This is critical to understanding his tenure as Chairman of the Broadcasting Authority. Andrews was of the same revolutionary generation as Lemass. Like the Taoiseach, he was a veteran of the War of Independence and the Civil War and believed Fianna Fáil was the only political party fit for government. But his support for the government was far from automatic. He drew the line when ministers demanded the identity of applicants for important positions or produced secret lists of 'known subversives' working at the station and rejected the carping of individual government ministers. Importantly, Andrews took a stand against the government when he supported the *Seven Days* programme on illegal money-lending, a programme that he nevertheless believed contained serious flaws. However, when the Fianna Fáil government intervened on major issues such as the Vietnam and Biafra projects he believed the responsible thing for a state-sponsored public broadcaster was to accept the government's instruction. Andrews was replaced as Chairman of the Broadcasting Authority by Dónall Ó Móráin.

Trouble continued to cause unrest within RTÉ for years to come. Much of this is recounted in detail in *Sit Down and Be Counted*, written by three seasoned producers at RTÉ, Lelia Doolan, Jack Dowling and Bob Quinn. All three grew increasingly alienated by what they considered the 'Anglo-Americanisation of the Irish mind by the mass-media' and what they considered the heavy-handed tactics employed by the Authority and new Director-General Thomas Hardiman.[116] Their book chronicles their growing disillusionment within the service, as they struggled to develop quality public service programming from within a hybrid commercial environment.

Considering the career of Lelia Doolan enables an understanding of this turmoil and also provides an opportunity to address the challenges that confronted women working for the national broadcaster. Doolan was a talented and creative senior producer who had held a number of different positions in broadcasting before Gunner Rugheimer hired her as a producer trainee in 1964. Rugheimer sent her to the USA for training where she observed American news programming including the *Huntley Brinkley Report* and the *CBS Evening News* presented by Walter Cronkite. When she returned to Dublin she worked in drama producing *The Riordans* before being asked to start up the current affairs programme *Seven Days* in 1966.[117]

Doolan was one of a number of talented high-profile women working in the television service in the 1960s; others included Maev Conway, Chloe Gibson, Shelah Richards and Carolyn Swift. Although these women held important positions, working as producers and department heads, women were not well represented in professional positions at the station. According to documentation in the RTÉ Authority Archive, in February 1970 of the 1,532 employees 424 were women.[118] More telling, only four women earned a salary over £3,000 while 174 men earned in excess of £3,000. Most women were employed in clerical positions, or as production assistants, and approximately 75 per cent of the women working full-time earned £2,000 or less.[119] RTÉ was not alone in this regard as women in the civil service and local authorities held only 7 per cent of senior positions in the late 1970s.[120]

Doolan makes it clear that, in spite of this, women were a critical force in keeping the television service running. 'The whole place was run by women. The male directors were kept on their feet by the production assistants who were all women, they often times stopped the men from making fools of themselves.'[121] However, many of these women were all but invisible; they were never named in the credits and seldom received the recognition

7   (Left to right) Lelia Doolan, Bob Quinn and Jack Dowling on *The Late Late Show* for a discussion about the book *Sit Down and Be Counted*, November 8, 1969. All were former producers at RTÉ and the book concerned their dissatisfaction with the state of Irish broadcasting.

they deserved. Doolan was a feminist and active member of the Irish Women's Liberation Movement (IWLM), which was established in 1970 and included a number of women who worked in the media. The founding members of the organisation included editors Mary Kenny, Mary McCutcheon and Mary Maher and a number of influential journalists including Mary Anderson, Nell McCafferty, June Levine and Nuala Fennell.[122]

In early 1971 the IWLM published a pamphlet outlining the demands of the group, titled *Irish Women – Chains or Change?* One of the key demands of the IWLM was for the removal of the marriage ban that restricted the ability of married women to be employed and promoted within the public sector. The IWLM was determined to make waves and call attention to the institutionalised discrimination that they argued relegated women to the role of second-class citizenship. They marched, demonstrated and held public meetings, exploiting every possible media opportunity even to the point of breaking the law.'[123] In March 1971 Gay Byrne offered the group *The Late Late Show* as a platform to present their case. Speakers included Senator Mary Robinson, the historian Mary Cullen, journalist Nell McCafferty and Lelia Doolan, who addressed issues concerning women, education and the media. In spite of the careful planning the programme became chaotic as the audience became involved in heated arguments. An unprecedented appearance by the uninvited leader of Fine Gael, Garret Fitzgerald, added to the excitement and confusion of the broadcast. Fitzgerald took exception to complaints by members that Dáil Deputies did not care about women's issues. Once again *The Late Late Show* proved itself an important outlet for presenting and debating controversial contemporary issues. As June Levine points out in the *Field Day Anthology of Irish Writing*: 'Many viewers may have been shocked, but they had not switched off their televisions. IWLM had arrived.'[124]

As the IWLM gained momentum RTÉ examined the practice of not hiring or retaining married women, with the intention of abolishing the ban. In 1971 the Authority was told that while there were no statutory obstacles to recruiting married women 'the general policy which has been followed since the Authority was first established has been not to do so. As part of this policy, women who hold permanent appointments must resign from employment in RTÉ on marriage'.[125] The prohibition against hiring married women was lifted by RTÉ on August 1, 1972 and for all public service employees in 1973. The director-general, Thomas Hardiman worked with the various union representatives and kept the national Commission on the Status of Women advised of the progress he was making, reporting later, 'we were most favourably regarded' by the organisation.[126]

Doolan was widely regarded within RTÉ as a talented force and some believed she would eventually become director-general. However she grew increasingly frustrated with the culture inside of the national broadcasting service and what she regarded as RTÉ's failure to produce high quality public service programming. One of her colleagues was Bob Quinn, who joined Radio Éireann in 1961, becoming a producer/director in 1964. He spent a number of years producing programmes and documentaries, but by 1968 he too became disillusioned, convinced that his work 'was only serving to ratify the commercial abuse of public broadcasting'.[127]

He resigned, and bought an old car that he drove to Teheran and back before returning to RTÉ as a contract producer. However, disenchantment set in yet again and after taking a film crew west to Clare Island he sent them back with a letter that articulated the frustrations of many producers in the station. Although unconventional, the letter captured the sense of misgiving felt by dissidents within the service as he railed against what he labelled 'the factory'. He argued RTÉ had become a

> bloated and swelling corpse, feeding the increasing number of parasites but incapable of directing itself because there is no life, no human spirit to quicken it. ... This despite the efforts of bright young men in advertising to string gaudy beads around the neck of the corpse, the vile body, in an effort to persuade the people of this country that their property is still working on their behalf. It is not. It is simply the vehicle for the frustrated fantasies of ad-men, the megalomania of insane technocrats and the sanctification of the acts of a conservative government. If one looks closely at those lines, one will see evidence of the greatest sell-out ever perpetrated on a nation – by the nation itself, through its sons.[128]

Quinn's letter caused a tremendous stir at the station, provoking a lively debate about the perceived failure of RTÉ to serve the nation as a public broadcaster. Shortly after the letter was received, producer Jack Dowling, who had been upset with the increasing power of advertisers, resigned. He had battled with his superiors over a programme he produced, *Home Truths* that clinically examined the claims of advertisers with often startling results. This created difficulties for advertisers as the programme discredited products being marketed on Telefís Éireann. *Home Truth*'s aggressive investigations upset a number of companies who complained that their products were being ridiculed, and some cancelled lucrative contracts the Authority was loath to lose. When his superiors began to question Dowling about the programme and insisted that he modify its tone and presentation, questions were raised by producers and directors about interference from the advertising division and the priorities of the station. Dowling had become increasingly frustrated as a producer and resented the growing pressure from the Authority and director-general. A Dutch television documentary about contemporary Ireland, made by Hans Keller in 1969 addressed these tensions in the Irish media. *Er Gaat Iedere Dag Een Boot* (*Every Day a Ship Leaves*) interviewed Jack Dowling, Bob Quinn and Lelia Doolan. When explaining why he resigned, Dowling cited the interventions that cancelled coverage of Vietnam and Biafra, noting that 'in quick succession a number of important programmes that were critical of the government or commercial interests were cancelled or delayed or abbreviated or interfered with'.[129] Inevitably the press began to report on these tensions forcing the Authority to issue a statement attributing these problems to growing pains and maintaining that there was no question about censorship or curtailing freedom of expression within the service. It also denied that advertisers were influencing programming.

After a series of exchanges in the *Irish Press* and the *Irish Times* where she accused management of 'hypocrisy, lack of candour, lack of trust, and trivialising prevarication'[130] Lelia Doolan was ordered by Hardiman to cease what he defined as a 'public campaign of dissent'.[131] Doolan regarded the director-general's order as an ultimatum and resigned, arguing that he was 'responsible for the deplorable state of affairs' at the station, complaining that the material being produced by RTÉ was 'dangerously and increasingly trivial, emasculated and contrary to the national cultural spirit'.[132] In fairness to Hardiman he was in a tremendously difficult position and regarded the resignation of Doolan as a great loss to RTÉ. Although he hoped to protect and nurture a generation of young and talented producers, he was under constant pressure to reign in some of the more provocative programmes being broadcast. As director-general he understood that the patience of the government was wearing thin and hoped to avoid direct state intervention.

The departure of these three producers was given extensive coverage in the press and created tremendous unease within the hierarchy of RTÉ and within the government. *Sit Down and Be Counted* remains a remarkable account of the short-lived careers of three extraordinary producers all of whom later appeared on *The Late Late Show* to tell their story. Although their departure was controversial, a current affairs programme addressing illegal money-lending broadcast later that same year provoked a harsh reaction from the government and added an exclamation point to the closing of the decade. The contentious *Seven Days* programme addressing illegal moneylending or 'loan sharking' in inner city Dublin will be considered in the next chapter.

Notes

1 See Chapter 8. The two men were not related. Interview of Kevin McCourt by John Horgan, February 24, 1997. According to McCourt, Todd Andrews was close to long-time Fianna Fáil minister Frank Aiken and this was his link to Eamon de Valera. Thanks to John Horgan for allowing me access to this interview.

2 C. S. Andrews, *Man of No Property* (Lilliput Press, Dublin, 2001), 276.

3 Ibid.

4 Ibid., 281–2. See also Fergal Tobin, *The Best of Decades* (Gill and Macmillan, Dublin, 1984), 185.

5 The News Division was a separate entity with its own manager, the head of news, who reported to the director-general.

6 The first director-general was American, the first controller of programmes was British and other senior members of staff were also drawn from Britain, the United States, Canada and as far away as Australia.

7 Author's interview with Maev Conway-Pikorski, Dublin, 1990.

8 RTÉ Authority Archive, Minutes of the Authority, October 6, 1965.

9 Ibid.

10 There were a number of impressive programmes made to mark the fiftieth anniversary of the 1916 Easter Rising. Several documentaries addressed the rebellion and interviewed survivors. Perhaps the most remarkable programme was the dramatisation *Insurrection*. See especially Roisín Higgins, '"I am the narrator over-and-above- ... The Caller of the Dead": Pageant and Drama in 1916', in *1916 in 1966: Commemorating the Easter Rising* (eds) Mary Daly and Margaret Callaghan (Royal Irish Academy, Dublin, 2007).

11 RTÉ Written Archives, John Irvine Papers, Memo from Kevin McCourt to the Authority, November 2, 1965.

12 Lelia Doolan, Jack Dowling and Bob Quinn, *Sit Down and Be Counted: The Cultural Evolution of a Television Station* (Wellington Publishers, Dublin, 1969), 62.

13 Author's interview with Lelia Doolan, November 20, 2008, Dublin.

14 Ibid.
15 Interview with Muiris MacConghail, April 18, 2007, Dublin.
16 Doolan, Dowling and Quinn, *Sit Down and Be Counted*, 75.
17 Ibid.
18 RTÉ Written Archives, John Irvine Papers, Memo from Kevin McCourt to the Authority, November 2, 1965.
19 Ibid.
20 Ibid.
21 Ibid.
22 Ibid., April 20, 1966.
23 Ibid.
24 See Chapter 8.
25 RTÉ Authority Archives, Minutes of the Authority, March 11, 1966.
26 Ibid.
27 Ibid.
28 Ibid.
29 Ibid.
30 Doolan, Dowling and Quinn, *Sit Down*, 75.
31 Ibid., 76.
32 This will be discussed in Chapter 5.
33 For an account of Childers's earlier tenure as Minister for Posts and Telegraphs see Savage, *Irish Television*, 31–6.
34 León Ó Broin, *Just Like Yesterday, an autobiography* (Gill and Macmillan, Dublin, 1985), 215.
35 NAI, 98/6/83, Childers to Lynch, December 21, 1966.
36 Ibid.
37 Ibid.
38 Ibid., Memorandum for the Government, January 11, 1967.
39 Ibid., Cabinet Meeting summary, January 17, 1967.
40 Ibid., Michael Carty to Lynch, January 27, 1967.
41 Ibid.
42 Ibid.
43 *Irish Independent*, April 29, 1967.
44 Ibid.
45 Ibid.
46 NAI, 98/6/83, Childers to Lynch, January 19, 1967.
47 Ibid.
48 Ibid., Childers to Lynch, undated but most likely January 1967.
49 Ibid., Memorandum for Government, January 11, 1967.
50 Ibid., Childers to Lynch, undated but most likely January 1967.
51 Ibid.
52 *Irish Press*, November 2, 1967.
53 *Sunday Independent*, March 26, 1967.

54 Ibid.

55 Ibid.

56 NAI, S3532/2E, letter to Andrews from Lynch, April 5, 1967. Notes in the file indicate the Taoiseach met with Aiken to discuss that matter.

57 NAI, S3532/2E.

58 Dáil Debates, Vol. 227, April 13, 1967.

59 Ibid.

60 Ibid.

61 Ibid.

62 Ibid.

63 *Sunday Independent*, April 16, 1967.

64 Ibid.

65 *Sunday Express*, April 17, 1967.

66 *Sunday Express*, April 16, 1967.

67 *Irish Times,* April 18, 1967.

68 *Irish Independent*, April 21, 1967.

69 NAI, S3532/2E, *Note by Department of External Affairs on Dáil Questions put down by Deputies Cluskey and Cosgrave on the question of sending a RTÉ Television Team to Vietnam* (undated).

70 *Irish Independent*, April 22, 1967.

71 *Irish Times*, May 2, 1967.

72 NAI, 98/6/83, memoranda to Lynch informed him of invitations extended by RTÉ for Ministers to appear throughout 1967.

73 Ibid. Garvey to Carty, August 15, 1967.

74 Ibid. Note of Conversation between the Minister for Finance, Mr Charles Haughey, T.D. and Michael Garvey, Controller of Programmes, Telefís Éireann, September 14, 1967.

75 Ibid.

76 Ibid.

77 Ibid., Childers to Michael Moran, November 10, 1967.

78 Ibid., Memorandum of November 14, 1967, meeting by Michael Carty, Fianna Fáil Party Whip.

79 Ibid.

80 Ibid.

81 Ibid., Department of Taoiseach Memorandum, November 1, 1967.

82 Ibid., Department of Taoiseach Memorandum, August 11, 1967.

83 Ibid., Childers to Moran, November 10, 1967.

84 John Horgan, *Broadcasting and Public Life* (Four Courts Press, Dublin, 2004), 52.

85 *Irish Press*, November 1, 1967.

86 Ibid.

87 Ibid.

88 RTÉ Authority Archives, 'Notes on Director-General's Policy meeting',

November 1, 1967.

89 Fergal Tobin, *The Best of Decades* (Gill and Macmillan, Dublin, 1984), 186.

90 Author's interview with Muiris MacConghail.

91 Ibid.

92 RTÉ Authority papers, 'Notes on Director-General's policy meeting'. January 25, 1968.

93 Ibid.

94 Ibid.

95 Later in the year the independent film company *Radharc* travelled to Nigeria to film a critically acclaimed programme on the crisis in Biafra, *Night Flight to Uli*. Although there were press reports of efforts to keep the programme off the air, these proved erroneous; in February 1969 the programme was broadcast on RTÉ and considered a major success for *Radharc*. Peter Kelly, who worked with the *Radharc* team, has written about the film, noting that it was screened in the British House of Commons and scheduled to be shown by the BBC programme *Panorama* before being withdrawn on short notice. See his unpublished M.A. dissertation at Dublin City University, 'Africa in Radharc Documentaries 1966 to 1993' especially Chapter 6 that addresses the Radharc programme on the Biafra crisis.

96 Andrews, *Man of No Property*, 285.

97 At the same time other programmes developed by *Seven Days* caused concern from management, including a feature on a dispute concerning planning permission for a commercial development in Mountpleasant Square. The programme was critical of the involvement by the Minister for Local Government, Kevin Boland, who intervened to overturn a decision by Dublin Corporation to prevent the building of a petrol station in an area defined as open under a draft development plan.

98 RTÉ Written Archive, file entitled, 'Seven Days Transfer', McCourt to all staff, February 12, 1968.

99 RTÉ Authority Archive, Minutes of the Authority, 146th meeting, February 1968.

100 Ibid., MacNeill memo February 15, 1968.

101 Ibid.

102 Ibid.

103 Dail Debates, Vol. 232, February 13, 1968.

104 Muiris MacConghail, 'David Thornley at RTÉ', in *Unquiet Spirit, Essays in Memory of David Thornley* (ed.) Yseult Thornley (Liberties Press, Dublin, 2008), 123.

105 Ibid.

106 Author's interview with Muiris MacConghail, April 18, 2007, Dublin.

107 *Irish Press*, December 9, 1967.

108 At the end of his tenure as director-general, surveys conducted for RTÉ recorded 420,000 television sets in the state, an increase of 34,000 from the previous year, and it was estimated that 60 per cent of Irish homes had television. The number of homes with multi-channel television (homes able to pick up either BBC or ITV stations) had increased 10 per cent from the previous year to 155,000. It was estimated that 250,000 urban homes had television while the number of sets in rural areas was 161,000 or 43 per cent.

109 Andrews, *Man of No Property*, 285. Conor Cruise-O'Brien applied for the position but was not interviewed.

110 Ibid., 293.

111 Ibid., 294.

112 Ibid.

113 Ibid.

114 Ibid., 295.

115 Ibid., 276–7.

116 Lelia Doolan, Jack Dowling and Bob Quinn, *Sit Down and Be Counted*, Appendix III, xlvii.

117 *The Riordans* was a popular soap opera set in 'a fictional farming community "Leestown", supposedly in County Kilkenny' that ran from 1965–79. See Lance Pettitt's *Screening Ireland: Film and Television Representation* (Manchester University Press, Manchester, 2000), 171 and Helen Sheehan, *Irish Television Drama: A Society and its Stories* (RTÉ, Dublin, 1987).

118 RTÉ Authority Archives, document listing 'distribution of all staff on basic salary as of February 15, 1970'. Of the 1,425 that were full-time members of staff 387 were women; 37 of the 107 contract employees were women.

119 Ibid.

120 See Diarmaid Ferriter, *The Transformation of Ireland 1900–2000* (Profile Books, London, 2004), 508.

121 Interview with Lelia Doolan, November 20, 2008, Dublin.

122 Myrtle Hill, *Women in Ireland: A Century of Change* (Blackstaff Press, Belfast, 2003), 154. For a comprehensive account of the Women's Movement in Ireland see Linda Connolly, *The Irish Women's Movement: From Revolution to Devolution* (Macmillan, Basingstoke, 2002).

123 June Levine, 'The Women's Movement in the Republic of Ireland, 1968–80', in *The Field Day Anthology of Irish Writing, Vol. V, Irish Women's Writing and Traditions* (eds) Angela Bourke *et al.* (New York University Press, New York, 2002), 177.

124 Ibid., 181.

125 RTÉ Authority Archives, *Policy on Employment of Married Women in RTÉ*. An internal document prepared for the Authority recorded that of

the 424 women employees 60 were married. Thirty-one of these married women were working in what were described as specialised roles while the remainder were in clerical positions. The role of woman's programming is an under-researched area that deserves attention. Although Edith Cusack was hired to oversee Woman's Programmes, innovative programming that addressed woman's issues struggled to find a place in television throughout the 1960s.

126 RTÉ Written Archive, Hardiman Papers, file entitled 'Employment of Married Women in Radio Éireann'. This small file includes documents that chronicle the 'releasing' of married women dating from 1962. Included in the file is a memo addressing the problem of too many women in the RTÉ Orchestra. It seems that there was a dearth of young men taking up stringed instruments and this was cause for concern as married women working on a contract basis were beginning to dominate, causing embarrassment 'all round when women in an advanced stage of pregnancy appeared on the concert platform'. These musicians were considered unable to 'give satisfactory performances' and those with 'young babies at home were unable to concentrate on their work'. One violinist who had been a permanent member of the orchestra before being married was trying to come back on a permanent basis but management was 'against any change in the present arrangement whereby women employed on the Orchestra and Choral staff must resign on marriage'. Ibid., memo from O hAnnrachain to the director-general, October 12, 1961.

127 Bob Quinn, *Maverick: A Dissident View of Broadcasting Today* (Dingle, Brandon Books, 2001), 11.

128 Ibid., xxxiv–xxxv. After leaving RTÉ, Quinn began a remarkable career as an independent filmmaker. Michael D. Higgins made him a member of the RTÉ Authority in 1995.

129 Jack Dowling interview, *Er gaat iedere dag een boot*, broadcast in Holland, October 30, 1969. Netherlands Institute for Sound and Vision; thanks to Bert Hogenkamp for tracking down this revealing documentary about Ireland in 1969.

130 Doolan, Dowling and Quinn, *Sit Down and Be Counted*, Appendix III; *Evening Press*, May 27, 1969.

131 Ibid., letter from Hardiman to Doolan, May 29, 1969.

132 Ibid., letter from Doolan to Hardiman, May 29, 1969.

5

'Irresponsible, amateurish, lacking in research, lacking in fact'?[1] The limits of public service broadcasting and the 1969 7 Days tribunal

On Friday November 14, 1969, Thomas Hardiman, Director-General of RTÉ, was working at his Donnybrook office when two detective superintendents of the Gárda Síochána called to see him. The detectives, who arrived unannounced, demanded he produce material relating to a recently broadcast 7 Days programme that examined the problem of illegal money-lending in Dublin. Hardiman was told they wanted 'recordings of the programme, transcripts, and information relating to the programme and [access] to RTÉ personnel whom they wished to interview', explicitly naming the presenter of the programme, Bill O'Herlihy, as a man they wished to question.[2] The detectives explained they were investigating allegations of criminal activity in the programme including the 'breaking of arms and legs and ... the burning of a car'.[3] Hardiman refused to cooperate, citing established RTÉ policy and the need of the station to enjoy freedom from government interference. In a detailed diary he explained that he did not think it appropriate to 'voluntarily agree to the handing over of recordings of programme transcripts' and the other materials the police wanted.[4] The two detective superintendents were sent away empty-handed having been told that without a court order the material would not be released.

The crisis that subsequently developed found the government setting up a formal judicial tribunal to investigate not the insidious practice of loan-sharking, but the veracity of the current affairs programming at RTÉ. The *Tribunal of Inquiry into the Television Programme on Illegal Moneylending* heard testimony for 51 days, calling 133 witnesses and costing taxpayers the considerable sum of £250,000 before publishing its conclusions in a 136-page report on August 5, 1970.

This remarkable episode is critical to understanding the increasingly complicated relationship between RTÉ and the government through the period under consideration in this study. After this crisis subsided the relationship remained troubled, leading to an even more drastic intervention by the government in 1972 when the entire RTÉ Authority was summarily fired for broadcasting political programming the state deemed problematic. In fact, the dramatic dismissal of the RTÉ Authority in 1972 has overshadowed this 1969 controversy in the historical literature. A more comprehensive understanding of this particular crisis offers valuable insight into how television helped transform Irish political culture in the 1960s, underscoring the pressures building in Irish society throughout the decade. It also places in context the government's extraordinary decision to punish Radio Telefís Éireann in 1972 by dismissing those responsible for overseeing the most important source for news and information in the country.

By November 1969 RTÉ was transmitting approximately fifty hours a week of programme material, seven hours of which were devoted to news and current affairs.[5] The flagship current affairs programme of the national television service was undoubtedly 7 Days, which also created tremendous discomfort for political, cultural, and religious elites. The producer, Muiris MacConghail, was a 28-year-old media-savvy Irish-speaking intellectual who assembled a team of ambitious reporters, presenters and researchers who possessed a spirited, if aggressive, attitude towards current affairs broadcasting. By the time of this particular broadcast MacConghail had overseen the production of close to two hundred episodes of 7 Days and was recognised as having been responsible for overseeing 'almost every major event involving politics and current affairs' for RTÉ.[6] Many of these programmes considered matters that were not easily broached in a society that was overwhelmingly Catholic, deeply conservative, and uncomfortable openly addressing difficult social issues. By the autumn of 1969, the programme had developed an audience of 620,000 viewers and tackled such thorny topics as alcoholism, gambling, emigration, the plight of unmarried mothers, and the challenges of poverty in contemporary Irish society.[7] In this context, *7 Days* excelled in helping to open up Irish society by exposing viewers to difficult and sometimes controversial subjects that had long remained outside the public domain.

The perspective of one young member of the *7 Days* staff provides a sense of what it was like to work for the critically acclaimed current affairs programme at an exciting time in the history of contemporary Ireland. Janet Moody, daughter of a longstanding member of the Authority, Professor Theodore W. Moody, joined the *7 Days* team as a researcher in January 1969. Janet Moody graduated from Trinity College in 1967 with a degree in Modern Languages before travelling to Africa to work as an English teacher in Madagascar. After a year abroad she returned to Ireland at the age of twenty-four, finding an entry-level position as a research associate with *7 Days* in RTÉ. For a young idealistic woman, joining the critically acclaimed programme was exciting. She became part of a community of ambitious and hard-working television journalists, describing the environment as a hectic but challenging one and a 'great place to work, we could do anything we wanted, most of the people were very young'.[8] Muiris MacConghail encouraged his young staff to take initiative to bring forward ideas and topics that the programme might address. Like many employees of RTÉ, those at *7 Days* were young, university educated and ambitious. There was a genuine sense of commitment and idealism that motivated the staff and Moody described her co-workers as 'a group of very bright people with a very strong sense of public broadcasting'.[9] The staff understood that many of the programmes produced by *7 Days* were provocative and would upset the government, but this did not intimidate the programme-makers. 'I think in many ways we wanted to sail as close to the wind as possible, that is the nature of that type of journalism … to see how far you can go.' When Moody joined *7 Days* there was no formal training; 'one was expected to be a quick learner as the staff all worked together in a small room with an open plan'. The staff were constantly working to meet deadlines for the programme that was broadcast twice a week. It was, she explained, 'one of these places where there was no introduction … you are just thrown in the deep end'.[10]

8   John O'Donoghue interviewing young Traveller children at Ballyfermot, Dublin for *7 Days*, in 1968. Dublin Corporation had just built new homes in Ballyfermot.

By January 1969, there had already been a number of clashes between the government and RTÉ and *7 Days* was often at the centre of these disputes. In the autumn of 1968, the Fianna Fáil Government suffered a humiliating defeat in a national referendum that rejected its attempt to abolish proportional representation. This angered many in the party who believed that a *7 Days* programme about the consequences of the abolition of PR was responsible for the defeat of the referendum. As was noted in Chapter 4, the programme had been moved recently to the News Division in an attempt to rein it, and its producer, Muiris MacConghail, in.

Janet Moody was well aware of this tension and the supervision the programme was under, recalling MacConghail continually meeting with the Head of News, James McGuinness to keep him informed of broadcast plans. As a young woman, Moody was in a minority; there were few women working in non-clerical positions at the time. Although women had a significant presence as producers, males tended to dominate in technical and managerial staffing. Two other women were on the staff of *7 Days*; production assistant Sheila Kane and another researcher, Susan Gadgeby (now Denham), who was later appointed to the Supreme Court. Moody had been at the station for about six months when she began research for a programme on illegal money-lending.

Another young member of the 7 Days team, Bill O'Herlihy, began a career in journalism as a correspondent for the *Cork Examiner* before joining Telefís Éireann and making his way to 7 Days. O'Herlihy was thirty years old when this particular programme was made. He recalls his associates as a group of young and talented journalists, including Rodney Rice and Ted Nealon, and two academics, Associate Professor in Politics at Trinity College Dublin, David Thornley, and Brian Farrell, a lecturer at University College Dublin who worked part-time for the programme.[11] O'Herlihy and his colleagues thrived in the demanding environment of 7 Days enjoying the hectic pace that made working on the programme professionally challenging.[12]

Even though the programme had stirred controversy it was regarded as an important one by the political establishment, having featured interviews with the Taoiseach Jack Lynch, members of his cabinet, and deputies from all political parties. By 1969, 7 Days had broadcast interviews with a number of elder statesmen including Seán Lemass, John Costello and James Dillon, lending it a degree of respectability that enhanced its prestige. According to Director-General Thomas Hardiman, it had become RTÉ's most popular current affairs programme, developing a reputation for high-quality investigative journalism. The director-general pointed out that surveys carried out by the station proved that the public held the programme in high esteem, regarding it as 'informative, well presented, balanced, and serving an important public purpose'.[13]

Despite Hardiman's claims, many elected officials had become increasingly uncomfortable with the programme. Although Kevin McCourt moved it to the News Division, 7 Days continued to create headaches for many politicians, especially Fianna Fáil ministers and deputies. Fianna Fáil had been in power throughout the life of Telefís Éireann and much of the tension between the national broadcasting service and the political establishment involved Ireland's largest and most powerful political party. The interventions mentioned earlier were regarded as necessary by Fianna Fáil governments concerned that RTÉ was becoming too aggressive and partisan in both its international and domestic current affairs programming.

In this highly charged environment, one particular programme about a social evil that preyed upon Dublin's working poor proved the final straw. According to the director-general, the November 1969 show investigating illegal money-lending was broadcast to favourable reaction from the public. However, when the Dáil met a week later, the programme and RTÉ were subject to what *Irish Times* Dáil correspondent John Healy defined as an 'unprecedented attack' by the Minister for Justice, Micheál Ó Moráin. The minister, a native of Mayo, was known for using colourful if crude language to abuse his political opponents. In what was undoubtedly a reference to Deputy David Thornley he once declared that the Labour Party had been taken over by a gang of 'Left-wing queers from Trinity College and Telefís Éireann' and also denounced Fine Gael Deputy Bernard Durkan as 'the maggot Durkan'.[14]

John Healy made it clear that this particular speech was not the creation of civil servants in the Department of Justice because, by the time he was finished, 'there was no mistaking the Mayo '"skin" on it'.[15] Ó Moráin was responding to a question put down by the leader of the Labour Party, Brendan Corish, asking if he was 'aware of the disturbing evidence disclosed by the television programme, *7 Days*, of unfettered unlicenced money-lending in Dublin city and of the strong-arm methods used by some of the illegal money-lenders to recover their money'.[16] Corish insisted Ó Moráin explain what steps his department would take to protect underprivileged victims of illegal money-lenders, demanding action be taken to bring these criminals to justice 'along with those whom they use to injure and intimidate people'.[17]

The Minister for Justice replied that unlicenced money-lending was a problem but denied it was as extensive as described in the *7 Days* programme. He explained that he had learned that it was notoriously difficult to prosecute illegal money-lenders because borrowers were reluctant to testify for fear of embarrassing themselves and their families. His initial response was measured as he placed the problem in a wider social context, defining it as a complex matter that was difficult to address. He advised the Dáil that according to the Garda Síochána, violence was not an issue associated with the practice. 'The difficulty is not the threat of violence or other reprisals, which is not a factor as far as they are aware, but the fact that those who borrow money in this way very often do so without the knowledge of other members of the family, especially husband or wife, and they are not willing to do anything that would reveal the transactions to their families, not to mention having them made public.'[18]

Ó Moráin then proceeded to launch into a scathing attack on RTÉ, denouncing as 'grossly exaggerated' the claim made in the programme that there were five hundred illegal money-lenders working in Dublin. He told the Dáil that the Garda Síochána had begun an investigation of the allegations made by 7 Days but had been obstructed by obstinate RTÉ officials who refused to turn over critical material relating to the programme. He claimed the police were able to identify, round up, and question the alleged money-lenders featured in the broadcast and concluded that the statements they gave were false. An animated Ó Moráin denounced the 7 Days broadcast as 'phoney', contending that those featured in the programme had spun a 'tissue of lies'.[19]

According to the minister, many of those interviewed had criminal records and were paid £20 to make statements they later told detectives had been fabricated. He complained that people featured in the programme had also been supplied with drink. An incredulous minister described one interview featuring a man who claimed on camera that he ordered a defaulting borrower's car burned as punishment. 'The more sceptical viewers no doubt asked themselves why a man such as this should agree to appear on a TV programme if indeed his story was genuine'. The minister claimed the man interviewed recanted his story when interrogated by the police: 'his statements on the programme were without foundation of any kind and were made solely because he was paid for making them and because he badly needed the money'.[20]

When Ó Moráin was finished, the Dáil was momentarily stunned into silence by the accusations; the opposition was knocked off balance. Before any other member could get in a word, Dáil correspondent John Healy maintained that the minister's colleague Flor Crowley 'indignation swelling his already ample figure was on his feet … and was asking for more information'.[21] He joined in the attack, asking, 'Would the Minister not also agree that producers and researchers in Telefís Éireann should declare beforehand their views, whether they are Leftist, Maoist, Trotskyites or Communists …'[22] Uproar filled the chamber as shouts, insults, and catcalls drowned out Ó Moráin as he struggled to continue.

Some members of the opposition took delight in seeing Fianna Fáil flailing away at RTÉ while others were concerned with the tone of the debate.[23] Garrett FitzGerald was one of the few deputies to try to defend the national broadcasting service by asking the minister if he had contacted RTÉ and asked for comment before deciding to pillory the broadcaster with his allegations. Ó Moráin refused to engage with FitzGerald and to shouts from his opponents, replied that RTÉ simply would not cooperate with the police investigation. David Thornley, a Labour deputy and former correspondent for *7 Days,* added to the excitement by offering an alternative interpretation for Ó Moráin's attack, arguing that his anger at the programme 'derives much less from the high moral tone which he takes up than from the fact that exposé programmes of this kind are not congenial to the Government or the Fianna Fáil Party'.[24] An indignant Ó Moráin informed an unruly Dáil that the police were conducting further investigations and that he would have more to report in the near future.

Ó Moráin's attack in the Dáil prompted Director-General Thomas Hardiman to issue a statement defending the programme as an honest attempt to address a real social problem that existed in Dublin. 'Nothing was contrived to present a dishonest picture. Those taking part were treated and paid in the normal way on such programmes. There was no question of the participants being paid fees to say things impliedly desired by RTÉ. RTÉ does not believe that its programme-makers were misled by the participants into distorting its presentation. It believes that the programme fairly reflected the serious nature of the activities involved.'[25]

Chairman of the RTÉ Authority Todd Andrews recalled

watching the programme at home, describing it as 'first-class viewing' and noting he 'thought it to be an excellent piece of investigative reporting'.[26] He thought that the programme may have overstated the extent of the illegal trade and intended to mention this to the director-general but was surprised to hear that the Department of Justice was upset. 'I could not, nor could anyone else, foresee that the programme would be interpreted by the Department of Justice as a deliberate attack on the competence of the Gardaí, although I knew the department was paranoid on the subject of RTÉ.'[27]

Andrews invited Hardiman and the new Minister for Posts and Telegraphs, P. J. Lalor to his home to view the programme and discuss how to handle what was becoming a major crisis for the government and RTÉ. Lalor had recently been appointed to Posts and Telegraphs, replacing Erskine Childers, a minister with considerable experience in broadcasting matters. Hardiman and Andrews again defended the programme and the staff that had made it, arguing that it was not the intention of *7 Days* to 'point a finger at the Gardaí or the Department of Justice: neither was it the purpose of the programme to produce conclusive evidence to incriminate those who took part: this being so, RTÉ did not want to get involved in arguments or debates about the detailed nature of what the *7 Days* reporters found'.[28] Although Lalor accepted that the programme-makers believed what they broadcast to be true, he could not understand the Authority's refusal to hand over material requested by the police. He also knew his cabinet colleague, the Minister for Justice, was going to raise the contentious issue in the Dáil once again the following week.

The next morning, a Saturday, the director-general was at home when he heard a knock at his front door. He was surprised to find the same two detective superintendents who had visited him earlier that week at his RTÉ office. Once again, the detectives asked that Hardiman produce all of the material related to the programme. Clearly annoyed at the tactics of the police but not intimidated by their arrival at his home, Hardiman refused and declined a further request that a stenographer be allowed to transcribe a private rebroadcast of the programme. Hardiman further recalled that the detectives were anxious to disassociate themselves from the politics of the investigation but 'recognised that I would be aware that their coming to my house on a weekend was related to Dáil questions which had been placed during the week for answering ... next week'.[29]

The two detectives were painfully polite and obviously uncomfortable with the situation in which they found themselves. They told the director-general they were sympathetic to his arguments for not handing over the material and, 'they proffered their own view that no other course of action would seem appropriate of RTÉ'.[30] Although the detectives maintained that their investigation had started the morning after the programme was broadcast, they were clearly under renewed pressure from superiors in the Department of Justice to keep after RTÉ.[31] Hardiman suggested a compromise, and the detectives were able to view a videotape of the programme and take notes. Although this satisfied the detectives, it did not assuage Micheál Ó Moráin's anger.

Once again the matter was the subject of furious debate in the Dáil, this time featuring an awkward intervention by the Taoiseach whose remarks intensified the controversy. As had been noted by the detectives, after the first debate opposition deputies interested in exploiting the government's difficulties put down a number of questions for the Minister for Justice. One came from the former Fine Gael Taoiseach Liam Cosgrave who asked for the establishment of a public inquiry to look into the issues raised by the programme and the controversy that it provoked. Cosgrave's contribution to the controversy illustrates that divisions existed within Fine Gael. Many politicians of Cosgrave's generation shared with their opponents in Fianna Fáil a strong distaste for the aggressive current affairs broadcasting employed by *7 Days*. The programme disturbed Cosgrave, who was upset with the implication that the police were not diligently performing their duties, and was especially concerned with the handling of the matter by the Fianna Fáil Minister for Justice. Younger members of Fine Gael were exasperated by Cosgrave's intervention, not wanting to see RTÉ put on trial. More politically astute members of the party, including Garrett FitzGerald, understood what was at stake and were quick to defend the national broadcasting service, believing a public inquiry would be a mistake.[32]

Once again Ó Moráin positioned himself as the defender of the Garda Síochána, rejecting allegations made in the programme about unfettered, unlicenced money-lending and strong-arm tactics, telling the Dáil that the programme's 'so-called evidence was worthless'. He was convinced the programme had insulted the police by suggesting they were incompetent for not aggressively dealing with a problem that he argued had been grossly overstated. Ó Moráin informed the Dáil that he had consulted senior members of the Garda Síochána who had investigated the allegations made by *7 Days* and concluded that they knew nothing of a 'money lending racket backed up by strong-arm tactics of any shape or form'.[33] According to the minister, police estimates placed the number of people involved in the illegal trade at between 12 and 15 and nowhere near the 500 that had been cited in the programme, a figure he described as 'grossly exaggerated'. Ó Moráin's reply caused more turmoil in the Dáil as shouts and heckling drowned out the minister's words. When again challenged to set up a public inquiry, he backed himself into a corner complaining of the 'amount of public uneasiness that has been fomented by the "phoneyness" of this show. People swallowed this fiction as fact. I do not know the number of people who have swallowed this. If I found that, notwithstanding the factual evidence of the Garda … the public still did not accept that these people were all "phoneys" I would consider a public inquiry.'[34]

Although he admitted he had not seen the programme, the Taoiseach got involved in the debate. Jack Lynch was careful at first to commend RTÉ for transmitting a programme 'exposing social evils'. However, he continued by making a statement that in retrospect appears bizarre: 'All this controversy could have been avoided if RTÉ had said at the outset of this programme that the characters and scenes to be portrayed in it were fictitious; otherwise there is the danger that, in future programmes, no matter how laudable or commendable, no matter how much they are put forward in the public interest, they would cause a cry of "wolf, wolf" in other words, that the credibility of any future RTÉ programme would be brought into question.'[35]

All along, RTÉ tenaciously defended the programme as factual while the Minister of Justice Ó Moráin denounced it as a fraud.

The Taoiseach's statement defining the work as fictitious further complicated matters. Garrett FitzGerald understood this, asking Lynch and Ó Moráin directly if they were 'aware that in making these allegations that the programme was fictitious they are contradicting the statement issued by the RTÉ authority?'[36] At this juncture, with senior members of the opposition demanding a public inquiry, Ó Moráin found himself in a difficult position. He could not easily back down given the statement he made in the Dáil about his willingness to hold a public inquiry if there remained any question in people's minds about the 'phoneyness' of the programme. The Taoiseach's defining the programme as fictitious directly contradicted the statement issued by RTÉ. A good deal hinged on how RTÉ would react: would it issue a statement that might try to defuse the controversy? Would it, in effect, back down?

The RTÉ Authority did not want to see an official inquiry take place and was annoyed that Ó Moráin had not followed established protocol by contacting Posts and Telegraphs or RTÉ before launching his attack in the Dáil. Andrews informed Lalor that any problems associated with the programme could be dealt with internally within the station. However, Lynch's remarks complicated the issue. Once they were made, Andrews recalls, 'I desisted from offering any further advice.'[37]

In these circumstances the director-general felt compelled to issue another statement, reiterating, 'the programme fairly reflected the serious nature of the activities involved'.[38] A short time later, a formal meeting of the Authority was called and members viewed the programme. Hardiman carefully outlined the events that had transpired since the broadcast of the programme, explaining the unexpected visits by the police to his office and home. Todd Andrews asked the Authority to consider what he identified as the three critical issues in the controversy. These were the charge by the Minister for Justice that the extent of illegal money-lending was 'negligible, the allegation by the minister that the lenders and borrowers portrayed in the programme were "fictitious" and the statement by the minister that the strong-arm methods do not exist as alleged in the programme'.[39]

Andrews told the Authority that both he and the Minister for

Posts and Telegraphs were convinced after discussing the matter with the director-general that 'fictitious characters were not used in the programme and that intimidation existed'.[40] Hardiman emphasised it was important to understand that the programme's approach 'was not to produce evidence leading to prosecutions but to look at the social problem which RTÉ was satisfied existed in a number of areas in Dublin: this was what he meant by saying that RTÉ had taken a journalistic approach to the problem'.[41] Hardiman provided additional information to the Authority, explaining how unofficial information had been gathered from a number of sources for the broadcast including the Dublin Health Authority, local clergy, welfare workers, credit unions, and the St Vincent de Paul Society. When addressing the programme's contention that there were five hundred illegal money-lenders in Dublin, he explained that the figure came from a representative of a credit union and that the real number could be much higher. According to Hardiman, 'the 7 Days team had selected the figure of 500 on a journalistic judgement on what was found in the preliminary studies and subsequent field work'.[42] After hearing the presentations of both the chairman and director-general and viewing the programme, the Authority expressed its unanimous support for 7 Days and quickly requested a meeting with the minister, P. J. Lalor.

When Lalor met with the RTÉ Authority he was chastised by the Chairman who took issue with the way the government had reacted to the programme. Todd Andrews complained about the tactics of the Minister of Justice, believing that raising the matter in the Dáil without consulting the RTÉ Authority or Posts and Telegraphs was unprofessional and unwarranted. Although he promised that his complaints concerning the behaviour of the police would not be made public, he criticised what he defined as inappropriate efforts made by Garda detectives to intimidate members of RTÉ staff.[43] He then told Lalor that the RTÉ Authority supported the programme and intended to issue a statement that would make this clear. This was an obvious challenge to the Minister of Justice, the Taoiseach and the Fianna Fáil Government. Lalor worried that by defying the government there would be difficult consequences, warning the Authority that issuing such a statement would 'intensify the controversy'.[44] However, Andrews explained there would be no backing down, noting the 'seriousness of the Taoiseach's statement, whereby the Board of a public organisation was seen to be publicly rebuked by the Head of Government and to have the credibility of its operation impugned by him'.[45] A deeply anxious Lalor told the Authority that any such communication should not be construed as having his approval, but was informed by Andrews that 'the matter at issue was the veracity of RTÉ'.[46]

The statement the RTÉ Authority issued noted that the board had met the minister and informed him of its position: 'The Authority told the Minister that the content of the programme was authentic, and that the people shown in it as moneylenders or borrowers were not fictitious. The Authority maintained the view that the programme did not present a distorted or exaggerated picture of the social problems of illegal money-lending in Dublin.'[47] The decision of the Authority and the director-general to stand by the programme provided a morale boost within RTÉ, especially the staff of 7 Days.[48] Given the remarks that had been made in the Dáil and the refusal of senior staff or indeed the Authority to give ground, the government established a special judicial tribunal on December 2, 1969. The tribunal was presided over by Justices Seán dé Buitléir, A. Denis Pringle and Cathal Ó Floinn.

The terms of reference under which the tribunal operated are critical to understanding how the formal inquiry functioned. If the tribunal had been instructed to investigate the allegations made by 7 Days into the existence and extent of illegal money-lending in working-class areas of Dublin, the results may have been quite different. However, the terms of reference focused on investigating the 'planning, preparation, arrangement, production and presentation' of the programme.[49]

These instructions required the tribunal to investigate the authenticity of the programme as well as the veracity of statements made by presenter Bill O'Herlihy and those interviewed. These terms of reference were written by a Fianna Fáil government that had little interest in exposing the shadowy practice of illegal money-lending in the nation's capital. Opponents of the government alleged that two of the three judges who presided at the tribunal were biased towards Fianna Fáil and would interpret the terms of reference to ensure the focus would remain on RTÉ. When considering strategy, counsel for RTÉ believed it imperative that the tribunal not focus narrowly on the programme. They hoped to provide enough information to 'help the Tribunal to conclude that there is a major problem with regards to illegal money-lending in Dublin and that the "Seven Days" Money-Lending programme sought to give a reasonable account of this problem'.[50]

The tribunal opened on January 6, 1970, and began to call witnesses from RTÉ, many of whom underwent often gruelling cross-examination in the witness box. Six weeks into the tribunal a status report by Oliver Moloney, secretary to the Authority, informed the director-general's Programme Policy Committee that the first thirty-two days were primarily taken up by the examination of witnesses from the programme. He predicted that as many as 180 further witnesses would be called. From his observations he believed that allegations of the programme using actors and paying bribes to those interviewed had been proven false, concluding the evidence supported the programme's contention that illegal money-lending was a real problem. According to Moloney, the weakest part of RTÉ's case were the allegations made 'of strong arm methods' used by money-lenders, predicting the programme would be open to charges of exaggerating the threat of violence associated with the illicit practice. He also reported that the use of hidden cameras and microphones had garnered much attention and could also be problematic.[51] Hidden cameras and microphones were used on unsuspecting individuals to try and capture illegal money-lenders plying their trade. Moloney took special note of the performance of the Attorney General, describing him as being scrupulously fair in ensuring that each side was able to call witnesses before the three judges.

John Irvine, Deputy Director General, attended many of the sessions of the tribunal and helped coordinate the defence of the programme with counsel for RTÉ. In a report to the director-general he later complained that counsel for the Gardaí launched a 'violent attack' on persons associated with *7 Days* and the programme itself, describing it as 'irresponsible, amateurish, lacking in research, lacking in fact'.[52] RTÉ was accused of descending to a level of journalism never seen in Ireland, and the tribunal was told that the real question was 'what should be done to RTÉ and its journalists … so that such a programme might never again be made'.[53] The staff of *7 Days*, especially Muiris MacConghail, Bill O'Herlihy and Janet Moody, found themselves under hours of intensive cross-examination from aggressive attorneys intent on discrediting the programme and its staff.

In spite of the terms of reference, the tribunal offered a glimpse of life in deprived areas of working-class Dublin as the 1960s came to a close. The testimony of social workers, priests, volunteers for the St Vincent de Paul Society and ordinary residents of Dublin's inner city reveal how this black market counter-economy functioned. One witness, a 44-year-old woman who was intimately acquainted with the trade, provided a detailed statement explaining that illegal money-lending caused tremendous suffering for disadvantaged residents of the city. She testified that she had moved to Dublin from Athlone at the age of nineteen and she lived with her aunt who worked as an agent for a female money-lender in Gardiner Street. She explained how the practice worked, noting that interest was deducted from the initial loans at a rate of 2s 6d on the pound. She recalled seeing 'men and women in tears as they beg to be let off repayments'. In the end these desperate borrowers would somehow come up with the money: 'They used to go to the pawn shop to pawn their goods or clothes.'[54]

This same witness testified that she later moved from Sean McDermot Street to Liberty House Flats and became friends with her next-door neighbour. The neighbour had fallen victim to illegal money-lenders, leading to misery for her family. She told the tribunal that at the time she was working at a restaurant in O'Connell Street and used to bring home scraps for her dog but that when her neighbour saw 'the scraps of food would ask me for them to feed her children'.[55] When her neighbour could no longer pay the loan, she fled to London. 'In fact she had to break up her home and put her two boys, Johnny and Paddy, in Artane School and her two girls in High Park Convent School, Drumcondra.'[56]

After settling in England she was eventually reunited with her family, but remained fearful of returning to Dublin: 'I sent her sons over with their names and addresses pinned on their collars. She collected the girls herself. She told me she sneaked back home to collect the girls herself. I left her out to Dun-Laoghaire – we took the back streets – she was afraid any of these people would see her.'[57] The source of the loan was a man who belonged to a notoriously violent organisation known as the Animal Gang. In the areas around Sean McDermot Street he was known as 'the coalman' because he sold coal in the neighbourhood frequently on credit, expecting everyone to purchase their supply directly from him. According to this witness the plight of her neighbour was not unique as she claimed there were hundreds, even thousands, like her. Her testimony and that of others identified enforcers with colourful names including Golly Green, Ginger, Mucker, Brambles and Blackman Doyle, all of whom were said to intimidate their victims.

Evidence submitted revealed that many of the borrowers were women, suggesting they were the ones who kept working-class families going in very difficult circumstances. The Irish Association of Social Workers prepared a memorandum confirming that illegal money-lending was widespread throughout the city and that strong-arm tactics were used. Echoing Ó Moráin's statements in the Dáil, it cautioned that the practice was notoriously difficult to deal with because victims did not want to come forward to testify for fear of being embarrassed. This was especially true for women who were susceptible to 'threats to inform their husbands but also by raising of voices at the door of [a] client's home, shouting about it so [they are] disgraced in front of her neighbours'.[58] If friends, relatives, or neighbours learned that a family had fallen into the grasp of loan sharks this would cause shame and embarrassment for the family involved. Witnesses indicated that any real fear associated with the unsavoury practice of illegal money-lending had more to do with a wife being afraid that her husband might find out rather than fear of trouble from an enforcer. If violence was part of the problem, the source was not likely to be a burly figure taking out brass knuckles on defaulting victims, but angry husbands upset with their wives. However, women were not just borrowers; many were deeply involved in the trade. Of the fifty-six individuals RTÉ listed as suspected moneylenders, thirty-eight were women.[59]

One reason the police tended to ignore the problem was that some of those involved in the practice were 'tots', or informers, and many detectives loathed losing sources – their ears and eyes on the street. Although there were not five hundred loan sharks working in Dublin in 1969, the scourge of the illegal money-lender was real. The practice was complex and operated at a number of different levels, from informal arrangements with the women fishmongers on Moore Street to dealing with more difficult characters in the pubs along the quays of the River Liffey. This practise became less of a problem in the 1970s not because of a renewed crackdown by police but because of other factors, including the rapid development of the credit union movement in Ireland, partly spearheaded by the Derry activist John Hume.

The experience of being summoned before a judicial inquiry to testify for hours or even days under oath created tremendous anxiety for members of the *7 Days* staff. During the proceedings, senior staff, producers and reporters were compelled to appear before the judicial tribunal to give evidence under oath and ordered to produce their notes, scripts, memoranda and tapes for examination. Many were convinced that an angry Fianna Fáil government was lashing out, seeking retribution for aggressive current affairs programmes that challenged the government and its policies. Members of the *7 Days* team regarded the tribunal as a witch-hunt, arguing that the presiding judges were doing the bidding of Fianna Fáil.

When the report of the tribunal was published it received widespread coverage in the national press, which reported that RTÉ had been criticised for significant failures and lapses in judgement. The research that was conducted for the programme was defined as deeply flawed, and one very junior member of the *7 Days* team, Janet Moody, was unfairly singled out for harsh criticism. Although the report admitted that the programme addressed a real social problem, its construction was found to be profoundly problematic. It was determined to be compromised by uneven research, a questionable methodology (the invasive use of hidden microphones and cameras), and the use of unsubstantiated statistics. Statements that referred to Dublin as a city 'living in fear' where five hundred loan sharks preyed on the working poor were defined as very wide of the mark. After hearing evidence from police, social workers, priests and others, the tribunal estimated that there were perhaps fifty active moneylenders in the capital. This was far fewer than the five hundred mentioned in the programme but many more than the twelve to fifteen claimed by Ó Moráin and the police. The use of what were defined as 'illustrative shots' was also questioned. These were reconstructed images of money or children's allowance books changing hands that had been filmed in the studio and inserted into the programme. Viewers were given the impression that these images were recordings of actual exchanges taking place when this was not the case.

The tribunal also complained that a false sense of violence had been woven into the fabric of the programme in order to make it more sensational. Statements maintaining 'violence is undeniable, always there is a threat of more' were singled out as unsubstantiated.[60] The tribunal criticised a section in the film in which the narrator discussed the topic of violence while unrelated film clips of men on crutches and in wheelchairs navigating the street of Dublin were shown. These images were filmed randomly and edited into the programme to suggest how defaulters were punished by enforcers working with illegal money-lenders. The tribunal pointed out that in the background the soundtrack played a song with the lyrics 'I'll pay you back in kind'.[61] These excessive techniques undermined the credibility of an ambitious investigative programme that had the best of intentions.

The tribunal admitted that the programme-makers were motivated by a real desire to expose a serious social problem. It deplored the practice of illegal money-lending and maintained that because the public had been made aware of the problem, 'the results of the programme have been beneficial'. However there could be no denying that the tribunal's report was damaging for RTÉ. 7 Days had made a number of mistakes and left itself exposed and vulnerable in producing a programme that had serious shortcomings. This was a blemish on the record of an otherwise remarkable current affairs programme.

In the end, the government had succeeded in inflicting a punishing whack at RTÉ. The consensus in the national press was that the national broadcasting service had been put in its place. RTÉ was found to have been guilty of serious failures in judgement. The tribunal and its findings succeeded in undermining the integrity of a prestigious programme and RTÉ itself. However, the creation of a formal tribunal was clearly a major over-reaction on the part of the government. The Minister for Justice, Micheál Ó Moráin, a politician who had earned a reputation for bluster and hyperbole before RTÉ came into his sights, bears part of the blame for the state of affairs. Rather than trying to communicate with his cabinet colleague in Posts and Telegraphs or senior officials at RTÉ, he decided that ham-fisted ambush was the best way forward.

The Taoiseach, Jack Lynch, also contributed to the controversy first by condoning the minister's vigorous attack on RTÉ and then by making reckless remarks about the programme being a work of fiction. One might hazard a guess that he was distracted by more ominous events. In the autumn of 1969, Northern Ireland seemed to be slipping into civil war, and violence was threatening to spill over into the Irish Republic. Partly because of this his cabinet was dysfunctional, deeply fractured by a number of ambitious and unscrupulous ministers who were openly challenging his authority and secretly plotting behind his back. A short time later the 'arms crisis' led to the dismissal of ministers Charles Haughey and Neil Blaney, and the forced resignation of a debilitated Micheál Ó Moráin.

The entire episode did not reflect well on the Fianna Fáil Government or, for that matter, its opponents in Fine Gael. While Fianna Fáil might be seen as the bully, throwing its considerable weight around in an effort to intimidate the national broadcasting service, Fine Gael had been the party that had insisted on the establishment of a tribunal in the first place. Although Liam Cosgrave had called for the tribunal, progressive elements in Fine Gael were appalled at the establishment of a formal tribunal that succeeded in putting RTÉ through the proverbial wringer. The 7 Days tribunal succeeded in harming the professional careers of a number of broadcasters, while putting in question the government's commitment to the freedom of the press. This experience damaged the careers of a number of people involved in the programme, most notably the young researcher Janet Moody and the presenter Bill O'Herlihy. When the report was issued both were singled out for blame, and each found it impossible to continue to work in current affairs broadcasting. Both went on to successful careers outside current affairs broadcasting, O'Herlihy becoming a tremendously popular businessman and icon in sports broadcasting while Janet Moody settled into a successful academic career.

The government's heavy-handed response to the programme had the intended effect of sending an ominous chill through the ranks of those working in RTÉ. Broadcasters became more careful in the aftermath of the tribunal and a degree of self-censorship, even paranoia, became part of the culture within the service, where a siege mentality took root. Todd Andrews regarded the entire affair as 'an act of political irresponsibility', blaming the opposition for calling for the inquiry and the government for establishing it.[62] He concluded, 'It proved nothing and changed nothing ... Its only effect was to create much personal anxiety to individual members of the RTÉ staff and to disrupt the organization for months.'[63]

The RTÉ Authority responded cautiously to the tribunal's report, issuing a statement that was mildly defiant. It accepted that 'certain defects' in the production of the programme had been identified, maintaining that 'careful account will be taken of the Tribunal's criticisms'. However, the Authority chose to highlight the report's positive remarks about the producers' motivations, which were defined as 'honourable', and pointed out that the programme was trying to address a serious social problem. Within RTÉ there was broad support for the statement issued by the Authority.[64]

The Authority expressed concern about the 'strongly condemnatory nature' of the report, especially that of researcher Janet Moody and reporter Bill O'Herlihy. After the programme had been broadcast and while the tribunal was hearing evidence, RTÉ began to review a number of practices employed in the programme, including the use of hidden devices such as microphones and cameras. Policies were put in place that provided guidelines banning the use of these devices without the approval of the director-general; the consensus of senior staff and programme-makers within the organisation was that these reforms should continue.[65]

When the *7 Days* staff returned from summer break in the autumn of 1970 there was a feeling of 'trepidation' although they were encouraged by the director-general's assurances that there would be no 'head chopping'.[66] A series of meetings were held, chaired by deputy director-general John Irvine, aimed at restructuring the *7 Days* programme to make it more accountable to Muiris MacConghail. The director-general was later told that the direction of *7 Days* would change and there would be '[l]ess regular concern with the demanding (in terms of resources and personnel) stories on social problems ... MacConghail said that a closer involvement in reporting on the medical and scientific field is envisioned, an aspect hitherto given little treatment. In the nature of programmes on such subjects, less of a preoccupation with deploring the ills of society is inevitably involved and this was welcomed by the *7 Days* staff.'[67]

When the tribunal's report was published in August 1970 the cabinet had been reshuffled and Gerry Collins was the new Minister for Posts and Telegraphs. Collins was not pleased with the Authority's response to the tribunal's report, defining it as 'unsatisfactory' and complaining that it created the impression that RTÉ was not taking the criticism seriously.[68] The relationship between Collins and RTÉ started out badly and deteriorated rapidly. He became RTÉ's nemesis.

Perhaps the most ominous consequence of this controversy was the complete rupture of the already troubled relationship between the government and the RTÉ Authority. The turmoil that led to the establishment of the judicial tribunal in 1969 offers insight into the critical role television played in a tumultuous and transformative decade. By continually challenging the government and questioning its priorities and policies television undermined the sense of deference and complacency that characterised Irish political culture prior to the 1960s. Despite the tribunal's findings, programme-makers continued to create difficulties for successive governments. RTÉ may have emerged battered and bloodied but it retained a conviction that difficult issues had to be explored, even if this would result in serious consequences for the service. As a result, the relationship between government and broadcaster was increasingly marked by mistrust, suspicion and foreboding.

This may partly explain the failure of the RTÉ Authority and especially the government to communicate more effectively a short time later as the state became increasingly concerned with coverage of the violence developing in Northern Ireland. It certainly helps place in context the extraordinary decision taken by the Lynch Government in 1972 to punish Radio Telefís Éireann by invoking Section 31 of the Broadcasting Act, then dismissing the Radio Telefís Éireann Authority, firing those responsible for overseeing Ireland's radio and television service.

Notes

1   RTÉ Authority Archives, Notes of the Programme Policy Committee, April 10, 1970.
2   RTÉ Written Archive, John Irvine Papers, Memorandum by Thomas Hardiman, dated February 5, 1970.
3   Ibid. *Tribunal of Inquiry into the Programme on Illegal Moneylending*, August 5, 1970, 85, section 149.
4   Ibid. John Irvine Papers, Memorandum by Thomas Hardiman dated February 5, for Haughey 1970.
5   By March 1969 there were 443,000 television sets in the country and 64 per cent of Irish homes had sets, meaning that individuals in television homes numbered over two million or approximately 72 per cent of the population. Of those television homes 64 per cent received RTÉ only while 36 per cent received at least one other station. Ownership of television sets remained predominantly an urban phenomenon; over 80 per cent of urban home had sets while the number in rural homes was 47 per cent. *RTÉ Chronology*, Vol. II, 1967–70 (RTÉ Written Archives).
6   *Tribunal of Inquiry into the Programme on Illegal Moneylending*, August 5, 1970, 3.
7   Ibid., 6.
8   Author's interview with Janet Moody, Limerick, Ireland, June 2005.
9   Ibid.
10 Ibid.
11 David Thornley left the programme when he was elected to the Dáil as a member of the Labour party in 1969.
12 Author's interview with Bill O'Herlihy, Dublin, September 19, 2007.

13   Ibid.
14   Quoted in the *Magill Book of Irish Politics* (ed.) Vincent Browne (Magill Publications, Dublin, 1981), 284. Ó Moráin was Minister for Justice during the arms crisis and was forced to resign by Lynch in May 1970. He later testified that he had passed information concerning the smuggling of arms to the Taoiseach, a claim Jack Lynch forcefully denied.
15   *Irish Times*, November 20, 1969.
16   Dáil Debates, Vol. 242, November 19, 1969, 1264.
17   Ibid.
18   Ibid.
19   Ibid., 1269.
20   Ibid., 1265.
21   *Irish Times*, November 20, 1969.
22   Dáil Debates, Vol. 242, November 19, 1969, 1266.
23   The veteran political correspondent for the *Irish Independent* Arthur Noonan described the attack as 'amazing' and was struck by the unanimous support it received from Fianna Fáil deputies speculating that the minister was expressing a 'government consensus'. *Irish Independent*, November 19, 1969.
24   Dáil Debates, Vol. 242, November 19, 1969, 1267–8.
25   RTÉ Written Archives, Irvine Papers, Memorandum by Thomas Hardiman dated February 5, 1970, 3.
26   C. S. Andrews, *Man of No Property* (Lilliput Press, Dublin, 2001), 290.
27   Ibid., 291.
28   RTÉ Written Archives, Irvine Papers.
29   Ibid. Irvine Papers, memorandum written by Hardiman, November 22, 1969.
30   Ibid.
31   A few days later Muiris MacConghail was interviewed by one of the superintendents who told him that the police were 'aware of quite a heap of questions coming up again in the Dáil ... These are all giving us certain difficulties naturally'. (Hardiman Papers, RTÉ Written Archives, transcription of telephone interview, November 25, 1969).
32   Author's interview with Garrett FitzGerald, Dublin, April 19, 2007.
33   Dáil Debates, Vol. 242, November 26, 1969.
34   Ibid.
35   Ibid.
36   Ibid.
37   Andrews, *Man of No Property*, 219.
38   RTÉ Written Archives, Irvine Papers, Memorandum by Thomas Hardiman dated February 5, 1970, 4.
39   RTÉ Authority Archives, Notes of the Programme Policy Committee dated December 2, 1969, 9.

40 Ibid.
41 RTÉ Authority Archives, Notes of the Programme Policy Committee December 2, 1969, 10.
42 Ibid.
43 Ibid.
44 RTÉ Written Archives, Irvine Papers, Memorandum by Thomas Hardiman dated February 5, 1970, 4.
45 RTÉ Authority Archives, Notes of the Programme Policy Committee, December 2, 1969, 12.
46 Ibid.
47 RTÉ Written Archives, Irvine Papers, Memorandum by Thomas Hardiman dated February 5, 1970, 5.
48 This was the consensus among those interviewed about the project including Muiris MacConghail, Bill O'Herlihy and Janet Moody.
49 *Report of the Tribunal Appointed by An Taoiseach*, 22 December 1969, 9. The terms of reference continued by ordering the tribunal to report on the 'authenticity of the programme and in particular, the adequacy of the information on which the programme was based, and whether or not the statements, comments and implications of the programme as to the number of unlicenced moneylenders operating in the city and county of Dublin and the scope of their operations, and the use of violence, to secure repayments of money lent, amounted to a correct and fair representation of the facts and ... reflected reasonable journalistic care on the part of those responsible for the programme.'
50 RTÉ Authority Archives, Notes of the Programme Policy Committee, December 23, 1969, 7.
51 Ibid., February 24, 1970, 2.
52 Ibid., April 10, 1970.
53 Ibid.
54 RTE Written Archives, John Irvine Papers, *Seven Days Money Lending File* 2.
55 Ibid., 1–2.
56 Ibid.
57 Ibid., 2.
58 Ibid., Irvine Papers, Irish Association of Social Workers Memorandum, December 21, 1969.
59 Ibid., Irvine Papers, document titled 'List of Suspected Money Lenders'.
60 *Report of the Tribunal Appointed by An Taoiseach*, December 22, 1969, 59.
61 Ibid., 57.
62 Andrews, *Man of No Property*, 292.
63 Ibid.
64 RTÉ Authority Archives, 'Programme Policy Meeting', August 21, 1970.

One internal report indicating 'it was felt the Authority acknowledged realistically the reasoned criticisms of the production process but also realistically expressed reservations at certain of the tribunals' findings and comments; it was noted that the Authority should not seem to be setting itself beyond criticism by a judicial Tribunal'.

65   Ibid., August 28, 1970, 2. Thomas Hardiman predicted that the government 'severely embarrassed by this costly Tribunal, may not find it sustainable to state that the RTÉ Authority is responsible for programme making and will take what action is necessary'. He believed that the Authority would have to craft a more elaborate response to the Tribunal, pointing to 'recent developments in programme policy in the organisation and the effect of this on improving standards of programme production and content'.

66   Ibid., September 11, 1970.

67   Ibid., 2. Although it appeared that *7 Days* was committed to producing a less 'aggressive' product only a month later it was targeted for criticism by the Director-General along with *The Late Late Show* and *Féach*. Hardiman complained that the station had been inundated with protests about the emphasis given to left-wing views, indicating that all three programmes had 'extensively dealt with and reported on societies and groups advocating social revolution'. All were scolded for featuring a Tass correspondent in their programmes, though MacConghail defended the use of the correspondent, noting that he was asked to represent the National Liberation Front in a discussion about the Vietnam War.

68   RTÉ Authority Archives, Minutes of the Authority, Letter from Collins to the Chairman of the Authority, September 22, 1970.

6

Religious broadcasting

The Catholic and Protestant Churches of Ireland greeted the advent of a native television service with a degree of trepidation. Although television signals from Britain and Northern Ireland allowed communities along the eastern seaboard and some border areas to view British programmes, the majority of the population were among the last western Europeans to have access to an indigenous television service. Both churches proved proactive in setting up television committees to monitor, influence and eventually partake in the new medium. The Catholic Church remained a remarkably powerful institution throughout the 1960s, and television provided opportunities and challenges for its leaders. Irish Protestant Churches shared many of the concerns articulated by their Catholic counterparts and also hoped to use the medium proactively. This chapter considers how these institutions, especially the Catholic Church, responded to the arrival of television in Ireland.

The Catholic Church in Ireland viewed the arrival of television with concern. There was tremendous anxiety that an unsupervised service could, through the broadcast of unsuitable material, not only corrupt the morals of the Irish people but also compromise the teachings of the church, ultimately undermining its influence.[1] Decades earlier this had been the case as radio developed and grew in popularity in Ireland. Long before television became a reality, radio, cinema and the popular press caused tremendous disquiet for the Catholic Church and contributed to the extraordinary censorship that helped define independent Ireland.[2] Church leaders wanted to ensure that broadcasts of the state-owned and state-operated radio service would not contradict their teaching, and awkwardly tried to find ways to use the medium to help support their work. In a country that was overwhelmingly conservative and Catholic, politicians and civil servants were keen to avoid controversy with the influential Catholic hierarchy. The relationship that developed between church and state was informal and characterised by a mutual desire to establish a non-confrontational relationship in which both would be comfortable. The hierarchy enjoyed a cordial relationship with Radio Éireann, which it hoped would continue once Irish television became a reality.

To assess how the Catholic Church responded and adapted to the challenge of television it is helpful to consider how the institution reacted to the development of the fledgling national radio service earlier in the century. The first Irish radio station, 2RN, began broadcasting in January 1926 via a fairly primitive, low-power transmitter based in Dublin.[3] Douglas Hyde, co-founder of the Gaelic League and future President of Ireland, opened the station with a broadcast in Irish, setting the tone for the new service. Extolling the richness of Irish culture and encouraging an appreciation of the Irish language, Hyde told listeners that he hoped radio would be used to support the Gaelic Revival. A short time later a second station opened in Cork, and these stations and the national service that emerged in 1932 as Radio Éireann, were operated by the Irish Post Office, later the Department of Posts and Telegraphs. The civil service staffed Radio Éireann until the 1960 Broadcasting Act created an independent public authority responsible for overseeing both radio and television. During this period Irish radio operated under considerable financial hardship as a resource-constrained government enterprise. It was managed by civil servants and monitored by a number of ministers from different political parties, some of whom had little interest in broadcasting.[4] Its programming supported the conservative ethos of the new state, emphasising that Ireland possessed a unique culture that had to be appreciated and supported. In supporting the Gaelic Revival with lectures, music and Irish language broadcasts, Radio Éireann generally reinforced an identity that many politicians and cultural nationalists were keen to promote.

The decision of the Cumann na nGaedheal government to designate the Post Office as the department responsible for radio was a controversial one. The minister of the department, James Joseph Walsh, strenuously opposed the decision, warning the Dáil: 'If this house determines that the Post Office must differentiate between rival organ grinders, rival tenors and people of that kind and even rival politicians who want to get control and preferential treatment, we will be able to do it at a price and it will be a very dear price.'[5] Walsh believed that political interference would be inevitable, and during his tenure as minister insisted radio avoid political and religious broadcasting; he advised the first director 'that it would be safe to steer clear as far as possible of religion and politics'.[6] Walsh feared political and religious programming would inevitably complicate his department's effort to manage radio. Unlike his contemporaries, he understood its potential to disseminate news and information that would inevitably address a range of social, political and religious issues.

In 1932 a high-powered radio transmitter began operating from Athlone in the Irish midlands, in effect introducing a truly national radio service. The new transmitter provided coverage to the majority of the Irish people who up until that time had only been able to receive broadcasts if living in close proximity to the two low-powered transmitters in Dublin and Cork. Brian Lynch, head of written archives at RTÉ, points out that the highlight of that year for Radio Éireann was the successful national broadcast of the Eucharistic Congress, a major Catholic event featuring an elaborate Mass celebrated for hundreds of thousands of the faithful in Dublin's Phoenix Park.[7] The successful broadcast of the ceremony, complete with greetings from the pontiff in Rome, was a milestone for the developing Irish radio service. Dr Frank O'Reilly, secretary of the Catholic Truth Society of Ireland, chaired the committee responsible for organising this logistically challenging event. This lay organisation was established in 1899 and became a powerful source of propaganda, publishing pamphlets that offered instruction and advice on moral issues to Ireland's Catholic population. Historian Louise Fuller notes that the 'pamphlets were written in a simple direct manner and concerned with giving information and advice about moral issues, and defending the faith'.[8] The Irish Bishops supported the organisation, and its pamphlets were a ubiquitous presence at the back of Catholic Churches throughout the country. A sample of the titles published provides a sense of its subject matter: *Divorce is a Disease*; *Marry Your Own*; *Mortal Sin and How to Avoid It*; and *What NOT to Do On a Date*. The Catholic Truth Society developed a strong interest in religious programming and hoped to build on the success of the 1932 Eucharistic Congress to encourage more Catholic broadcasting in Ireland.

However, the hierarchy did not match their enthusiasm as many bishops remained suspicious of radio and uncomfortable with a technology some considered vulgar. In 1934 T. J. Kiernan, the new director of Radio Éireann, proposed the occasional broadcast of religious programmes but encountered resistance from bishops who remained sceptical of the medium and ambivalent about broadcasting lectures and talks. Despite this reluctance, significant pressure for substantial religious programming continued to build from the Catholic Truth Society and its secretary Dr Frank O'Reilly.[9] This organisation remained an outspoken advocate of religious broadcasting and continually lobbied for a strong Catholic voice in Irish radio. O'Reilly enjoyed direct access to members of the hierarchy and took it upon himself to try to determine what type of Catholic broadcasting would work best in an Irish context. In the course of his research he corresponded with the American director of the *Catholic Program Hour*, a programme presented by Fr Charles Coughlin, the famous radio priest and notorious anti-Semite. The Canadian-born Coughlin was a pioneer in using radio to reach mass audiences and during the 1930s estimates place his audience at over forty million. O'Reilly later tried unsuccessfully to convince the director of Radio Éireann to relay material broadcast from the newly opened Vatican Radio station through the high-power transmitter in Athlone, targeting not only Ireland but the United Kingdom as well.[10] When this proposal failed, he lobbied for the establishment of an independent Catholic radio station and pitched this idea to a sceptical Thomas Morris, Archbishop of Cashel.

In 1937, accompanied by members of the hierarchy, he met with the Taoiseach, Eamon de Valera, to press the need for increased Catholic broadcasting. RTÉ archivist Brian Lynch points out that de Valera was sceptical of these plans and 'wary about religious broadcasting schemes in general, and he drew the attention of the three bishops to the necessity for fairness to all interests'.[11] It is interesting to note that de Valera was reluctant to embrace formal Catholic broadcasting during the same year the constitution that he had become intimately associated with recognised the 'special position of the Holy Catholic Apostolic and Roman church'.[12] However de Valera was never afraid to carefully resist pressure from the Catholic Church. Throughout his career he engaged in a number of quiet confrontations with John Charles McQuaid, the powerful archbishop of Dublin.[13] He was clearly uncomfortable with the initiative and wary of using radio to proselytise. After this meeting, the Taoiseach established an informal, highly confidential advisory committee that included O'Reilly; T. J. Kiernan, Director of Radio Éireann; and Sean Moynihan, Minister of Finance. This committee was set up to offer advice about religious broadcasting to the Taoiseach who remained unconvinced about the matter. In typical de Valera style, he continually delayed making any commitment or endorsing any particular scheme, much to the chagrin of O'Reilly and members of the Catholic Truth Society. Sensing the ambivalence of the bishops and wary of antagonising other denominations, the government continually baulked at the request for formal Catholic broadcasting on Radio Éireann. The Taoiseach's confidential advisory committee enabled him to stay informed about any initiative that might come forward and effectively sideline any scheme that could develop through a deliberate policy of procrastination and obstruction.

After meeting de Valera, the Irish hierarchy established its own Episcopal Committee of three bishops chaired by Revd L. Lyons, Lord Bishop of Kilmore, to consider how the Church could develop Catholic programming for Radio Éireann. This small committee of bishops turned to the Catholic Truth Society, asking it to establish the formal and much larger Catholic Broadcasting Committee to study the subject and offer advice. Revd Dr Kissane of Maynooth was appointed its chair and served as liaison officer between the newly formed Catholic Broadcasting Committee and the director of Radio Éireann. The Catholic Broadcasting Committee consisted of twenty-three members, including two clerics who became intimately involved in the question of television broadcasting: the Archbishop of Cashel, Thomas Morris, and the future Archbishop of Dublin, John Charles McQuaid. When the Catholic Broadcasting Committee first met, it was told in 'strict confidence' about the small group de Valera had set up to report directly to him on the question of formal Catholic broadcasts. Members were informed that all of their work was highly confidential and warned not to engage in any 'outside discussion about the activities of the Broadcasting Committee, or of the intention to institute Catholic Broadcasts. Non-Catholic bodies would surely make applications for official broadcasts if they were aware of what was afoot, and it was desirable that the Catholic broadcasts should commence quietly, without undue publicity or stunting.'[14] The existence of these and subsequent Catholic broadcasting committees and their relationship with Radio Éireann and the government remained highly confidential.

In October 1938 the Catholic Broadcasting Committee developed a formal plan for regular religious programming that was accepted by the hierarchy.[15] Revd Dr Kissane presented a scheme to de Valera calling for three programmes a week commencing in the autumn of 1939 and featuring special broadcasts for Lent, Advent and Easter. However, this initiative was left to wither on the vine as de Valera and the director of Radio Éireann decided not to embark on any formal regime of Catholic broadcasting. Instead, a decision was made to maintain the informal policy that allowed the director of Radio Éireann to work quietly with Revd Dr Kissane, Chair of the Catholic Broadcasting Committee. This collaboration allowed for the occasional broadcast of lectures or talks by members of the Church.

Nevertheless, the following year 'a very elaborate scheme was put forward' to the bishops by the Catholic Broadcasting Committee, and this was again presented to de Valera.[16] Although the Taoiseach accepted a modified version of the proposal, which called for 'a Benediction Service from a church and a 10-minute talk from the studio every Sunday night' this scheme was also dropped.[17] A meeting of the hierarchy decided 'practically unanimously, to drop the scheme for Catholic broadcasts ... the Bishops considered that regular broadcasts of this type might give rise to a good deal of dissension and controversy and might only result in defeating the object in view'.[18] After thinking through these propositions and considering its options, the hierarchy decided that it was happy with the status quo and the quiet, informal arrangement it enjoyed with Radio Éireann and the civil servants from Posts and Telegraphs who operated it.

The bishops were convinced it was best not to have any official relationship with Radio Éireann and were satisfied that the service was not disseminating material they found offensive, concluding that those overseeing it were 'looking after the matter reasonably well in the course of their ordinary programmes and that it would be better to leave it at that'.[19] The Catholic Church therefore enjoyed an informal relationship that quietly continued over the next thirty years. During this time occasional religious broadcasts and talks, sanctioned by the bishops, were transmitted. The hierarchy knew it could rely on officials in Posts and Telegraphs and Radio Éireann and that nothing would be broadcast that might be inimical to its interests. In the unlikely event that problems developed, they were handled in confidence through informal channels.

In 1940, León Ó Broin became Secretary of the Department of Posts and Telegraphs and quickly established himself as a resourceful civil servant with a keen interest in broadcasting and an important intermediary between the hierarchy and Radio Éireann. Ó Broin later emerged as a critical voice in the debates concerning television broadcasting, and remained interested in television over the next twenty-five years. That same year, John Charles McQuaid, a close confidant of Eamon de Valera, became Archbishop of Dublin. He proved a deeply conservative and highly controversial archbishop who was comfortable intervening in the political and cultural affairs of the nation when he believed issues of faith and morals were at stake. Historian Tom Garvin describes McQuaid as 'a kind of ecclesiastical dictator of the Dublin Archdiocese', noting:

His influence was pervasive, affecting schools, housing developments, newspaper advertisements, marital relationships, university
life and appointments, schoolteachers' employment and relationships
between Catholics, Protestants and Jews. His word was law in large
sections of the Catholic Church, parts of the civil service, Dublin
Corporation, the university colleges and, of course, the primary and
secondary school systems.[20]

As Ó Broin and McQuaid took up their appointments, direct
but informal lines of communication were already in place that
enabled each to communicate with the other without having to
use official channels or formal procedures. Although Ó Broin may
have bristled at some of the decisions of the authoritarian archbishop, he enjoyed a constructive relationship with McQuaid,
who valued Ó Broin's advice on broadcasting matters. This relationship served both men as each became intimately involved in
the development of an Irish television service.

McQuaid had a strong interest in Radio Éireann and because its
studios and offices were in Dublin believed that it was his responsibility to make the national service more Catholic. By 1948, at
his instigation, Radio Éireann was regularly broadcasting High
Mass on Sunday mornings. Up until that time Mass had been
broadcast only sporadically; seventeen times in 1945, thirteen
times in 1946, and falling to twelve broadcasts in 1947.[21] Later,
at the suggestion of McQuaid, Radio Éireann inaugurated the
daily broadcasts of the Angelus, the first taking place on the Feast
of the Assumption, August 15, 1950. This was done after special
technical devices were installed at Dublin's Pro-Cathedral and at
the General Post Office, home of Radio Éireann. The inaugural
tolling of the Angelus bells was described as creating 'great interest
… the newspapers carried photographs of the archbishop bless-
ing the mechanism, both in the G.P.O. and the Pro-Cathedral
roof'.[22] The ease by which the Angelus made its way into the daily
programming of Radio Éireann underscores the very comfortable
relationship between Radio Éireann and the Catholic Church.
This new initiative was not in any way controversial in a country
that was overwhelmingly Catholic and deeply conservative. When
Telefís Éireann went on the air twelve years later, the Angelus made
the transition from radio to television, again without controversy.

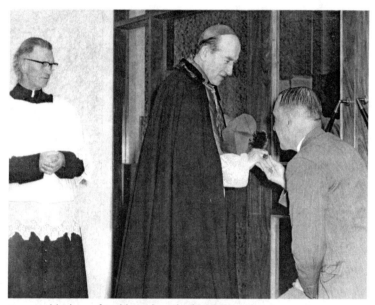

9   Archbishop of Dublin John Charles McQuaid.

Maurice Gorham served as director of Radio Éireann from 1953 until 1960 and on his retirement wrote an informative history of Irish radio, *Forty Years of Irish Broadcasting*, published in 1967. Gorham worked in a number of positions in the BBC, directing its wartime broadcasts to the USA and founding the Allied Expeditionary Forces Programme before returning to Ireland to take up the position of director of Radio Éireann. In his study he claimed the 'broadcasting service has been singularly free from interference by the Hierarchy of the Catholic Church'.[23] The programming featured on the national radio service mirrored the conservative society it served, and the close working relationship between Radio Éireann and the Catholic Church meant that there was little reason for the hierarchy to interfere.

When any hint of controversy or discord arose, it was dealt with quickly and quietly. For instance, in February 1956 a broadcast of an Emmet Lavery play, *The First Legion*, caused discomfort for the Archbishop of Dublin. The play, set in an American Jesuit house, concerns three novice priests experiencing doubts about their vocation and features a spurious miracle that turns the house into a short-lived shrine. After the broadcast, Gorham wrote to a close associate of McQuaid, Cannon Cathal McCarthy, in a code suggesting the archbishop was upset with the broadcast: 'I was talking to León Ó Broin about the question you raised with him the other day and we thought the best thing would be if I were to come and talk to you about it.'[24] A notation by McCarthy at the bottom of the file reveals there had been a 'complaint by the archbishop' and a review of the play from the *Irish Times* was attached to his correspondence.[25] The cleric Gorham contacted about the matter, Canon Cathal McCarthy, became a close confidant of the archbishop and acted as his advisor on broadcasting well into the 1960s.

As a member of the Catholic Broadcasting Committee since the 1930s, McQuaid illustrated a keen interest in Radio Éireann that would lead to a similar interest in television. As archbishop he understood that television could be much more harmful than radio in undermining the authority of the Church and he was keen to influence its development. He was not alone in fearing television could threaten the morals of Catholic Ireland. This became clear as debates about how television might come to Ireland were taking place inside the government and in the press. In 1958 the archbishop proactively set up his own diocesan Television Committee to explore how the new medium could enhance the work of the Church and defend its interests. The formation of this committee coincided with the government's establishment of an official Television Commission set up to examine the complicated question of how television should be introduced to Ireland.[26] McQuaid's committee was influenced by advice offered to the Irish bishops on a number of occasions by Agnellus Andrew, a Scottish Dominican priest who was Deputy Head of Religious Broadcasting for the BBC. Andrew was a frequent visitor to Ireland, offering much valued information and counsel to the hierarchy about television.[27]

McQuaid provided his committee terms of reference, mandating it 'report on what preparations should be made to safeguard

Catholic interests' in the event that a television service was established.[28] The committee was instructed to study the Papal Encyclical Letter on Films, Radio and Television, *Miranda Prorsus*, published by the Vatican in September 1957. Later in the year it produced a report embracing the Vatican document, emphasising that television should be considered 'of great importance in human history' and that it provided the Church with 'high hopes' as well as 'serious anxiety'.[29] The committee thoughtfully offered suggestions to McQuaid on how the Church should respond to the establishment of an Irish service.

Although the government's Television Commission had not yet issued its report, McQuaid's committee knew from press reports that an Irish television service would inevitably have a significant commercial component. The archbishop's committee carefully considered how the Church might work with such an entity, concluding that it should not insist that a Catholic priest be formally named to any potential television authority. Instead it proposed a cleric be identified who could gain specialised training in Britain and the United States before being appointed to consult with the authority and to offer advice and guidance. The committee hoped that the new service would set aside time for religious broadcasts, but recognising television would be a commercial enterprise, supported the notion of purchasing time for religious programmes. The majority of members thought that underwriters could be identified and suggested the 'Knights of Columbanus, the G.A.A., Catholic publishers, etc. might be asked to act as sponsors'.[30] A minority argued that there was no need to find sponsors because 'in this predominately Catholic country … Catholic programmes would naturally be acceptable to even commercial sponsors, who tend to cater for the needs of their audience'.[31] All members of McQuaid's television committee agreed that televised Mass should be a regular feature on Sundays and should not be sponsored.

The report advocated establishing links with countries that had Catholic television bodies. Acknowledging that Irish television might be years away, it nevertheless pointed out that there were thousands of sets in Ireland receiving broadcasts of British programmes. Again referring to the Papal Encyclical *Miranda Prorsus*, it recommended steps should be taken to 'educate the faithful, especially the young, in the way they should look at and judge the various programmes presented to them'.[32] The report also maintained that a national organisation be established to coordinate all the Church's initiatives with the new medium.[33] Understanding that setting up such an organisation was years away, the committee advocated that placing television on the agenda of the Board of Studies of the Dublin Institute of Sociology would suffice until a more formal body was established.

Although the committee knew that foreign material would inevitably be featured in Irish broadcasts, it hoped that quality programmes produced in Ireland would be featured. 'Let us not be content with "blackthorn sticks and leprechauns" as a main ingredient of our T.V. films. Through the members of the National Film Institute, the Catholic Stage Guild, the Knights of Columbanus and other lay Apostolate associations, the positive and urgent part Ireland can play in the world of T.V. should be prudently but effectively emphasized'.[34] The report served as an important point of departure for McQuaid who appreciated the need to be proactive. He accepted the conclusion of the committee that argued, 'We must not allow the initiative to pass into the hands of those by whom the Catholic system of values can be disregarded or ignored.'[35]

As Secretary for the Department of Posts and Telegraphs León Ó Broin was in an influential position as debate about an Irish television service developed because all proposals and queries concerning the medium came to his department. Archbishop John Charles McQuaid trusted Ó Broin's judgement and confided in him when his committee issued its report. He sent a copy to Ó Broin suggesting that it be brought to the attention of the official Television Commission. When McQuaid offered to have his committee testify before the Television Commission, Ó Broin strongly opposed the idea, understanding that the Television Commission would already be sensitive to the concerns of the hierarchy and that any formal presentation was unnecessary and could be counterproductive. The Television Commission included clerics from both the Catholic and Protestant Churches appointed to represent religious interests. One member of the Commission, Dr Henry

Robert McAdoo, Dean of St Finbar's Cathedral in Cork and later Church of Ireland Archbishop of Dublin, recalled that members were fully aware of concerns the Catholic Church might have. He described Ireland in the late 1950s as a country where 'Catholic triumphalism' permeated society, noting that all members of the Television Commission were well aware of the anxieties that the Catholic Church would have. He made it clear that the Church of Ireland shared many of the concerns about the broadcast of immoral material that animated its Catholic counterpart.[36]

Ó Broin told McQuaid that he appreciated the committee's recommendations, especially the argument that an Irish service broadcast indigenous material, assuring him 'that is the best way … to ensure that the religious traditions of the Irish people will be respected' but he did not see anything specific in the report that needed to be brought to the attention of the Television Commission.[37] Ó Broin told McQuaid that he supported the Committee's opinion of opposing the appointment of a priest adviser to any new television organisation, arguing that other religious bodies would also request they be represented: 'Our experience here – and I think yours – favours an unofficial arrangement such as has worked out so well on the sound broadcasting side. I refer, of course, to the arrangement involving Fr. Cathal McCarthy.'[38] Ó Broin wanted to maintain the informal relationship that he had with the Church, believing it would save embarrassment for all concerned. He also understood that McQuaid could be a difficult and aggressive force that could alienate members of the Television Commission wary of interference from the archbishop's palace.

By this time McQuaid's advisor on broadcasting, Canon Cathal McCarthy, had become the unofficial priest-advisor to Radio Éireann and had developed a close working relationship with León Ó Broin. The archbishop valued McCarthy as an important intermediary, telling him 'Your value to me lies in your present anonymity and your established good relations with Radio Éireann and Mr. L. Ó Broin.'[39] Canon Cathal McCarthy became one of McQuaid's most trusted advisors on the developing issue of television. The domineering archbishop wanted to exert as much influence as possible over the emerging medium and made it clear to McCarthy that he expected him to continue to act as a liaison between him and the new television service.

Like the Archbishop of Dublin, Archbishop of Cashel Thomas Morris had been a member of the Catholic Broadcasting Committee since the 1930s and shared McQuaid's interest in radio and television. As the dawn of Irish television broadcasting loomed, a rivalry developed between the two archbishops, McQuaid believing that television should be in his bailiwick because the new service would be set up in his archdiocese. Morris and other members of the hierarchy were wary of McQuaid and worked to keep him from dominating the Church's relationship with television. In the summer of 1959, a formal General Meeting of the Hierarchy established an Episcopal Television Committee when the bishops discussed the imminent arrival of an Irish service. The Committee included the Bishops of Derry, Clonfert, Nara and Neve and, tellingly, not John Charles McQuaid. This group presented its first report to the General Meeting of the Irish Bishops that autumn.

The *Report of the Episcopal Television Committee* outlined some of the problems that would challenge an Irish television service, explaining that because of the costs involved in producing material 'three of every four programmes [would] be imported'.[40] The bishops were told that in countries where television had been introduced it made 'a most profound social impact, which shows little sign of decreasing ... The fact that it brings its visual programme for long hours into the very heart of the home gives it particular moral and religious significance.'[41] The Episcopal Committee believed that television would be a transformative force in Irish life, warning that the Church would have to pay close attention to its development. The hierarchy was told that the arrival of indigenous television could be a positive development if the Church were proactive and used it to reach out to Catholics and non-Catholics alike, thereby bringing the teachings and ceremonies of the church to a wide audience.

However, television was also seen as highly problematic, and the bishops were warned to be alert to the 'potential danger of harm being caused to the faith and morals of the people, particularly in view of the fact that most of the programmes will have to be produced abroad'.[42] The Episcopal Committee was especially wary of immoral foreign material being broadcast by the new television service, material that could work to undermine the teachings of the Church. The report advocated that steps be taken immediately to ensure the Church 'as custodian of the faith and morals, has the machinery to make her influence felt on the new medium from the very beginning'.[43] It maintained that some form of censorship had to be formally established for television and the existing Film Censor was considered a model to replicate.

Sensing the importance of the new medium, the committee proposed a delegation of bishops meet with government leaders quickly to outline the views of the Church. The group recommended that the hierarchy be given direct access to the broadcasting authority by having a link 'by which the Bishop's views could be communicated to the highest levels in the service'.[44] It was also suggested that a pastoral letter be issued by the hierarchy to coincide with the launch of television to address the significance of the new medium and give 'advice to parents… stressing the importance of a healthy and articulate public opinion with regard to programmes'.[45]

Using the BBC as an example, the report proposed the government establish a religious advisory committee that could work closely with television officials. It recommended that the advisory committee should have a proportion of Catholics that would broadly correspond with the percentage of Catholics in the country. It stipulated that the members should 'be nominated by the Hierarchy and *not* the Government'.[46] The report suggested the chair of the advisory committee not only be Catholic but a member of the hierarchy. As an alternative to a religious advisory committee it was proposed that 'a representative of the Bishops be officially accredited to and perhaps be a member of the Television Authority'.[47] The committee wanted bishops to have direct access to the authority and were not interested in the government choosing their representative. The Episcopal Television Committee also argued that steps should be taken quickly to ensure that members of the clergy be 'thoroughly trained in television work with the object of forming a panel of technical advisors who could be availed of by the representative of local Ordinaries when television programmes are being transmitted from their diocese'.[48]

The next meeting of the hierarchy decided that the Episcopal Television Committee should continue its work in studying television under the direction of Archbishop of Cashel Thomas Morris. It is important to note that, despite his unmistakable interest in television, McQuaid remained *outside* the Episcopal Television Committee, underscoring the tension that existed within the hierarchy. Bishops who had seen John Charles McQuaid dominate Church–State relations regarding Radio Éireann understood the controlling nature of his personality and were wary of letting him dominate the Church's relationship with the emerging television service. Joseph Dunn, a priest who became involved in religious broadcasting in Ireland, addressed this in his book, *No Vipers in the Vatican*. According to Dunn, the hierarchy chose the Archbishop of Cashel to direct the committee in an effort to 'make the church interest in broadcasting a national rather than a local affair'.[49] Morris in turn appointed an advisory group to work with him and, in an effort to mollify the concerns of McQuaid, appointed McQuaid's close confidant in media matters, Cannon Cathal McCarthy, to the Episcopal Television Committee as his assistant.

A press release was prepared by Morris announcing the formation of the Episcopal Television Committee and forwarded to McCarthy for formal distribution. Morris believed that the Church should be seen by the public as proactive and prepared for the introduction of television. Until this time, all discussions and meetings concerning television – and, for that matter, radio – had been held in secret. Morris worried that a sudden statement to the press would suggest that the Church was just getting around to thinking about television and had not being adequately prepared for its inauguration. In writing to McCarthy, he warned him of a critical article written by Antoinette Fortune that recently appeared in *Hibernia*. He told McCarthy to be prepared to deal with questions from the press, upset over being 'kept in the dark' ,and that he would have to dispel any notion of the Church 'having slept on TV'.[50] McCarthy was later interviewed by the *Catholic Herald* and explained the work the committee would undertake, denying it would act as a censor and maintaining 'I've represented the Archbishop for 15 years with Radio Éireann. I've never had any difficulty, and there's never been a question of censorship, nor have we ever thought in terms of it … I have complete faith in the television Authority, whom I regard as safe as any Vigilance Committee could be.'[51] McCarthy's reference to a vigilance committee referred to an informal group brought together by McQuaid that reported to him about deviant anti-Catholic behaviour.[52] He explained that the committee he was chairing was an interim one and that eventually a national office of cinema, radio and television would be established; in the meantime he would act as liaison between the hierarchy and the new broadcasting authority. Over the next few years, with very mixed results, this committee and its successor, the Catholic Television Interim Committee, worked to gain influence over the emerging television service.

In the months leading up to the opening of Telefís Éireann, Archbishop Morris met with both the Chairman of the Radio Éireann Authority, Eamonn Andrews, and the Director-General Edward Roth on two separate occasions to discuss the hierarchy's views on television broadcasting. The Episcopal Television Committee Morris chaired had communicated with both Ulster Television and BBC Northern Ireland, learning that Catholic priests served on formal advisory committees for both broadcasters in the province. Wary of Episcopal meddling, Roth and Andrews explained to Morris that the new Irish service did not envision maintaining such an advisory committee. Morris was told that Telefís Éireann was 'strongly in favour of the idea of an official representative of the Hierarchy who would be available for consultation by directors and producers not only in connection with specifically religious programmes but also in connection with other programmes where the interests of religion would be involved. Such consultations would mean frequent and sometimes urgent meetings with directors and producers.'[53] Both Andrews and Roth wanted to maintain an informal relationship with the Catholic Church and were comfortable with communicating with a representative of the hierarchy. Neither had any interest in allowing the Church to have a formal presence in the new television service or on the Radio Éireann Authority.

In October 1961, a few months before Telefís Éireann was scheduled to go on air, the Episcopal Television Committee delivered a second report to the hierarchy. Repeating the recommendations of the committee McQuaid had set up a few years earlier, it called for the establishment of a permanent national organisation for cinema, radio and television that would advise and report annually to the hierarchy on matters related to the electronic media. In doing so it was following the recommendations of Vatican publications concerning mass media. The report suggested that the president of the organisation be a member of the hierarchy and that a priest be appointed and dedicated to the organisation. It is important to recognise that the attitude of the Catholic Church towards television was not simply one-dimensional and reactionary. The notion of being proactive, of using the medium in an innovative manner, resonated with more progressive members of the clergy. Although a decision to officially sanction a permanent organisation was postponed, Morris was named president of what was now rather awkwardly titled the Catholic Television Interim Committee (CTIC) and £1,000 was voted to help the group begin work on investigating how the Church could both monitor and exploit television.[54]

With the opening of the new service only a few months away the bishops believed that instead of a pastoral letter being issued a more public statement should be released to the press. The *Statement of the Hierarchy on the Inauguration of the Irish Television Service* was drafted and released in October 1961, ten weeks before the service began broadcasting. It praised television technology and maintained that a native service would be of great importance to Irish society. The hierarchy recognised the tremendous power of television to improve the lives of people 'as a medium of healthy education, in the dissemination of truth, in the diffusion and encouragement of true cultural values and in the formation of high standards of public taste ... But this same medium can also do great harm, not merely in the diffusion of the erroneous ideas of those who are lacking in deep or accurate knowledge of religious truth but also in the broadcasting of programmes which offend all reasonable standards of morals and decency.'[55] Emphasising that television entered into the home directly in a manner that cinema did not, the document warned parents to be vigilant in protecting their children from unsuitable material. The statement expressed confidence that Telefís Éireann 'will respect true Christian values and standards' but still reminded officials and viewers alike of their responsibilities in regard to Irish and foreign-made programmes.[56]

Earlier in the year McQuaid was able to secure the unofficial permission of the hierarchy to choose a priest who would represent the Church and act as liaison with the new Radio Éireann Authority. Cannon Cathal McCarthy had worked as an intermediary between Radio Éireann and Dublin's archbishop for a number of years, and McQuaid wanted him to serve in the same capacity for television. McCarthy had been appointed by Morris earlier to assist the Episcopal Television Committee and, when this organisation was formally established as the Catholic Television Interim Committee (CTIC), Morris appointed him chair. The Archbishop of Dublin felt increasingly marginalised by Archbishop Morris and the CTIC, and McCarthy became a critical link to television for Dublin's archbishop. McQuaid therefore worked diligently to see him promoted as liaison between the hierarchy and the new television authority.

The impatient Archbishop of Dublin did not want to wait for the next meeting of the bishops to formalise McCarthy's position, and began pressuring Morris to make the appointment formal. However, the Archbishop of Cashel, responding as president of the CTIC, told McQuaid to be patient, explaining that there were procedures that had to be followed. He insisted that nothing could be done until a formal General Meeting of the Hierarchy considered making the appointment permanent. It is clear that McQuaid's anxiety created a degree of friction between the archbishops, but Morris held firm. Acting unilaterally, McQuaid had already begun putting pressure on Director-General Edward Roth, insisting he accept McCarthy as the hierarchy's official Catholic religious advisor. The ensuing 'behind the scenes' wrangling between the bishops leaked out to both Edward Roth and Eamonn Andrews, both of whom balked at accepting McCarthy as a formal representative of the Church without the official sanction of the hierarchy through the CTIC. Neither wanted to get caught in a battle between the bishops.

McQuaid's relationship with the American director-general had not started off well and deteriorated quickly. In the spring of 1961 he was upset that Roth had reported to Revd G. T. Fehily, Director of the Dublin Institute of Catholic Sociology, and that although Protestant groups had appointed a clergyman to represent their interests, nothing had been heard from the Catholic Church.[57] An irate McQuaid retorted, 'Mr. R[oth] was given 1½ hours of my time during which I asked Fr. McC[arthy] to call over. Mr R[oth] was at once to phone Fr. McC[arthy] to see him. Since that good day he has never given any sign of life. If Mr. R[oth] thinks that we can take that treatment he is mistaken.'[58] McQuaid told Fehily that Roth had been told unequivocally that McCarthy had been appointed what he defined as the 'Catholic Representative'.[59]

Only when the General Meeting of the Hierarchy formally appointed McCarthy to his position in October 1961 did Roth formally acknowledge he was named 'to coordinate all radio and television religious activities on behalf of the Hierarchy'.[60] Eamonn Andrews also wrote to McCarthy to compliment him on his appointment, pointing out that the Archbishop of Cashel informed him of the news. Both Roth and Andrews were careful to communicate directly with the President of the CTIC, not McQuaid. Although McCarthy had been named the hierarchy's liaison with Telefís Éireann, he did not have a formal position within the new service and was not a staff member.

Just as the station was about to begin broadcasting Roth contacted McCarthy telling him he was 'both disturbed and annoyed' at information he had received and asked for an urgent meeting.[61] Roth told McCarthy he was troubled at having learned there was 'strain and strife between Dublin and Cashel' and that it was because of this tension he had decided to 'lie low'.[62] McCarthy denied that there was any feuding or discord between Morris and McQuaid and took the opportunity to inform the American director-general that McQuaid was disturbed that he had not worked more closely with the Dublin Archdiocese. He was told the archbishop 'was disappointed that he [E.J.R.] had not kept his promise to see me – nearly 12 months ago'.[63] Roth's failure to heed the advice of McQuaid and call on his lieutenant Cathal McCarthy the previous year infuriated the archbishop, who expected more from the director-general.

Despite these difficulties Roth worked with McCarthy and succeeded in convincing the archbishop to visit the Donnybrook studios to provide a benediction on the opening night of Telefís Éireann. McCarthy reported to McQuaid that the director-general was delighted that he would come to the station and thought this would signify his encouragement for the new service in an 'eloquent way'.[64] Attempting to improve a difficult relationship, McCarthy arranged a meeting between Roth and McQuaid hoping that Michael Barry, the Controller of Programmes, would also attend. He believed Barry should be courted by the archdiocese, explaining 'he is a gentlemanly person, educated and cultured and very favourable to us'.[65] McCarthy hoped Barry would develop extensive contacts with the hierarchy, viewing him as a sympathetic and important figure in the new television service.

Although McQuaid and Morris were pleased that Andrews and Roth accepted McCarthy as the liaison between the Radio Éireann Authority and the hierarchy, they wanted this arrangement formalised. Again looking to the BBC as a model, both expected that the new service would take this 'priest advisor' into Telefís Éireann as a member of staff, providing him with an office and salary. However, Andrews and Roth wanted to keep McQuaid at bay, knowing his reputation as an imperious and demanding figure. There was also a history in the Andrews–McQuaid relationship that influenced the actions of the Chairman of the Broadcasting Authority. As a young member of the Catholic Stage Guild, he learned firsthand how difficult McQuaid could be. According to Joseph Dunn, Eamonn Andrews resented the manner in which a friend of his had been treated by the archbishop earlier in his career when he was a member of the Guild. It appears that McQuaid had abruptly dismissed a popular chaplain that worked with the Guild and Eamonn Andrews 'never forgot nor forgave' the way his friend had been treated. When he became Chairman of the Television Authority, Andrews 'resolved that Archbishop John Charles McQuaid would be allowed to interfere with it as little as possible'.[66] Both Andrews and Roth were wary of allowing him to appoint a priest to the staff of Telefís Éireann, a priest who would technically report to the Hierarchy but in reality report directly to the intrusive archbishop.

Andrews, Roth and his successor, Director-General Kevin McCourt delayed making any decision on accepting Cathal McCarthy as a permanent, paid staff member much to the consternation of Morris and especially McQuaid. As the inauguration of Telefís Éireann approached, the tension between McQuaid and Archbishop of Cashel Thomas Morris dissipated and both men worked to have McCarthy appointed formally to the staff of Telefís Éireann. One can't help but believe that the incessant pressure from McQuaid had worn down Morris, who had come to recognise that it would be impossible to sideline the aggressive Archbishop of Dublin.

Unsurprisingly, McQuaid's desire to micromanage religious broadcasting through McCarthy alienated senior staff at Telefís Éireann. As the television service was preparing to go on the air McQuaid instructed McCarthy that as religious advisor he should be consulted about all Catholic programming. When he found out that plans were being developed to broadcast Catholic services in Wicklow, he recorded his response: 'I asked Cannon [McCarthy] to insist with Telefís Éireann no religious broadcast or telecast on T. E. be permitted without the Canon's sanction. This is an absolute rule, binding all orders, congregations, or societies, for divine worship is the exclusive care of the archbishop.'[67] McCarthy had the full confidence of McQuaid who wanted to keep a close watch on the new Irish television service, telling his assistant that priests appearing on the short *Recollection* programme should not be allowed to go on the air unless their scripts were first cleared by him.[68] 'I think it would help Telefís Éireann if it were understood that the text of every Recollection to be given by a Catholic priest must first be submitted to … you.'[69]

McQuaid's edict that no cleric should appear on Telefís Éireann without his permission could produce a severe reprimand if questioned or violated. One unfortunate victim of the archbishop was the Reverend Mother of the Missionary Sisters of St Columban, who made the mistake of seeking the archbishop's permission to appear in a programme about missionary work. His terse response, angrily refusing the request, caused the Superior-General of the Maynooth Mission to China to write to McQuaid complaining about the 'rather sharp rebuke' that he considered 'undeserved'.[70] An unapologetic McQuaid responded, telling the Superior-General that his policy concerning sisters being seen on television was a simple one: he did 'not sanction such appearances'.[71]

During the first year of broadcasting Andrews and Roth succeeded in blocking McQuaid's efforts to insert McCarthy formally onto the staff of Telefís Éireann. The archbishop became increasingly uncomfortable with a sense of drift that he believed character-ised the relationship between the new broadcasting service and the Church, and wanted a formal relationship established to allow him significant influence on Telefís Éireann. Both McQuaid and Morris believed that it was urgent that action be taken quickly to ensure that a Catholic voice – one appointed by the hierarchy – be institutionalised within the broadcasting service before its struc-tures became too rigid. Although Morris remained the President of the CTIC, McQuaid continued to assert himself, insisting that Telefís Éireann formally establish a paid position for a priest advisor at the Donnybrook station. McQuaid wrote to Morris, complaining 'Sooner or later we must face a choice and get a grip of the situation. I believe the sooner the better for time is pressing and methods are being established.'[72]

At this juncture McQuaid wanted to approach the Radio Éireann Authority directly to insist that Canon McCarthy be for-mally appointed to a paid position on the staff as religious advisor. However, Morris tried to dissuade McQuaid from approaching the Authority, once again arguing that there were procedures that had to be followed and that the issue had to wait until it could be discussed fully at the next formal General Meeting of the Hierarchy. Nevertheless, McQuaid wrote to both Morris and McCarthy impatiently complaining again about the impasse and offering to arrange a meeting with Edward Roth to pursue the matter, complaining that the present policy was 'dilatory, timor-ous and piecemeal'.[73] McQuaid was writing from Rome where he was attending the meetings of Vatican II but was still agitated enough about the appointment to claim 'the Holy See is pressing us to put our house in order'.[74] Morris finally relented, agreeing McQuaid should approach Roth when he returned to Dublin: 'negotiations on this point must come sooner or later and I have more confidence in your ability to secure good terms than in my own'.[75]

McQuaid later met with McCarthy, explaining that he wanted Telefís Éireann to formally appoint him to a position at the station as director of Catholic broadcasting. McCarthy, who was experiencing health problems at the time, was President of Clonliffe College, the Dublin seminary. McQuaid wanted him to leave that post and take up the full-time position in television. Although McCarthy was interested, he balked at the proposal, advising the archbishop that he needed a young, energetic priest to work as his executive assistant – someone who could 'move around, organise (and) go abroad'. McQuaid chose a young priest from the archdiocese, Joseph Dunn, 'on condition that he *not* be responsible for policy and that Telefís Éireann pay him a good salary'.[76] McQuaid planned to meet Roth so he could present the scheme to him. In an effort to expedite his request, and put pressure on Telefís Éireann, McQuaid had a word with President Eamon de Valera, an old friend with whom he remained on good terms. De Valera contacted Seán Lemass, who in turn spoke with Eamonn Andrews to inquire about the status of the appointment. Joseph Dunn mentions that this attempt to pressure Andrews into making a decision was a 'counterproductive move since it would only have reinforced Chairman Eamonn Andrews in his fear and distrust of the archbishop'.[77]

A General Meeting of the Hierarchy in October 1962 formally granted McQuaid his wishes, deciding Fr Joseph Dunn, who had undertaken a number of television courses, should be appointed 'whole time executive assistant for religious broadcasting' to Telefís Éireann. Dunn was placed under the control of the President of the CTIC, Thomas Morris, and told to work with Canon McCarthy, designated liaison between the hierarchy and Telefís Éireann. Dunn was expected to develop plans for religious programmes, assist with the training of religious broadcasters, and generally gather information about the medium.[78]

At this same meeting an agitated McQuaid made a series of startling revelations causing great distress in the ranks of the hierarchy. The bishops, already frustrated by their inability to have their candidate formally appointed to the staff of Telefís Éireann, only grew more anxious as they learned about two secret reports McQuaid received. Minutes of the meeting indicate that there was alarm and consensus that 'the position in regard to Catholic television in Telefís Éireann had worsened considerably. It was agreed therefore, that the archbishops of Dublin and Cashel should approach the Taoiseach without delay to express the grave concern of the Hierarchy concerning the personnel in Telefís Éireann and to protest against the appointment of unbelievers to key posts.'[79]

The information that had caused such distress was contained in two confidential reports that McQuaid received denouncing key personnel at Telefís Éireann. The first, from Dermot O'Flynn, Supreme Knight of the Knights of St Columbanus, revealed that he had collected damaging information from a 'reliable source' about the 'mental outlook of the liberals' who held important positions in the new television service.[80] The report identified a number of alleged extremists who it complained were constantly being interviewed on current affairs programmes. The list included members of the Fabian Society at Trinity College Dublin, identified as a 'known Communist cell'.[81] It listed a number of troublemakers including Dominic Behan, brother of Brendan Behan, who was denounced as a Communist 'well known for his activities to promote strikes in England', the maritime historian and political activist John de Courcy Ireland and the Secretary of the Irish Congress of Trade Unions, Rory Roberts. After listing those deemed objectionable the report concluded, 'There is an urgent need for the selection and training of an elite to recover these vital lines of communication of ideas to the general public.'[82]

However, it was the second report from one of McQuaid's ubiquitous unidentified sources that caused the most distress. This document reviewed the religious preferences and marital status of senior staff that held critical positions within the new service and undoubtedly provoked the Hierarchy to urgently request a meeting with Seán Lemass. Although Eamonn Andrews, Edward

Roth and the Controller of Programmes Michael Barry were all acknowledged in the document to be practicing Catholics, the religious make up of others in Telefís Éireann was seen as highly problematic. The document emphasised that of the sixteen producers, only four were Catholic and many of the Catholics were considered compromised. Gerard Victory and Chloe Gibson were categorised as the only producers in Telefís Éireann who were practicing Catholics.

Producer James Fitzgerald, who had been denounced by the Knights as a Communist, was scorned because he had 'started a fund for Carolyn Swift and her former husband when their production of Tennessee Williams's play, "The Rose Tattoo", was stopped by the Gardai on the grounds of indecency'.[83] James Plunkett was described as a 'Left-wing trade unionist and writer' and it was noted that he had travelled to the Soviet Union in 1955 at the invitation of Communists.[84] Other producers regarded as objectionable included Shelah Richards, described as a 'divorced actress who has been associated with numerous left-wing groups'; Peter Collinson, regarded as 'an Englishman, violently anti-clerical'; Patrick Kearney, 'believed to be a Catholic but he has stated that he is anti-clerical and against all forms of censorship'; and Jack White, a 'non-Catholic and one of the leading liberals here'. The report also listed the aforementioned Carolyn Swift who was classified as 'a divorced Jewess. She has been associated with the production of indecent plays in Dublin for some years.'[85] Head of News Pearse Kelly and Public Relations Officer James McGuinness were singled out as objectionable as both were former members of the IRA and interned at the Curragh during the Second World War.

Armed with this information, McQuaid and Morris met with Seán Lemass on October 3, 1962, to complain about the 'appointment of unbelievers' in critical positions within Telefís Éireann. Lemass asked Padraig O'Hanrahan, Director of the Government Information Bureau, for information about some of these broadcasters, including Jack White. He received a vicious report from O'Hanrahan, denouncing White as a person 'having no national outlook in the broadest sense of the word and has no loyalties [and] would think of Ireland as a place where those, like himself, who are "liberal" in outlook must suffer as best they may'.[86] Lemass took no action against any of those identified by the archbishops as unsuitable. Given his ambivalent attitude towards clerical involvement in politics, Lemass appears to have listened to their complaints politely but ignored their demands, despite his own growing unease with Telefís Éireann.

McQuaid remained highly annoyed with Telefís Éireann and especially the American director-general, Edward Roth. He grew increasingly upset with Roth's unwillingness to accept his pronouncements and the director-general's failure to effectively communicate with him. The American director-general simply did not display the sort of deference that the imperious archbishop had come to expect. Roth was, by all accounts, a conservative Catholic, having grown up in a close-knit Irish-American neighbourhood in Boston's Mission Hill. Throughout his professional career Roth worked with Catholic bishops and priests, first at the University of Notre Dame in South Bend, Indiana, and later in Peru and Mexico. However, his own Catholic background and his impressive résumé had not prepared him for the likes of Archbishop John Charles McQuaid.

After meeting Lemass, McQuaid wrote to Roth, informing him that the concerns of the hierarchy had been taken to a higher authority. He took pleasure in letting the director-general know that he had effectively gone over his head and that of the Chairman of the Broadcasting Authority, Eamonn Andrews: 'I have the pleasure in informing you that at the meeting of the Hierarchy the question of Catholic policy in television was again fully considered. At the request of the Hierarchy His Grace of Cashel and I today called on the Taoiseach to discuss a policy, which involves the people of the whole country in regard to the Faith. The Taoiseach will duly communicate with you and the Authority.'[87] The correspondence proved to Roth and Andrews what level of interference the Catholic Church was prepared to engage in. The Taoiseach contacted Eamonn Andrews a short time later to tell him of the visit by the two archbishops and discussed the matter in some detail with Edward Roth. Lemass's attitude towards the Church was a typically pragmatic one. He viewed it as a powerful interest group that had to be dealt with but was not

as receptive to ecclesiastical pressure as his predecessor had sometimes been. If the two archbishops expected Lemass to intervene
in the affairs of Telefís Éireann to remove liberals, Protestants,
Jews, divorcees, or others, they were mistaken.[88] The intervention
of McQuaid and Morris was counterproductive. It once again
proved to both Roth and Andrews that the hierarchy – especially
McQuaid – would be a meddling and invasive presence if they
were allowed to appoint a priest to a position at Telefís Éireann. In
these circumstances, officials in Telefís Éireann continued to resist
taking a priest into the television service.

Andrews later wrote to McCarthy explaining in detail why he
thought the request by the bishops was a bad idea. He maintained that if a Catholic priest was appointed a member of the
Telefís Éireann staff, appointments to members of other religious
denominations would also have to be made, arguing 'we cannot
risk the accusation that Catholic Ireland offers less to a minority than Protestant Britain does'.[89] Andrews maintained that the
best option was for the hierarchy to appoint and pay for a full-
time religious advisor, stating that Telefís Éireann would provide
facilities at the station and access to staff and studios. In these
circumstances, there would be no need to make formal appointments to other denominations. The argument was a calculated
and somewhat cynical ploy intended to delay the initiative of the
Hierarchy. Andrews also made it clear what he thought the duties
of a religious advisor should be: 'The ideal function … is not to
make religious programmes, but to advise and to watch and to
help permeate the whole output with a basically Catholic atmosphere. Religious programmes, as such, will seldom if ever attract
majority audiences, no matter how well received by, for instance,
the press.'[90] Andrews pointed out that the Authority had followed
this example when dealing with supporters of the Irish language:
'we resisted the strong temptation to appoint someone with the
responsibility of watching over the Irish language because in doing
so we felt we would isolate the language and build it up into something of an irritant to individual producers'.[91] Andrews asked
McCarthy to explain his position to the hierarchy and expressed a
willingness to bring up the matter at the next meeting of the Radio

Éireann Authority, but cautioned, 'You are aware, of course, that two members of our Authority are not Catholics.'[92]

The Chairman of the Authority was willing to make a gesture to the Hierarchy but clearly wanted to keep the archbishop at arm's length. Although he knew of the complaints McQuaid and Morris had made to Lemass, he was not impressed and was not going to be bullied. He had no intention of accepting the demands of the bishops or removing staff from their positions due to their religious outlook or alleged political beliefs. Both Roth and Andrews shared the Taoiseach's tendency to see the Church as simply another, albeit very powerful, interest group that had to be dealt with and somehow placated.[93] This attitude and the slow and very difficult negotiations that took place infuriated McQuaid who expected his wishes to be quickly accepted.

McCarthy forwarded Andrews's letter to McQuaid who was again in Rome with Thomas Morris and preoccupied with meetings of the Second Vatican Council. At this time it was increasingly clear that McCarthy, who continued to serve as McQuaid's adviser on radio and television and as the Hierarchy's liaison with Telefís Éireann, was under tremendous stress and becoming seriously ill. McCarthy complained to McQuaid that he was suffering from high blood pressure and that his doctor had ordered him to take time off from work. McQuaid understood his key adviser on media matters was not physically fit to continue and in these circumstances Joseph Dunn emerged as the leading candidate to take over from the ailing McCarthy.[94]

The fact that McQuaid was distracted in attending the Second Vatican Council in Rome and that his long-time associate was incapacitated at an important juncture in the evolving and difficult relationship between the Church, State and Telefís Éireann presented a challenge to McQuaid and Morris. McQuaid responded angrily to the communication from Eamonn Andrews stating that neither he nor Morris was concerned with the needs of Protestant denominations. Once again the archbishops insisted that they be able to name a priest to the staff of Telefís Éireann and that he be given 'all necessary facilities for advising, watching and if need be, producing or directing production, and contribute a reasonable sum to his upkeep, seeing he will be a whole-time appointment'.[95]

When McCarthy reported these demands to Eamonn Andrews they were firmly rejected. Andrews telephoned McCarthy from London and outlined the reasons that the terms set out by the bishops were unacceptable. McCarthy was told that the Radio Éireann Authority had never received a direct, formal, written request from the bishops indicating that the unofficial oral submissions that had been made by McCarthy, McQuaid, and Morris were not acceptable. Andrews also made it clear that if a formal written application were submitted, the Authority would carefully consider the proposal and decide about any position that might be created. McCarthy was told that the Radio Éireann Authority, not the Hierarchy, would define any position that might be created and decide who would be appointed to it. This was a critical point that Andrews and the Radio Éireann Authority wanted the bishops to understand. Andrews insisted that because of the Authority's statutory position these issues were not negotiable. However, in an effort to provide a compromise, a degree of flexibility was offered on the question of the actual appointment. Andrews seemed to accept that a position would be created and explained that if the Hierarchy submitted a short list to him the Authority could act on 'a choice of names submitted'.[96]

The tense negotiations underlined the fact that any special relationship that the hierarchy had enjoyed with the old Radio Éireann regime no longer existed. Here it becomes evident, too, that the 1960 Broadcasting Act changed the nature of broadcasting in Ireland. Under the old Radio Éireann, the Hierarchy and the government were comfortable with an informal relationship that allowed civil servants responsible for radio to communicate confidentially with the bishops. Quiet conversations between representatives of the bishops and senior civil servants could quickly resolve any difficulties that might arise. However, the 1960 legislation empowered the Radio Éireann Authority to make critical decisions as an independent entity. The act provided a substantial degree of protection to the Authority, enabling it to resist pressure from powerful interests including the Catholic Church. Like many politicians of the day bishops were slow to learn that the 1960 act gave the Radio Éireann Authority a considerable degree of independence.

The Catholic Television Interim Committee considered the conditions set down by Andrews and reported back to the bishops in November 1962. At this juncture the CTIC illustrated that it too was willing to compromise with the Authority. The group reported that extensive consideration had been given to the question of the appointment, how it might be made, and where it should be based. The CTIC saw two options: the first, which had been supported by McQuaid and Morris but rejected by the Authority, argued for an executive director to be chosen by the Hierarchy as a salaried official of Telefís Éireann. The alternative, which Andrews had originally suggested, called for the official to be chosen and salaried by the Hierarchy and given offices and access to other facilities at the Donnybrook station. The CTIC regarded the ability of the bishops to appoint the person as critical and therefore argued that it believed that the best course of action would be for the Hierarchy to accept the second option and both appoint and pay for a priest executive.[97] When McQuaid was told of these developments he described himself as 'surprised' by both the Radio Éireann Authority's refusal to accept the demands he and Morris had made to Eamonn Andrews and by the CTIC's offer to compromise.[98] At the time these negotiations were taking place McQuaid was still in Rome attending the meetings of Vatican II. The positions of both the Authority and the CTIC were simply not acceptable to him; he had no interest in capitulating. The end result was a prolonged stalemate.

Kevin McCourt replaced Edward Roth as Director-General in January 1963, and his appointment provided an opening for the bishops to try once again to convince the Authority to appoint a priest advisor of their choosing as a permanent member of the Telefís Éireann staff. McCourt, a businessman and Fianna Fáil supporter, was a graduate of Blackrock College where McQuaid had been Principal prior to becoming Archbishop of Dublin. This change suited McQuaid, as he no longer had to deal with Edward Roth. Archbishop Morris was still the President of the CTIC and saw McCourt's appointment as providing an opportunity to once again advocate for the creation of a staff position within Telefís

Éireann. He contacted McQuaid who was again in Rome at the start of the New Year, telling him he was going to meet McCourt and asking if Joseph Dunn would still be available for the position they wanted established at Telefís Éireann. He told McQuaid that he wanted to propose that Dunn be taken on as a paid consultant or advisor and that the Hierarchy would contribute to a salary as he would be working for both Telefís Éireann and the CTIC.[99] McQuaid agreed with Morris's strategy but warned that Cathal McCarthy was seriously ill and might not recover to 'grip the T.E. situation. It is better for me to look for a substitute in case he cannot prove active in close quarters, in the day-to-day difficulties.'[100] It is interesting to note that McQuaid was claiming that he should be the one to find a substitute, even though he was not on the CTIC. It was agreed that Dunn would be the Hierarchy's choice to be appointed to a position in Telefís Éireann and eventually replace the ailing McCarthy as chair of the CTIC.

A short time later Morris reported to McQuaid that he had a very pleasant meeting with Kevin McCourt, describing the new director-general as being 'sincerely concerned that relations between the TV service and the Hierarchy should be harmonious. He was anxious to probe matters giving rise to anxiety on the part of the Hierarchy and I wished that I had briefed myself more accurately on persons and programmes.'[101] McCourt explained that he was still settling into his position and would not be expanding the staff in the near future but gave Morris the impression that he looked favourably on bringing Joseph Dunn on board, even asking what a fair salary for Dunn might be.[102] By the next time the Hierarchy met the CTIC had succeeded in getting Dunn formally appointed to a three-year term as secretary to the Committee.[103]

It appeared that everything was falling into place for McQuaid, Morris and the Catholic Hierarchy. A former student of the Archbishop of Dublin at Blackrock College was director-general and seemed much more sympathetic to the needs of the Church. McQuaid had been pleased with the report he had received from Morris, noting the 'first contact was gratifying'.[104] All of this changed when McCarthy received a startling phone call from Kevin McCourt advising him that the Radio Éireann Authority had appointed not Joseph Dunn as Adviser for Religious Programmes but Romuald Dodd, a Dominican priest.[105]

McCarthy contacted McQuaid in Rome telling him, 'I must say the news came as a great shock to me for more reasons than one. I felt sure that Father Joe Dunn would be accepted. However Mr. McCourt was very emphatic and asked me to inform Your Grace and the archbishop of Cashel.'[106] This was a major blow to McQuaid; he expected Joseph Dunn would be appointed to the staff of Telefís Éireann as priest adviser. Dunn was the archbishop's hand-picked candidate, he had supported Dunn's training in London, Manchester and New York and believed he would provide a valuable service in keeping Telefís Éireann under his supervision.[107]

McQuaid, still at the Irish College in Rome, was furious and responded to McCarthy's news, telling him that he had written to Kevin McCourt complaining about the appointment: 'though I am the sole authority in the Diocese in which his station is situated, I know neither the priest concerned nor his competence'.[108] McCourt responded, stating he was 'distressed' at the archbishop's 'note of disapproval' and defended the appointment.[109] He pointed out that prior to his coming to his position as director-general the wish of the CTIC that a priest adviser be appointed 'had foundered' and that he had sought to rectify the situation after meeting with Archbishop Morris, CTIC President. McCourt explained that the Committee had agreed that a priest adviser would be chosen from a list submitted to him and that of the three names submitted, 'it seemed to me that Father Romuald Dodd, O.P., in all respects would be the most suitable'.[110] Unbeknownst to McQuaid, the proposal made earlier by Eamonn Andrews had been accepted by Morris and the CTIC as the bishops believed the procedure was simply a formality and that Dunn, whose name was on the list, would be chosen. Interestingly Archbishop Morris may have quietly helped undermine Dunn's appointment. Interviewed many years later, Kevin McCourt explained that Morris warned him strongly against taking Dunn into RTÉ telling him he was: 'chained and trained by McQuaid, you'd have McQuaid himself there if you had Dunn'.[111]

The director-general cannily explained to McQuaid that although he sensed the archbishop disapproved of the decisions of the CTIC he was in no position to question an ecclesiastical committee 'understood to be appointed by the Hierarchy'.[112] Kevin McCourt was not about to back down and was pleased to resolve a difficult dilemma that had troubled his predecessor, Edward Roth. But McQuaid was bitterly disappointed and on receiving McCourt's reply responded quite forcefully. 'I must regret that I knew nothing of a list presented, that I was unaware of a priest being appointed, that I received the news of an appointment at second-hand and that I do not know the priest appointed in my Diocese, where the archbishop ... is responsible for religious affairs.'[113] Wary of an intrusive archbishop, McCourt, Eamonn Andrews and the Radio Éireann Authority had cleverly outmanoeuvred McQuaid. Dublin's archbishop never forgot this slight and remained an often aggressive and embittered critic of Telefís Éireann, but with the appointment of a Dominican, who did not report to him, his ability to create difficulties within Telefís Éireann was curbed greatly.

Joseph Dunn was aware that his name had been mentioned as a priest adviser and had even been told by the editor of the Catholic journal *The Furrow* and a member of the CTIC, Dr. J. G. McGarry, that he would be appointed to the staff of Telefís Éireann. McGarry told him to prepare for the position and Dunn assumed his appointment was imminent. Dunn maintains that the CTIC believed that his appointment was settled, 'that [although] this had been verbally agreed with RTÉ they felt that as a formality they should submit more than one name'.[114] Desmond Forristal, who had trained and worked with Dunn in New York, was the second name and on the advice of a member of the CTIC the Dominican Fr Dodd was also nominated. According to Dunn, 'when the list came in to Eamonn Andrews's hands he saw his chance. Romuald Dodd's name was submitted by the CTIC, so no bishop could complain if he were appointed. RTÉ could have a priest but one from a religious order who was not directly subject to the Archbishop of Dublin ... the CTIC felt it had been tricked but could do nothing about it. John Charles was, needless to say, not at all pleased. I was instructed by him to have nothing to do with Fr. Dodd.'[115]

Although upset with the failure to get Dunn appointed to the post of Religious Adviser the CTIC met with Dodd and outlined the relationship that he would have with the organisation. Although he was given complete authority for the planning and presentation of all religious programmes, the Committee instructed Dodd he would be required to report to them regularly. The minutes of the meeting between Dodd and the Committee indicate that this was a critical point as far as the CTIC were concerned as they told Dodd he should, 'appreciate the status of this Committee as a policy making body responsible to the Hierarchy and [should] keep the Committee informed as far as possible of his general plans'.[116] Although the CTIC accepted that all communications from the Committee that concerned Catholic programmes would be sent to the Television Authority through Dodd, the Committee made it clear that other communications, 'relating to matters of policy or criticism will be otherwise conveyed'.[117] In other words the bishops reserved the right to communicate or complain directly to the Television Authority or director-general, circumventing Fr Dodd. McQuaid did not hesitate to complain to Kevin McCourt when he felt that he had been ignored or offended. He still believed that no cleric of any order, society, or organisation should appear on Telefís Éireann without written permission from his office.

While the Irish Catholic Church was working to formalise its relationship with Telefís Éireann, the Protestant Churches were also interested in the new television service and hoped to find ways to use it for their own purposes. The Church of Ireland established a Sound and Broadcasting General Committee at its General Synod in April 1961. The committee replaced an older one that had met in the past to oversee sound broadcasting. The Sound and Broadcasting General Committee consisted of two groups, one for Northern Ireland and another for the Irish Republic. Each sub-committee was chaired by a bishop and included six additional members; three clerical and three lay, nominated by the General Synod. The island-wide committee was expected to meet annually while the two sub-committees met on a monthly basis. These committees were expected to serve as a resource for clergy and laity interested in all matters concerning radio and television and to develop close, meaningful relationships with the authorities responsible for broadcasting. In addition they were charged with coordinating all Church of Ireland religious broadcasts with the relevant authorities, identifying members of the Church with experience in broadcasting, and developing 'a general Church of Ireland policy in sound and television broadcasting'.[118] It was also expected these committees would promote radio and television training courses for clergy, help identify playwrights and script writers for religious programmes, and develop 'Look Listen' groups in as many parishes as possible. These groups had been organised in Britain and it was hoped they could be developed throughout Ireland to 'provide a body of Christian comment upon broadcasting of all sorts, which would enable the voice of the Church to be heard at the local level, and would supply a stream of Christian opinion which could be analysed centrally and submitted periodically to the broadcasting authorities'.[119] The Catholic Church was also interested in developing a network of 'Look Listen' groups to monitor broadcasts on the new station.

In reading through the minutes of what was referred to as the Southern Sub-Committee it is clear that members were not primarily focused on trying to keep immoral material off the airwaves in the Irish Republic. It was understood that the Catholic Church would have strong opinions about the transmission of objectionable material and would be vigilant in this regard.[120] In the Republic, the Church of Ireland Committee worked to find its own voice on Telefís Éireann and, like its Catholic counterpart, looked for talented clerics who could make use of the airtime the Authority granted to the Church. The first meeting of the committee, chaired by the Bishop of Limerick, met in October 1961 approximately ten weeks before the new service opened. It addressed working with Director-General Edward Roth to organise the broadcast of services from Christ Church Cathedral during Holy Week and arranging dates for additional talks and services.[121] The Church of Ireland Committee assigned a young cleric, Revd Fergus Day, the rector of Dún Laoghaire parish, to meet with Roth. Day may have been chosen due to his interest in the performing arts and service as a chaplain of the Actor's Union Church.

Day later met Roth and was told the Authority wanted to deal 'with one person only to represent all Protestants'.[122] He also learned that all churches would be invited to take part in a short epilogue each evening as the station was about to go off the air. Roth defined these as non-sectarian although Day was assured the station would make provision for midweek talks enabling Protestant and Catholic Churches to reach their members. The committee formally appointed Revd Day as Television Adviser and asked him to develop a training course to familiarise Church of Ireland clergy with the medium. When the General Committee met after Telefís Éireann went on the air a decision was made that each of the two sub-committees should prepare its own annual report to the Standing Committee of Bishops. Day soon found himself representing not only the Church of Ireland but also the major Protestant Churches in the Irish Republic as the coordinator of Protestant Religious Programmes at Telefís Éireann.[123]

Day's relationship with staff at Telefís Éireann was professional and by all accounts uneventful, and the few complaints that emerged from the committee were passed onto the Radio Éireann Authority and dealt with quietly. One early complaint addressed the habit of broadcasters on both radio and television to lump all Protestant Churches together by using the term 'non-Catholic'. After communication with other Protestant denominations Day reported that he had discussed the matter with television officials and that the issue of 'three denominations being regarded as one has now been solved'.[124] It took a while for the request to sink in, and three years later the committee reported that the term 'non-Catholic' was 'not so much used now by Telefís Éireann'.[125]

Although Day's relationship with senior staff in Telefís Éireann was constructive, there remained a degree of frustration at the inability of the Church of Ireland to use the medium more effectively. This was articulated in the pages of the *Church of Ireland Gazette* as early as March 1963 when an editorial expressed dismay that the Church had failed to 'present to the country at large the true image of the Church of Ireland'.[126] The *Gazette* criticised the Church's approach to the medium, noting that it moved with a 'characteristic lack of urgency' relying on 'a large and unwieldy committee' to handle television matters. It expressed some sympathy for Day, pointing out that all the work had fallen to one 'fully occupied individual' while at the same time criticising Telefís Éireann for not providing greater notice of available programme time.

The *Gazette* called for a 'a thorough re-examination of the position and that, if necessary, representations should be made to the television authorities with a view to a revision of their regulations regarding religious programmes'.[127] Acknowledging the work of the Revd Day as Co-ordinator of Protestant Programmes and pointing to the policy in Northern Ireland, the paper called on Telefís Éireann to pay for his services. Later in the year the *Gazette* was critical of the short programme *Recollection*, broadcast at the close of each evening's programming. The paper pointed out that no matter what denomination was featured it 'requires something more than average strength of personality to make an impact on minds that have been soaking in a conglomerate diet of *Bat Masterson, Jackpot, Rescue 8*, and the highly specialised efforts of ad-men, with a "thought for the night"'.[128] The editorial questioned the need to continue the programme, complaining that there was no system in place to audition, select, reject or support those participating. Given the performances of the various clerics that had been featured it suggested that if *Recollection* were to continue Telefís Éireann should identify a competent producer to work with the hapless clerics featured each evening. The *Gazette* watched the evolution of Telefís Éireann closely, applauding programmes it thought were worthwhile and complaining of others.[129]

Revd Day's position evolved into an important one and the Southern Sub-Committee recognised this, granting him a salary, allowing him to appoint an assistant, and paying for both to enrol on television courses in England. A delegation from the Church of Ireland Committee travelled to London for meetings with BBC officials involved in religious broadcasting and was delighted to learn that the BBC would be of assistance in providing additional support and training for Revd Day. By March 1964 Day had settled into his position, collecting a modest salary from the Church of Ireland and a further £250 from the Broadcasting Authority. He felt obligated to distribute £50 each to his Presbyterian and Methodist colleagues.[130] Later, a decision was made by the Protestant Churches to provide a more formal role for each denomination when a Joint Committee was established in April 1964. The Joint Committee included representatives of the three Protestant Churches in an effort to bring together all three denominations to share ideas and address broadcasting issues in both Northern Ireland and the Republic.

Revd Fergus Day continued to represent the three Irish Protestant Churches in the Irish Republic and each agreed to a formula that allowed them to share time allocated by the Television Authority for Protestant broadcasts. All three defended the arrangement when an article appeared in the June 1966 issue of *Focus* criticising Telefís Éireann by maintaining that the station was marginalising the Protestant Churches because it 'lumped together' the denominations. A distraught controller of programmes approached Day requesting he publicly reject the allegations of discrimination and a special meeting of the Church of Ireland Sound and Television Committee was quickly summoned. It sent a strong letter of protest to the publication to 'Refute any idea of discrimination'.[131] The letter to the editor of the magazine argued 'this is in no sense an accurate assessment of the situation. The Church of Ireland, the Presbyterian and Methodist Churches have freely agreed to accept the position whereby programme time available to the minority churches is shared in order to spread the impact over the greatest possible viewing public.'[132] The Church of Ireland Committee enjoyed a cordial relationship with Telefís Éireann, reporting at the end of 1966 that nineteen broadcasts had taken place over the course of the year, then passing a motion 'to express its thanks to the Radio Éireann Authority for its courtesy at all times'.[133]

Although the Church of Ireland had been satisfied with arrangements to share time with the other Protestant Churches, by 1969 this had changed. In a report to the Standing Committee of Bishops the committee maintained that although the Church of Ireland represented approximately 75 per cent of the Protestant population in the Republic, it was sharing time with the other Protestant Churches equally, arguing that the agreement precluded it from effectively serving its members. The Church had become more comfortable with television and more confident about developing its own programmes. It hoped to revise the station's policy, noting 'we are somewhat handicapped by the policy of the

RTÉ Authority'.[134] It suggested the Church of Ireland be given a greater share of the time allotted to the Catholic Churches but changes in the television services made the issue a moot one. The establishment of a formal religious department in Telefís Éireann enabled all of the churches to be directly involved in broadcasting and addressed the committee's concerns. It later concluded it 'was the unanimous opinion of the Committee that the new situation of religious broadcasting was an improvement, and that it felt the closer co-operation between all churches to be in keeping with Church of Ireland policy in general'.[135]

Throughout the 1960s Protestant Churches enjoyed a cordial relationship with Telefís Éireann, which provided an outlet for each church to both reach its members and present itself to citizens of other faiths. The Church of Ireland became comfortable working with a number of progressive Catholic clergy who were interested in building bridges and using television as a means to facilitate contact and communication between the Irish Churches.

The Church of Ireland may have been comfortable with the programmes being transmitted by Telefís Éireann but this was not the case with BBC broadcasts received in Northern Ireland. In this respect it shared many of the concerns expressed by the Catholic Church south of the border. For instance, in 1965 a petition read out at all Church of Ireland services in County Londonderry sharply criticised the BBC for belittling what was termed a Christian way of life. Parishioners were urged to sign a petition which objected to 'the propaganda of disbelief, doubt and dirt that the BBC pours into millions of homes through the television screen. Crime, violence, illegitimacy and venereal disease are steadily increasing yet the BBC employs people whose ideas and advice pander to the lowest in human nature, and accompany this with a stream of suggestive and erotic plays which present promiscuity, infidelity and drinking as normal and inevitable.'[136] Other complaints about television also targeted BBC programmes for presenting Church of Ireland clergy in stereotype as 'ineffectual and often as mere caricatures' while Catholic priests were presented as heroic.[137]

From the establishment of the BBC Northern Ireland radio service in 1924 religion proved a contentious subject, first with radio and then with television.[138] Many Catholics in the province considered the station an instrument of a unionist majority that ignored their interests and culture. The Catholic community was deeply alienated from the Unionist government, initially boycotting all of the institutions in the province including the BBC. The station enjoyed what historian Jonathan Bardon describes as a 'cosy relationship' with the unionist government and for twenty years the Catholic Church refused to send a representative to the BBC Northern Ireland Religious Advisory Committee. Twenty years after the station went on the air, the Church relented and sent Monsignor A. H. Ryan to attend a meeting of the committee. Ryan was joined a short time later by the future Cardinal and Archbishop of Armagh, Cathal Daly, who at the time was teaching moral philosophy at Queens University in Belfast. BBC Northern Ireland radio (and later television) studiously avoided controversy when dealing with religion, featuring church services, concerts and talks. Discussion programmes such as *Meeting Point* were carefully arranged by producers to avoid topics that could provoke disagreement.

A short time after Romuald Dodd's appointment as Catholic Religious Adviser to Telefís Éireann, Archbishop McQuaid expressed displeasure at the appearance of Gregory Baum, a Canadian Augustinian priest who was a widely respected expert on ecumenism. During the meetings of Vatican II, Baum was theological advisor to the Ecumenical Secretariat, the commission responsible for three documents: *On Religious Liberty, On the Church's Relation to Non-Christian Religions* and *On Ecumenism*.[139] In an interview with Peter O'Kelly, Baum addressed the transformation of the Church in the aftermath of Vatican II. His comments about ecumenism and the changing role of bishops in the Church infuriated Archbishop McQuaid. The statement that most unnerved the archbishop maintained, '[i]n the past we thought of the influence, which the church had played in the world as being the actions of the Princes of the church, of the Bishops in touch with the leaders of society and in that way seeking to influence the development of the world. Today we know this time has passed.'[140] The archbishop felt threatened by these sentiments, believing they undermined the power and prestige of the hierarchy.

The interview provoked an angry letter from McQuaid who wrote directly to the director-general, ignoring the recently appointed Dominican Religious Advisor Romuald Dodd. The archbishop asked McCourt 'to state by whose authority the stranger priest Rev. Gregory Baum O.S.A. was invited to speak and did speak in my Diocese on matters of faith and morals'.[141] The incident captures an unsettled archbishop confronted by a medium that questioned his understanding of the place of the hierarchy in Irish society. The fact that this challenge emanated from within his archdiocese was a profoundly disturbing experience. Kevin McCourt rejected the archbishop's criticism and responded by defending the interview describing Baum as a 'well known expert on the ecumenical movement', pointing out that he was a member of the Ecumenical Council that had met in Rome and was 'well qualified to comment on proceedings there'.[142] McQuaid chose not to respond to his former pupil's letter. He understood that television was subverting the power and influence of the Church and undermining his influence as archbishop.

The Irish Catholic Church followed up on earlier advice of the Vatican, included in the Papal Encyclical *Miranda Prorsus*, issued by Rome in 1957 and embraced in the Second Vatican Council. The publication *Inter Mirifica* called for the establishment of communication centres throughout the Catholic world dedicated to educating and training religious and lay people interested in exploiting television for the Church.[143] As the name suggests, the Catholic Television Interim Committee was set up to assist the hierarchy in overseeing the introduction of television into the country until a permanent organisation could be established. When he was appointed to work with the hierarchy on television matters, Joseph Dunn was assigned the task of setting up a communications institute designed to teach priests, nuns and lay people how to use television technology to develop religious programming. Joseph Dunn was formally appointed director of the Communications Centre in the summer of 1964 and identified a site for the new centre near Telefís Éireann, which was purchased by the hierarchy from the Christian Brothers.[144] The Catholic

Truth Society generously funded construction of the project, committing £55,000 to building and equipping the centre, while a grant of £12,000 from the Vatican paid for operating costs in the first year. Dunn oversaw the building of a modern facility complete with studios, classrooms, and an extensive media library. He developed courses taught by colleagues, some of whom worked with him on the *Radharc* television series that was making programmes for Telefís Éireann.

The Communications Centre was opened in Booterstown, County Dublin, in February 1967, illustrating that the Irish Catholic Hierarchy would be proactive in using television for its own purposes. While the rhetoric of pre-Vatican II could still be heard denouncing the evils of television, these attitudes were giving way to an understanding by the Church that advances in technology were having a transformative effect on Irish life. A generation of young priests and nuns, excited by the new emphasis on engaging with the laity promised in Vatican II, understood that technology could enhance their educational and pastoral work.

Joseph Dunn and his staff offered courses for clergy working both in Ireland and those engaged in missionary work around the world. Although the centre developed educational films for a domestic audience, it increasingly focused on helping Irish missionaries use television in their pastoral and educational work. A visit to the centre by journalist Patrick Nolan in 1968 found a young group of priests and nuns in the midst of an intensive nine-week training course learning the basics of television production. Nine of the twelve students he observed worked as teachers abroad, representing the six thousand Irish-born missionaries working in developing countries. Some had recently returned from postings in Nigeria, Hong Kong, Burma and Sierra Leone, while others were preparing for work in Botswana and Nigeria. All were required to write, direct and produce a thirty-minute programme during the course. Peter Lemass, a priest who worked with Dunn in the television programme *Radharc,* was the assistant head of training at the centre. He explained that the centre was not necessarily training students for careers as producers but wanted its graduates to be positioned to influence television services being established in developing countries. 'We try to let the priests and sisters see what's involved. If you don't know anything about television it is difficult to be an educational or religious advisor to television.'[145]

Dunn understood the value of bringing technology into the classrooms where many of the missionaries worked and believed the courses offered by the centre could enhance the work of these teachers. He explained to one reporter: 'One had to come to terms with the electronic world. We are providing an opportunity of handling equipment – tape recorders, cameras, projectors and so on. This is useful for people connected with education. Irish missionaries have one basic way of working – through the schools.'[146] He maintained that the Catholic Church had lost out on radio; that it had 'failed to even keep pace with other Christian Churches in this regard'.[147] However, television was different and he took a longer view, seeing the role of the Communications Centre as evolving. He explained that in funding the centre the Church hoped that in twenty years' time the 'training of a selective group of its members in television appreciation and the uses and application of the media will pay dividends'.[148]

The Communications Centre also made an effort to reach out to the Protestant Churches in Ireland and encouraged Revd Fergus Day, Co-ordinator of Protestant Religious Programmes, to use the facilities and take advantage of the courses it offered. In January 1967, Day reported to the Church of Ireland Television Committee that he was working with Dunn on a joint programme on church unity to be broadcast later that month. Dunn made a positive impression on Fergus Day, and when the Communications Centre opened the Church of Ireland Committee decided, after consulting with the Archbishop of Dublin, that 'friendly approaches should be made to the R.C. Communications Centre regarding T.V. Courses'.[149] Courses were made available for Protestant clergy who were able to take advantage of the studios and staff to improve their religious programmes. By the end of the decade, Church of Ireland bishops, divinity students, clergy and lay people – including staff from the *Church of Ireland Gazette* – were enrolling in courses at the Communications Centre.

Throughout the period under consideration in this study a number of incidents provoked the Catholic Church to complain about broadcasts it regarded as offensive or indecent. These have been chronicled over the years by a number of historians and cultural critics.[150] Perhaps the most famous incident occurred in 1966 and is simply known as the 'bishop and the nightie' episode. This unfolded on the iconic *The Late Late Show* hosted by Gay Byrne when a contestant in a quiz revealed that she might not have been wearing a nightdress on her wedding night. The subsequent criticism emanating from Dr Thomas Ryan, Bishop of Clonfert, denouncing the episode as indecent, received widespread coverage in the national and regional press. The station issued an apology and although some viewers may have been upset by the incident the bishop was widely ridiculed for his awkward intervention.

Byrne's programme proved to be one of the most provocative features on Irish television and deserves all the credit it has received for helping to open up Irish society. Byrne was a master performer and mediator who provided a popular and accessible forum for the discussion of a wide array of often controversial topics that had previously been taboo in a public setting. For instance television critic Nora Relihan singled out a programme that considered the lives of Travelling people. 'This show's extraordinary success was due in no small measure to Mr Byrne's approach. One might have thought in advance that he would be both patronising and facetious. To his credit he was neither, and in fact displayed a gentleness and kindness which in different situations might easily be labelled "soft".'[151] Cultural historian Lance Pettitt notes that the programme 'provoked legislative changes and shifted the boundaries of taboos in Irish social discourse on a variety of topics including unmarried mothers, Travellers rights, infanticide, different kinds of sexuality, marriage and clerical celibacy'.[152]

Another iconic moment featured a frustrated young student, Brian Trevaskis, lashing out at Bishop Browne of Galway in particular but Irish Catholicism in general on *The Late Late Show*. In March 1966 he criticised Bishop of Galway Michael Browne, referring to him as a 'moron', suggesting he was forcing the people of Galway to pay for the cathedral he described as a 'ghastly monstrosity'.[153] The episode underscores how television not only eroded a sense of deference, but also enabled a stinging critique of the established order to be delivered live on one

10   Gay Byrne (left) with playwright and Trinity College Dublin student
      Brian Trevaskis on *The Late Late Show*, February 22, 1969. Trevaskis
      had famously called the Bishop of Galway 'a moron' on the programme
      three years earlier, on March 26, 1966.

of the country's most popular and cherished programmes. Again
there was widespread reaction in the press, and RTÉ was attacked
for supporting anti-clericalism and undermining the work of the
Church.[154] Bishop Brown received an apology from the director-
general and a flood of letters from supporters upset with Byrne's
programme.[155] Galway's bishop remained sensitive to any criticism emanating from RTÉ. Later that year Brown complained
to McCourt about a *Newsbeat* programme presented by Frank
Hall, defining it as insulting. It appears that in opening a story
concerning drinking in hotels Hall remarked that the 'bishop of
Galway is waving his crozier again'.[156] Brown contacted McCourt
to complain he was 'the subject of offensive and slighting remarks
… I sincerely hope that television is not being used to subvert religion in this country'.[157] Although these episodes provoked debate
in some quarters about the intrusion of a vulgar popular culture
into a respectable conservative society, they tended to be isolated
incidents. Nevertheless they proved that no one was immune to
criticism, fair or unfair, from a medium that often featured live,

unscripted material that captured the tensions emerging in Irish society in the 1960s.

As the decade moved to a close, the Irish Catholic Church became much more comfortable with the medium. A new generation of priests with engaging personalities and interests in developing innovative programmes made their way into television. Members of the hierarchy also made an effort to use television to reach the faithful and appeared on news and current affairs programmes. For instance, by 1970 Cardinal Conway had appeared as a guest on *The Late Late Show*, and other bishops began to make their way onto television for interviews demonstrating an accessibility that contrasted sharply with many older members of the Irish hierarchy who remained suspicious of the medium, many avoiding it at all costs.[158] In spite of efforts by RTÉ, Archbishop McQuaid refused to be interviewed on the national television service.

A number of innovative Catholic broadcasts enabled the Church to reach a wide audience with intelligent and creative programmes that were topical, expressing an interest in issues of social justice. One such programme was *Outlook*, a short feature that addressed issues of poverty in contemporary Ireland. In the spring of 1967 the radical Dominican, Austin Flannery, presented a series of *Outlook* programmes that addressed poverty and the housing crisis in Dublin. One of the more remarkable broadcasts included four guests: a Jesuit priest, two members of Sinn Féin and Michael O'Riordan, general secretary of the Irish Workers' Party, the official Irish Communist party. While the broadcast created unease among politicians and members of the clergy, it illustrated that Ireland was changing. It was only a few years earlier that members of the Hierarchy had met with Seán Lemass to complain about communists holding important positions within RTÉ and appearing as programme guests. As Louise Fuller observes, 'The fact that the general secretary of the Irish Communist Party appeared on national television on a religious programme, at the behest of a clergyman, and on a discussion panel with another priest, underlines how much Irish society had changed in a decade.'[159]

There were other innovative programmes that challenged the teachings of the Catholic Church during the 1960s. Michael

Viney, described by historian Diarmaid Ferritter as 'one of the most outstanding journalists of his generation' for his investigative reporting on social problems also worked with RTÉ.[160] In late 1966 he produced a remarkable programme about contraception titled *Too Many Children?* The broadcast featured 'Dublin mothers discuss[ing] frankly their attitudes to family planning'.[161] However, the most influential religious programme of the period was undoubtedly *Radharc* which will be considered in detail in Chapter 7.

Notes

1 See Robert J. Savage, *Irish Television: The Political and Social Origins* (Cork University Press, Cork, 1996), 108–10.

2 On the extent of censorship in Ireland during this period see Michael Adams, *Censorship: The Irish Experience* (University of Alabama Press, Tuscaloosa, AL, 1968), and Kevin Rockett, *Irish Film Censorship* (Four Courts Press, Dublin, 2004).

3 The designation 2RN was given to the Irish Free State by the British Post Office. See Richard Pine, *2RN and the Origins of Irish Radio* (Four Courts Press, Dublin, 2002), 39–40.

4 There were exceptions as some ministers took a real interest in radio, most notably Erskine Childers.

5 See Savage, *Irish Television*, 1–6.

6 See Brian Lynch, 'Steering Clear: Broadcasting and the Church, 1926–1951,' *New Hibernia Review*, 4:2 (Summer 2000), 28.

7 Ibid.

8 Louise Fuller, *Irish Catholicism since 1950: The Undoing of a Culture* (Gill and Macmillan, Dublin, 2002).

9 According to its mission statement the Catholic Truth Society of Ireland was organised at the meeting of the Maynooth-Union in 1899, with the stated purpose of diffusing 'by means of cheap publications sound Catholic literature in popular form so as to give instruction and edification in a manner most likely to interest and attract the general reader [which would] create a taste for a pure and wholesome literature, and will also serve as an antidote against the poison of dangerous or immoral writings'. In the first ten years of its existence 424 penny publications, with a circulation of over five million copies, were issued. It also printed a prayer book and other works in Irish.

10 Vatican Radio began broadcasting in February 1931. Later in the decade the Vatican experimented with television, however the Vatican did not begin television broadcasting until the 1990s.

11 Lynch, 'Steering Clear,' 33.
12 *Bunreacht na hÉireann*, Article 44, 1937.
13 See Diarmaid Ferriter, *Judging Dev* (Royal Irish Academy, Dublin, 2008), 117–222.
14 Dublin Diocesan Archives, Cathal McCarthy Papers, [hereafter DDA] DDA/P/10/III, Broadcasting: *Catholic Truth Society Broadcasting Committee 1939*, 'Strictly Confidential Report', April 27, 1939.
15 NAI, Department of Foreign Affairs, 96/2/14. León Ó Broin to Hugh McCann, Secretary of External Affairs, April 9, 1965. The history of these events is addressed in this document.
16 Ibid.
17 Ibid.
18 Ibid. The bishops also rejected a proposal that Revd Kissane be appointed to a paid position in Radio Éireann as director of religious broadcasts and another that the Church purchase time on Radio Éireann for religious talks and lectures.
19 Ibid.
20 Tom Garvin, *Preventing the Future: Why was Ireland so Poor for so Long?* (Gill and Macmillan, Dublin, 2004), 71–2.
21 Maurice Gorham, *Forty Years of Irish Broadcasting* (Talbot Press, Dublin, 1967), 180.
22 Ibid., 196.
23 Ibid., 180.
24 DDA, Cathal McCarthy Papers, DDA/P/10/ III, Broadcasting, Gorham to McCarthy, February 20, 1956.
25 Ibid., *Irish Times*, February 14, 1956.
26 For a detailed account of the work of the Television Commission, see Savage, *Irish Television*, Chapters 7–9.
27 His contribution to religious broadcasting will be considered in greater detail in the following Chapter 7.
28 DDA, McQuaid Papers AB8/B/XXVI/a/2, Report of the Television Committee, June 2, 1958.
29 Ibid.
30 Ibid.
31 Ibid., 2.
32 Ibid., 2–3.
33 When the Second Vatican Council published *Inter Mirifica*, calling for the establishment of communication centres around the Catholic world, the Hierarchy responded. This recommendation was later realised when the Communications Centre was established in 1967 in Booterstown, County Dublin.
34 DDA, McQuaid Papers AB8/B/XXVI/a/2 Report of the Television Committee, June 2, 1958.

35 Ibid.

36 Author's interview with Dr McAdoo, December 12, 1990, Dalkey, Ireland.

37 DDA, McQuaid Papers AB8/B/XXVI, Ó Broin to McQuaid, November 10, 1958.

38 Ibid., Ó Broin to McQuaid, November 12, 1958.

39 DDA, Cathal McCarthy Papers, DDA/P/10/ III, Broadcasting, McQuaid to McCarthy, November 24, 1960.

40 DDA, General Meeting of the Irish Hierarchy, Report of the Television Committee, October, 1959.

41 Ibid.

42 Ibid.

43 Ibid.

44 Ibid.

45 Ibid.

46 Ibid. (emphasis added).

47 Ibid.

48 Ibid.

49 Joseph Dunn, *No Vipers in the Vatican* (Columba Press, Dublin, 1996), 267.

50 Cashel Diocean Archives, (hereafter CDA) Morris Papers, Morris to McCarthy, November 18, 1961.

51 *Catholic Herald*, December 12, 1961.

52 See John Cooney, *John Charles McQuaid, Ruler of Catholic Ireland: The Man and the Mask* (O'Brien Press, Dublin, 1999), 308. Cooney indicates that McQuaid asked this group to gather information for him about a number of organisations and people, including the Irish Housewives' Association, the Irish Workers' League and the IRA.

53 CDA, Morris Papers, Report of the Episcopal Television Committee, October, 1961.

54 Here one can see the influence of the Agnellus Andrew O.P, Religious Advisor for the BBC who offered advice to the Irish Hierarchy about religion and television.

55 CDA, Morris Papers, Cashel, *Statement of the Hierarchy on the Inauguration of the Irish Television Service*, October 10, 1961.

56 Ibid.

57 DDA, McQuaid Papers AB8/B/XXVI/a/9, Fr G. T. Fehily to McQuaid, May 2, 1961.

58 Ibid., McQuaid to Fehily, May 2, 1961.

59 Ibid., McQuaid to Fehily, May 15, 1961.

60 DDA, Cathal McCarthy Papers, DDA/P/10/ III (12), Broadcasting, Roth to Brother Conan, December 6, 1961.

61 Ibid., Roth to McCarthy, December 4, 1961.

62 Ibid., McCarthy memorandum, December 4, 1961.

63 Ibid.

64 DDA, McQuaid Papers AB8/B/XXVI/a, McCarthy to McQuaid, December 28, 1961.

65 Ibid., 2.

66 Dunn, *No Vipers*, 269.

67 DDA, Cathal McCarthy Papers, DDA/P/10/ III, Broadcasting, memorandum January 12, 1962.

68 *Recollection* was a very brief programme that simply featured a priest giving an informal talk about religious matters.

69 DDA, Cathal McCarthy Papers, DDA/P/10/ III, Broadcasting, McQuaid to McCarthy, January 15, 1962.

70 Ibid., Timothy Connolly to McQuaid, February 6, 1962.

71 Ibid., McQuaid to Connolly, February 7, 1962.

72 Ibid., McQuaid to Morris, September 6, 1962.

73 Ibid., McQuaid to McCarthy, September 16, 1962.

74 Ibid.

75 Ibid., Morris to McQuaid, September 20, 1962.

76 Ibid., memorandum of meeting with Canon Cathal McCarthy by McQuaid, September 23, 1962 (emphasis added). McQuaid believed the Authority should pay the priest advisor an annual salary of £850.

77 Dunn, *No Vipers*, 270.

78 DDA, McQuaid Papers, Minutes of the General Meeting of the Irish Hierarchy, October 1, 1962.

79 Ibid.

80 DDA AB8/B//XXVI/a/3. Letter and report from the Knights of Columbanus to McQuaid, March 7, 1962.

81 Ibid. David Green, Anthony Coughlan, James Fitzgerald, Andrew Boyd and the editor of *The Plough* Massie MacConnell were all signalled out as left-leaning political deviants.

82 Ibid.

83 DDA, McQuaid Papers, Minutes of the General meeting of the Irish Hierarchy, October 1, 1962, undated memorandum titled *Report on Radio Telefís Éireann Staff.*

84 Ibid.

85 Ibid.

86 Quoted in John Horgan, *Broadcasting and Public Life* (Four Courts Press, Dublin 2004), 30. Horgan notes that this document was one of the few Lemass took with him when he left office.

87 DDA, AB8 XXVI/a, McQuaid Papers, McQuaid to Roth, October 3, 1962.

88 Cooney, *John Charles McQuaid*, 347–8.

89 DDA, AB8 XXVI/a, McQuaid Papers, Andrews to McCarthy, October

24, 1962.

90 Ibid.

91 Ibid., Andrews to McCarthy, October 24, 1962, 2.

92 Ibid.

93 See Robert Savage, *Seán Lemass* (Historical Association of Ireland, Dublin, 1999).

94 Dunn worked as McCarthy's assistant and recently had been appointed to the CTIC where he made a very good impression among the bishops. He had also taken extensive courses in television production in Britain and the United States and was being cultivated by McQuaid and the Hierarchy to continue to work in television.

95 DDA, AB8 XXVI/a, McQuaid Papers, McQuaid to McCarthy, November 5, 1962.

96 Ibid., *Appointment of Priest Executive Director to Telefís Éireann*, Report of the Interim TV Committee, November 29, 1962.

97 Ibid. 'It is the belief of the Committee that the presence of such an independent appointee would be calculated to have a more potent and welcome influence in all departments of television and would appear to serve better the interests of any future National Committee of TV and radio'.

98 Ibid., McQuaid to McCarthy, December 11, 1962.

99 Ibid., letter and memorandum from Morris to McQuaid, January 14, 1963. At the time Dunn was working for him and the CTIC as an executive assistant and helping Canon Cathal McCarthy.

100 Ibid., McQuaid to Morris, January 19, 1963.

101 Ibid., Morris to McQuaid, January 24, 1963.

102 Ibid.

103 Ibid., June 25, 1963. Importantly, the Hierarchy agreed to establish and underwrite the Catholic Communication Centre that would take over the work of the CTIC. A fund was set up to support this initiative, which envisioned the building of studios and extensive facilities to train clergy in television broadcasting. The Hierarchy wanted to appoint 'men with flair' to act as diocesan representatives to consult with the organisation. The infrastructure for what became the Catholic Communications Centre was being built. After receiving technical advice on the construction of the facility from Kevin McCourt, Thomas Hardiman and George Waters, the Centre formally opened in Booterstown, County Dublin in April 1967. See Dunn, *No Vipers in the Vatican*.

104 Ibid., January 25, 1963, marginal note on Morris's January 24, 1963, letter.

105 At the time of his appointment Dodd was teaching biblical archaeology at the Dominican House in Tallaght, County Dublin. A statement issued by the station reported that the new religious advisor for Telefís

Éireann had spent twelve years in Rome working in the Vatican Archives studying medieval history before becoming interested in the electronic media and taking a communications course at RAI, the Italian state television service.

106 DDA, AB8 XXVI/a, McQuaid Papers, McCarthy to McQuaid, November 1, 1963.
107 See Chapter 7.
108 DDA, AB8 XXVI/a, McQuaid Papers, McQuaid to McCarthy, November 8, 1963.
109 Ibid., McCourt to McQuaid, November 13, 1963.
110 Ibid.
111 Interview of Kevin McCourt by John Horgan, February 24, 1997. McCourt had become friendly with Morris who didn't always agree with the other bishops, including McQuaid. Thanks to John Horgan for allowing me access to this interview.
112 DDA, AB8 XXVI/a, McQuaid Papers, McCourt to McQuaid, November 13, 1963, 2.
113 Ibid., McQuaid to McCourt, November 15, 1963.
114 Dunn, *No Vipers*, 272.
115 Ibid. In his memoir Dunn maintains that he was not overly enthusiastic about taking up the new job and was not interested in the 'fighting and politicking for resources' that would be required within Telefís Éireann. He also was concerned about being caught in the middle of what he knew would be a difficult relationship, explaining 'I felt the advisor might have difficulties at times liaising between a strong archbishop like John Charles and the Broadcasting Authority.'
116 DDA, McCarthy Papers, DDA/P10/, Minutes of the Catholic Television Interim Committee, November 20, 1963.
117 Ibid.
118 Representative Church Body Archive, Dublin (hereafter RCB), Church of Ireland Sound and Television Broadcasting Scheme.
119 Ibid.
120 This point was made in an author interview with the former Archbishop of Dublin Dr Henry Robert McAdoo, December 12, 1990, Dalkey, Ireland.
121 RCB Archives, Minutes of the Church of Ireland Sound and Television Broadcasting Committee, October 17, 1961.
122 Ibid., November 15, 1961.
123 Day represented the Church of Ireland, the Methodist and Presbyterian Churches in the Republic. He later informed the group that the Baptist Union of Ireland had written to him asking about Baptist ministers appearing on the new television service.
124 RCB Archives, Minutes of the Church of Ireland Sound and Television

Broadcasting Committee, June 17, 1963.
125 Ibid., December 18, 1966.
126 *Church of Ireland Gazette*, March 1, 1963, 1.
127 Ibid.
128 Ibid., May 31, 1963.
129 Ibid. The *Gazette* also ran advertisements for Murdochs Stores, telling readers their television 'worries' could be 'cured' by purchasing televisions on extended payment plans, January 12, 1962.
130 RCB Archives, Minutes of the Church of Ireland Sound and Television Broadcasting Committee, March 10, 1964.
131 Ibid., Minutes of a special meeting, July 20, 1966.
132 Ibid., letter from the Secretary of the Church of Ireland sub-committee to the editor of the periodical *Focus*, July 22, 1966.
133 Ibid., minutes, December 13, 1966.
134 Ibid., December 10, 1968.
135 Ibid., February 18, 1970.
136 *Church of Ireland Gazette*, April 2, 1965, 6.
137 Ibid., March 20, 1964, 4.
138 Jonathan Bardon, *Beyond the Studio: A History of BBC Northern Ireland* (Blackstaff Press, Belfast, 2000), 7.
139 Baum was Professor of Theology and Sociology at Saint Michael's College, University of Toronto, and subsequently Professor of Theological Ethics at McGill Univerity's Faculty of Religious Studies. From 1962 to 2004, he was the editor of *The Ecumenist*, a review of theology, culture and society, as well as a member and frequent editor of the international Catholic review, *Concilium*.
140 John Cooney, *John Charles McQuaid*, 365.
141 DDA, AB8 XXVI/a/3, McQuaid Papers, letter and draft, McQuaid to McCourt, December 12, 1963. Also quoted in Horgan, *Broadcasting and Public Life*, 32.
142 Ibid., McCourt to McQuaid, December 17, 1963.
143 See *Decree on the Means of Social Communication*, Vatican II Inter Mirifica: 4, December, 1963.
144 DDA, AB8 XXVI/b/15, McQuaid Papers report from Dunn to McQuaid, December 12, 1964.
145 CDA, Archbishop Morris Papers, article in the journal *Pioneer*, February 1968, 8.
146 Ibid., *Pioneer*, 6–7.
147 Ibid.
148 Ibid., 6.
149 RCB Archives, Minutes of the Church of Ireland Sound and Television Broadcasting Committee, October 18, 1967.
150 See esp. Horgan, *Broadcasting and Public Life*; Louise Fuller, *Irish*

Catholicism Since 1950 (Gill and Macmillan, Dublin, 2002); and Gay Byrne with Deirdre Purcell, *The Time of My Life* (Gill and Macmillan, Dublin, 1989).

151 *The Corkman*, December 12, 1969.

152 Lance Pettitt, *Screening Ireland: Film and Television Representation* (Manchester University Press, Manchester, 2000), 169–70.

153 Fergal Tobin, *Best of Decades* (Gill and Macmillan, Dublin, 1984), 141.

154 See Pettitt, *Screening Ireland* and also Maurice Earls, 'The Late Late Show, Controversy and Context in Television and Irish Society', in *21 Years of Irish Television* (eds) Martin McLoone and John MacMahon (Irish Film Institute, Dublin, 1984).

155 Galway Diocean Archives, Brown Papers, B/12/160, McCourt to Brown, April 5, 1966. The file contains many letters of support for the bishop from private citizens and many local and county organisations upset with RTÉ. The Mayor of Galway, the Galway County Council, the Gort Chamber of Commerce, the Letterkenny Urban Council, and the GAA were among those that condemned the programme. Hostile editorials were published in a number of provincial newspapers including *The Longfor Leader*. Trinity College Dublin maintained that it regretted that one of its students offended Bishop Brown but a spokesman would not comment on Brown's statement that 'he was not surprised at being called a moron by a student of Trinity College'. (*Independent*, March 30, 1966).

156 Ibid., Brown to McCourt, November 3, 1966.

157 Ibid., Brown to McCourt, October 25, 1966.

158 By 1970 Archbishop Morris of Cashel, and bishops from Ossory, Killaloe, Galway, Ferns, Kildare and Leighlin, and Down and Connor had been interviewed. J. H. Whyte, *Church and State in Modern Ireland, 1923–1970* (Gill and Macmillan, Dublin, 1971), 355.

159 Fuller, *Irish Catholicism*, 134.

160 See Ferriter, *Transformation*, 536. Viney's writing was featured in the *Irish Times*.

161 Whyte, *Church and State*, 358.

7

Radharc, the Catholic Church and cultural shift in modern Ireland[1]

Perhaps the ~~most influential voice in Catholic religious broadcast-ing in Ireland in the late 1950s and into the 1960s was a Scottish one, that of Dominican Priest Agnellus Andrew.~~ Andrew enjoyed a long and distinguished career in broadcasting and proved to be a prominent international voice in Catholic radio and television. Born outside Glasgow in 1908 and ordained in 1932, he established the National Catholic Office for Mass Media at the Catholic Communications Centre in Hatch End, London. He later became Deputy Head of Religious Broadcasting for the BBC, serving in that capacity until 1967 when he moved to the Independent Broadcasting Authority to work as religious adviser. Recognising Andrew's role in religious broadcasting, the Vatican promoted him to titular Bishop of Numana and summoned him to Rome in 1980 to serve as the vice president of the Pontifical Commission for Social Communications.[2]

He first caught the attention of the Irish Hierarchy in 1951 when he was invited to attend a conference organised by Charles Kelly, Director of Radio Éireann. Kelly arranged the conference in an effort to seek technical advice to improve religious broad-casting, especially the transmission of the Catholic Mass. A few years later Andrew was invited back to lecture on religious broad-casting and contributed an article to the *Irish Ecclesiastical Record*. His essay addressed both the challenges and opportunities that television presented to the Irish Catholic Church.[3] Andrew told the Irish bishops they should prepare for the introduction of a native television service by following the example of the American Catholic Church. In the United States a number of Catholic universities, including Fordham University in New York and the University of San Francisco, had organised departments of communication designed to feature highly specialised courses in television broadcasting.[4] He explained that these courses were established to educate a generation of bright, young Catholics in the new medium, thereby enabling the American church to have the expertise required to harness the power of television. Andrew urged the Irish bishops to follow suit and to set up a committee to consider the challenges and opportunities that the new medium would provide. He pointed out that hundreds of Catholic programmes were being broadcast weekly not only in the United States but also in France, Germany, Holland, Italy and other nations across Europe.

Andrew warned of the dangers of television and was particularly concerned that children might be corrupted by an unsupervised service. Calling for close parental supervision of the medium, he went so far as to suggest lockable shutters be attached to sets, enabling parents to protect their children from harmful programmes. He described Pope Pius XII as tremendously apprehensive about the perils of the medium and quoted the Pontiff at length to underscore his argument:

> The painful picture of the evil and disturbing power of the cinema is present before our minds. But it is impossible not to be horrified at the thought that through the medium of television it may be possible for that atmosphere poisoned by materialism, fatuity and hedonism, which is too often breathed in so many cinemas, to penetrate within the very walls of the home.[5]

Andrew was later invited back to Ireland to address what he told his superiors in the BBC was a private symposium on television 'designed to create an informed opinion amongst some of the educated Dublin people so they might approach the question in a proper way'.[6] He outlined for the bishops the manner in which religious broadcasting was handled in the UK, suggesting that an Irish service follow the BBC model, which had religious advisers from the main churches appointed to its staff. Over the decade Agnellus Andrew became a frequent and influential visitor to Ireland, gaining the respect and admiration of a conservative hierarchy uncomfortable with the medium of television, and a generation of young priests excited by the prospect of using it to enhance their work.

Another influence in the development of religious broadcasting came from the US, specifically from the Archdiocese of Boston. In April 1959 Cardinal Richard Cushing visited Ireland accompanied by Monsignor Walter Flaherty, Director of the Catholic Television Studios in Boston, a project funded and controlled by Cardinal Cushing. While in Dublin, Flaherty was approached by Thomas Fehily, Director of the Dublin Institute of Catholic Sociology, which had been interested in broadcasting for much of the decade. Fehily's interest in television underscored the fact that there were clerics who understood that the establishment of an Irish television service was inevitable and warranted the attention of the Church. The two men had a long discussion about television coming to Ireland and specifically how the Irish Church should prepare for its arrival.

Fehily reported the details of his conversation to the Archbishop of Dublin, John Charles McQuaid, carefully explaining the advice offered by the American cleric. McQuaid was told the Bostonians were convinced 'it would be of inestimable value to us to have a priest trained in television work, if possible even before T.V. starts in this country'.[7] The American director maintained that after an Irish service was up and running there would be no shortage of qualified staff in the various areas of television. However, if qualified priests trained in the field *before* an Irish service went on the air the Church would be in a strong position to influence its development. Flaherty suggested if such a priest 'were available in the first few months when training would be at a premium, he would gain an advantage and status which he would never lose'.[8] He urged the Irish Hierarchy to identify candidates to enrol in a specialised course in television broadcasting at the School of Radio and Television in New York City. If an Irish priest completed the intensive course in New York, Flaherty promised that he would personally see to it that the cleric would have an opportunity to work at the Boston Catholic Studio and 'guarantee his ability to prepare and direct T.V. programmes'.[9]

Thomas Fehily also contacted Agnellus Andrew, whom he had met in Dublin when the BBC Deputy Head of Religious Broadcasting was advising the hierarchy. Andrew agreed whole-heartedly with the advice of the American and urged the Irish bishops to seize the initiative, recommending an additional course that was being offered by ABC, one of the independent broadcasting companies in Manchester. The course was specifically designed for clergy interested in religious broadcasting and included Anglicans, Catholics, and what Andrew described as 'Free Churchmen', offering a rigorous course in religious programming. Andrew volunteered to help the hierarchy place priests in additional courses run by his employer, the BBC, and in classes he ran as the Director of the Catholic Communications Centre in London.

The Catholic Communications Centre was situated in Hatch End, on the outskirts of London in a rambling old house that became a meeting place and school for Catholics and non-Catholics alike interested in religious broadcasting. The centre was established with the financial support of Cardinal Griffin and the English Catholic Church; it became the centre for Catholic broadcasting in the UK. Andrew received the support of the English hierarchy by successfully arguing that it was imperative the Catholic Church possess 'a well equipped church sponsored centre where people interested and involved in religious broadcasting could meet, and where [a] substantive training course in radio and television could be organised'.[10]

With the help of Andrew a place was secured for an Irish priest to train at the course offered by ABC in Manchester. On the advice of Canon Cathal McCarthy, the Dean of Holy Cross College, the diocesan seminary in Dublin and the archbishop's adviser on broadcasting, Joseph Dunn's name was submitted to the Archbishop of Dublin. McCarthy knew the young Dublin priest had an interest in broadcasting, having made mock radio programmes in religious classes he taught in vocational schools in the city. McQuaid approved Dunn's participation in the course, setting in train a remarkable career in television. Joseph Dunn was an intellectually gifted young man who grew up in Sandymount, the product of a Dublin middle-class family that owned a well-known fish business in the heart of Dublin.[11] Although educated by the Jesuits, when Dunn decided to become a priest he recalled that as a boy he 'didn't like Jesuits' and did not want to work as a teacher. Pierce Perkins, a priest from his own parish who regularly visited the family in their Sandymount home, and Bishop Dunne, whom he described as 'wise, urbane and quite possibly holy', influenced Dunn's decision to become a Catholic priest.[12]

Joseph Dunn enjoyed his experience in England and became a close friend and great admirer of Agnellus Andrew. He described the Catholic Radio Centre in London fondly, capturing the sense of community that developed there: 'Hatch End became the ashram, and Agnellus the guru of Catholic Broadcasting in the English speaking world, while the relationship between the churches and the BBC became the model which the Irish Hierarchy were anxious to see established.'[13] Dunn remembered the house as a comfortable ecumenical Mecca for those interested in religious broadcasting where 'one could find oneself sitting down to dinner beside a clerical student from Sierra Leone, or an American media executive, or the Director General of the BBC'.[14] Over the years Dunn returned to Hatch End on a number of occasions, rubbing shoulders with Hugh Carlton Greene and Charles Curran, both of whom served as BBC Directors-General. Other guests he encountered there included Grace Windham-Goldie, head of BBC current affairs programming, who developed the influential *Panorama* programme and a host of directors, managers and programme-makers in British and American television.

When he completed the courses in Manchester and Hatch End, Dunn sent the first of many detailed reports to Archbishop John Charles McQuaid, explaining that his time in England had proved an invaluable experience. He carefully described the course, detailing how much he enjoyed being immersed in television while working in studios and meeting with experts in the field of broadcasting: 'Thinking and talking about television everyday with other priests helped everyone to clarify his own ideas in its potentialities and limitations.'[15] His experience led him to believe that there were tremendous possibilities for the use of television by the Church in Ireland. He told McQuaid, 'English Catholics are naturally conscious of being a minority group, conscious too of the many "uncommitted millions", most of whom are kept far from the Church by inbred prejudices which must be removed before conversion becomes a possibility. Not having to face such problems, we have a far greater opportunity of presenting really Catholic programmes and imparting solid Catholic teaching.'[16]

McQuaid liked to delegate projects to clerics he trusted and regarded as capable and energetic, and quickly decided that Dunn was the ideal candidate to groom for a television portfolio. He accepted Agnellus Andrew's suggestion that Dunn take additional courses that the BBC was offering and the advice from Boston concerning the Academy of Broadcasting Arts in New York City. At the urging of McQuaid, inquiries were made about sending Dunn and another priest, Desmond Forristal, to enrol in courses in both Britain and the United States. Enrolling on the BBC course proved problematic as students had to be nominated by a national radio or television service and at this juncture McQuaid did not want to approach Radio Éireann. While this proved a short-term obstacle, enrolling priests in the American courses was quite simple. Dublin's archbishop financed the travel and education that Dunn and Forristal received in New York, regarding the money spent as a wise investment. McQuaid wrote to Cardinal Spellman in New York to advise him of the priests' arrival and offering their services in the New York Diocese.[17]

While in New York Dunne again sent regular reports to McQuaid, carefully describing the courses he and Forristal were taking as practical, maintaining that they were both gaining critical experience in all matters of television. Dunn was initially terrified of the archbishop, recalling how when he was first called to the archbishop's house the summons was enough to 'induce cardiac arrest'.[18] But the young Dublin priest skilfully developed a relationship with McQuaid, earning the archbishop's trust and confidence. The correspondence between Dunn and McQuaid reveals an intellectually engaged young priest immersing himself in the study of television and writing enthusiastically to a supportive, if laconic, archbishop. It also illustrates that Dunn was politically savvy, his letters containing the deference McQuaid expected, as he repeatedly acknowledged the generosity, wisdom and foresight of his superior. Once the course was over, Dunn requested additional time to stay in New York to observe rehearsals and to visit film studios at the American network, CBS. McQuaid agreed and encouraged the young priest to pursue his interests.

When the two young men returned to Dublin they presented an extended report to the archbishop, explaining the courses they had taken and addressing developments in American television. Living and studying in America profoundly influenced the careers of both men as well as the direction of broadcasting in Ireland at a critical juncture in the development of an Irish mass media culture. The courses in New York were taught by practitioners working in the field and, by the time the two Dublin priests were finished, they had produced programmes and worked as directors, assistant directors, switchers, audio controllers, floor managers, boom microphone operators, and cameramen. Importantly, they made friends and socialised with a diverse group of professionals from varied ethnic and religious backgrounds, an experience that would have been impossible to replicate in 1959 Ireland. Both men reported to McQuaid that studying in New York had been invaluable, that the instructors had been highly skilled and provided 'a very good knowledge of television techniques'.[19]

The report included observations concerning many aspects of television broadcasting in the US. Dunn explained that Catholic religious broadcasting had been delegated by the American bishops to the National Council of Catholic Men (NCCM), an organisation that was responsible for producing both television and radio programmes. The NCCM worked under the supervision of the Pontifical Commission for Radio and Television and had an ecclesiastical censor. Although the American Hierarchy made occasional suggestions for programmes, the organisation, headed by two men based in New York, was left on its own. The organisation was financed by a subvention from the American Bishops and by donations.

Dunn pointed out that the American religious programmes ran on commercial and public service networks and that the Federal Communication Commission (FCC) expected each licensee to provide airtime for programmes that were of service to the public. These broadcasts addressed 'civil defence, social problems, education, politics and religion'.[20] He also explained that the FCC was responsible for ensuring that nothing indecent, obscene or deceptive would be aired and that a violation could result in a fine or the revocation of a broadcasting licence. Dunn reported that while in the United States both he and Forrestal watched as much religious television as possible, but that they also saw a good deal of non-religious material, remarking, 'Much of it was trite and commercial but there was very little that was morally objectionable. In this respect U.S. television seems to be superior to British'.[21]

When the course in New York was finished Dunn travelled to Boston where he spent a week meeting with Monsignor Flaherty observing the Boston studio and visiting the local commercial and public service affiliates. He described in detail the equipment needed to operate the studio of the Boston Archdiocese outlining both capital and operational costs. While Dunn was in Boston Desmond Forristal travelled to the University of Notre Dame to observe how the university ran their station, WNDU. He reported that WNDU was a small commercial affiliate of the NBC network and only produced two hours of very simple material each day. He explained that the station operated in almost complete independence from the university administration but still provided courses for undergraduates in television production. Forristal also reported that WNDU was required to abide by FCC regulations and did not produce much Catholic programming, pointing out that the week he was in South Bend the five minutes allocated for religious broadcasting had been taken up by a talk by a Protestant minister.[22]

The report itself provided valuable information for the archbishop as it illustrated that religious broadcasting could function quite well in a commercial setting. McQuaid carefully read the report submitted by Dunn and Forristal and believed his investment in the two priests produced satisfactory results. His response, though concise, indicates that he valued the work of both men and the way that they had undertaken it. He told the priests the report was helpful: 'What I sought. Clear, well-ordered, complete.'[23]

As has been noted, McQuaid's ultimate goal was to secure a formal position for Joseph Dunn in the nascent Irish television

11   Father Joe Dunn and colleagues on a training course (he was giving the course).

service. He wanted Dunn appointed the station's religious adviser, expecting he would report directly to him. While the archbishop's efforts were delayed by a wary director-general and were ultimately unsuccessful, he encouraged the creative interests of Dunn, recognising his talent, energy and drive. The young Dublin priest in turn remained very careful in dealing with the archbishop, always sending him detailed reports that were informative, illustrating that he was interested in taking what he had learned in the classrooms and studios of England and the USA and making something of it. After returning from the USA he was appointed chaplain at University College Dublin, a position that enabled him to experiment with filmmaking during holiday breaks and in the summer. He quickly illustrated a knack for filmmaking on a shoestring budget, making it clear he wanted to produce additional films and offer critical and informed advice to his superiors.

The first film Dunn and Desmond Forristal made was *La le Bride*, an Irish language film about Saint Bridget's Day, the first day of spring. The National Film Institute of Ireland recognised it as the most outstanding Irish language film in 1960.[24] The following year he wrote to McQuaid indicating that '[a] few fellow priests, Father Forristal and myself included, have dabbled in a little film making in recent months. We felt some practical knowledge of the problems involved might be of value.'[25] Dunn explained that both he and another priest with an interest in film, Donald Flavin, had shown one of their short films to a representative of Gevaert, a Belgian company that manufactured cameras and other products associated with filmmaking. The company invited Dunn and Flavin to Antwerp to attend a twelve-day course that would allow them to use film stock, which could be processed immediately, enabling the priests to learn 'the complicated mechanics of film making in a short period'.[26] Again McQuaid granted permission for Dunn to take the course in Antwerp believing it made sense to encourage and invest in the young dynamic priest. Although Dunn had gained an education in television production and had a basic understanding of what it took to make television programmes, filmmaking was another matter. Dunn became interested in making 35 mm films knowing that the television service scheduled to go on the air later that year could provide an outlet for his work.

In April 1961 Dunn submitted a carefully crafted, five-page proposal to McQuaid addressing the challenges that television would present for the Catholic Church in Ireland. He argued that because Telefís Éireann was being established as a commercial enterprise, the Church had to be proactive and adopt a strategy for developing innovative religious programming that could exploit the medium for religious purposes. He argued that religious broadcasting in Ireland would quickly be confronted with a number of problems. Because television would be commercial, it had to be accepted that religious broadcasts would take place during 'valley periods' that were not popular with viewers. This was a reality that he maintained had to be accepted. He told the archbishop that commercial television's primary function was to generate revenue and that finding and holding an audience and keeping it from changing stations was critical. Dunn pointed out that this was 'a matter of hard cash because advertising rates depend on the estimated number of viewers'.[27]

He reported to the archbishop that most people looked at television for entertainment and that religious programmes would struggle to find an audience. Dunn reported that in the United Kingdom surveys had concluded that three-quarters of all viewers were tuned into ITV programmes at any given moment, the commercial alternative to the more cerebral BBC. He also maintained that broadcasters had to consider the socio-economic demographic of viewers, maintaining that 'By far the majority and by far the most persistent of viewers are those whose education ceased at the primary level.'[28] In these circumstances he believed it imperative that religious broadcasting in Ireland develop a programme format that would be innovative and flexible, not simply didactic. He told the archbishop that Catholic programmes should follow a 'magazine format', ironically pointing to more 'high brow' BBC programmes including *Tonight*, *Panorama* and *Monitor* as the best examples of this type of television.

Dunn believed such a format would work in an Irish religious context, explaining that the magazine format, if topical, would have something for everybody. He regarded this point as critical, pointing out that '[a]ny subject can in fact be made topical with a little ingenuity'.[29] While in the USA, Dunn and Forrestal had viewed a number of religious programmes and found that some of the most important, such as *The Catholic Hour*, were well produced and informative but ultimately dull and tedious. Rather than try to force religious or educational programmes upon an indifferent audience, Dunn felt it important to show a bit of creativity. 'To get viewers to watch items with really serious content, it may be necessary to sugar the pill, i.e. to introduce items of quasi-religious or humorous nature. This could be done with brief items in a magazine programme, but hardly in another format.'[30] He understood that television audiences liked to see familiar faces that were both charismatic and articulate, noting that 'the personality cult is very important in TV'.[31] Convinced a magazine format containing a number of short segments would be a safe alternative to a longer formal programme, Dunn concluded, 'Not every item in the magazine can be a dud.'[32]

McQuaid was told that the problems associated with developing a magazine-type program were manifold. Budgets would be a major factor, as production costs were very high. Moreover, the work was labour intensive and technicians, if they could be found, were expensive, commanding as much as $15 per hour in the United States. Dunn pointed out that the new American director-general of Telefís Éireann, Edward Roth, had made it clear that home-produced material would be limited not only due to the costs involved, but also because there were few trained technicians available in Ireland. Dunn knew Telefís Éireann would be under tremendous pressure to produce home-made material but could not dedicate limited resources to produce religious programmes, features that Dunn pointed out would be expensive to produce and shown at unpopular off-peak hours.

In these circumstances he argued that, at best, religious programme-makers would have limited access to the facilities 'unless there was some way for the Church authorities to provide their own'.[33] He carefully and logically built a case that argued for the establishment of a film unit, staffed by priests, to develop programmes for the new television service, concluding, '[m]any people would not give such a project much chance of succeeding. Even so I respectfully suggest that it might be worth a trial … because the stakes are high, and worth a gamble, even at long odds.'[34] McQuaid read the proposal closely, underlining sections and making marginal notes. He found Dunn's argument convincing, and offered qualified encouragement, telling him to 'try a magazine format as an experiment' and responding to the proposal of a film unit being made up of priests, in much the same manner by telling him to 'form it by way of experiment'.[35]

Dunn's proposal soon bore fruit. In the summer of 1961 he was able to complete a number of short films that were screened for the archbishop in the autumn, films that made their way onto television in January 1962. Telefís Éireann featured Dunn's work in its first month of operation to critical acclaim. The programme was titled *Radharc* and quickly found an audience that enjoyed the work of Dunn and his fellow priests. True to form, the magazine format featured three short films described by the press as being presented by a 'slim, dark haired young priest'.[36] The first broadcast featured three segments addressing a Croagh Patrick Pilgrimage, a story of a penal era Mass Rock in Donegal, and the life of an urban parish in the heart of Dublin. The film on the urban parish was a unique exploration of life in working-class Dublin. A modest Dunn echoed the words of the archbishop when he cagily explained to the press that the programme was 'an experiment'. The *Irish Press* praised the effort as 'outstandingly successful. Fr Dunn and his colleagues seem to ... have hit on a worthwhile formula in these film-magazine type of programmes. In a Catholic country where religious broadcasting is to a certain extent bound to be preaching to the converted their naturalistic presentation of aspects of Catholic life is a sensible approach.'[37]

In 1962 and throughout 1963 Dunn's *Radharc* experiment enjoyed critical success much to the delight of Ireland's bishops (and the Catholic Television Interim Committee). At this time McQuaid was engaged in a battle with the Radio Éireann Authority to get Dunn appointed as a member of the Telefís Éireann staff. While McQuaid was in Rome attending the Vatican Council and struggling and ultimately failing to get Dunn appointed to this paid position, Dunn was demonstrating his talents as a producer and director. Archbishop Morris collected a compilation of reviews, which he sent to McQuaid in Rome, extolling the work of *Radharc*.[38] Reviews from the *Evening Mail, Evening Herald, Irish Independent, Irish Times* and *Sunday Independent* all praised the work of the *Radharc* team, arguing that it had produced some of the best material yet screened by Telefís Éireann.[39] It is important to point out that Joseph Dunn did not work alone but was assisted by a team of able priests, including Desmond Forristal, Peter Lemass and later Dermod McCarthy. All played a critical role, volunteering their time to help write, present and produce programmes. Later these men were responsible for producing some of the best and most innovative *Radharc* programmes.

In 1963 *Radharc* beat out the popular *The Late Late Show* and an early current affairs undertaking, *Broadsheet,* to receive the Jacobs Award for most enterprising programme. Shortly afterwards Dunn wrote to McQuaid, asking to meet with him to talk about the future of the *Radharc* film unit. At this juncture the status of the programme, begun as an experiment, was not financially secure. Dunn was anxious to try to exploit the popularity of the programme, which he pointed out to the archbishop had an audience of over four hundred thousand viewers. Dunn enjoyed making programmes and wanted *Radharc* to have the financial and organisational stability he thought it deserved. Ever the politician, Dunn explained, 'I would like to tell your Grace all that we have learned over the past two years, and discuss the possibility of continuing the work, should your grace so decide.'[40] In a clever gesture of gratitude, he told the archbishop that he wanted to present him with the Jacobs trophy that *Radharc* had won.

Prior to meeting McQuaid, Dunn forwarded a comprehensive proposal requesting formal support for *Radharc* and explaining the state of Irish broadcasting. Dunn was again deferential and diplomatic but knew he was approaching McQuaid from a position of strength. He underscored the fact that the fate of the *Radharc* project was in the hands of the archbishop: 'It would not be fair to think that we value this work too highly. We believe that the primary work of a priest is pastoral work'.[41] He required McQuaid's continued support to make films but to do this he needed access to the other priests that had been part of the production team. These men had helped Dunn in their spare time and used their vacation to contribute to *Radharc*. For the programme to continue, men such as Desmond Forristal would have to be released from their pastoral responsibilities to work on *Radharc* projects. In case the archbishop thought that Dunn and his associates were getting too self-focused, Dunn also addressed the alleged 'glamour' of the work. He reported that while the work from the outside might seem alluring, 'we have done enough of it now to see some of the glamour wear off, and to appreciate the tedious, exacting, worrying, frustrating, aspects of the work as well'.[42] Dunn knew unless he received continued support from McQuaid the enterprise would not be viable, explaining 'we believe that we have proved something – that religious television can be good and popular. That is enough to have made the experiment worthwhile'.[43]

Although the tone of the report may have been obsequious, it was also cleverly pitched to what Dunn perceived were the needs of the Church and the interests of the archbishop. He argued carefully, though forcefully, for the continued support of a production unit for television, maintaining that educational television was a significant trend that would have an impact in schools and universities. Because the Catholic Church had such an important interest in education he argued that keeping his film unit together was important for the future. He pointed out that in other countries including France, Germany and the UK, Catholic television was supported by the Church and was making important religious programmes for television and for distribution to schools and parishes.

Dunn understood that television was becoming a powerful force in society and argued that the Church had to appreciate its importance. Keeping a production crew intact would enable the Church to get off the sidelines and become fully engaged with the medium, offering 'opportunities for doing a good public relations job for the Church and the clergy'.[44] Dunn underscored the fact that having a team of priests developing religious programmes enabled clergy to shape all of *Radharc*'s work, advising the archbishop that this was tremendously important. He maintained that in *Radharc* clergy were involved at every stage of the production process – from choosing themes to writing scripts to 'interviewing, editing, and even in the choice of pictures photographed'.[45] This was an obvious but critical point that Dunn was keen to emphasise, stressing that this sort of control would not be possible under any other circumstances.

One of the many attributes of early *Radharc* programmes was its ability to tap into an important network of local clergy throughout the country. This enabled Dunn and his associates to gain access to local knowledge through local people who trusted them. Dunn pointed out that many of the critics had singled out this quality of the programmes for praise, telling the archbishop 'the ease and frankness of ordinary people on our programmes has been called its most significant characteristic'.[46] Once again emphasising access to an estimated four hundred thousand viewers, Dunne argued that there was tremendous potential to build on its successes.

Dunn cleverly pointed out that *Radharc* was in an advantageous position, having succeeded in getting a foothold inside Telefís Éireann. He understood quite clearly the difficulty and frustration

McQuaid needs Raharc to maintain relationships w/ RTE – Dunn

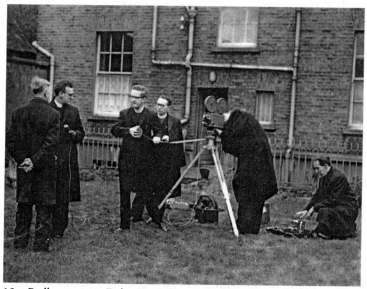

12   Radharc priests Father Peter Lemass (holding the microphone about
to do an interview), Father Billy Fitzgerald (with measuring tape),
unidentified Priest, Father Joe Dunn (crouching behind camera), and
Father Des Forrestal (with the sound gear).

McQuaid had encountered with the Radio Éireann Authority and
carefully exploited this. He knew that it would prove impossible
to regain the type of access that he enjoyed, explaining 'we had
programmes ready at the beginning when T.E. were desperate for
material'.[47] Dunn informed the archbishop that the Controller of
Programmes, Michael Barry, who had recently left Telefís Éireann,
had been a critical ally when the broadcasting service was getting
off the ground. He quoted Father Agnellus Andrew, who praised
Barry '[a]s a man with almost too much reverence for the priest-
hood', pointing out that the 'same personal interest could hardly
be expected ... of the present holder of that office'.[48] When the
archbishop read this part of the report he carefully made reference
to the new controller, writing in the margins, 'Mr. Rugheimer a
Lutheran Swede.'[49]

Dunn was convinced that *Radharc* was in a strong position and
that it would be a serious mistake to walk away from the very

[handwritten annotation: Appealing to his desire for power/control]

favourable circumstances that had developed. He pointed out that
he and his team had full control over its material and that Telefís
Éireann would only view programmes prior to broadcast to screen
for any possible legal complications. 'The fact is that absolute
control is at present being given to a group of clerics independent
of T.E. with respect to a significant part of religious programming.
I think this would have been very difficult to obtain: in fact it just
happened without anybody thinking much about it.'[50] He mentioned that a considerable financial investment had already been
made as another reason that the project should continue.[51]

The concluding arguments summed up quite clearly the strong
position that *Radharc* was in. Dunn was careful to make the case
that it was McQuaid who retained the real power and that it was
he who was operating from a position of strength. He argued that
the television critics had made it clear that they valued the work of
Radharc and 'the Jacob's award will strengthen our hand vis-à-vis
T.E'.[52] He was certainly correct in stating that the service was under
mounting pressure to provide more home-produced material and
that *Radharc* programmes were 'pure gain' for the service. Dunn
understood the commercial implications of a popular programme
and the need of the station to maintain high audience numbers.
He believed that *Radharc* had the largest audience of any broadly
defined public service programme beyond news and sports and
that the director-general and the Radio Éireann Authority would
loathe losing such a profitable, home-produced programme.

He concluded by suggesting that it was his impression that
Telefís Éireann would 'like to be accommodating with us in the
hope that it might please Your Grace. This may not be a very
worthy motive on their part; however, if your Grace should wish
to take advantage of the fact, there seems no reason for not doing
so.'[53] Moreover, the programmes developed by Dunn and his associates were not dry, tedious lectures on some aspect of Catholic
theology but innovative programmes that caught the attention
and engaged the imagination of the viewing public. Put simply,
Radharc satisfied a number of concerns for an Authority under
intense pressure to feature first-rate indigenous programmes. The
programmes could be broadcast in prime time, attracting advertising revenue. The fact that it was the product of an independent

contractor took pressure off the limited resources of the new station. Importantly, because it was classified as religious programming it had the added advantage of enabling Telefís Éireann to mollify ecclesiastical critics.

Dunn was a shrewd operator and knew how to play to the interests of both Dublin's demanding archbishop and senior officials in Telefís Éireann. McQuaid had long felt ignored and later outmanoeuvred by the Chairman of the Radio Éireann Authority Eamonn Andrews and Director-General Edward Roth and his successor, Kevin McCourt. In *Radharc* McQuaid knew he had a foothold inside Telefís Éireann, one that he did not want to give up. When he met with Dunn to discuss the future of *Radharc* he proved sympathetic to the argument put forward by the young filmmaker. He understood that Dunn wanted to continue to make films and needed to have both Fr Desmond Forrestal and Fr Peter Lemass work with him if the project was to continue. McQuaid told Dunn to talk to the new director-general to ascertain what the broadcaster was willing to pay for *Radharc* productions. The notes the archbishop kept of this meeting explain in no uncertain terms that he wanted it understood by all parties where the authority for the initiative lay. 'I stressed that they are a Dublin unit independent of T.E. or ... [Catholic] Advisory Committee or Father Dodd, new director: subject to me and in religious matters to my liaison officer Canon McCarthy.'[54] McQuaid encouraged Dunn and his work, telling him 'I am very grateful for your clear explanation of *Radharc* and its needs. You just keep on pursuing the way you have been following so well.'[55] Before leaving the meeting the ever-resourceful Dunn was able to convince the archbishop to write a £500 cheque for an editing machine.

Dunn followed the archbishop's advice and entered into negotiations with Director-General Kevin McCourt and later the Controller of Programmes Gunnar Rugheimer. He reported to McQuaid that the terms he reached were generous and that Telefís Éireann had more than doubled their previous offer for the programmes. One sticking point remained the relationship between *Radharc* and the religious adviser that the Broadcasting Authority had hired, Romuald Dodd O.P. Dunn was under strict instructions by McQuaid to avoid him at all costs, and Dunn took these instructions seriously.[56] Dunn reported to the archbishop that he had met with Dodd and spoke to him 'nicely but quite bluntly … the upshot is that Mr. Rugheimer has promised to write to me directly. This seems to set the correct precedent'.[57] McQuaid was pleased, describing the news as 'good' and noting that Dunn had 'succeeded in following my council to stand clear apart of Father Dodd O.P. You are not "religious programmes" and you are subject directly to me in your work.'[58]

The new director-general of Telefís Éireann, Kevin McCourt, met with Dunn and informally agreed to terms that required Radharc to deliver eight programmes over the course of the year. Radharc would be paid £250 per episode, and provision was made for additional programmes to be purchased if acceptable to Telefís Éireann.[59] Before the agreement could be formalised, trouble developed when McQuaid hesitated to release the priests Dunn needed for his work. This caused a certain amount of drift and anxiety that was halted when Kevin McCourt intervened and contacted McQuaid directly, requesting that he release Fathers Forristal and Fitzgerald from their pastoral duties so they could work on Radharc. Dunn had made it clear to the director-general that without a commitment from Forristal and Fitzgerald the verbal agreement could not be formalised as a written contract.

Dunn engaged in a degree of brinksmanship, telling McCourt that without Forristal and Fitzgerald the experiment was over, and Radharc would falter. This forced McCourt's hand and he contacted the archbishop directly, telling him that Radharc was 'inoperable' and that the agreement he had reached with Dunn was in danger of collapsing. He told McQuaid that he wanted to give Radharc 'every encouragement and opportunity' but that the agreement was void unless the priests were made available.[60] McCourt asked the archbishop 'to consider most sympathetically if these two priests could not be freed to work as soon as possible with Father Dunn in an exercise which has an appreciable contribution to make to Irish Television'.[61] McQuaid agreed to release the two priests, delighted that a deferential McCourt had made a point of calling to thank him for releasing the priests, noting, '[h]e was very pleased, wanted at all costs to keep this group together and will see Father Dunn to arrange matters'.[62]

McQuaid was delighted at the turn of events and enjoyed the fact that the director-general was now coming to him to plead for help. The change in the relationship between McQuaid and the station could not be more striking. It had been just a short time earlier that an angry McQuaid complained bitterly that he had been betrayed by McCourt and the Authority over its decision to appoint Fr Dodd O.P., not his personal choice, Joseph Dunn, as Religious Adviser. This is not to say that the relationship between the Hierarchy and Telefís Éireann prospered from this point forward. However, *Radharc* under the careful guidance of the ever-diplomatic Joseph Dunn, emerged as a programme that everybody, broadcaster and bishop alike, not only wanted but needed. Dunn kept Telefís Éireann at a distance, resisting later efforts to bring the programme formally into the national television service. The income derived from selling programmes to Telefís Éireann enabled Dunn and his associates to maintain its distance from the archbishop, and Dunn quietly established *Radharc* as Ireland's first independent television production company.

That summer *Radharc* filmed eight programmes and by December four had been delivered to Telefís Éireann while the others were in production. Many of the early films were pioneering documentaries about contemporary Ireland and some of the social problems that confronted Irish society. They included a segment on urban destitution, *Down and Out in Dublin*; a feature on the plight of young emigrants arriving in London, *Meeting the Irish Trains at Euston Station*; and films set in rural Ireland that addressed the morality of smuggling livestock across the border, and another about fairs in rural Ireland titled *Is there an Honest Man at an Irish Fair?* One of the earlier films considered the involvement of the clergy in the Rebellion of 1798, *Father John Murphy of Boulavogue*. Other *Radharc* programmes proved to be groundbreaking, such as *The Young Offender* (1963), which brought cameras inside a prison for the first time. This particular segment featured a day in the life of young boys at St Patrick's institution, exposing the difficult lives of the young inmates. Watching the programme more than forty years later the viewer can't help but feel somewhat uncomfortable as deferential young boys respond to awkward questioning by priests who may have had the best of intentions in highlighting the grim regime of institutional life behind the wall of St Patrick's. A suspicious Minister for Justice and future Taoiseach Charles Haughey agreed to be interviewed for the programme only *after* viewing the finished product. A film about life in the seminary that many of these priests attended provided a glimpse of life at Clonliffe College in 1965.

Later, a programme about alleged teenage prostitution in Cork caused outrage and controversy because many believed the film was less than convincing. The use of an invasive hidden camera in the film raised questions about ethics in making contemporary documentary film, questions that would cause more concern and controversy at the end of the decade when a current affairs crew used these same techniques. The Catholic Church did not criticise the programme, but an avalanche of letters from angry citizens of Cork barraged RTÉ and appeared in the press accusing *Radharc* of sensational programming that slandered the city.

Radharc was highly mobile, travelling around Ireland making popular programmes about local events outside metropolitan Dublin. The priests knew they could count on a network of parishes around the country and, using the magazine format, offered programmes that considered current affairs in Kerry, Clare, Kilkenny, Armagh, Donegal, Galway and Mayo. Dunn and his crew were one of the few television teams to travel to Northern Ireland in 1964 to film a programme about life in the province. Inevitably the film addressed contentious issues including gerrymandering and institutionalised discrimination in Derry. This was one of the very few television programmes made by Irish or British broadcasters about Northern Ireland before the outbreak of 'the Troubles' in 1969. Gunner Rugheimer refused to screen the programme and it is unclear if the Lemass Government stepped in to prevent it from being broadcast. The feature was made while Lemass and his counterpart Terence O'Neill were working to improve North–South relations and RTÉ did not want to complicate government policy. Dunn later explained: 'We were disappointed but anxious at the same time to be seen to accept the Contoller's authority in such matters without question.'[63] Lance Pettitt in his book about Irish film and television representation points out the programme was 'prescient because it identified the key issues in the civil rights

13 (Left to right, foreground) Fathers Billy Fitzgerald, Joe Dunn, Peter Lemass and Des Forristal (all with their backs to camera) filming in Kenya 1966.

campain that followed'.[64]

By 1970 John Charles McQuaid had become disillusioned with *Radharc* and its programmes. Once Joseph Dunn became director of the Catholic Communications Centre, Desmond Forristal became director of *Radharc* and Dermod McCarthy, who had worked with *Radharc* since 1965, took up a prominent role directing and producing programmes. According to McCarthy one particular feature, *Eggs in the Hay*, broadcast in 1969, about relics of pagan superstition, upset McQuaid and led to his abrupt transfer to the small, remote village of Athy in County Kildare.[65] The programme, a clever and irreverent commentary on the close relationship between superstition and religion annoyed the archbishop who decided to punish McCarthty by expelling him from *Radharc* and banishing him to a small rural parish. Desmond Forristal wrote to McQuaid asking that he reconsider the transfer, arguing that the programmes produced by *Radharc* had become 'an integral part of the work of the Dublin diocese' that

239

14   Radharc in Kenya, 1966, filming for a programme on missionary
     work.

had reflected 'credit on our diocese both at home and abroad'.[66]
McQuaid refused Forristal's request stating McCarthy 'must cease
to work for Radharc'.[67] He told Forristal, 'I regret that I cannot
see how Radharc has "become part of the diocesan apostolate",
or "an integral part of the work of the Dublin diocese," I can see
that a success achieved in producing films here, and especially
abroad, can in its own way, reflect credit on the diocese, for the
reasons only that Dublin priests produce them.'[68] Later when
questioning a request for support for an overdraft at a local bank
he complained to Forristal, that he was 'not at all clear about the

nature of *Radharc*, its financial position and its responsibility to the Archbishop.'[69]

Dermod McCarthy returned to *Radharc* from Kildare in 1972 after McQuaid had left his position as archbishop and was replaced by Dermot Ryan. He made a number of innovative films over the following decade and did not experience any interference from Archbishop Ryan. Among the provocative programmes he made were two that questioned why the Irish Church was slow to institute the reforms of Vatican II. *Are Nuns Human?* and *Convent Walls are Falling Down*, both made in 1971, were filmed inside the convent walls of the Presentation Sisters and the Sisters of Mercy. McCarthy remembers that he had heard stories of a young nun who was refused permission to attend the funeral of her father. When he started to ask awkward questions, some older nuns he knew told him to back off while younger members asked that he do more to address their plight. At the time enormous changes were taking place in women's religious orders, especially in the way that nuns wanted to be perceived. The reforms did not come without opposition from some Church authorities and these programmes opened a window into these secretive institutions enabling viewers to better understand the challenges of convent life.

McCarthy became the Religious Adviser for RTÉ after leaving *Radharc* and when interviewed in his Donnybrook office just prior to his retirement in 2007 still felt strongly that Dunn should have challenged the archbishop when he was banished to Athy in 1970 as punishment for him producing a programme the archbishop found objectionable. Given this experience, he takes issue with Dunn's contention that the archbishop never interfered with *Radharc*.[70] According to McCarthy, Dunn was 'playing it safe' and did not stand up to the archbishop, fearing that if he did the programme would be shut down.[71]

Radharc excelled when the team began to travel outside Ireland, exploiting a deep network of Irish missionaries in Africa, Asia, South America and Latin America. The team travelled to Nigeria, Kenya, El Salvador, Chile, Nicaragua, Vietnam, Haiti, Burma and the Philippines, addressing the challenges that confronted these missionaries and the people they served. Not surprisingly these films addressed the plight of the poor and dispossessed and considered issues such as poverty, corruption and political violence. Programmes highlighted the work of Oscar Romero in El Salvador, the role of the Church in revolutionary Nicaragua, the horrors of the civil war in Guatemala, and the challenges of land reform in the Philippines. By the mid-1980s, *Radharc's* priests had been deeply influenced by liberation theology and were broadcasting programmes highly critical of American-backed dictatorships in the developing world.

Informed, well-written, provocative programmes enabled Irish viewers an alternative to the steady diet of British and American reports produced by BBC, ITN and American networks either re-broadcast on RTÉ or picked up from UK-based transmitters. The international dimension of these programmes played a critical role in widening the horizons of Irish viewers, exposing them to issues and events that Telefís Éireann could not afford to address. The series helped Irish society become aware of complex political and social problems both at home and abroad. Many of the programmes were purchased by British and European networks as well as PBS in the US. By the time *Radharc* ceased production it had made 420 films addressing issues of faith, peace and justice both at home and abroad. *Radharc* was a key part of the cultural shift that helped transform Ireland in the 1960s. It is ironic that John Charles McQuaid, long considered a reactionary bully by his enemies, an archbishop who intimidated many and was deeply uncomfortable with modernity, was responsible for *Radharc* and therefore a key, if unwitting, agent in the transformation of Ireland.

Notes

1 *Radharc* was the name of the documentary television series developed by Joseph Dunn, a Dublin Diocesan priest; translated from Irish it would be 'view', or 'vision'. The Radharc Trust maintains a website (www.radharcfilms.com) where many of the films made by the film company can be purchased.

2 Every bishop is assigned a diocese. Bishops that are not the 'ordinary' of a diocese, are assigned a 'titular see', which are historical dioceses that are no longer in existence. The ordinaries of jurisdictions below

the class of diocese (such as vicariates) are also often assigned titular sees. Andrew was appointed titular bishop in February 1980 and held the appointment until his death in January 1987.

3   See Robert Savage, *Irish Television: The Political and Social Origins* (Cork University Press, Cork, 1996), 109–11. The article 'Television and Religion' appeared in the *Irish Ecclesiastical Record*, 83 (1955), 15–17.

4   Ibid.

5   Ibid., quoted in Savage, *Irish Television*, 110.

6   Ibid.

7   DDA, McQuaid Papers, AB8/B/XXVI/a (4), Thomas Fehily to Revd L. Martin, secretary to the Archbishop of Dublin, May 6, 1959.

8   Ibid.

9   Ibid.

10   Joseph Dunn, *No Vipers in the Vatican* (Columba Press, Dublin, 1996), 265.

11   In fact, the Dunn shop located on Westmoreland Row features in James Joyce's *Portrait of an Artist as a Young Man*.

12   Joseph Dunn, *No Lions in the Hierarchy* (Columba Press, Dublin, 1994), 12. Bishop Dunne was not related to Joseph Dunn.

13   Ibid.

14   Ibid., 263.

15   DDA McQuaid Papers, AB8/B/XXVI/a (4), Dunn to McQuaid, July 1, 1959, 7.

16   Ibid.

17   Ibid., McQuaid to Spellman, September 4, 1959. Spellman replied September 23, 1959, thanking McQuaid for offering the services of the two priests.

18   Joseph Dunn, *No Tigers in Africa* (Columba Press, Dublin, 1986), 1.

19   DDA McQuaid Papers, AB8/B/XXVI/a (4), report from Forristal and Dunn to McQuaid, January 22, 1960.

20   Ibid., 7.

21   Ibid., 8.

22   Ibid., supplemental report from Forristal to McQuaid, 13.

23   Ibid., note by McQuaid, January 25, 1960.

24   See Harvey O'Brien, *The Real Ireland: The Evolution of Ireland in Documentary Film* (Manchester University Press, Manchester, 2004), 159.

25   DDA, McQuaid Papers AB8/B/XXVI/a (5), Dunn to McQuaid, April 6, 1961.

26   Ibid., 2.

27   Ibid., *Some Problems for Religious TV in Ireland*, submitted by Joseph Dunn, April 7, 1961.

28   Ibid.
29   Ibid., 2.
30   Ibid.
31   Ibid.
32   Ibid.
33   Ibid., 3.
34   Ibid., 5.
35   Ibid., 2–3.
36   *Irish Press*, January 16, 1962, 9.
37   Ibid.
38   DDA, McQuaid Papers AB8/B/XXVI/a (5), Morris to McQuaid, March 30, 1963.
39   Ibid.
40   Ibid., Dunn to McQuaid, December 6, 1963.
41   Ibid., Dunn to McQuaid, December 9, 1963.
42   Ibid.
43   Ibid.
44   Ibid., Dunn's Memo: *Some Reasons for Continuing a Production Unit for TV.*
45   Ibid.
46   Ibid.
47   Ibid., 2.
48   Ibid., 3.
49   Ibid. Gunnar Rugheimer had replaced Barry as Controller of Programmes and quickly developed a reputation as a hardworking and somewhat difficult professional dedicated to developing serious current affairs programming.
50   Ibid.
51   Ibid. He estimated the amount at approximately £4,300.
52   Ibid.
53   Ibid.
54   Note by Archbishop McQuaid, December 10, 1963.
55   Ibid., McQuaid to Dunn, December 10, 1963; the archbishop suggested Dunn consider a programme about adult education in a remote part of the diocese and a feature on Clonliffe, the Dublin seminary.
56   See Dunn, *No Vipers*, 272.
57   DDA McQuaid Papers AB8/B/XXVI/a (6), Dunn to McQuaid, January 16, 1964.
58   Ibid., note written on the Dunn letter, January 17, 1964.
59   Ibid., contract memorandum, January 11, 1964.
60   Ibid., McCourt to McQuaid, May 21, 1964.
61   Ibid.
62   Ibid., notes written by McQuaid, May 28, 1964.

63 Dunn, *No Tigers in Africa,* 134.
64 See Lance Pettitt, *Screening Ireland: Film and Television Represntation* (Manchester University Press, Manchester, 2000), 84–5. The film was screened by RTÉ as part of a *Radharc* retrospective in 1989.
65 Author interview with Dermod McCarthy, June 18, 2007, Dublin.
66 DDA McQuaid Papers AB8/B/XXVI/a (8), Forristal to McQuaid, July 4, 1970.
67 Ibid., McQuaid to Forristall, July 7, 1970.
68 Ibid.
69 Ibid., McQuaid to Forristal, October 13, 1971.
70 Dunn, *No Tigers in Africa.* See Chapter 6, 'Life with J. C. McQuaid'; Dunn does not address McCarthy's banishment to Athy and indicates that the few examples of interference by the archbishop were inconsequential.
71 Author's interview with Dermod McCarthy, June 18, 2007, Dublin.

8

Finding a voice? The Irish language and Irish television

To get a sense of the unbridled passion that the state's language revival policy continued to generate in the 1960s one might consider an extraordinary incident that occurred at Dublin's Mansion House in the autumn of 1966. This involved the recently founded Language Freedom Movement (LFM), an organisation established in 1965 to oppose the state-sponsored Gaelic revival. One of the key aims of the LFM was reforming the state's school curriculum targeting compulsory Irish. The LFM believed that the state's emphasis on the Irish language disadvantaged Irish children by denying them access to subjects they believed were more important and practical. The organisation argued it was especially unfair and counter-productive to require students to pass Irish as part of their Leaving Certificate exam. At the time, students who failed Irish in their Leaving Certificate exam failed the entire exam.

The various groups dedicated to the revival of Irish were disturbed that the organisation had dedicated itself to abolish what they considered a cornerstone of the language revival.[1] The LFM booked Dublin's Mansion House, a venue steeped in symbolic importance for Irish nationalists, for a public debate to address the question, 'Can it be shown that replacement of the English language by Irish is for the common good?' Amid a large police presence of more than fifty uniformed officers and many plain-clothes detectives, more than two thousand people jammed into the hall. Many more were stranded outside, and it quickly became clear that most of the boisterous crowd were not members of the LFM but supporters of the Irish language. When the chairman rose to open the meeting, heckling erupted followed by the derisive waving of Union Jacks and singing of *God Save the Queen* mocking the LFM as anti-nationalist British stooges. In the jostling that ensued, a tricolour was forcibly removed from the stage by protesters while objects were hurled at the podium and a stink bomb set off.

As fistfights broke out, the future Cardinal Tomás Ó Fiaich asked that representatives of the Irish language organisations be allowed to speak. The request was denied and, when playwright John B. Keane was introduced as the first speaker, cheering and heckling once again disrupted the meeting. Amidst the ensuing mayhem, Dónall Ó Móráin, founding Director of Gael-Linn and member of the Broadcasting Authority, took the stage and appealed for calm.[2] 'We must have discussions here with all points of view represented. I don't care how anti-Irish any speaker on this platform is, I will defend his right to speak as long as the other spokesmen for those who represent my viewpoint are allowed an opinion.'[3] Although Ó Móráin's intervention may have avoided a full-scale riot, the fact that the opponents of the LFM had disrupted the meeting and demanded equal access to the podium at an event organised and paid for by the LFM suggests what Fergal Tobin describes in his iconic book, *The Best of Decades,* as 'a queer notion of the right to freedom of speech'.[4] The LFM repeated their demand that a national referendum be held on abolishing compulsory Irish in the schools, denying they were 'anti-Irish, pro-British, West Britons or shoneens'.[5] Press reports described the chaotic meeting coming to a farcical close. While the President of Sinn Féin appealed for 'unity to attain a "free and Gaelic Ireland," a group of men climbed onto the platform and pulled the microphone from his grasp. Blows were exchanged and the stage curtain was drawn closed. At one side a man was seen trying to set fire to the curtain.'[6]

These dramatic events spilled out across the pages of the national press and were covered extensively by the state's radio and television services; the current affairs programme *7 Days* devoted a broadcast to the meeting. The Mansion House mêlée suggests that the battle lines of these culture wars were simple, that they were contested by modernising reformers determined to liberate

Irish society from the tyranny of a narrow, dogmatic policy that was retarding the progress of the nation. A more accurate assessment would find that most supporters of the language were not wild-eyed zealots intent on 'ramming Irish down the neck' of the people but citizens motivated by a genuine love for a rich and complex language struggling for survival.[7] Many were alarmed at what they regarded as the arrogance of the LFM and were determined to challenge its efforts to eliminate a critical component of revival policy.

Debates about the place of the language in society were not new to Ireland in the 1960s but they were now occurring while Ireland was experiencing significant economic change. Throughout the 1960s and into the 1970s economic development brought with it changing social trends and as Tony Crowley points out: 'Though the Irish language remained a core symbol of Irish national identity, there is no doubt that its role as the constitutive factor of Irishness began to diminish in this period'.[8] These cultural debates about the language were taking place while Fianna Fáil was pushing forward a reformist agenda which deftly tried to argue that the principles on which the state were founded would not be compromised by a more 'pragmatic' approach to the revival of Irish. These arguments were being made while the state was introducing and defending from intense criticism a hybrid television service that was charged with both entertaining and informing the public. This chapter will consider how television became a key battleground for a culture in transition.

Before considering the state's effort to support the Irish language it makes sense to try and define what was meant by the term 'Irish Language Revival'. Sociologist Pádraig Ó Riagáin addresses the confusion often associated with the term noting that the Irish case was never one of pure language revival, as the language was not extinct at the time of independence but was spoken by a minority in the western regions of the island. Although some assumed 'revival' meant displacing English with Irish, he points out, '[w]hatever may have been the views of individual politicians or spokespersons of the language movement, the constitutional and legislative provisions made for Irish in the 1920s and 1930s do not suggest anything other than the establishment of a bilingual state'.[9] In spite of this the term 'revival' remained problematic through much of the period considered in this study. Politicians, civil servants, supporters of the Irish language and those opposed to the state's language policies interpreted the term differently. The advent of television as a commercial public service forced the state to address uncomfortable questions concerning the level of support it was willing to provide to the Irish language. When confronted with the prospect of taking substantial financial risks to promote the language and thereby jeopardising the viability of RTÉ, the state began to redefine the term 'revival' while at the same time hoping to find other institutional partners to accept the responsibility of supporting the Irish language.

What might broadly be defined as the Irish language lobby proved the most difficult and certainly the most persistent pressure group that challenged the Irish television service throughout the 1960s. The restoration of the Irish language was a key goal of political and cultural nationalists active in the revolutionary period of the late nineteenth and early twentieth centuries. Both Cumann na nGaedheal and Fianna Fáil governments defined this as a national priority and its special place in Irish life was embraced in the Constitution of the Irish Free State in 1922 and in the 1937 Constitution where it was recognised as the first language of the nation.[10] The language policy developed by the state had four goals: maintaining the language in Irish-speaking regions, increasing the number of Irish speakers through the schools, encouraging the use of Irish in the public service, and standardising or modernising the language.[11] Initial efforts to restore the language focused on the classroom, as the language was an essential part of the elementary and secondary curriculum. Irish was made compulsory for passing public examinations, including the Intermediate Certificate (1927/28) and the Leaving Certificate (1933/34).[12] The Irish National Teachers' Organisation soon came to regard teaching through the Irish language a mistake, noting in a study conducted in 1941 'that in all subjects except singing and needlework the result was the relative retardation of the child'.[13] Despite the fact that the language was integrated into the state's schools, beyond the classroom it struggled to find a place in a country where the majority of people continued to speak English.[14] Although the state defined the revival as a priority and surveys continually indicated a majority of citizens appreciated its cultural importance, government initiatives to support the revival were not broadly successful.

Historian Joseph Lee points out that government failed to develop imaginative, comprehensive planning that would support the language once students completed their education. Although Irish was required for some appointments in the civil service there was no concerted effort to bring Irish into the everyday life of politics or a determined effort to make it the language of the civil service. Lee argues that 'the refusal of all governments since the foundation of the state to practise what they preached alerted an observant populace to the fact that the revival was a sham'.[15] While governments continued to pay lip service to the revival, the number of native Irish speakers declined from approximately 200,000 in 1922 to 100,000 in 1939 and 50,000 in 1964.[16] This decline was due to a number of complex factors including heavy emigration from economically depressed Irish-speaking areas, and was not simply the result of failed linguistic policy. In fact it would be a mistake to dismiss all of the linguistic efforts of the state since independence as going for naught. Historian Gearóid Ó Tuathaigh argues that despite the deficiencies of government policies, by the 1950s 'a substantial cohort of secondary bilinguals, of varying levels of competence, had emerged from the schools, and Irish had achieved a degree of penetration and a presence in public domains in Ireland from which it had been excluded from centuries'.[17]

While Irish-speaking districts in the west of Ireland seemed to be in terminal decline and debate developed concerning its place in schools, a remarkable renaissance in Irish literature unfolded. Irish writing in the post-war period flourished as authors and poets produced some of the most impressive Irish literature of the century. Brian Ó Nualláin, Máirtín Ó Cadhain, Mártín Ó Direáin, Máire Mhac an tSaoi and Seán Ó Ríordáin, for example, all published intriguing, innovative works in Irish. Moreover, young urban-based Irish language intellectuals who were committed to Irish began to question, even ridicule, simple Gaelic

Revival ideology that cherished a rural way of life that they found antiquated and even absurd. In this environment a number of new cultural organisations formed that had different ideas regarding the role the language should play in the cultural life of the country. In his groundbreaking social and cultural history of twentieth-century Ireland, Terence Brown maintains that 'an awareness grew among concerned individuals and in the organisations they founded that the only hope for its future was to encourage interest in the language in the towns and cities'.[18] In these circumstances, a proliferation of organisations adapted to changed conditions understanding that rhetoric employed by many advocates of the language about linguistic exchange was unrealistic. A number of these groups, including the National Gaelic Congress, Comhdháil Náisiúnta na Gaeilge were comprised of university graduates and professionals becoming inventive advocates of the Irish language.

At the start of the 1960s, Fianna Fáil continued to argue that it was fully committed to the revival, although many supporters of Irish regarded the party's rhetoric as pure political posturing. Even so, advocates of the language understood the power of television and viewed the establishment of an indigenous TV service as a new and perhaps final opportunity to force the state to make good on its commitment to the revival, arguing that the medium should fully support their aims. Many in the language lobby considered television a critical tool in saving Irish from oblivion, making this clear in countless submissions to governments, directors-general of Telefís Éireann, and broadcasting authorities. Throughout the decade language supporters were relentless in their criticism of Telefís Éireann, continually arguing that the system was guilty of gross negligence for failing to support what, at least on paper, was a national priority. These critics maintained that both the state and officials in television were ignoring cultural mandates spelled out in Section 17 of the 1960 Broadcasting Act. The section stipulated that in the course of performing its duties 'the Authority shall bear in mind the national aims of restoring the Irish language and preserving and developing the national culture and shall endeavour to promote the attainment of these aims'.[19] Despite these complaints, the language struggled mightily to develop a meaningful presence on Telefís Éireann throughout the 1960s, creating tremendous tension between the service and advocates of Irish.

The commercial structure of Irish television complicated the efforts of supporters of the language to promote its revival and protect what they believed was a frail national culture teetering on the brink of extinction. By 1965, the unrelenting pressure of the language lobby succeeded in forcing the government of Seán Lemass to make significant changes in the composition of the Broadcasting Authority. These changes provoked intense controversy within Telefís Éireann, leading to the resignation of Eamonn Andrews, Chairman of the Authority. Andrews was convinced that the government erred in trying to placate what he considered a noisy minority of zealous cultural nationalists.

The language had been a controversial part of programming on Radio Éireann from its origins in the 1920s, and its experience is worth considering as this strongly influenced decisions made about the place of Irish on television. Ireland's first radio station opened in 1926 with an address by Douglas Hyde, who in 1892 had encouraged the de-Anglicisation of Ireland in the foundational polemic of the Gaelic Revival. In his remarks Hyde argued the new radio service 'was a sign to the whole world that a great change has come about when we can take our place among the nations of the world and make this wire-less instrument work in our own language like every other country'.[20] He once again cautioned against Anglicisation, telling listeners:

> There were two tides in Ireland – one of them coming in on this side of Ireland and the other going out on the west coast. The tide of Gaelic was ebbing there and leaving behind a bare, cold ugly beach in its wake. The fine, Gaelic water had ebbed away and was replaced by the mud, slime and filth of English.[21]

In the early decades, a concerted effort was made to develop programmes in Irish, and this proved controversial. The station failed to impress the leader of the Irish Free State, William Cosgrave, who considered it simply a vehicle for Irish-Ireland propaganda. Cosgrave complained about monotonous programming and of a general assumption that '2RN is an Irish-Ireland institution and that there is only abuse awaiting any criticism'.[22] Irish language programming on Radio Éireann was not popular according to the station's own surveys which indicated that the numbers of listeners to Irish programmes had declined to as low as 1 per cent in the 1950s. In March 1953, a confidential report reviewed a recent listener survey conducted by Radio Éireann admitting that the low numbers were 'disappointing'. A cabinet meeting later that year rejected demands made in the Dáil and national press to publish the report 'in light, particularly, of the very poor showing of programmes in the Irish language'.[23]

When, in 1963, the Gaelic League proposed that the state develop an Irish language television service, León Ó Broin dismissed the idea as simply replicating earlier demands for an all-Irish radio service. He recounted earlier efforts to develop an Irish language radio service and in doing so pointed to tension between Dublin-centred intellectuals interested in Irish broadcasting for ideological reasons and community activists advocating the creation of a station to serve the economically depressed Gaeltacht. Ó Broin referred to a proposal made to the government in 1934 by the Galway branch of the Gaelic League, a plan supported by the Galway Urban District Council. The proposal argued for an Irish language service that would originate in the Gaeltacht and serve its residents. The proposal was denied by the Director of Radio Éireann who argued that the best way to address the needs of the Gaeltacht was to increase the amount of Irish language material on Radio Éireann and provide opportunities for special programmes to be broadcast from Galway.

Almost a decade later, Eamon de Valera inquired about the establishment of something quite different, an Irish language radio station powerful enough to reach listeners across Ireland and in Scotland. The director of broadcasting did not consider the idea practical, noting that there would be technical difficulties in organising such a service, including gaining access to the proper wavelength. Additionally 'the Emergency' complicated matters as obtaining a 100-kilowatt transmitter would be impossible while the Second World War distracted most of Europe. Although de Valera accepted there would be difficulties due to the war he instructed Radio Éireann and Posts and Telegraphs to begin planning and to 'be prepared (staffing, programme schemes etc.) as would make it possible to proceed with the scheme when circumstances permitted after the Emergency'.[24]

Little was done to follow up on de Valera's request, but in 1945 a small committee was set up, chaired by León Ó Broin, including civil servants from Posts and Telegraphs and staff from Radio Éireann. This group, described by Ó Broin as being made up of 'Gaelic enthusiasts', looked into developing a service for the Gaeltacht. It determined that 'even where sets existed (10% of households in the rural Gaeltacht) programmes in Irish were listened to in comparatively few of these houses'.[25] The committee concluded, 'The Gaeltacht dweller was very seldom an enthusiast for the Irish language and was impatient and suspicious of other dialects. The Committee was satisfied that programmes in Irish were more extensively listened to in areas outside the Gaeltacht. Even then these programmes were not as widely supported as the enthusiasts would have one believe.'[26] Irish speakers living in these economically deprived areas were more interested in jobs and economic development than a Dublin-based Gaelic revival.

Ó Broin's committee placed a great deal of emphasis on how difficult it was to develop quality programming in Irish and was sceptical, complaining about a 'paucity of talent … There was no flow of suitable material from the Gaeltacht. The restricted life of the Gaeltacht greatly limited the amount of broadcast material from the Gaeltacht'.[27] The committee concluded rather paternalistically that it made no sense to establish an Irish language station for the Gaeltacht believing more could be done by supporting Irish within the existing structure of Radio Éireann in Dublin. De Valera agreed but hoped Radio Éireann would encourage and recruit scriptwriters, producers and actors who could develop quality programmes for the national radio service.

In spite of government inaction there continued to be calls for an Irish language station that would serve Irish-speaking areas of the country. A decade later, Muintir na Gaeltachta (People of the Gaeltacht) demanded the establishment of a station that could both relay Irish language material from Radio Éireann and develop its own programming when Radio Éireann was broadcasting in English. Muintir na Gaeltachta was established in the 1930s to demand rights for residents of the Gaeltacht. It underscored the tension that existed between supporters of the language and supporters of the Gaeltacht, claiming that the Gaeltacht was 'thoroughly dissatisfied with 70% of the present programmes in Irish'.[28] This proposal for an Irish station – like those before it – came to nothing.

However, another organisation that formed in March 1969, Gluaiseacht Chearta Sibhialta na Gaeltachta (the Gaeltacht Civil Rights Movement), had more success. The movement, influenced by civil rights campaigns in the United States and Northern Ireland and the unrest roiling university campuses across Europe and the Americas, challenged the state and its policies directly. The organisation lobbied for 'industrial development for the region, for proper schools and villages, for autonomous local authority and for a broadcasting service in the native language'.[29] Activists in the movement insisted the government recognise that the Irish-speaking community was a minority that should have full rights of citizenship including the right to a broadcasting service in Irish. It gained national attention by launching a picket outside the Teach Furbo Hotel in the Connemara Gaeltacht, protesting the recording of the popular television quiz show *Quicksilver* because it was recorded mostly in English. Although the programme's presenter, Bunny Carr, was bilingual and questions to the audience were asked in both languages, much of the programme was broadcast in English to the dismay of supporters of the language. Pickets also went up outside RTÉ studios in Donnybrook, and the director-general expressed sympathy for the protest, believing that the bilingual work on the programme had been 'less than adequate'. Thomas Hardiman, an accomplished Irish speaker, met a group of a dozen young protesters led by the president of the Gaelic League, Maolsheachlainn Ó Caollaí, and reported that after a frank exchange of views protesters seemed 'more appreciative of RTÉ's attitude, position and policies'.[30] However, as part of a broader campaign, the group repeated demands that the government set up a Gaeltacht-based Irish radio service to cater to their needs. In 1970, civil rights campaigners set up a pirate station in Ros Muc, Connemara, challenging the government to address their demands. The government's response was the establishment of Raidió na Gaeltachta in Casla, the heart of the Connemara

Gaeltacht, which began broadcasting on a part-time basis on Easter Sunday 1972, before expanding to a full-time service with studios in Kerry, Mayo, and Donegal.[31]

The failure of Irish language radio programmes to attract a significant audience in the early 1960s strongly influenced official thinking on television. León Ó Broin advised his minister that given the experience of Radio Éireann, the Gaelic League's 1963 proposal to establish an Irish language television service was 'unrealistic and extravagant'.[32] Assuming the service would be a commercial one, he argued advertisers 'would not open their purses ... The experience gained in sound radio shows that sponsors of commercial programmes, despite preferential rates, are most reluctant to use the language.'[33] In a service dependent on advertising revenue the Irish language was consistently sidelined and often ignored as senior officials focused on the service maintaining its financial viability.

In the late 1950s, supporters of Irish played a key role in undermining proposals from private firms interested in establishing commercial television. When the Television Commission was set up to consider how a service should be introduced, a Joint Committee of Gaelic Bodies testified that television should be exploited to enable the restoration of Irish as the primary language of the Irish people. Members of the Television Commission who were well aware of the position of the language lobby later met with representatives of Gael-Linn, an organisation that had made a number of films and earned a reputation for innovation in promoting the language and supporting the Gaeltacht. Gael-Linn submitted a comprehensive proposal that was clearly focused on using the medium for didactic purposes. The Commission turned down the application, believing it was far too narrow and that its programmes would not find an audience substantial enough to be financially viable. When the Television Commission completed its report it addressed the language issue, arguing for what it defined as an 'enlightened approach' and stating that it was 'preferable that little be done well rather than much be done badly and that there should be a gradual and natural increase in the use of the language in programmes'.[34]

Undaunted by the failure of Gael-Linn to win the concession, many supporters of the language remained hopeful that the 1960 Broadcasting Act which created Telefís Éireann would require the new station to make a concerted effort to feature a significant amount of material in Irish. Many considered television an important resource that should be fully exploited by the state, and tremendous tension developed over how best to use it to further the cause of the revival. Understanding that the most vocal in the language movement were focused on exploiting the new television service to restore the Irish language as vernacular throughout the state is a critical point, as this attitude not only contradicted government policy but alienated civil servants, politicians, ministers and senior administrators in television. Repeatedly, directors-general and management in Telefís Éireann told advocates of the language that the 1960 Broadcasting Act established a commercial public service that needed to pay its own way by featuring programmes that would generate advertising revenue. In these circumstances, they argued Telefís Éireann could not dedicate a significant portion of programming to support the revival of Irish. Officials in government and broadcasting were convinced that many of the more extreme demands of the language lobby were simply unreasonable and not acceptable. What government officials considered a simple commercial reality some advocates of the language defined as another example of the government supporting the crass materialism undermining a frail linguistic culture. Supporters of Irish were dismayed by this attitude and by the paltry amount of Irish language broadcasting that made its way onto Telefís Éireann.

While the Television Commission was deliberating the question of how TV should be structured, another government-appointed board was simultaneously in session, the Commission for the Restoration of the Irish Language (CRIL). This Commission issued its final report in 1963, but not before it published an interim report timed to coincide with the publication of the Television Commission's final report in 1959. In March 1959, two months before the Television Commission issued its final report, the *Interim Report of the Language Commission* was submitted to the Taoiseach, Eamon de Valera. This *Interim Report* emphasised that television should assist in the goal of restoring Irish as the vernacular of the nation. The report denied that leaders of the revival movement wanted to exploit television 'continuously or even frequently for the purpose of propaganda or indoctrination' but instead wanted to encourage the development of a service that would 'portray sympathetically the many facets of our native culture and our traditions'.[35] The best means of realising this goal was for television to foster a deep appreciation of Irish culture by embracing the Irish language. The Language Commission's *Interim Report* claimed that the government had failed in its efforts to encourage the restoration of Irish and believed that television would be an important test, indicating just how seriously it was committed to what politicians defined as a 'national priority'. While at first glance the report might seem eminently reasonable, it became less so as it continued. There was a tone of desperation that permeated the Language Commission's *Interim Report* as it pleaded for a national television service that would help save Irish. According to the *Interim Report*, there would be dire consequences if the state failed to exploit the medium, as the Commission believed that the efforts to revive the language would be 'doomed'.[36] The report argued that only Irish speakers should be hired to work at the new television service, that advertisers should broadcast in Irish, and that a firm commitment be made to allow for a significant amount of Irish language broadcasting during peak viewing periods. It also demanded extensive Irish programming for children.

León Ó Broin, a critical voice in the deliberations that were taking place inside the government, reviewed the Commission's *Interim Reportt* and regarded it as being 'completely out of touch with reality'.[37] Although he was sympathetic, he understood that the type of commercial service that would emerge would not be able to promote Irish to the degree that the Commission desired. Gearóid Ó Tuathaigh commenting on the work of the Language Commission, which issued its final report in 1963, notes that few of its recommendations were accepted and the *Interim Report* certainly suffered the same fate.[38] However, the anxiety of the language lobby articulated in the *Interim Report* was cleverly used by Ó Broin to help scuttle a number of proposals from foreign corporations looking to gain a licence to establish commercial television in the country.

As early as the autumn of 1959 when the government established an Advisory Committee to help purchase equipment and look into acquiring land for studios and transmitters, the National Gaelic Congress, Comhdháil Náisiúnta na Gaeilge, protested to the Taoiseach, Seán Lemass, that the members were not Irish language speakers. The Congress was a voluntary association that had been encouraged to come together by the government to coordinate the myriad efforts and voices of those working in support of the Irish language. The state saw an advantage in one group speaking for the language and encouraged the development of a consensus among the various cultural groups who supported Irish. The Congress understood that members of the Advisory Committee would be invited to sit on the formal Broadcasting Authority and was concerned about the absence of Irish speakers. The Taoiseach's office responded to the complaint by assuring the Congress that 'every aspect of the nation's welfare will be borne in mind when the appointment of the members of the Authority is being considered'.[39]

When American Edward Roth was named director-general, he quickly learned that the language lobby would be a strong and persistent critic of the new service. Roth understood that language supporters could create real and lasting headaches with demands he and his colleagues regarded as unrealistic. The Chief Secretary of the Gaelic League, Donncha Ó Súilleabháin, wrote to Roth in February 1961 asking for detailed information on the plans that were being made to develop Irish language broadcasting. Roth replied in firm but diplomatic terms, first apologising for replying in English, explaining, 'I feel that it would be insincere of me to sign a translation of this letter to you in Irish which I myself would not understand.'[40] He assured Ó Súilleabháin that as director-general he was well aware of his responsibilities under the 1960 Broadcasting Act. In replying to complaints about the hiring of non-Irish speakers, he explained that the primary concern in appointing staff was hiring 'experienced television people' with the necessary technical expertise. He noted that he had every intention of encouraging the development of Irish language material but was evasive in providing the details that the Gaelic League requested. He cautioned that it would be premature to answer

specific questions about the extent or nature of Irish language programmes or timing of their broadcast. He tried to assure the Gaelic
League that it was his intent to support the language: 'Attractive
Irish language programmes will, I hope, find their place in the
originated programmes which we will undertake.'[41]

Roth was explicit in stating that there were other considerations of which the Authority had to be conscious. He stressed
that the service was under an obligation to be financially independent as quickly as possible and that developing a large viewing
audience was paramount. In these circumstances he made it
clear that a large proportion of programmes broadcast would be
foreign-made. Roth was a realist and understood that although
the language lobby might not like his response he saw no reason
not to be straightforward, explaining 'the Irish television service
must attract and hold a large viewership and this consideration
will have to be given substantial weight in determining programme content.'[42] Financial considerations were indeed critical
and Roth made it clear that there were other challenges in this
regard. He pointed out that the Authority was also, as of June
1960, responsible for sound broadcasting which was 'operating
at an annual deficit of £200,000 with also, as has been demonstrated by surveys, very low listenership interest in many of its
programmes'.[43] Although he did not come out and say it, the
implication was quite clear: Irish language radio programmes were
unpopular and this certainly weighed on Roth's mind as demands
from the language lobby were made.[44] The Gaelic League was
deeply disappointed by Roth's response and at its annual meeting
the director-general was denounced as an enemy of the language.
Some made it clear they were offended that Roth's reply was in
English and there was an extended debate about whether or not
his letter should even be read to the assembly. Suggestions from
the floor that the director-general be instructed to study and learn
Irish indicate the contempt his response generated from some of
the more passionate delegates. These events were reported widely
in the press indicating that there would be difficulties ahead for
the American director-general.

In the spring of 1961 Roth held a pre-arranged press conference to provide a status report, explaining where the service was

some eight months before the first programme was scheduled for broadcast. When the question of Irish language broadcasting came up he pointed out that the recent Nielson reports had indicated Radio Éireann's Irish language broadcasts had 'the lowest ratings received'.[45] Anticipating questions concerning the language, he had shrewdly released his letter to the Gaelic League to the press beforehand. The director-general explained that many of the demands of the Gaelic League were simply unreasonable and told the press that he and the Broadcasting Authority were well aware of their obligations under the Section 17 of the Broadcasting Act. His remarks, which had the full backing of the government and Eamonn Andrews, illustrate that he was not afraid to challenge his harshest critics.

The Irish language movement was animated by other concerns in the early 1960s as debates about the state's language policy provoked a lively and sometimes ugly cultural war that lasted through much of the decade. In February 1960 Noel Browne, who referred to the 'disquiet and dissatisfaction among responsible authorities and among parents and pupils alike about compulsory methods', put forward a motion in the Dáil calling for a referendum 'to ascertain whether a majority of the people would favour the replacement of compulsory methods, where used, in the attempted revival of the language by voluntary schemes for its encouragement'.[46] Although the motion provoked a lively debate, it was easily defeated. Fine Gael also raised questions about the subject and in 1961 a section of the party's election platform promised to abolish compulsory Irish in public schools, maintaining 'Fine Gael believes that the present methods of reviving Irish have not been successful, and that, in the interests of the Irish language, a change must be made.'[47] This provoked a firestorm of debate as the language and the state's role in its revival became part of the political rhetoric of the election campaign.

Editorials in the *Irish Times*, the *Longford Leader,* and the *Galway Observer* praised the courage of Fine Gael, arguing that for over forty years the policy had been tried 'without success'.[48] However, Seán Lemass used the occasion to question the patriotism of his opponents, denouncing the notion of eliminating compulsory Irish as 'irresponsible'. 'Fine Gael seems to be soliciting support for a policy of retreat. I want no misunderstanding of Fianna Fáil's aim. It is to bring the language into common use in the daily life of the nation. We are not prepared to lower our target by even a fraction.'[49] Despite the Taoiseach's hyperbole, the reality was that his attitude towards the language was at best ambivalent; his remarks were spoken in the heat of an election and illustrate that when it suited Fianna Fáil, traditional rhetoric could be deployed, maintaining the party was fully supporting the language. The ensuing debates about the revival of the Irish language and its place in a national television service need to be seen in the context of a society experiencing rapid change that challenged traditional cultural nationalist ideology. By the early 1960s questions concerning long-held commitments to seemingly sacrosanct cultural policy began to undermine the state's language policy. Fine Gael's decision to talk about 'preserving' the language instead of 'restoring' it unsettled many in the language movement who felt threatened by government inaction and the expressed policy of the state's second largest political party. Fine Gael issued a policy statement in 1966 'calling for an end to the mandatory pass in Irish necessary to qualify for the award of the Intermediate and Leaving Certificate examinations'.[50]

Underscoring the complexities of these debates one of the most important Gaelic literary figures of the period, Séamus Ó Grianna, published a number of letters that actively supported the work of the Language Freedom Movement. Ó Grianna was a prolific novelist, short story writer and satirist who had also served as editor of *An Claidheamh Soluis*, the Gaelic League's official newspaper.[51] *The Lights of Heaven*, a collection of his short stories, essays and letters, edited by Nollaig Mac Congáil, includes a series of letters he penned to the *Irish Times* in the spring and summer of 1966. In these letters he denounced the 'Murder Machine of compulsory Irish' arguing that the state's educational policy was 'killing what is left of the language'.[52] He later argued: 'Irish is an old language whose growth was arrested centuries ago. It was a beautiful language; even what remains of it is beautiful. For that reason, every assistance should be given to anyone who wants to study it. But there is a world of difference between fostering a love of Irish and the attempt to make it, by brutal compulsion, the one and only language of the nation.'[53]

Unhappy with what was perceived as Roth's indifference to their concerns, the National Gaelic Congress wrote to the Chairman of the Radio Telefís Éireann Authority, requesting a formal meeting with the board in the autumn of 1961. Eamonn Andrews declined, explaining that their work was at a critical stage; instead he asked that concrete suggestions be submitted, promising that he would help facilitate a meeting at a later date. The Congress responded with a six-page, twelve-part submission that outlined what it defined as the 'minimum principles' that had to be accepted by the new service. These were core demands that the language lobby would return to time and again as it tried to force Telefís Éireann and the government to take the aim of restoring the Irish language seriously. The ensuing correspondence set the stage for a decade of tension and frustration for both broadcasters and advocates of the Irish language alike.

The confrontational document employed the type of heated rhetoric that characterised many subsequent communications from advocates of the language. It sharply reminded the Authority of its responsibility under Section 17 of the Broadcasting Act and asked that 'urgent consideration' be given to its submission 'sufficient to reassure this representative body that the best use in the interests of the language is going to be made of the Service, in spite of the many signs, at present, to the contrary'.[54] The Authority was told that a war had been fought to preserve the Irish nation, a war that was the culmination of centuries of struggle for independence and that the founders of the state and all subsequent governments understood the vital role of the language as an 'essential part of Irish nationality'.[55] In these circumstances, the state had done much to support the language, notably through requiring that it be part of the curriculum in schools throughout the nation. Although the Congress deplored the mistakes that had been made in the past – including a failure of governments to develop comprehensive planning to support the language – it still believed that huge strides had been made. The Congress argued that the state educational policy had given a degree of Irish to most citizens but lamented that this was lost once schooling ceased, arguing this was 'due principally to the absence of a progressive policy towards the language in the cinema, theatre, press and other mass media of entertainment and communication'.[56] The submission singled out the media as being responsible for transmitting a foreign popular culture that it believed was antithetical to its efforts to support a frail indigenous culture.

After citing the support from the Catholic Hierarchy and the Protestant Churches, the Congress cleverly quoted the Taoiseach's address at the November 1960 Fianna Fáil Ard-Fheis. In that speech Lemass lashed out at opposition politicians who had campaigned to 'disparage the language and belittle the efforts to restore it', arguing that Fianna Fáil 'stood firm on the issue of the language, refusing compromise with expediency or truck with despondency, which has held the national line of battle intact'.[57] In extraordinary language, Lemass had exclaimed that it was vital for members of Fianna Fáil to understand the commitment his party had to Irish, maintaining that 'if our section of the national front should break or sag, all hope for victory would begin to fade'.[58] Again, one could question the sincerity of the Taoiseach's remarks spoken in the excitement of a political convention. Lemass had little interest in the Gaelic ideology that animated de Valera but this did not prevent him from returning to spirited nationalist rhetoric if he judged it politically expedient. In employing the Taoiseach's language in its report, the Congress argued that the government fully backed their position.

The Congress also highlighted statements made by the minister for Posts and Telegraphs, Michael Hilliard, when the minister introduced the Broadcasting Act in the Dáil, assuring deputies that 'the use of Irish in broadcasting has to be one of active assistance in the restoration of the language'.[59] The Congress, which regarded itself as the most important national organisation charged with overseeing a coherent language policy, believed that it was the responsibility of the Radio Éireann Authority to play a major role in restoring the language as an essential feature of Irish life. Because it regarded the Authority as acting irresponsibly and in violation of Section 17 of the Broadcasting Act, it demanded action be taken to avoid what it believed was a national crisis.

The submission by the Congress criticised the Authority for appointing people to positions in Telefís Éireann with little interest or knowledge of Irish, maintaining that the number of those appointed with no appreciation or understanding of the language was 'very great'.[60] It expressed particular disappointment with comments made by the Chairman, Eamonn Andrews, who was quoted as stating it was not the intention of the Authority to 'ram the language down the throats, eyes or ears of the viewers'.[61] These statements were regarded as counterproductive as they 'tended to mislead the uninformed rather than enlighten public opinion'.[62] Complaints were also made about the decline in the amount of Irish programming on Radio Éireann since the Authority assumed responsibility for radio. The Congress believed that the solution to these problems lay in the Authority's agreeing to only employ enthusiastic Irish speakers willing to use Irish in an imaginative and meaningful fashion.

Although the Authority regarded much of the document as unrealistic, there were a number of suggestions that Telefís Éireann understood it could work with. In some respects the document illustrates that within the Congress there was tension between those willing to accept compromise and hard-liners. For the majority of the Radio Éireann Authority being reminded of its responsibilities under the Broadcasting Act not once but on several occasions was seen as beyond the pale. Many demands were simply unrealistic, including one that stipulated that no person should appear on television on a regular basis unless they spoke Irish. The demand that Irish programmes be broadcast at peak hours illustrates that the Congress did not appreciate the financial pressure the service would be under nor understand the hostile reaction this would provoke from the majority of viewers. If these demands were strategic ones, designed to place a marker from where future negotiations might take place, this strategy failed. Television officials took them seriously and repeatedly argued that if Irish language programming were to enjoy parity with English language programming the service would not be economically viable.

The Congress looked to children as part of the solution, arguing that Irish language programming for children should be 'predominant', believing that because advertisers 'are not interested in advertising to children ... the Authority should not lose financially by such a policy, even if it could be shown that the viewing ratings were lower because of this policy'.[63] It also advocated the establishment of training courses for television which would be under the direction of Irish speakers and insisted that any publication of the Radio Éireann Authority, including programme guides, be published in Irish. The report concluded in a tone that was less hectoring than the *Interim Report from the Language Commission*: 'Unless the Authority adopts an enthusiastic, positive policy towards the language, the television service will cause irreparable damage', concluding that the demands set out were 'the minimum necessary to carry through such a progressive policy'.[64]

Shortly after submitting its report, the Congress wrote to Edward Roth, this time alarmed by notices appearing in the national press. These advertisements for female announcers did not stipulate applicants had to be fluent in Irish. The Congress again argued that it was imperative that only fluent Irish speakers be appointed and expressed the 'fear' that the Authority was ignoring its responsibilities under Section 17 of the Broadcasting Act. An anxious Congress also asked for an early reply to the detailed document that they had submitted to Eamonn Andrews. Roth responded to both the complaint and the submission in an extended letter, once again reminding the Congress that he had to consider the entire Broadcasting Act and not simply Section 17. Roth believed that the Congress did not appreciate that the Broadcasting Act required television to be financially self-sufficient, pointing out that Telefís Éireann was not established to restore the Irish language. He maintained that the Radio Éireann Authority knew that the service had to have a definite Irish character but emphasised it also had to be capable of 'attracting the audience necessary for its financial well being'.[65]

The director-general claimed that the authority would give 'due recognition' to the national aim of the Gaelic Revival but was uncompromising in maintaining that it 'does not interpret this obligation with regard to the language as over-riding its general obligations'.[66] He informed the Congress that interpreting the

Act was the responsibility of the Authority, although he allowed that suggestions would always be welcome. However, the director-general was not going to be dictated to and once again pointed to the fact that the state had made a national investment of £2,000,000, which the Authority had the statutory responsibility to repay. That meant that the television service would be 'dependent for an essential part of its revenue on income from advertisements' which required the cultivation of a large audience.[67]

Roth rejected as 'unrealistic' demands that appointments to the station require proficiency in Irish and dismissed as financially impossible the notion that he hire Irish-speaking assistants to work alongside new appointments. Responding to complaints about the hiring of foreigners, he maintained that every effort was being made to keep the non-Irish appointments within the service at a minimum but pointed out that it was difficult to find Irish people with the technical expertise necessary to fill critical positions. Roth concluded by promising that other suggestions outlined in the proposal would be studied but that the Authority had decided against meeting and discussing the report with representatives of the Congress. The Congress was furious with Roth's response and vented its frustration in the press, which was intrigued with developments in the new service. Newspaper reports predicted a 'showdown', maintaining that the refusal of the director-general and the authority to meet the Congress meant 'that they have no alternative but to go over Mr. Roth's head to Mr. Lemass'.[68] An unidentified representative for the Congress complained about the large number of foreigners working in Telefís Éireann and about the 'indifference' to the need for Irish language programming.[69]

At a contentious annual meeting of the Congress in November 1961, a month before Telefís Éireann began broadcasting, Liam Ó Luanaigh, its president, lambasted the Lemass Government, telling the delegates 'it was obvious that the Government in nominating the Television Authority was not primarily concerned with the welfare of the Irish language'.[70] Ó Luanaigh maintained that as far as the Congress was concerned it was better not to have a television service than to have one that did not support the language, arguing that the opening of the station should be postponed until a commitment was made to providing 'suitable programmes in Irish'.[71] Although the Congress was a confederation of groups interested in supporting the language, there was considerable tension within the movement between moderate and more extreme elements. The president found himself defending his efforts and strategy from angry members arguing that he was not aggressive enough in dealing with the government.

A resolution was passed criticising the Television Authority 'for its failure to make a firm decision on the place of the Irish language in the new service'.[72] A formal letter of protest was delivered to Roth denouncing the director-general and the authority for refusing to meet with the Congress. Roth was told the organisation was 'disappointed and alarmed' by the Authority's position.[73] The Congress lamented what it considered was a misguided policy adopted by Telefís Éireann 'to give absolute priority to attracting advertising revenue, and considers that any use of Irish in the service would interfere with that aim'.[74] Once again the director-general was reminded of his responsibility under the Broadcasting Act and the Irish Constitution to support a cultural policy that was critical to the nation. Roth was criticised for interviews where he talked about featuring 'thriller and cowboy films' as these programmes would inevitably harm the Irish language.[75] The Congress was writing five weeks before the service was scheduled to go on the air and therefore maintained that it was, 'a matter of the utmost national urgency' that it be assured that the language would be secure.[76]

The Congress was 'extremely anxious' that a number of promises be given as quickly as possible, demanding that it be assured that Irish feature in the opening broadcast. It asked for details concerning the amount of Irish language material scheduled to be used in the first month of broadcasting, and that it be told what steps had been taken to feature Irish in all aspects of broadcasts including news, sports, announcements, advertisements and children's programmes. In a telling remark, the Congress expressed resentment at being treated like any other interest or cultural group, arguing that 'we cannot accept that we, the state-sponsored representative body of all the language organisations, should be regarded by you as an "outside body" any more than the Churches could be regarded as outside bodies in regards to religious programmes'.[77]

Reiterating its 'extreme anxiety' it once again demanded a meeting with a delegation from the Authority as quickly as possible. As tensions developed in the days before Telefís Éireann was to go on the air, Peter Black of the *Daily Mail* caught up with an exasperated Roth who remarked, 'I've started up six television stations. This is the toughest, including the one in Peru where I got embroiled with Communist politics.'[78]

Unfortunately for the Congress, and, for that matter, for the Catholic Church, Roth, Eamonn Andrews and Seán Lemass regarded the Congress as another, albeit relentless, interest group that somehow had to be mollified. When questions about the complaints of the Congress were raised in the Dáil, the Minister, Michael Hilliard, backed the position of Telefís Éireann. He maintained that the Radio Éireann Authority was concentrating its effort in getting the service on the air and would be always mindful of its duty to support the language. Later, when addressing Gaeltacht affairs, an agitated Lemass emphasised that the Congress, Comhdháil Náisiúnta na Gaeilge, was not an official government body. He pointed out it was a voluntary organisation that had been encouraged by the government to establish itself to give some semblance of unity and cohesion to the variety of language organisations.[79]

The Congress, meanwhile, continued its relentless criticism of evolving television policy, a short time later complaining that the publication of the *RTV Guide* was yet another example of the Authority's failure to appreciate its concerns because of the English language programming that dominated and because it was not published in Irish.[80] A few days later a much more comprehensive letter of protest was sent to Roth complaining that the schedule contained no arrangements for Irish or bilingual programming with the exception of a few minutes at the start and end of transmission. 'We are therefore utterly dismayed at the programme plans, and we note that the press is equally dismayed, not alone in relation to the use of Irish but in regard to the low cultural level of programmes in general.'[81] Roth was also taken to task for an interview in the publication where he was said to have described 'Irish as merely a minority interest and presumes to suggest that the language would best be served by having very little of it on either the television or sound services'.[82] The Congress was upset with the position taken by Roth and the Authority and demanded an 'immediate conference' stating that 'in the meantime, as a matter of the utmost urgency, we would ask that you revise the opening week's programme schedule so as to endeavour even at this late stage to give due prominence to the Irish language'.[83] Roth tried to assuage the Congress by providing assurances that the Authority was conscious of its complaints and took them seriously. He claimed he wanted to try to work with the Congress and promised to meet a delegation from the Congress in the New Year, after the service was up and running.[84] This willingness to meet a delegation from the Congress did not defuse the situation as it maintained it was 'appalled' with the Authority's attitude and upset at the 'complete disregard' for the advice that they had provided.

A short time later Gael-Linn caused considerable alarm within the government by lambasting the Broadcasting Authority in an article titled: 'We have held our piece [sic] …' published in the weekly racing pools card that had a national circulation exceeding two hundred thousand. The article, written by Dónall Ó Móráin, founding director of Gael-Linn, maintained that the organisation had held back criticising Telefís Éireann because it wanted to give the service time to 'find its feet', especially in light of the fact that it had been an unsuccessful applicant for the television concession. But with the publication of the *RTV Guide* listing the programmes to be broadcast, it felt obligated to speak out. The article accused the Authority of scheduling programmes that were 'deliberately going to debase the cultural and other values of our community', pointing to the first week of programming as proof.[85] Reporting that not one programme was entirely in Irish, the article argued the Authority 'is proposing with your money, to subject the Nation to worthless programmes which seek the most uneducated and unenlightened section of the community as their audience'.[86] The publication of such a hard-hitting critique two weeks before the service was to go on the air received extensive coverage in the national press.[87]

One particular line caught the attention of the Lemass Government. 'Now is the time to act … tell the Authority,

Opposition, tell everyone that you will not stand for it. You are prepared to pay for something distinctively Irish and worthwhile: you are not prepared to help pay for a service which ITV can give you for nothing.'[88] The Department of Justice was alarmed with this language, interpreting it as inciting civil disobedience by advocating that citizens withhold the payment of licence fees. The matter was discussed by the Attorney General, the Taoiseach and the Minister for Posts and Telegraphs; a decision was made to write formally to warn the organisation that the article could be construed as 'an incitement to the public to refuse to make payment of the prescribed fee in respect to television receiving instruments'.[89]

Gael-Linn denied that the intent of the article was to incite the public to commit a criminal offence, arguing it was simply reminding people of the commitments the Authority were required to honour under Section 17 of the Broadcasting Act. In writing to Hilliard, Ó Móráin wryly maintained, 'we thought that the Minister would be very pleased with this attitude rather than the opposite'.[90] The fact that the Department of Justice made inquiries into the incident and that Seán Lemass took part in the discussions illustrates that the government did not want to see the financial footing of the new service undermined by a mischievous strategy developed by Gael-Linn. In an interview conducted years later, Ó Móráin explained that Gael-Linn was hoping to send a message but that 'it didn't strike us that they would take us seriously … it showed their jumpiness at the time'.[91] Dónall Ó Móráin continued to agitate the Authority until he was drafted onto it in 1965, becoming chairman a short time later. He firmly believed that the Authority was negligent for not supporting the language holding that television more than any other instrument could decide whether Irish was going to 'prosper or become extinct'.[92]

Roth and a subcommittee of the Authority eventually met with a delegation from the Congress in March 1962 to try to find common ground. By the time the meeting took place many members of the Authority and senior staff at Telefís Éireann had become frustrated with the aggressive tactics and harsh critique used by members of the language lobby. Members of the Congress were tremendously frustrated with the dearth of Irish programming and angry that Telefís Éireann had not addressed their concerns. The meeting was chaired by Professor T. W. Moody and included Edward Roth; John Irvine, head of management; and James Fanning, a member of the Authority who had serious reservations about the demands that the Congress had made. Liam Ó Luanaigh, the President of the Congress, Dónall Ó Móráin, Director of Gael-Linn, and David Greene, Professor of Irish at Trinity College and author of the government-sponsored publication, *The Irish Language*, represented the Congress. Records of the meeting underscore the substantial gap that existed between the expectations of the Congress and the realities of broadcasting as seen by Roth. Liam Ó Luanaigh argued strenuously that Telefís Éireann had failed to use Irish in a substantial manner and urged the Authority to do more, arguing that it 'should be accepted as fact that most viewers are competent to understand Irish'.[93] David Greene maintained that the declared policy of the state was to change the language of the Irish people from English to Irish and that Telefís Éireann had to assist in getting Irish 'out of the school and into the street'.[94] His statement illustrates the degree of confusion concerning the policy of the Lemass Government, highlighting the conflict between the rhetoric and reality of the state's policy.

James Fanning was not impressed by these arguments, telling the delegation that '[f]undamental facts had emerged – the country, by and large, was not behind Irish and its use'.[95] He claimed that initially sales of television sets in Ireland had been very slow and blamed this on his belief that many members of the public were concerned television would follow the example of Radio Éireann and broadcast unpopular Irish language programmes. This led to a debate about the popularity of Irish language broadcasting on radio with members of the Congress arguing that the programmes were unpopular not because they were broadcast in Irish but because they were of inferior quality. Ó Luanaigh told the sub-committee that the Irish people would 'tolerate' a good deal of Irish broadcasts, maintaining that 'by and large the population as a whole does not resent Irish as much as many people think'.[96]

Dónall Ó Móráin argued that Telefís Éireann was a state service and 'was not a commercial enterprise'; moreover, the state had a duty to use the service to support the language. He pointed to the public service remit of Telefís Éireann, arguing that although it relied on advertising it nevertheless had an obligation to serve the public and support stated government policy. John Irvine tried to explain to the delegation just how dependent Telefís Éireann was on commercial revenue, pointing out that in the next financial year it was committed to an expenditure of approximately £1,250,000. He patiently explained that the 65,000 licences issued as of March 1962 would cover only one-third of these costs, with the remainder coming from advertising revenue. This was before considering the obligation the Authority had to repayment of government-granted capital. Irvine argued that given the hybrid nature of the service it was imperative that it cultivate a large audience with popular programmes, pointing out that it was simply not economically feasible for the station to accept their demands. He told the delegation from the Congress that in setting up television the government never envisioned using it as a means of 'Gaelicising' the population.

Roth was blunt, arguing that unless advertising was forthcoming 'Telefís Éireann would collapse'.[97] Although he had only been in Ireland a short time, Roth informed the delegation that from his own experience the majority of people were not interested in the Irish language having a prominent place in television, noting 'a great resistance to the Irish language'.[98] He had never been impressed with Radio Éireann, informing the delegation that one of the reasons people were hostile to the language being deployed in television was due to the way it was used on radio. In a revealing remark he noted that one of the reasons Radio Éireann had been unpopular 'was because R.E. was identified too much with intellectuals'.[99] Roth saw television as primarily a means of entertainment and believed the service he was overseeing would not be economically viable if it were to accept the demands that the Congress was making. He remembered quite clearly the warnings about the finances that had been made by Lemass through Hilliard and remained determined that Telefís Éireann would not become a financial burden to the state.[100] What becomes obvious in reading through the minutes of this meeting (and in subsequent correspondence) is a singular lack of trust between representatives of the Congress and Telefís Éireann. This was based on the perception that neither side could grasp the 'realities' that exercised the other.[101]

Although the members of the Congress may have come away from the meeting with a better appreciation of the financial challenges confronting the service, they remained angry and deeply frustrated. The meeting had ended with a long discussion about audience research, Ó Móráin complaining that the surveys conducted to measure audience response to programmes were not fair, as they were not developed to include Irish-speaking families who would be advocates of Irish language programming. Roth replied that staff at Telefís Éireann would consider his protests in its reports but argued 'what the statistics people were trying to do was rate the television, not the language'.[102]

Ó Móráin developed this argument a short time later in an article published in *An tUltach*, the official journal of Comhaltas Uladh, the Ulster branch of the Gaelic League. He lamented the failure of Telefís Éireann to develop Irish language programming, maintaining that from the time the station went on the air until March 17, 1962 – a period of three-and-a-half months – only 1.25 per cent of output was in Irish.[103] He argued that the contract that the Broadcasting Authority had entered into with the firm hired to measure audiences, Television Audience Measuring (TAM), was flawed and worked to the detriment of the Irish language because the monitoring equipment was not placed in the homes of people interested in Irish. The claim by Ó Móráin that '24% of the population have Irish' could be open to question but his critique of Telefís Éireann was closely monitored by the government.[104]

His article was translated and summarised by civil servants in Posts and Telegraphs who were dismissive:

> Mr. Ó Móráin's theory is that the majority of the Authority are not against Irish but that they have a mental illness or phobia about the size of the viewing audience; that this is a result of bad advice; that they have been persuaded that Radio Éireann was no good under the *ancien régime* [sic] and that this was due to an excess of Irish, of symphony music, of traditional music, and of cultural programmes. Accordingly he feels that the majority of the Authority consider that

it is more important to have 200,000 listening to a programme which imitates Radio Luxembourg than have 50,000 listening to a lecture on Irish history.[105]

As far as Ó Móráin was concerned, the Authority had to be convinced that people were sympathetic to Irish and that the language could be used without affecting advertising revenue. He called on supporters of Irish to remind the Authority and 'people above them – of the will of the [Irish] Movement and of the will of Irish nationality'.[106]

During that first summer of television broadcasting in 1962, Ó Móráin remained on the offensive, frequently denouncing Telefís Éireann and the Authority. Throughout that summer Controller of Programmes Michael Barry attempted to take the pressure off his staff, deciding to screen more foreign-made pre-recorded programmes and concentrate on the production of indigenous programming for the autumn. As more American Westerns and crime dramas were screened, Ó Móráin's criticisms and the language he used became increasingly excited, gaining considerable coverage in the press. The relentless attacks did not escape the attention of the government, the Radio Éireann Authority, or senior staff at Telefís Éireann. In the summer of 1962, Ó Móráin addressed the Combined Universities Irish Society, An Comhchaidreamh, an organisation of university graduates and professionals interested in supporting the Irish language. His remarks were typical of the rhetoric that continually chastised Telefís Éireann: 'Irish television has acquired a shape which, if left undisturbed will earn it the reputation for the Authority of being the greatest depravers of public taste and cultural values in the history of the country.'[107]

Ó Móráin pointed to debates in the UK about American Westerns and crime dramas and the generally poor quality of commercial programming featured on the Independent Television Network. He referenced the report of the Pilkington Committee on Broadcasting, which was set up to consider the future of broadcasting in the UK and had issued its report to Parliament in June 1962. The report heavily criticised the Independent Television Network's emphasis on popular programming, arguing it was trivial and did not properly reflect British social values. The director of Gael-Linn hoped that Telefís Éireann would be influenced by its recommendations and develop intelligent programming instead of transmitting 'dim-witted American comedies'. According to Ó Móráin, in its first six months of broadcasting viewers were willing to be patient while Telefís Éireann was getting itself organised. However, after six months he believed opinion had changed. He pointed out that television had come to Ireland at 'a time when, internationally, a reaction had set in against the cult of the cowboy and the mindless American kitchen comedy'.[108]

Professor Dáithí Ó hUaithne added his voice to the critique of Telefís Éireann but signalled that the Authority was the problem, maintaining that things would be different if 'we had the right sort of Authority. My only complaint about the members of the present Authority is that they don't make a good board'.[109] Others at the meeting argued that some members of staff of Telefís Éireann were anti-Irish and anti-national, although these were regarded as a minority. The problem centred on the people who 'do not understand what is at stake or are indifferent'.[110] Although Ó Móráin's critique of programming may have found support among viewers tiring of the older American material in the summer of 1962, his recipe for remedying the problem did not. There is little evidence that viewers believed the answer lay in transmitting extensive Irish language programmes. Reporting on the growing critique of the language lobby, the *Irish Times* made the point that the most vocal and hostile critics were not necessarily speaking for all revival supporters. Two factions within the movement were described as those who wanted extensive Irish language programming and a more pragmatic group indicating that the more passionate advocates may be 'more vocal, but it is doubtful if they are the stronger' than the moderates.[111]

Almost one year to the day from which the Congress had submitted a document listing what they had described as the minimum steps to take to ensure that the language would be treated appropriately, and after two meetings with representatives of the Congress, Eamonn Andrews provided an extensive reply outlining the Authority's position on Irish language in television. The response of the Authority illustrates the frustration that Andrews, Roth and various Authority members were experiencing in regard to the language issue. His reply was made as the station was being pilloried by supporters of Irish and other critics upset with programmes that had been broadcast in the initial eight months of 1962. Andrews methodically addressed the critique made by the Congress, setting the tone early by stating that although the Authority recognised the 'special position' of the Congress it did not see any contradiction in defining it as an 'outside body'.[112] Andrews wanted the organisation to clearly understand the Authority's position in this regard. He and his colleagues regarded the Congress as one of a number of interest groups out to pressure the Authority.[113]

Andrews also rejected the incessant criticism of the Congress, which repeatedly referred to the Authority's statutory duty under Section 17 of the Broadcasting Act. He dismissed as fallacious its position that the state opted for a government-owned service to ensure that the language would be supported. The Comhdháil/ Congress were told that the Authority understood its obligations under Section 17 but did not interpret this section of the Broadcasting Act in a narrow manner. Instead, he emphasised that this section had to be understood within a much wider context and read as a part of a general obligation to 'maintain a national broadcasting system providing entertainment, information and education for a popular audience'.[114] Andrews pointed out that Section 24 of the Act required the Authority to operate the service in a responsible financial manner and to ensure that it would be economically viable and self-sustaining. He also emphasised that television did not derive its income from the state, maintaining that the £2,000,000 in start-up costs would be repaid to the government: 'No one is compelled to be a listener or a viewer or an advertiser, but it is from licence fees and advertising revenue that the service is financed.'[115] Andrews argued that to generate advertising revenue it was imperative that the service broadcast popular programmes at peak times. He dismissed demands that Irish language programmes be featured during these times as unrealistic, arguing they would not attract large audiences. In explaining the financial imperatives of Telefís Éireann, Andrews pointed out that the government was fully aware of these issues when setting up the service and understood that the television would 'not be conducted primarily as a means of promoting the restoration of Irish'.[116] In answering demands that the service use the language in an imaginative and positive manner and that it progressively increase the amount of Irish programming, he insisted that this was precisely the policy of Telefís Éireann.

Andrews dismissed demands made about staffing as simply impractical. The notion that all assistants to department heads, newscasters, announcers, interviewers and commentators be fluent in Irish was defined as unreasonable. He pointed out that the service required personnel with special technical and manage-rial skills that were not readily available in Ireland and that if this condition was accepted the professional standards of the service would suffer. Andrews explained that the Authority accepted the argument that it was important to recruit staff that were compe-tent Irish speakers but rejected the demand that only Irish speakers be hired, refusing to exclude promising candidates due to a lack of Irish language skills. Moreover, Andrews rejected outright the notion that the *RTV Guide* should be published in Irish, again defining the request as 'impracticable'.

The chairman reported that the Authority's policies were prag-matic and reasonable, unlike the demands being made by the Congress:

> The Authority considers that, in the interests both of Irish itself and of its revenue, it must carry out its duty to the language with tact and moderation. In determining the timing, duration and type of items to be televised in Irish, it must ensure that viewers are not wantonly driven away from Telefís Éireann and into hostility to Irish. Items in Irish transmitted during peak viewing period should, as a rule, be short and should not be close together. Larger items should generally be transmitted outside of the peak period.[117]

This distilled the attitude of Roth, Andrews, and – for the moment – the Broadcasting Authority. The Authority's report was not wholly negative or confrontational and tried to identify common ground between the demands of the Congress and its own policies. Although it agreed that there should be a substantial percentage of children's programming produced in Irish, there was little in Andrews's correspondence to appease the Congress.

The nine-page response was the most extensive statement

that had been issued by the Authority on the place of Irish in Telefís Éireann. Andrews made it clear that the Authority would not accept many of the demands that had been made via correspondence, in face-to-face meetings, or in the press. There was also a good deal of frustration that found its way into the report. Although Andrews hoped that dialogue could continue in a positive and friendly manner, the conclusion was a slap at the tactics of the Congress. It is clear that Andrews did not appreciate that earlier confidential discussions between representatives of the Authority and the Congress were leaked to the press. Andrews told the Congress that the Authority

> ... observes with regret that individual members of the Comhdháil have not respected the spirit of these negotiations; and it considers that the resulting publicity has damaged Radio Éireann's own efforts on behalf of the Irish language by accentuating the divisions on the question that exist in the country, by inflaming extreme views on both sides, by causing unsettlement among the staff of the television service, and by creating apprehension among viewers that the service is being turned into an instrument of propaganda.[118]

Andrews understood that the document he was producing for the Congress would find a wide audience and was prudent in sending a copy to both the Taoiseach and his minister, Michael Hilliard. He told the Congress that the Authority 'is convinced that the best hope of contributing to the restoration of the language through Telefís Éireann lies in using Irish attractively, persuasively and realistically, and in disassociating it from all rancour, dogmatism and make-believe'.[119]

Comhdháil Náisiúnta na Gaeilge held its annual meeting at the Mansion House in Dublin shortly after the Authority's report was forwarded to its president, Liam Ó Luanaigh. In addressing the annual meeting, Ó Luanaigh bitterly complained of the failure of Telefís Éireann to accept the organisation's advice, 'that a good deal of what we had described as essential and practicable now seemed to the Authority impossible or inadvisable'.[120] He complained particularly about the fact that Telefís Éireann had begun a search for a Controller of Programmes to replace Michael Barry, and that the advertisements for the position did not stipulate the candidate should be an Irish speaker.

Throughout these negotiations, Andrews was sensitive to what he defined as the 'one sided arguments presented in the press' and was careful to keep both Seán Lemass and Michael Hilliard informed. When sending a copy to the Taoiseach and minister he explained how 'serious and conscientious' the Authority had been in addressing these issues.[121] He maintained that he had not released the document to the press 'in the belief that too much controversy can do more harm than good to the language'.[122] At question time in the Dáil, the Minister for Posts and Telegraphs was confronted with queries about the controversy. Interestingly these questions were from deputies who had different ideas about the role of the language on Irish television. Labour Deputy Sean Treacy was sympathetic to the complaints of the Comhdháil, while Deputy Eamonn Rooney complained that more Irish language programming would force licence-paying Irish viewers to switch stations. Rooney asked the minister if he would consider the 'whole position of the use of Irish in Telefís Éireann programmes', suggesting that there was too much Irish language material.[123]

When preparing an answer for the Minister for Posts and Telegraphs, a pragmatic León Ó Broin pointed out that the pressure from both sides would continue and that 'it was obviously impossible to please everybody. The Authority cannot overlook its statutory obligation under Section 17 but neither can it overlook the fact that undue emphasis on Irish would adversely affect the size of the viewing audience and its income, not alone from advertisements but also from licence fees. It therefore considers that in the interests both of Irish itself and of its revenue it must carry out its duty to the language with tact and moderation.'[124]

Civil servants in Posts and Telegraphs understood that the pressure from the Irish language lobby was not going to cease and looked abroad for advice. In September 1962, the department wrote to the BBC asking for advice specifically looking at the way in which the BBC was working with the issue of the Welsh language. The Pilkington Report, which had been published earlier that year, had not only been critical of the commercialisation of television in Britain but also recommended the establishment of a second BBC channel. This second public service channel was expected to devote resources to regional television broadcasting and make additional provisions for Welsh language broadcasting. BBC officials were sympathetic to the query from Dublin, providing documents they had submitted to the Pilkington Committee including information about the future of Welsh television programming. This indicated that in 1962 the BBC was broadcasting five hours per week for a Welsh audience, three and a half hours of which was in Welsh. The BBC hoped to build an additional transmitter in Wales that would enable more Welsh language programming to a large Welsh-speaking population. By October 1962 British officials were reporting to their Irish counterparts that plans were in place to develop a BBC Wales television service that would broadcast twelve hours per week, with about seven hours in Welsh. The BBC reported they hoped the Welsh service would go on the air in 1964.[125] As noted, politicians and civil servants in Dublin were not interested in establishing an Irish television station; in fact, it would be decades before Telefís na Gaeilge made its debut in the autumn of 1996.

Within the Authority there were at least two strong supporters of Irish, the most substantial being Ernest Blythe. A native of Lisburn, County Antrim, Blythe was a 'rare example ... of an Ulster Protestant embracing cultural and political nationalism'.[126] As a young man Blythe joined the Gaelic League where he became a passionate advocate of the Irish language. He was an active republican and imprisoned by the British in the aftermath of the 1916 Easter Rising. He served as Minister for Finance from 1922 until 1931 in Cumann na nGaedheal governments, where he earned a reputation for frugality, going so far as to reduce Old Age Pensions in order to balance the budget of the Irish Free State. After 1940, Blythe left politics and became the managing director of the Abbey Theatre from 1941 until 1967, insisting that the theatre not hire actors or actresses unless they were Irish speakers. In naming Blythe to the Authority, the Lemass Government was able to satisfy two constituencies with one appointment as he was both a well-known political opponent of Fianna Fáil and a dedicated advocate of the Irish language. Philip O'Leary, who has written extensively about the Irish language, points out that Blythe had long been interested in using television to support the revival of Irish. He was president of the Comhdháíl Náisiúnta na Gaeilge in 1950 when it submitted a memorandum to the government that looked beyond film, targeting television as a means to support the revival of Irish.[127]

Blythe became increasingly frustrated with the failure of Telefís Éireann to develop and broadcast Irish material. Though Dónall Ó Móráin considered Blythe an ally inside the Authority, he became increasingly upset with his friend's failure to effect policy change. He described Blythe as a man who

> bull-dozed ahead, but one of the interesting things in that behaviour that you would find with that type of a goer and doer of things … he could be quite aggressive then suddenly become very mild when up against somebody like Eamonn Andrews. I remember well this kind of behaviour at a meeting where he said "ah we'll have to go ahead with this … sure Eamonn knows everything we better let him go ahead" a total u-turn as it were. He was the only help we could possibly expect on the Authority and he had that so called weakness.[128]

In fairness to Blythe, he was certainly in a minority, although Áine Ní Chanainn, one of the two women on the Authority, also advocated for a greater emphasis on Irish language broadcasting. Ní Chanainn had considerable experience in brodcasting Irish programmes with Radio Éireann dating back to the late 1930s.[129]

In truth, Blythe was not as passive as Ó Móráin believed and did his best to encourage more Irish broadcasting. In the summer of 1962 Blythe protested against what he saw as 'obstruction within the establishment' of Telefís Éireann that was inhibiting efforts to get Irish into broadcasts.[130] He complained openly to the Radio Éireann Authority and was particularly upset that more had not been done to get the language into the current affairs programme *Broadsheet*. Blythe became a persistent critic from within the Authority, believing that there was 'stonewalling' taking place in an effort to block his efforts to get more Irish on the air. Controller of Programmes Michael Barry disputed Blythe's critique as unfair and defended *Broadsheet,* insisting that he was constrained by the realities of a service that had to rely on advertisement for sustenance, maintaining 'to act without discrimination would quickly lead to bankruptcy. Our aim has been to walk a tightrope between needs of a national service and the exigencies as I have been given to understand them of commercial service.'[131]

As previously mentioned, Barry was actually trying to take the pressure off production staff by cutting back on the broadcast of indigenous programming that summer, filling the void with imported material while trying to stockpile home-made programmes for the autumn. Eamonn Andrews tried to reassure Blythe that his concerns would be taken seriously, telling him that he had already dealt with complaints from the Church, politicians, and the language lobby, all of whom were upset with programming, explaining that 'in all cases, the programme has been dubbed as suspect'.[132] Although he told Blythe he was concerned over Barry's insistence that Telefís Éireann reduce its home-produced programmes, he counselled patience. 'I feel we will get a better result if we can coax rather than compel. After all, it is the basis of our overall policy and perhaps we should use it internally as well.'[133] Nevertheless, Blythe remained convinced that Barry and producers in the service were ignoring his efforts to encourage Irish language programming.

Supporters of Irish became increasingly frustrated with the paltry amount of Irish language programming on Telefís Éireann and were relieved by a report that added pressure on the station to take their complaints seriously. The Commission on the Restoration of the Irish Language issued its final report in late 1963, acknowledging that there was much work to be done if Irish was to survive as a viable living language, never mind a restored vernacular. Among 288 recommendations made by the Commission were 16 designed specifically for broadcasting, with 9 of those targeted for Telefís Éireann. Not surprisingly the report recommended 'there should be a progressive extension of the use of Irish in television programmes', pointing out that as television reception had made its way into the West material should be developed that would engage the Gaeltacht.[134] Many of the recommendations were reasonable and were accepted, albeit in modified form, by the Radio Éireann Authority. For instance, the service accepted suggestions that television news in Irish be separated from news bulletins in English as reasonable although trying to work additional Irish material into the nine o'clock evening news proved more difficult. The request that sporting events and public ceremonies be broadcast in Irish and that more attention be given to bilingual programmes were suggestions that had been made earlier, and television service management maintained they would be supportive of these suggestions, provided that changes were made carefully and gradually.

The Commission advocated for an increase in Irish language broadcasts for children, the creation of a magazine programme in Irish, and the development of broadcasts that would interest viewers without a great knowledge of Irish, including 'musical programmes, panel games, travelogues etc. rather than straight talks and debates'.[135] Additionally, the Commission asked for programmes for adult learners of Irish and wanted the *RTV Guide* used to support weekly lessons. While many of these recommendations were ones Telefís Éireann could (and eventually did) work with, the report returned to demands that had previously been dismissed as impractical. The Commission argued that 'programmes in Irish and more bi-lingual programmes should be scheduled for peak viewing periods' and concluded that the 'Authority should henceforth ensure fluency in Irish on the part of members of its staff who prepare programmes or appear in them'.[136] This was a clear reference to staff working in all programming at Telefís Éireann, not just Irish language programmes.

Gearóid Ó Tuathaigh points out that from the late 1950s and into the 1960s 'one can identify a decisive shift in the ideological basis of state policy, and rhetoric, in independent Ireland'.[137] The government of Seán Lemass was committed to addressing the economic crisis challenging the country and keen to utilise experts to develop coherent planning that would support economic development, improve living standards and put a brake on emigration. As Ó Tuathaigh argues, the emphasis on ending protectionism and embracing a new openness influenced the government's position on the Irish language. Shortly after the publication of the Commission's report, Seán Lemass addressed a Fianna Fáil Ard-Fheis, telling delegates that the report and recommendations would be studied carefully. He also promised that a formal White Paper would be published outlining an unambiguous policy which his government would put in place. Lemass introduced a note of honesty into the speech indicating that a more prag-matic approach to the language had to be taken if any substantial progress would be made. He explained that he wanted to establish a set of clear goals that could be realised by taking careful, meas-ured steps, drawing an analogy with the successful *Programme for Economic Expansion*. His statement that the government would do its part but that 'this great national work cannot be discharged by the Government without widespread and whole-hearted public support' created cause for concern among some Irish language advocates. Language in his speech, which was widely covered in the press, referring to the 'redefinition of our aim' and his acknowl-edgement that 'we recognise that in practise English will remain the general vernacular' alarmed the more outspoken supporters of the language who recognised a shift in government policy.[138]

The speech was clearly a mild effort by Lemass to introduce a sense of realism into the debate about the place of Irish language in society. Accepting English as the vernacular of the majority of the Irish people and arguing for a commitment to bilingualism was a shift away from what Lemass and many others considered was the unobtainable goal of restoring Irish to everyday use throughout the state. The implied admission that a more realistic approach was needed was a departure from Fianna Fáil policy that some-times gestured to the notion of restoring Irish as the vernacular of the Irish nation. It contrasts sharply with the rhetoric Lemass had employed to denounce political opponents who in the past had called for a re-evaluation of the state's revival policies. In this respect, critics of the government's language policy were correct in noticing a marked shift taking place.

The Gaelic League in Cork quickly issued a statement that illus-trated the level of opposition from some quarters to the perceived change in government policy. It denounced Lemass, arguing that he

> has clearly shown that he has abandoned the National ideal and that his policy is to give second-rate status to the Irish language, while giving pride of place to the language of the conqueror. It is now obvious that the Government's promised White Paper will give birth to a weak leukemic underling, which will never reach maturity and will be incapable of encompassing the national ideal of re-establishing

> Irish as the spoken tongue of the people … Any patriot worthy of the
> name who is prepared to accept anything less (than a Gaelic nation) is
> a traitor to his heritage and to those that made the supreme sacrifice
> to ensure that Ireland should truly be made "a nation once again."'[139]

Lemass, of course, was a veteran of the 1916 Rising, the War
of Independence, and Civil War; his brother Noel had been kid-
napped, tortured, and killed by Free State forces in the Civil War.

The future Cardinal Tomás Ó Fiaich, who chaired the
Commission on the Restoration of the Irish Language, wrote to
Lemass expressing his concern with his comments at the Ard-
Fheis. With a national meeting of the Gaelic League only a few
days away, Ó Fiaich asked for a meeting with Lemass or a clarification of his position, explaining that there were efforts underway
within the organisation to draft a statement denouncing the government, particularly the Taoiseach. Press reports indicated that
many members of the Gaelic League were incensed with Lemass,
especially his statement that English would 'remain the general
vernacular' of the Irish people. Ó Fiaich was anxious to meet
the Taoiseach, explaining that he was worried about the 'wild
elements' at the meeting.[140] Lemass tried to defuse the controversy by carefully responding to Ó Fiaich in a letter that was read
out to the national meeting of the Gaelic League. The Taoiseach
declared that too much had been read into one sentence in his
speech and that it was not the aim of Fianna Fáil to 'keep English
as the general vernacular'.[141] Lemass had tried to speak honestly
and frankly about the language but was forced to backtrack and
argue that he had been misunderstood. He now maintained that
the White Paper, when published, would 'leave no cause for complaint or apprehension to any rational language enthusiast'.[142]

The attempt by Lemass to call for careful measured steps to
implement a rational language policy and his statement that
English would remain the spoken language of the Irish people was
incompatible with the thinking of the many cultural nationalists
intent on a policy of restoration. Lemass had tested the waters and
been scalded. The fact that such a firestorm would erupt when
trying to revise what many understood was an unrealistic policy
illustrates just how sensitive the issue remained. It also highlights
the political difficulty in accepting the reality of a failed cultural

policy that had been a key component of Irish cultural nationalism and Fianna Fáil political rhetoric for decades.

Although there may have been scepticism over using television to
promote the language, there was broad public support for and an
attachment to the Irish language. In 1964, Irish Marketing Surveys
Limited conducted an extensive study to gauge what it defined as
the 'climate of opinion among the Irish adult population to various
aspects regarding the Irish language question'.[143] The survey was
carried out with a sample of 1,961 men and women in fifty different areas of the country where trained members of the polling
company met respondents in face-to-face interviews. The results
were tabulated to indicate the response of urban and rural dwellers
in 'upper and middle income' groups and those in 'lower middle
and lower income groups' and were classified by age and gender.
When asked, 'Do you think that the Irish language could ever
replace English as the language most commonly used for ordinary
conversation in Ireland?', 83 per cent responded no.[144] There was
little discrepancy between urban and rural respondents.

When asked, 'Would you yourself like to see the Irish language
used by most people for ordinary conversation in Ireland?', 33 per
cent of those surveyed responded yes, and again there was little
discrepancy between rural and urban respondents.[145] When asked,
'Do you think that the Irish language could ever become a commonly used second language to English in Ireland?', 53 per cent
answered yes, while 42 per cent replied in the negative, but 76 per
cent responded that they would like to see Irish used as a second
language. Again the difference between urban and rural respondents was minimal. Women were marginally more optimistic about
Irish as a commonly used second language.

When asked if they approved or disapproved of Irish being
taught in national schools, 76 per cent indicated that they approved
but when the question was modified to, 'Do you yourself think
that the teaching of Irish should be compulsory or voluntary in
Secondary schools?', 72 per cent replied that it should be taught
on a voluntary basis. When it came to questions of advantages in
Irish society there was a broad consensus, with 72 per cent stating
that those who knew Irish had a distinct advantage in society.

Those that answered, yes, saw benefits in obtaining jobs, especially in the civil service, while other advantages included getting into university, conversing with native speakers, and having a better understanding of Irish literature.

Although the survey illustrates that there was broad support for the language, it also indicates there was a good deal of scepticism about the aims of the more ardent members of the language lobby. The poll also underscores the fact that compulsory Irish in secondary education was broadly unpopular. Tomás Ó Fiaich forwarded a copy of the entire report to Lemass, arguing that it demonstrated that there was a wealth of support for the language that needed to be cultivated, imploring him to take the lead on the issue. 'I state quite frankly that I believe you yourself as Taoiseach are the only one in Ireland today capable of getting things moving.'[146] Ó Fiaich discounted the results in the poll that demonstrated opposition towards compulsory Irish being taught in schools by defining the word 'compulsory' as problematic, labelling it a 'dirty name'. He maintained that if the term was taken out and a question simply asked 'Should Irish be taught in secondary schools?', the results would have been considerably more favourable.[147] This deliberately ignores the point that Irish was compulsory for public examinations and certification in secondary schools and that this form of 'compulsion' was unpopular with a large body of citizens.

Another major study commissioned in 1970 and published in 1975 regarding attitudes towards the language also reveals that there was considerable support for Irish. Many respondents believed it was important to 'national or ethnic identity, or as a symbol of cultural distinctiveness'.[148] This particular study indicated that the language was understood by a majority of the Irish people as an important part of Irish culture and argued that 'when interpreted in this sense [Irish] has favourable support from about two-thirds of the national population'.[149] The report indicated that the teaching of Irish in schools had considerable backing, but that there was widespread dissatisfaction with the methodology used in the schools because many believed it did not prepare students to speak the language after finishing their education.

When the Language Restoration Commission's Report was

published in 1963, the Department of Finance was charged with drafting the definitive White Paper that Lemass had promised. The Broadcasting Authority was asked by Finance for a detailed response to each point that had been raised in the Language Commission's report that related to broadcasting. The Authority responded by trying to identify recommendations that it could work with, pointing out that some had already been taken on board. Nonetheless, fundamental disagreements remained. In responding to the two chapters of the Commission's Report that addressed broadcasting, the Authority made this abundantly clear. Once again the Authority argued that it had a statutory responsibility to make ends meet, maintaining this was a critical point that had been missed by all language advocates: 'In general, it is difficult to avoid the conclusion that the obligation in regard to Irish set out in the Broadcasting Act has been interpreted by the Commission as requiring the Authority, without sufficient regard for its wider obligations, to operate broadcasting with the revival of Irish as a central feature of its general programme policy.'[150] It rejected the Commission's demand that there be an increase in Irish language programming in peak viewing periods in both television and radio, arguing that this would risk the financial stability of the national broadcaster. Pointing to the growing public opposition to obligatory language teaching in the schools, it argued that forcing Irish into prime time would 'generate resentment and the charge that the Language was being rendered compulsory for viewers and listeners'.[151]

Although the Authority was not opposed to exploring how more could be done with the language in drama and in children's programming, the general tone of its response was not positive. It was willing to make some concessions as long as these did not impede its ability to find and hold an audience, arguing 'the use of Irish on a substantial scale in television programmes would result in a major loss of audience, would antagonise large sections of the public and would have a marked effect on its finances. Increase[d] use of Irish must … be gradual, be well judged and be matched by a corresponding rise in acceptability by the public'.[152] This position represented the opinion of Eamonn Andrews and senior staff in both radio and television. As Secretary of the Department of Posts and Telegraphs, León Ó Broin evaluated the Authority's response and was broadly sympathetic. Although he was an advocate of public service broadcasting, and an Irish-speaking intellectual with tremendous affection for the language, he informed the Department of Finance that the Authority's position was valid. He argued that in drafting the White Paper the Department of Finance had to accept the fact that Irish programming was not popular and that the commercial remit of the service did not provide the Authority with much room to manoeuvre.

The Department of Finance realised that it had stepped into a political and cultural minefield and asked Ó Broin for help in defining exactly what the term 'restoration' meant in the context of the language. Ó Broin responded and in doing so helped the government reorient one of the most contentious cultural debates of the decade. His definition influenced the White Paper and sub-sequent government policy and provided a degree of 'wiggle room' for the government. It accepted the reality that there was not going to be a linguistic exchange any time soon, and instead addressed the need to patiently encourage the use of Irish. Although critics of the state's language policies had made similar arguments, Ó Broin succeeded in providing a degree of legitimacy to a critique that forced a re-evaluation of government policy. '"Restoration" means, in the long term, the restoration of Irish as the language in main use in Ireland. In the short term, it means the maintenance of Irish as the language in main use in the present Gaeltacht areas and the systematic extension of the knowledge and the use of Irish in the rest of the country.'[153]

Ó Broin then deftly shifted the emphasis to the need for the government to encourage economic development in the remote and economically deprived Irish-speaking areas of the state. Believing that support for the Gaeltacht was politically popular, he argued that if one accepted his definition of restoration, then the most important priority was the stability and prosperity of these Irish-speaking areas. He advised Finance it was critical that these areas be developed economically to stem the tide of emi-gration that plagued the Gaeltacht. If residents could be assured that they would enjoy a reasonable standard of living, only then would they be willing to remain and retain Irish as their primary language. In addressing the challenges inherent in restoration outside the Gaeltacht, he argued that the greatest obstacle was not ideological but practical, maintaining that there was a significant lack of knowledge of the language that had to be systematically but patiently addressed. He believed that a concerted effort could be undertaken but that progress would take over a generation or more. Ó Broin cautioned that none of this would work unless the right atmosphere existed, an atmosphere of genuine support for Irish. 'The arguments for the restoration of the language need to be studied and propagated persuasively and with the most modern techniques.'[154] He understood that unless society was genuinely interested in supporting the Irish language, the 'effort would fail and the Gaeltacht will not survive since the people of these areas are unlikely to wish to remain different from the rest of the country indefinitely'.[155]

The 1965 White Paper produced by the Department of Finance, *The Restoration of the Irish Language*, emphasised the critical need for public support in trying to restore the Irish language. Ó Riagáin notes that the government's Irish language policy between 1948 and 1970 was 'slowly detaching and distancing itself from leadership and prime responsibility for language policy'.[156] This is certainly made clear from the White Paper, which shifted at least partial responsibility to the general public.[157] Terence Brown has pointed out that the White Paper marked a 'turning point' because the government recognised and stated clearly that the English language was necessary even in Gaeltacht areas. A shift had taken place, as 'bilingualism not linguistic exchange became the new aspiration'.[158] Although the White Paper was sympathetic to many of the recommendations articulated by the Commission, it proved that the government was not willing to move quickly for fear of alienating public opinion. Brown notes in the publication a degree of ambivalence in this regard, as it vaguely sketched a set of goals that were to be reviewed on an annual basis: 'Phrases and terms such as "will recommend," "will encourage," "desirable," and "target" suggest a government caution and ambiguity almost amounting to equivocation.'[159]

Tony Crowley who has written extensively on the politics of the Irish language in Ireland maintains that although the White Paper reiterated the government commitment to the language, a close reading would lead advocates of the language to 'despair'. He too identifies a shift defining the White Papers as a 'classic example of political evasion and ambiguity … [concluding] In effect the state was withdrawing from its leadership role in the restoration project, despite its acknowledgment of the still integral role of the language in definitions of Irish identity'.[160] The clear and decisive strategy Lemass had called for at the Fianna Fáil Ard-Fheis gave way to a lukewarm plan marked by caution and ambivalence.

The White Paper called for the establishment of an organisation that would monitor the implementation of its recommendations and advise the government about progress and policy. This led to the creation of yet another body, Comhlacht [Council] Comhairleach na Gaeilge, which was set up to be 'representative of public and private interests, which will help to review policy and advise on its future development, with particular reference to the extension of the use of Irish in spheres other than that of public administration'.[161] This group comprised a range of individuals representative of public life and was to be overseen initially by Minister for Finance Dr James Ryan. When the Minister for Finance first met the council in the spring of 1965, he suggested 'television as one topic with which the Council might profitably concern itself'.[162] Ryan was keen to get the Council to aggressively investigate the role that television could play in reviving the language 'and was particularly anxious that the Council should examine the question thoroughly'.[163] After raising expectations, he and his department distanced themselves from the issue by referring all subsequent questions regarding television to a highly annoyed Department of Posts and Telegraphs.

When the required progress report addressing Irish in television was being drafted a year later a palpable degree of tension had developed between the two departments, as neither wanted anything to do with the contentious issue. The Minister for Posts and Telegraphs met with a group from Comhlacht Comhairleach na Gaeilge and told the delegation that 'he would welcome its detailed ideas on programmes and assumed that it would furnish its recommendations thereon to the Minister for Finance who had appointed it'.[164] He also informed the deputation that he 'would do his best to ensure the Council's views would be put into effect'.[165] Posts and Telegraphs instructed the group to communicate directly with the Department of Finance and wanted to avoid getting involved in contentious negotiations. Upon being contacted by the group, Finance quickly made it clear that it was not interested in questions concerning Irish language broadcasting, insisting that Posts and Telegraphs address the matter. The language was the proverbial hot potato that neither department wanted to hold.

Responding to pressure for a more substantial presence of Irish language material in Telefís Éireann, Kevin McCourt informed the Authority that an editor of Irish programmes would be appointed. He assured the Authority that the editor would be a 'key person in the organisation, would require to be possessed of high qualities of character and competence and would have the positive support of the Director-General in fulfilling his duties'.[166] Liam Ó Murchú was appointed editor of Irish programmes in April 1964 in an effort to address the critique of many Irish language supporters. After spending a month at a BBC training course in London he returned to Dublin and was expected to become the station's 'point person' on Irish language broadcasting. His responsibilities included developing programmes for Irish lessons, working with all departments to improve and increase the amount of Irish language broadcasts, recruiting bilingual personnel and assisting all departments in identifying appropriate Irish language material for broadcast. He was also expected to develop new programmes and find talented performers for productions that would be broadcast in Irish.[167] He experienced mixed results and was often frustrated in his efforts to find support for projects but was able to oversee a number of programmes that proved successful in finding an audience.

Ó Murchú's memoir, *A Time to Love?* recalls the struggles he encountered in trying to develop quality Irish language programming. An early success was *Labhair Gaeilge Linn*, developed as a short but innovative programme to provide language instruction to viewers. It was promoted by the station as an important development and described as a 'refresher course … made in the form of short playlets'.[168] According to Ó Murchú its success was due to his desire to make it attractive to 'the new urban-orientated mind' and communicate a sense of style that the language 'had a place in modern situations and which young people especially could identify with'.[169] Minister for Education Donogh O'Malley provided critical support for another popular programme that was designed to run with a new set of Irish lessons that the department was publishing. The programme *Buntús Gaeilge* was popular, running for three seasons, and the 250,000 books published to accompany the programme quickly sold out. Ó Murchú was interested in developing accessible bilingual programmes and later developed a popular variety programme that was broadcast both from the studio and on location around the country. *Trom agus Éadrom* won a Jacobs Award and realised Ó Murchú's desire to develop a programme that would make the language accessible by carefully integrating it into a programme thereby making it appealing to an audience that was not fluent in Irish.[170]

In an effort to bring the language into sports commentaries Kevin McCourt directed Ó Murchú and the Head of Sport, Michael O'Hehir, to develop a policy that would bring Irish into Gaelic games. An understanding was reached that this would be done 'in such a way as not to diminish general communication or detract from the general appeal of the programme'.[171] It was agreed that a concerted effort would be made to feature more Irish 'by way of phrases, comment, etc., but this must not be done in such a way as to give the impression that information is being given in one language and not the other'.[172] In spite of some success Ó Murchú was frustrated by more passionate supporters of the language who 'seemed to feel that I was as much in their employ as in that of RTÉ – a kind of honorary, unpaid, Graham-Greene-like "Our Man in Havana" – who had nothing to do but put on *their* Irish language programmes'.[173] As editor he was convinced that Irish language programmes broadcast in prime time would not be watched and that a concerted effort had to be made to provide innovative educational and bilingual programming. He believed broadcasts had to be geared to four programme categories: to native speakers in the Gaeltacht; to viewers that had lost touch with the language since leaving school; for enrichment, teaching viewers about the role of the language in Irish culture; and, lastly, for teaching Irish at different ages and levels. Ó Murchú concluded that planning was not really difficult but the implementation of policy was always problematic. 'The successes were few, and all of them hard won; the abortions, miscarriages and outright failures many, and too bitter to bear remembering.'[174]

Within the Broadcasting Authority, tension concerning the absence of substantial Irish programming came to a head when Ernest Blythe penned a fifteen-page critique to the director-general in the autumn of 1964. The letter, which was circulated to members of the Radio Éireann Authority, focused on what he defined as the failure of the Authority to make a sincere effort to support Irish. Seemingly not impressed by the appointment of Ó Murchú, he once again expressed disappointment at both the amount of material featured and its quality, arguing that what was broadcast was nothing more than 'scraps' he defined as useless. He argued that when Irish was featured in decent viewing time the quality was abysmal, 'indicative of varying types of indifference or contempt, being mostly what I have described as incestuous or ghetto-minded or non-adult'.[175] Blythe told the director-general that the Authority was duty bound to serve not simply an Irish-speaking minority but all viewers, and called for regular, if brief, Irish broadcasts in prime time and the use of the language in popular programmes such as *The Late Late Show*. He urged the station to make an effort at broadcasting short plays in Irish and in popular home-produced programmes such as *Jamboree, Jackpot, World of Sport* and *Strictly Politics*. Blythe argued that the most important viewers were young children and teenagers that needed the lessons they learned in school reinforced at home.

He was convinced that efforts to develop imaginative Irish lan-guage programmes were being thwarted by what he referred to as 'the resistance of the Establishment which in some instances amounted almost, if not quite, to sabotage'.[176] Again, he argued that even when the Radio Éireann Authority was working with the best of intentions to get staff within Telefís Éireann to do more for the language, its efforts were being subverted or undermined. 'Only the strongest directives from the Authority or the Director-

General will prevent the efforts of the minority of our officials who would like to do the right thing by the Irish language, from being thwarted or circumscribed by the steady pressure of the majority who personally have no use for it and when something is proposed to be done in Irish will almost invariably contend that it should be done in English.'[177]

The director-general replied to Blythe, explaining that the Broadcasting Act did not stipulate that the television service go so far as to feature Irish at peak viewing times. He reiterated his belief that while this might satisfy those who knew and understood Irish, the policy 'would do injustice to far greater numbers who could not but be driven, most of them, to the seductive light-weight material normally being transmitted at peak viewing time on British channels'.[178] Blythe's letter was the focus of a regularly scheduled meeting of the Authority in January 1965, and the minutes of that meeting illustrate where the fault lines lay in relation to increased Irish language broadcasting. Blythe argued that he was trying to be reasonable but believed it imperative that television reach out to young adults, especially those who had recently completed school. Once again he pleaded for Irish language broadcasting during peak viewing times, arguing that every effort should be made to improve the quality of Irish programmes. He believed that the language could successfully be integrated into popular domestic programmes, arguing that Irish should not be used primarily in instructional programming but also in creative entertainment with what he defined as a 'strong narrative element'.[179] Although he accepted that prime-time Irish programmes might decrease the station's revenue, he believed this should be accepted and 'a case should be made to the Government if the Authority's revenue earning capacity was thereby unduly impaired'.[180] Although Áine Ní Channainn, who believed that Irish could be used in *The Late Late Show* and *On the Road*, endorsed his position, none of the other members of the Authority supported him.

Authority member Edward McManus, who was regarded as a strong Fianna Fáil supporter, rejected the proposal to extend Irish programmes into peak viewing periods because of the risks to revenue that would be at stake.[181] James Fanning, who had already made it clear that he believed viewers were not interested in Irish language broadcasts, also criticised Blythe's interpretation of the Broadcasting Act and made it clear that it was not the responsibility of Telefís Éireann to restore the Irish language. He was sceptical of developing programmes for young people, maintaining 'the Authority knew very little of the viewing habits of the young adults at whom Mr. Blythe sought to direct more Irish, and it would be exceptionally dangerous to risk loss of viewers by greater emphasis on the language at a time when the position of the pattern of television advertising was under consideration'.[182] Another member, Commander Crosbie, editor of the *Cork Examiner*, also disagreed with Blythe, stating he had spoken with 'a large number of Irish speaking viewers, all of whom were satisfied with current Irish broadcasting'.[183] Blythe found little support for his proposals from other members of the Authority. Charles Brennan and Fintan Kennedy maintained that although they were sympathetic they were worried about the financial implications of a loss of viewers, believing the Authority should move slowly and carefully. Brennan accepted that more could be done to develop quality Irish programming while Kennedy claimed that he noticed a growing public sympathy for the language throughout the country, believing this was 'mainly attributable to television which had helped to increase respect for the language'.[184]

Eamonn Andrews assured members that they were fulfilling their obligations under the Broadcasting Act, and that the best way to address the critique put forward by Blythe was to increase the quality of Irish programming and carefully consider when and how additional material could be broadcast. Director-General Kevin McCourt also believed that Telefís Éireann was doing its part in helping efforts to revive Irish, but that this was not enough for what he referred to as 'dedicated enthusiasts'. During these discussions, he took the opportunity to make it clear that the new Controller of Programmes, Gunnar Rugheimer, who had replaced Michael Barry, should not be targeted for criticism due to his non-Irish background. He asked the Authority not to see his status as a foreigner 'as preventing him from sharing a feeling for the Authority's objectives'. McCourt praised Rugheimer as being responsible for 'building up the image which the station enjoyed today as a consequence of the switch of emphasis from inexpensive U.S. material to more and better quality home origination'.[185] He singled out Ó Murchú's successful Irish language programme *Labhair Gaeilge Linn*, an instructional programme that had been praised by supporters of the language, as an initiative that Rugheimer had developed. Despite these arguments, Ernest Blythe remained frustrated at his inability to push the Authority to increase both the quality and quantity of Irish language broadcasts.

While these debates were taking place within the Authority and in the pages of the national press, attention began to focus on the fact that the term of the Broadcasting Authority was about to expire. In May 1965, speculation mounted about what the Lemass Government would do when the term of the first Authority ended. The *Irish Press* reported that there was growing speculation that Eamonn Andrews would not stay on as chair, given his commitments to the BBC in the UK. The paper also reported that the Broadcasting Authority had prepared a report for the Minister for Posts and Telegraphs on its five-year term. The paper claimed that although members believed there was always room for improvement the Authority was convinced it had succeeded in 'achieving a fairly high standard, and that any dissatisfaction which has been expressed with the service has come from a minority of viewers'.[186]

The government met on June 1, 1965 and reappointed Eamonn Andrews to a one-year term as a member and Chairman of the Authority. Five years earlier, when the first Broadcasting Authority was established, he had been consulted closely about the make-up of the Authority but, tellingly, this was not done in the summer of 1965. The government decided not to reappoint Charles Brennan, Ernest Blythe, Commander George Crosbie, and one of only two women on the board, Áine Ní Chanainn. The new board included existing members Eamonn Andrews as Chairman, Professor T. W. Moody, James Fanning, Edward McManus, Fintan Kennedy, and new members including Dónall Ó Móráin, Michael Noonan, Phyllis Bean Uí Cheallaigh and Ruairí Brugha. All the appointments were made for a period of one year, which provided the government a degree of flexibility as the last board had a fixed term of five years.[187]

The appointment of Dónall Ó Móráin was an extraordinary attempt to try to blunt the relentless criticism emanating from one of the most outspoken advocates of the language. By including Ó Móráin the government tried to appease or co-opt one of its harshest critics. Ó Móráin found allies in the widow of the late president Seán T. O'Kelly, Phyllis Uí Cheallaigh, and the son of Cathal Brugha, Ruairí Brugha, both of whom advocated for increased Irish language programming. The Broadcasting Authority subsequently fractured as it came under renewed pressure from within to increase Irish language programming, creating serious divisions that complicated national broadcasting policy. This change in the make-up of the Authority was addressed in the Irish language publication *Inniu* (Today).[188] An article written by an unidentified correspondent engaged in research to determine if the changes in the make-up of the Broadcasting Authority would have any real effect on the status of Irish on television. The reporter did not identify sources but concluded that 'it is likely that the situation will improve somewhat'.[189] After explaining the dynamics of the old Authority where there were two identified as supporting the language, four against and three somewhere in between it was reported that the balance of power within the Authority had shifted in favour of Irish.

The new Authority was reported as having three members identified as friends of the language, three defined as 'anti-Irish', and three neutrals. It was hoped that this new dynamic would work to the benefit of those that wanted an increased presence of Irish in television broadcasting. Special mention was made of the government's appointment of 'one member of the newly appointed authority who used to complain strongly about the neglect of Irish by the old Authority'.[190] This was certainly a reference to the appointment of Dónall Ó Móráin, one of the most withering critics of Telefís Éireann. The article pointed out that his appointment should send a message to the neutrals on the new authority that 'the Government wants greater and more effective concern with Irish on television in the future than was the case up to now'.[191] There was some speculation that this was in fact a Machiavellian move to try to quiet the government's critics, but the reporter believed that the constitution of the new board signalled that change was imminent. The reporter warned that the government should not leave the fate of the language in the hands of 'a group as foreign-minded as are the majority of the Authority, especially since most of the paid staff of Telefís Éireann are unenthusiastic about the language'.[192] Although the writer did not see ill will or an anti-national sentiment behind the neglect of the language, it was argued that nothing would change unless the entire Authority underwent further transformation or until the government made it clear that more Irish language programming be provided immediately.

Under the terms of the 1965 White Paper, Posts and Telegraphs was required to produce a progress report to the Department of Finance detailing what steps had been taken to bring more Irish into television broadcasting. This information would be used for a larger, more comprehensive report that would be submitted to the Cabinet in a formal *Memorandum for the Government*. The department duly submitted a report, maintaining that two improvements had been made that would benefit the cause of the language. The first was the reconstitution of the Broadcasting Authority to include both Dónall Ó Móráin and Ruairí Brugha, a man described as an active member of the language movement.

The second accomplishment was the publication of an official policy statement on the place of Irish that had been widely circulated in the press. When he joined the Authority, Ó Móráin drafted this policy statement titled simply *Irish on television,* and after some discussion it was accepted by the Authority and distributed throughout the radio and television service. The document signalled a new commitment to making a concerted effort to help with the revival, stipulating that staff had a 'responsibility to nurture the Irish language by presenting it in a sympathetic and imaginative way.'[193] The document illustrates the influence of Ó Móráin, Uí Cheallaigh and Brugha and is remarkable for what it implied. In promising that the service would not be used to 'present unbalanced discussion on the national aim of restoring Irish', it suggested that there was a conspiracy afoot within Telefís Éireann to undermine and ridicule efforts of revivalists.[194]

The policy statement outlined a renewed effort to bring Irish into sports, news, children's and current affairs programming, announcing that new initiatives would be developed in Irish. Furthermore, bilingualism would be required for specific jobs, and it was strongly suggested that Irish speakers would find it easier to advance through the ranks within Telefís Éireann.

In addition to increasing the amount of Irish language broadcasts, Telefís Éireann would 'increasingly help to build a better public consciousness of national identity by means of programmes on history and culture in Ireland'.[195] One can sense here the influence of T. W. Moody who succeeded in getting a commitment to bring informative history projects onto Telefís Éireann.

The new Authority proved to be aggressive in inserting itself into programming decisions, challenging the director-general and controller of programmes on a number of occasions. One can sense that this new-found comfort in involving itself in the day-to-day operations of Telefís Éireann became a distraction for senior administrators, producers and writers. The director-general announced the new policy to a bewildered staff in an impromptu meeting held in a studio at the Donnybrook station. The new emphasis on quantity was made clear by the director-general as producers, writers and presenters were encouraged to use Irish as much as possible in all aspects of programming. During the meeting with McCourt questions and comments illustrated a wide range of emotions from 'sheer bewilderment to polite rage'.[196] Within the service even senior producers committed to the Irish language had reservations, believing that it would be a mistake to do too much too fast. Aindrias Ó Gallchóir, a veteran producer who later became controller of the Irish language radio service, Radió na Gaeltachta maintains that this was understood within the television service; 'you had to go to the degree that people would accept, you had to go with the audience, you can not go so far ahead that the dog cannot hear the whistle'.[197] The fact that the new policy did not produce a marked increase in Irish programming concerned Ó Móráin who expressed his frustration at the 'decline of the quantity of Irish' to the Authority that spring.[198] Looking ahead to the autumn season, Ó Móráin hoped more could be done for the language; he suggested that news broadcasts could be made easier to understand, maintaining 'there should be slowly read Nuacht headlines at 8 p.m.'[199]

By April 1966, almost one full year into the tenure of the new Authority and with an understanding that the same group would be reappointed, Eamonn Andrews abruptly resigned as chair of the Broadcasting Authority. He was deeply unhappy with the make-up of the new Authority and the efforts to insert more Irish into programming. In his letter of resignation to Seán Lemass, Andrews explained that he believed broadcasting was headed in the wrong direction. He pointed out that seven years earlier when Lemass asked him to chair the Radio Éireann Authority his views on its composition were sought. He lamented the fact that this was not the case when the second Authority was appointed and was clearly upset with the appointments of Ó Móráin and his allies. One year earlier when Andrews learned of the make-up of the new board, he was so distraught he cut short a trip to the USA, returning to Ireland where he considered tendering his resignation. He explained to Lemass that he had accepted the invitation to continue with reservations. 'I was concerned, among other things, to save any possible embarrassment to yourself or the Minister and to see through the important and difficult 1916 celebration year.'[200] Andrews had become profoundly uncomfortable with the new board, complaining that the new emphasis on Irish was a mistake and that concessions made to appease the language lobby were undermining the service. He informed the Taoiseach, 'I have tried to compromise to the point beyond which honesty will not permit me to go. I fear very much that if the present RTÉ policies in this respect are pursued, the service will get so far ahead of public acceptance that it will lose the Irish viewer to cross channel services as happened in radio.'[201]

Andrews was convinced that it had been a serious mistake to try to placate the language lobby by bringing in members who wanted to promote the language with what he believed was no conception of the financial realities of broadcasting. He told Lemass that the new emphasis on the Irish language was causing discord and that he had 'distressing evidence of repercussions within the service itself. For the most sincere reasons members are pressing an unrealistic policy which I believe may have both artistic and financial repercussions of an unfortunate kind. Enough practical board room experience of Public Service budgets and balance sheets is not available to counterbalance the idealism that, no doubt, inspires the present course of action; and the wish to have what is desirable is not being related to what is either possible or acceptable.'[202] As noted earlier he was also upset with the Authority's decision not to reappoint Gunnar Rugheimer Controller of Programmes.

Lemass was troubled by the resignation and tried to get Andrews to change his mind. Andrews responded that, 'If my understanding that the Authority is to be re-appointed en bloc is correct, then, for the reasons I have given you, I could not change my mind.'[203] Andrews met with Lemass and later wrote to him explaining that as 'nothing has changed' he would resign and advise the members of the Authority of his decision. He also told Lemass that when his resignation became public he would explain that he resigned as a matter of principle. 'I will not do this to add to the controversies that already exist about such things as the Irish language, but to emphasise, if only to my former colleagues, the danger and short-sightedness I believe to be synonymous with the present policy.'[204]

Many years later Dónall Ó Móráin disputed this version of events, which were largely supported in an interview John Horgan conducted with Gunner Rugheimer for his authoritative biography of Seán Lemass. Rugheimer maintained that Authority members were unreasonable in pushing for more Irish language programming; he specifically mentioned Phyllis Bean Uí Cheallaigh and Ernest Blythe: 'I got hell from these two. They wanted to operate on the basis of a belief that everybody spoke Irish, and that the appropriate thing to do would be to sprinkle Irish throughout the programming: this was complete rubbish.'[205] Rugheimer maintains that Andrews resigned because he thought it was 'unreasonable and unfair' for the Authority to force RTÉ to assume responsibility for the revival of the Irish language.[206]

In a 1999 letter to the editor of the *Irish Times* Ó Móráin argued that Eamonn Andrews knew he was not going to be reappointed to the Authority when his term expired later in the year. According to Ó Móráin when the second Authority was established 'there was virtually no Irish used on the television service' and when he worked with Phyllis Bean Uí Cheallaigh and Ruairí Brugha to make modest proposals Andrews and other members were opposed. Eventually some members 'turned against the chairman's general broadcasting policy and were open to compromise. Eventually, by majority vote, the [A]uthority, in its generosity, decided to allow 30 minutes of programming in Irish per week!.[207] Ó Móráin was not impressed with the resignation of the Chairman, arguing that Andrews' dramatic resignation a few months before his term was due to expire simply 'made a virtue out of necessity'.[208]

The government moved quickly in finding a replacement for Andrews; less than a month after receiving Andrews's letter of resignation a decision had been made to offer the position to Christopher Stephen (Todd) Andrews. The position was not advertised, and there was no formal search. Lemass met Todd Andrews at the end of May and offered him the position.[209]

At the start of the 1960s, the Sinn Féin ideology that had defined de Valera's Ireland had run its course. Seán Lemass, Ireland's great moderniser, opened up a closed economy and encouraged the development of what he described as a modern 'vigorous nation seeking efficiency'.[210] Inevitably modernisation undermined powerful institutions that had become entrenched in the fabric of life in independent Ireland. As television became more confident and assertive the Catholic Church and many political elites found themselves on the defensive, forced to answer difficult questions about their decisions and policies. Advocates of the Irish language were also challenged by television and chafed at being treated as yet another interest group. As television permeated Irish society, it provoked debates about the place of the language in contemporary Ireland. Increasingly questions about the state's cultural priorities were complicated by television's relentless presence. The medium exposed cultural policies that had been accepted, at least on paper, through much of the life of independent Ireland to a bright and discomforting light.

It would be inaccurate to argue that there was a simple bipolarity between traditionalists and modernisers that squared off in the cultural wars of the 1960s. In fact the term 'language lobby' is highly problematic as it suggests there was one cohesive organisation driven by consensual politics. This was far from the case as supporters ranged from those committed to the actual restoration of the language as the vernacular of the Irish people to moderates who hoped to both support the Gaeltacht and cultivate an appreciation of a rich and varied literary and oral tradition. Many had little time for the traditional rural Gaelic ideology that de Valera embraced. Others were interested in social justice and focused on urban and class issues and hoped to use the language to open up Irish society making it more pluralist.

Within RTÉ there were certainly many progressive voices that were keen to use the language to challenge the status quo. Seán Mac Réamoinn, Aindrias Ó Gallchóir and Breandán Ó hEithir all understood that many of the demands of the Gaelic League were unrealistic. Aindrias Ó Gallchóir argued that the producers and writers he worked with were interested in preserving and nurturing the language and that they considered the term 'conservation' more appropriate that 'restoration'.[211] However all were happy enough to exploit the constant pressure on RTÉ to develop successful programmes that often featured hard-hitting critiques of governments, politicians and the conservatism that characterised Irish society throughout the 1960s.[212] Mention has already been made of a controversial edition of *An Fear Agus A Sceal*, which was cancelled in the autumn of 1963 provoking charges of censorship from members of the Labour Party and the national press. At the time Proinsias Mac Aonghusa who produced the programme rattled the political sensibilites of Kevin McCourt for conducting an interview with an outspoken former Clann na Poblachta Dáil Deputy, Con Lehane, who attacked the Catholic Church and Fianna Fáil.

When Eoghan Harris joined the staff of RTÉ in 1966 as a bright 22-year-old producer trainee he understood that Ireland was undergoing a period of remarkable change. He quickly emerged as a talented producer determined to use television to undermine the conservative nature of Irish society that he found suffocating. 'I had an agenda … I wanted to punch holes in the three legs of Daniel Cokery's Ireland, land, religion and nationalism.'[213] He knew the language could have a radical, progressive voice and developed programmes about the challenges of urban

15   *Féach* presenters Brendán Ó hEithir (right) and Eamonn Ó Muirí.

life for working-class viewers, programmes that often times were critical of Fianna Fáil economic and social policy. He also wanted to exert maximum pressure on the Chairman of the Broadcasting Authority, Eamonn Andrews, who opposed the extension of Irish language programming.[214] Harris maintains that a confident 'Gaelic Mafia' emerged within the national radio and television service that included Mac Réamoinn, Ó Gallchóir and Ó hEithir and that by 1966 there was a marked improvement in the quality and popularity of Irish language programming.

Harris worked with Breandán Ó hEithir producing a re-energised *Féach,* a current affairs programme with a radical agenda that targeted the political and religious establishment of the time. Their guests included advocates for affordable housing, campaigners for economic development in the Gaeltacht, and leaders of a number of organisations including the Northern Ireland Civil Rights Association, People's Democracy and the Irish Women's Liberation Movement. Their programmes were meant to be provocative, for instance when President Nixon visited Ireland in the autumn of 1970, *Féach* telecast a mock trial of the President from outside the American Embassy. This 'highly improper' broadcast caught the attention of the Minister for Posts and Telegraphs who would not have been impressed.[215] According to Harris, a network of Irish speakers within the government and civil service tolerated the iconoclasm of *Féach* and offered some degree of protection because it produced quality programming in Irish. 'Their attitude was "ok that young guy Harris may be a communist but he's doing great programmes in Irish, let's put up with the anti-clericalism and anti-nationalism".[216] John Horgan notes that although many of these producers in this 'Gaelic Mafia' did not share a clear set of political convictions they were all 'united in their desire to push the envelope of the new medium, and protected that enterprise by the fact that they were doing it in the first official language'.[217]

In his exhaustive study *Gaelic Prose in the Irish Free State 1922–1939*, Philip O'Leary addresses the fractious debates that divided supporters of the Irish language.[218] Disputes between native speakers and learners of the language and between what O'Leary defines as nativists and progressives created controversy among supporters of the language soon after independence and these tensions persisted well into the years covered in this study. Throughout the 1960s there was a high degree of tension between the more conservative leadership of the Gaelic League and the producers of Irish language programming within RTÉ. Many leaders of the Gaelic League 'detested' the Irish language producers within the television service, regarding them as a 'gang of trendy Irish speaking lefty progressives'.[219] While many supporters of Irish understood that trying to force the language on an uninterested population was counter-productive and doomed to failure, these voices were often drowned out by reactionaries in the language movement, by what one long-serving Irish speaking director-general referred to as 'language fascists'.[220]

Many 'modernisers' chose to dismiss the language lobby as one-dimensional, maintaining that although they were not hostile to the language they were firmly committed to seeing Ireland prosper and fully engage with the modern world. In the formative years of Telefís Éireann, Eamonn Andrews and Edward Roth argued that many of the demands made by the language lobby were impossible to accept for a television service dependent on advertising revenue to remain financially viable. Seán Lemass who was determined to see RTÉ become a financially viable enterprise accepted this interpretation. Many supporters of the language considered their arguments a convenient 'smoke screen' meant to hide the fact that these men had little real sympathy or interest in the Irish language. It was understood that unlike his predecessor, Eamon de Valera, Seán Lemass had no command of the language and therefore no real appreciation for it.[221] His commitment to the language was regarded as highly suspect in spite of the colourful rhetoric he employed during elections. Many supporters of the language considered the first chairman of the Radio Telefís Éireann Authority Eamonn Andrews as highly suspect because his reputation and experience were both established in the UK. Telefís Éireann's first Director-General, Edward Roth, was a capable American technocrat dedicated to completing the difficult task of getting a commercial public service off the ground and on the air. He was bewildered by demands made by supporters of the language and never fully comprehended or appreciated the cultural context of the arguments being made. These men were focused on the establishment of a viable hybrid service and were unfamiliar and perhaps unconcerned with the complex arguments pertaining to mass media and language shift.

As the decade unfolded, more Irish language programming slowly made its way onto Telefís Éireann, and much of it was remarkably creative and successful. *Labhair Gaeilge Linn*, *Féach* and later *Trom agus Éadrom*, found impressive audiences and proved to be engaging programmes. However the issue of Irish language programming continued to cause controversy and towards the end of the decade tactics shifted once again as many advocates began to successfully argue for Irish language programming as a minority right.[222] Instead of insisting the government feature more Irish material on the national service support grew once again for a separate television station that would serve Irish-speaking communities. This resulted in the establishment of Teilifís na Gaeilge which went on the air in 1996. Although it experienced intense opposition as it was being organised, and serious growing pains once it was up and running, it has tried to use the medium to make Irish interesting, engaging, and relevant.

Notes

1 One writer and activist who supported the language, Risteárd Ó Glaisne, described the LFM as 'Protestants, descendants of those who collaborated with the British, upper class "Castle Catholics", those influenced by Anglo-American culture, "an ambitious stratum within the Roman Catholic middle class" and people who have failed the Leaving Certificate Exam'. Quoted in Tony Crowley, *War of Words: The Politics of Language 1537–2004* (Oxford University Press, Oxford, 2004), 179.

2 Gael-Linn was established in 1953 to promote Irish culture with an emphasis on the Irish language. It developed entrepreneurial projects in the Gaeltacht including fish farms, and was committed to exploiting developing technologies for the language. It produced a remarkable number of innovative films that were screened in cinemas throughout the country in the late 1950s and early 1960s. It also helped popularise traditional music by producing records on the Gael-Linn label. The group was an unsuccessful applicant for a television broadcasting licence in 1958. Dónall Ó Móráin, the founding director, was a former army officer and supporter of Fine Gael. He was interviewed by the author in Dublin in December 1990.

3 Quoted in Fergal Tobin, *The Best of Decades: Ireland in the 1960s* (Gill and Macmillan, Dublin, 1984), 153.

4 Ibid.

5 *Irish Independent*, September 22, 1966.

6 Ibid.

7 NAI DT, S14996D, the language is from a memorandum written by Lemass to Moynihan, April 1960.

8 Crowley, *War of Words*, 184.

9 Pádraig Ó Riagáin, *Language Policy and Social Reproduction, Ireland 1893–1993* (Clarendon Press, Oxford, 1997), 269.

10 See Niamh Nic Shuibhne, 'The Constitution, the Courts and the Irish Language', in *Ireland's Evolving Constitution 1937–1997* (eds) Tom Murphy and Patrick Twomey (Hart Publishing, Oxford, 1998).

11 Ó Riagáin, *Language Policy*, 15.

12 Gearóid Ó Tuathaigh, 'The State and the Irish Language: An Historical Perspective', in *A New View of the Irish Language* (eds) Caoilfhionn Nic Pháidín and Seán Ó Cearnaigh (Cois Life, Dublin, 2008), 29.

13 Joseph Lee, *Ireland 1912–1985* (Cambridge University Press, Cambridge, 1989), 134.

14 For an in-depth consideration of Language policy and education see Adrian Kelly, *Compulsory Irish, Language and Education in Ireland 1870s–1970s* (Irish Academic Press, Dublin 2002).

15 Lee, *Ireland 1912–1985*, 135.

16 Ibid., 134.
17 Gearóid Ó Tuathaigh, 'The State and the Language', 30.
18 Terence Brown, *Ireland: A Social and Cultural History, 1922 to the Present* (Cornell University Press, Ithaca, 1985), 149–50. Brown addresses developments in the 1940s as a 'watershed for the fortunes of the Irish language'.
19 Broadcasting Act, 1960, Section 17, 23, Dublin Stationery Office, 1960.
20 Opening address of 2RN, Douglas Hyde, January 1, 1926. The address began in English for 'any strangers listening in'. He then completed his talk in Irish and these quotes are taken from that part of the address. Thanks to Nollaig Mac Congáil for the translation.
21 Ibid.
22 Ronan Fanning, *Independent Ireland* (Helicon, Dublin, 1983), 79.
23 NAI, Department of Taoiseach, SP15580, report and minute, September 25, 1953. Although the listener surveys may say something about the quality of Irish language programming there is little doubt that the low numbers created real concern when Telefís Éireann was finding its feet as a commercial enterprise.
24 NAI, Department of Communications, TV 11361.
25 Ibid., the statistic of 10 per cent seems very small and does not take into account unlicenced sets, but the Gaeltacht was one of the more chronically impoverished regions of the country. Although de Valera proposed that free radios be distributed to residents, nothing was done to follow through on his proposal.
26 Ibid
27 Ibid.
28 Ibid. Iarfhlaith Watson's research into radio schedules gives an idea of the amount and type of Irish language programming being broadcast in the 1950s. For one particular week in October 1955, over eight hours of Irish programming included news, talks, songs and music, and children's programmes. See his *Broadcasting in Irish* (Dublin, Four Courts Press, 2003), 34.
29 Declan Kiberd, *Inventing Ireland* (Jonathan Cape, London, 1995), 568.
30 RTÉ Authority Archive, Notes on Programme Policy Meeting, March 22, 1969.
31 See Breandán Delap, 'Irish and the Media', in *A New View of the Irish Language* (eds) Nic Pháidín and Ó Cearnaigh.
32 NAI, Department of Communications, TV 11361.
33 Ibid.
34 Robert Savage, *Irish Television: The Political and Social Origins* (Cork University Press, Cork, 1996), 181–2. The efforts by the language lobby to influence the Television Commission and the government are

addressed in detail in this book.

35 Ibid., 194.

36 Ibid.

37 Ibid., 196.

38 Gearóid Ó Tuathaigh, 'Language, Literature and Culture in Ireland Since the War', in *Ireland 1945–1970* (ed.) Joseph Lee (Gill and Macmillan, Dublin, 1979).

39 NAI, Communications, TW 6086, Ó Muineacháin to Donnacha Ó Laoire, October 20, 1959.

40 RTÉ Written Archives, Irvine Papers, Roth to Ó Súilleabháin, March 28, 1961.

41 Ibid.

42 Ibid.

43 Ibid.

44 Depending on their equipment Irish listeners had a choice of stations available including the BBC, American Armed Forces Radio, and 'pirate' stations including Europe Number One, Radio Luxembourg, and later Radio Caroline.

45 RTÉ Written Archives, Irvine Papers, transcription of Roth's press conference, April 7, 1961.

46 Dáil Debates, Vol. 179, February 17, 1960.

47 Quoted in the *Irish Times*, September 14, 1961.

48 *Galway Observer*, September 16, 1961.

49 NAI S13180 D/61 Lemass Speech at Fianna Fáil Headquarters, Dublin South-Central Dáil Constituency, September 20, 1961.

50 Kelly, *Compulsory Irish*, 38. Fine Gael also advocated the elimination of required tests in Irish for appointment to the Civil Service and local authorities. When Fine Gael formed a government in 1973 changes were made and the requirement to pass Irish in order to pass the Leaving Certificate, Intermediate Certificate and Group Certificate was dropped.

51 Séamus Ó Grianna stepped down as editor in 1929.

52 Letter to the editor from Séamus Ó Grianna, 'Compulsory Irish', *Irish Times*, May 19, 1966, in *The Lights of Heaven* (ed.) Nollaig Mac Congáil (Arlen House, Galway, 2006), 203. See also Philip O'Leary's, *Gaelic Prose in the Irish Free State, 1922–1939* (University College Dublin Press, Dublin, 2004).

53 Ibid. Ó Grianna to *Irish Times*, June 6, 1966, 207.

54 NAI, Department of Communications, TW 11292, September 21, 1961. Submission to the Radio Éireann Authority on Telefís Éireann.

55 Ibid.

56 Ibid.

57 Ibid., 2.

58 Ibid.
59 Ibid., 3.
60 Ibid., 4.
61 Ibid.
62 Ibid.
63 Ibid., 5.
64 Ibid.
65 Ibid., Roth to Donncha Ó Laoire, Secretary, Comhdháil Náisiúnta na Gaeilge October 26, 1961.
66 Ibid.
67 Ibid.
68 *Evening Mail*, November 11, 1961.
69 Ibid.
70 *Sunday Press*, November 19, 1961.
71 *Irish Times*, November 11, 1961.
72 Ibid.
73 NAI, Department of Communications, TW 11292, Ó Laoire to Roth, November 28, 1961.
74 Ibid.
75 Ibid.
76 Ibid., 2.
77 Ibid.
78 *Daily Mail*, December 2, 1961.
79 *Dáil Debates*, November 29, 1961. The organisation originally formed in 1943 as a student group interested in the revival of the language.
80 NAI, Department of Communications, TW 11292, Ó Laoire to Roth, December 5, 1961.
81 Ibid., Ó Laoire to Roth, December 12, 1961.
82 Ibid.
83 Ibid.
84 Ibid., Roth to Ó Laoire, December 8, 1961.
85 NAI TV 11361 *Gael-Linn,* pamphlet, December 17, 1961.
86 Ibid.
87 Ibid. Articles appeared in the *Evening Press*, the *Irish Independent, Irish Times*, the *Evening Mail*, and the *Limerick Leader,* among others.
88 Ibid.
89 Ibid., Scannell, Department of Posts and Telegraphs to Gael-Linn, December 19, 1961.
90 Ibid., Mac Gabhrann to Posts and Telegraphs, December 21, 1961. The response was shared with the Taoiseach Seán Lemass.
91 Author's interview with Dónall Ó Móráin, December 1990, Dublin.
92 *Irish Independent*, February 12, 1962.
93 Department of Communications, TW 11292. Meeting of Authority

with Comhdháil Náisiúnta Delegation, March 10, 1962.

94 Ibid.

95 Ibid.

96 Ibid., 2.

97 Ibid., 3.

98 Ibid.

99 Ibid.

100 Ibid.

101 Thanks to Gearóid Ó Tuathaigh for his observations on the wrangling between the Congress and broadcasters.

102 NAI, Department of Communications, TW 11292, meeting of the RTÉ Authority with Comhdháil Náisiúnta Delegation, March 10, 1962, 3.

103 Ibid., summary of Dónall Ó Móráin's article in Irish in the April 1962 issue of *An tUltach* – the official journal of Comhaltas Uladh, 2.

104 Ibid., 3. Television Audience Measurements (TAM) was the company contracted to measure viewership by the Authority.

105 Ibid. Radio Luxembourg was established as a commerical radio station in 1933 in Luxembourg, broadcasting across international boundaries. It quickly became a popular and influential source of contemporary music including blues and rock and roll.

106 Ibid., 4.

107 *Irish Press*, August 6, 1962.

108 Ibid.

109 *Irish Times*, August 8, 1962.

110 Ibid.

111 *Irish Times*, August 21, 1962.

112 NAI, Department of Communications, TW 11292. *The Place of Irish in the Television Service*, September 19, 1962, with cover letter, Andrews to Ó Laoire.

113 Ibid. Andrews explained 'The Authority does not admit to any right in the Comhdhail to dictate broadcasting policy or to prescribe how the broadcasting service should be conducted'.

114 Ibid.

115 Ibid., 2.

116 Ibid., 3.

117 Ibid.

118 Ibid., 10.

119 Ibid.

120 *Evening Press*, October 20, 1962.

121 NAI, Department of Communications, TW 11292 Andrews to Hilliard, October 21, 1962.

122 Ibid.

123 Dáil Debates, Vol. 197, October 31, 1962.

124 NAI, Department of Communications, TW 11292. Supplementary Information for the Minister of Posts and Telegraphs, October 30, 1962.
125 NAI, Department of Communications, TV 11361, Woolard to Ingoldsby, October 26, 1962.
126 Sean Connolly, *The Oxford Companion to Irish History* (Oxford University Press, Oxford, 1998), 49.
127 Quoted from Philip O'Leary's upcoming volume, *Writing beyond the Revival: Facing the Future in Gaelic Prose 1940–1951* (University College Dublin Press, Dublin, forthcoming): 'We do not, of course, suggest that the allocation of seven to ten minutes of every film programme to Irish would be satisfactory as a permanent arrangement. It would, however, be acceptable for, say, five years. Then, as the future in store for television became more clearly defined and the percentage of citizens able to understand Irish increased, the matter could be re-examined.' Comhdháil Náisiúnta na Gaeilge, *Films in Irish*, 13.
128 Author's interview with Dónall Ó Móráin, Dublin, December 14, 1990.
129 Thanks to my colleague at Boston College, Philip O'Leary for pointing this out.
130 UCD Archives, Blythe Papers, P/24/1182, Blythe to Irvine, August 27, 1962.
131 Ibid., P/24/1185, Barry to Roth, October 15, 1962,.
132 Ibid., P/24/1186.
133 Ibid.
134 Report of the Commission on the Restoration of the Irish Language, summary in the *Irish Times*, January 11, 1964.
135 Ibid.
136 Ibid.
137 Ó Tuathaigh, Gearóid, 'The State and the Irish language', 33.
138 NAI, S13180 D/95.
139 NAI, S13180 D/95, Statement by Cork Gaelic League, November 20, 1964.
140 Ibid., record of a call from Ó Fiaich to the Taoiseach's Office, November 25, 1964.
141 Ibid., Ó Fiaich to Lemass that quotes the November 26 letter, December 1, 1964.
142 Ibid., Lemass to Ó Fiaich, November 1964.
143 NAI, S13180 D/95 Irish Marketing Surveys Limited, 1964 Report.
144 Ibid.
145 Ibid.
146 Ibid., Ó Fiaich to Lemass, March 4, 1964.
147 Ibid.

148 *Report of the Committee on Irish Language Attitudes Research,* Dublin 1975, quoted in Brown, *Ireland, A Social and Cultural History,* 209.
149 Ibid.
150 NAI, 2001/78/78, *Memorandum of observations as requested by the Minister for Posts and Telegraphs,* May 7, 1964, 4.
151 Ibid., 5.
152 Ibid., 8.
153 Ibid., Ó Broin to Finance, August 17, 1964.
154 Ibid.
155 Ibid.
156 Pádraig Ó Riagáin, *Language Policy,* 22.
157 *The Restoration of the Irish Language,* White Paper (1965, 10), quoted in Ó Riagáin, *Language Policy,* 23.
158 Brown, *Ireland: A Social and Cultural History,* 209.
159 Ibid.
160 Crowley, *War of Words,* 178–9.
161 NAI, 2001/78/78, Department of Posts and Telegraphs memorandum, February 18, 1966.
162 Ibid.
163 Ibid.
164 Ibid.
165 Ibid.
166 RTÉ Authority Archive, minutes of the Authority, October 31, 1963, 4. Liam Ó Murchú was appointed February 19, 1964, as Irish Language Editor.
167 RTÉ Authority Archive, memorandum from the director-general to the Authority, October 17, 1964.
168 *Radio Éireann Annual Review,* 1965, RTÉ Library.
169 Liam Ó Murchú, *A Time to Love?* (Gill and Macmillan, Dublin, 1986), 103.
170 The programme was first broadcast in April 1975.
171 RTÉ Authority Archives, *Memorandum on Irish in Sports Commentaries,* November 6, 1965.
172 Ibid.
173 Ó Murchú, *A Time to Love?,* 107.
174 Ibid., 109.
175 UCD Archives, Blythe papers, P24/1191 Blythe to McCourt, November 6, 1964.
176 Ibid., 11.
177 Ibid.
178 Ibid., P124/1142, McCourt to Blythe, November 7, 1964.
179 RTÉ Authority Archives, Minutes of the Radio Éireann Authority, January 14, 1965.

180 Ibid.

181 John Horgan makes the point that McManus was understood to be a strong backer of Fianna Fáil, referring to Deputy Jack McQuillan's retort, 'When Eddie says no, it's curtains for the show' (*Irish Press,* September 25, 1962), quoted in John Horgan, *Broadcasting and Public Life* (Four Courts Press, Dublin, 2004), 49.

182 RTÉ Authority Archives, Minutes of the Radio Éireann Authority, January 14, 1965.

183 Ibid.

184 Ibid.

185 Ibid.

186 *Irish Press,* May 25, 1965.

187 NAI, Department of the Taoiseach, S16837, Government Minutes, June 1, 1965.

188 *Inniu* was one of the longest running Irish language weeklies, running from 1943–84. See Delap, 'Irish and the Media', 153–6.

189 NAI, 2001/78/78, Department of the Taoiseach. S16837 *Inniu* (probably August 1965) article translated and included in the file.

190 Ibid.

191 Ibid.

192 Ibid.

193 RTÉ Authority Archive, Minutes of the Authority, January 5, 1966.

194 Ibid.

195 Ibid. One year later the Authority reviewed the policy statement concluding that although it was still unhappy with the amount of Irish in television programming 'a favourable attitude' towards the language was developing within RTÉ. A report indicated that over 300 employees were enrolled in 25 Irish language classes. 'The Use of the Irish Language in Broadcasting', RTÉ Written Archives, Hardiman Papers February, 1967.

196 Lelia Doolan, Jack Dowling and Bob Quinn, *Sit Down and Be Counted: The Cultural Evolution of a Television Station* (Wellington Publishers, Dublin, 1969), 73.

197 Author's interview with Aindrias Ó Gallchóir, June, 2007, Dún Laoghaire.

198 RTÉ Authority Archives, Minutes of the RTÉ Authority, April 20, 1966.

199 Ibid.

200 NAI, Department of the Taoiseach. S16837, Andrews to Lemass, April 25, 1966.

201 Ibid.

202 Ibid.

203 Ibid., Lemass to Andrews, April 28, 1966, and Andrews to Lemass, May

1, 1966.

204 Ibid., Andrews to Lemass, May 12, 1966.

205 See John Horgan, *Seán Lemass, the Enigmatic Patriot* (Gill and Macmillan, Dublin, 1997), 320.

206 Ibid.

207 Letter from Dónall Ó Móráin to the editor of the *Irish Times*, January 1999, reprinted in Liam Mac Con Iomaire, *Breandán Ó hEithir, Iomramh Aonair* (Cló Iar-Chonnachta, Indreabhán, Conamara, 2000), 297–8. Original emphasis.

208 Ibid. No documentation has been found to support Ó Móráin's contention that Andrews was not going to be reappointed. However, all members of the second Authority were given one-year appointments – the first Authority's term was five years.

209 NAI, Department of the Taoiseach. S16837, Department of Taoiseach Memorandum, May 17, 1966. (See p. 90.)

210 NAI, Department of the Taoiseach, S14996D, Lemass to Moynihan, March 30, 1960.

211 Author's interview with Aindrias Ó Gallchóir, Dublin, June 2007.

212 This was made clear in author interviews with Seán Mac Réamoinn (Dublin, June 2006), Aindrias Ó Gallchóir (Dublin, June 2007) and Eoghan Harris. (Dublin, March 2009).

213 Author interview with Eoghan Harris, Dublin, March, 2009.

214 Ibid.

215 National Archives of Ireland, 2001/78/38. The programme, chaired by Proinsias Mac Aonghusa, featured a 'trial' in English followed by a discussion in Irish with Ruairí Brugha.

216 Harris maintains that when he first came to Telefís Éireann he was protected by senior civil servants including León Ó Broin and later Dónall Ó Móráin. Author's interview with Harris, Dublin, March 2009.

217 Horgan, *Broadcasting and Public Life*, 51.

218 See O'Leary, *Gaelic Prose in the Irish Free State, 1922–1939*.

219 Author's interview with Eoghan Harris, Dublin, March 2009.

220 Author's interview with Thomas Hardiman, Dublin, December 5, 1990.

221 See Diarmaid Ferriter, *Judging Dev* (Royal Irish Academy, Dublin, 2008), especially Chapter 13 for a consideration of de Valera's relationship with the language as a cultural priority.

222 See Watson, *Broadcasting in Irish*. Watson traces the change in tactics pursued by supporters of Irish who adopted a minority rights aproach to the Irish language.

9

A box of troubles: television and Northern Ireland

Television formally came to Northern Ireland in the spring of 1953 when a small temporary transmitter began relaying BBC programmes to viewers in the Belfast metropolitan area. The BBC was especially keen to transmit the coronation of Elizabeth II, understanding the event would be popular with many viewers and hoping the coronation would spur demand for televisions and licences. Once the permanent Divis transmitter became operational in 1955, coverage was extended throughout the province and across the border, enhancing the ability of some viewers in the Irish Republic to tune into BBC Northern Ireland. Many viewers along the East Coast of Ireland were already picking up BBC programmes from Britain, creating a level of discomfort for political, religious and cultural elites.[1] In Northern Ireland, as in the Irish Republic, the arrival of television proved transformative, challenging a conservative society and ultimately undermining the status quo. Its arrival especially upset the political and cultural hegemony that unionist elites had worked hard to cultivate and that defined the state since its creation in 1920. This chapter will consider how the arrival of television slowly eroded the image of the province and helped accelerate the demise of what its critics argued was a one party state.

Rex Cathcart's seminal study of the BBC in Northern Ireland, *The Most Contrary Region, the BBC in Northern Ireland 1924–1984*, points out that BBC television made a number of programmes about Northern Ireland in the 1950s that were for the most part complimentary. This created unrealistic expectations from political leaders within the province who thought that complimentary features such as *The Pattern of Ulster* and a feature in the series *About Britain* would be typical of future programmes.[2] There was certainly a degree of naivety in official thinking that BBC television would continue to provide positive publicity for an audience throughout the UK. Cathcart notes that the unionist government and the unionist majority never thought that television would have 'anything other than a positive, promotional role'.[3]

This was partly due to the evolution of the BBC's radio service in Northern Ireland, which timidly avoided upsetting or challenging the unionist-controlled government at Stormont. Radio came to the province in 1924 when Northern Ireland's first station, 2BE, went on the air. This became BBC Northern Ireland when a Royal Charter established the BBC a few years later in 1927. BBC Northern Ireland transmitted the national programme from London, and in Belfast was overseen by a small, mainly English, staff. During the inter-war years, the unionist establishment came to appreciate the importance of the BBC, seeing it as an important link to a British culture they considered their own. The Catholic minority in the province tended to view it as a mouthpiece of unionism and tuned into Radio Éireann for information and entertainment.

After the Second World War, the British government sought to decentralise radio broadcasting throughout the UK but found unionist politicians wary of devolution, unsure it would work in the province for a number of reasons. This reluctance to accept more responsibility for broadcasting can be detected in Stormont's reaction to the report of the Beveridge Committee in 1949. The Beveridge Committee was established by Parliament to consider the state of broadcasting throughout the UK and to advise the government on developing a new charter for the BBC. Although the committee did not include a representative from Northern Ireland, its recommendations were problematic for the unionist government because it encouraged greater regional autonomy. Senior civil servants at Stormont complained that when it came to radio and questions of extending television to Northern Ireland, the province was being ignored by London. However, their political masters were ambivalent, unconvinced that the province should have more direct control over broadcasting. Many unionist politicians were hesitant to see regional radio or indeed television programmes develop that would inevitably touch upon the sensitive issue of divisions within Northern Irish society. As discussions about the expansion of the electronic media in the UK gained momentum, apprehension among unionist politicians grew, as they began to realise that much was at stake with the arrival of television in Northern Ireland.

When the Beveridge Committee issued its final report in 1951 it addressed regional radio broadcasting, suggesting that Scotland, Wales and Northern Ireland each have its own commission that would enable each region to 'initiate and decide on a Home Service programme in its region and should have powers in relation to finance, accommodation and staff'.[4] While there certainly was anxiety over reporting on local conditions and addressing local problems, the Prime Minister of Northern Ireland, Sir Basil Brooke, expressed other concerns. He was worried that devolution would cut the province off from London and British culture. The Stormont government's position underlines the high degree of insecurity that existed within the unionist leadership at the time. In the end, the Cabinet decided it was not in favour of Northern Ireland's gaining greater autonomy and accepting the accompanying responsibility for regional broadcasting.[5]

This was partly due to the urging of the controller for BBC Northern Ireland, Andrew Stewart, who at the time was responsible for BBC radio programming in the province. At the invitation of the Prime Minister, Stewart attended a Cabinet meeting telling ministers that divisions within the province's society would inevitably make their way into the proposed Northern Ireland Broadcasting Commission. It was his professional opinion that the unionist majority would always prevail in any disagreement that might arise, leading to bitterness and controversy. He argued Northern Ireland was unable to assume responsibility for broadcasting because 'the minority would feel constantly put down and the majority would always appear bloody-minded. In the end the representatives of the minority would resign and there would be public scandal.'[6] These cabinet discussions addressed the realities of a province that remained bitterly divided.

Minister for Home Affairs Brian Maginess had no such qualms about accepting the autonomy that was on offer. He argued that the unionist government should accept the recommendations of the White Paper published after the Beveridge Committee issued its report. Maginess pointed out that both Scotland and Wales were confident enough to accept the responsibility of a broadcasting council, arguing critics would ask 'If the Scots and Welsh are capable of being entrusted with the virtual direction of broadcasting ... are we not so capable?'[7] He maintained that there was simply no answer to such a question. 'If we insist on the present position standing, we confess to an inferiority complex, we strike a grave blow at the prestige of the Government and still more at the prestige of Northern Ireland. We will be the butt of opponents and friends will be forced to make apologetic excuses. We who have run the country successfully for 30 years are confessing that we have not sufficient confidence in ourselves to direct a regional broadcasting service.'[8]

The minister assumed that the unionist government, not the BBC, would have control over appointments made to the regional commission, emphasising that this would keep the government's opponents from gaining control. Even if county councils got involved in helping make appointments Maginess knew unionists would maintain control of appointments to the regional commission, as the Ulster Unionist Party enjoyed a virtual monopoly on political power at the local and regional level through much of the province. Nationalists or Labour politicians would not have accepted his argument that 'the Government represents and speaks for all of the people of Northern Ireland, not just one party'. Maginess denied that a Northern Ireland Broadcasting Commission would try to exert political influence or that appointments would be made 'only from our own ranks', stating that this type of favouritism was simply not practised in Northern Ireland.[9] When making his case, Maginess referenced a pronounced discomfort that many unionists experienced when BBC broadcasts from London featured traditional Irish music. Broadcasts from London especially on Saint Patrick's Day often created controversy within a unionist community upset with the emphasis on

'Gaelic' music especially in the inter-war years. Many unionists did not want to be associated with a Gaelic culture they considered nationalist and complained regularly to the BBC that their British identity was being compromised. According to Maginess, if regional control came to the province the perceived emphasis given to manifestations of Gaelic culture such as céilí bands could be addressed and 'the situation should be bettered and not worsened if we're running the show ourselves'.[10]

After considering these arguments Brookeborough decided that any autonomy coming to the province would have to be conditional. He consulted the Executive Committee of the Ulster Unionist Council who agreed to support a regional broadcasting commission 'provided the Government had the power to choose its members; otherwise they would prefer that the Council for Northern Ireland should continue to be advisory'.[11] Maginess's argument for the change found support inside the Cabinet from ministers who believed that the establishment of a regional broadcasting commission would enhance the power and prestige of the unionist government. The Cabinet favoured the change with the stipulation that it be given the sole power to appoint members to the regional authority. When Brookeborough reported back to the Cabinet that the BBC refused Stormont the exclusive authority to make such appointments, the government rejected devolution. Unlike other regions within the UK, the province continued with the older, paternalistic system in which decisions concerning broadcasting in the province were made in London. Martin McLoone, who has written extensively about Irish popular culture, argues that unionists feared 'that the BBC, under less direct influence from the Unionist Government, might become something of a Trojan horse smuggling in all kinds of nationalist culture under the benevolent eye of a liberal central authority'.[12]

The Belfast newspapers, the existing BBC Advisory Council and other political parties accepted this decision. For various reasons all were comfortable with London making appointments to the existing Advisory Council and were wary of a regional commission that might be susceptible to political bias. In Dublin, the *Sunday Independent* suggested that unionists were not keen on seeing a true regional service, as it would inevitably expose the fractured political landscape while 'Anti-Partitionists and Labourites are naturally afraid of the Belfast station being controlled from Glengall Street and used for Unionist propaganda.'[13] However, Brookeborough did accept the recommendation of the Beveridge Committee that Northern Ireland be represented on the BBC Board of Governors. The unionist government was able to appoint the member, ensuring that its political interests were represented and enhancing the influence of the Ulster Unionist Party. Sir Henry Mulholland, who at the time was the Chairman of the Regional Advisory Council, was named Northern Ireland BBC Governor. This set a precedent as all subsequent chairmen of the Regional Advisory Council were appointed to the Board of Governors.[14] Devolution proved too politically complicated for an anxious and insecure unionist government. As Rex Cathcart observed, 'In any event, Northern Ireland had been offered a measure of control of the Home Service, and had rejected it because no one believed that power-sharing would work.'[15]

However, BBC Northern Ireland did make an effort to develop regional broadcasts. In the post-war period the station began to carefully increase regional programming, recruiting writers that included Sam Hanna Bell and John Hewitt. Although some producers regarded this effort with a degree of scepticism, Gillian McIntosh's study of unionist identities, *The Force of Culture*, points out that 'the influx of locals did bring the station closer to the indigenous population'.[16] BBC Northern Ireland trod carefully, wary of antagonising the unionist establishment while simultaneously making cautious overtures to the minority community. However, many nationalists in the province tended to view BBC Northern Ireland as overly sympathetic to the unionist community and focused on representing a culture that was not their own. Well into the 1950s the station employed few Catholics and featured little cultural programming that could be defined as Gaelic or Irish.[17] The service had an established record of being overly sensitive to the concerns of the unionist community as illustrated by accepting Prime Minister Lord Craigavon's request to stop reporting results of Gaelic Athletic Association games in the province. Broadcasting officials complied, accepting that the Sunday broadcasts 'were hurting the feelings of the large majority of people in

Northern Ireland'.[18] Unionists worked to marginalise the nation-alist community and its culture and were determined that the image of Ulster presented to the outside world was a British one. Unionist elites remained deeply uncomfortable and embarrassed by any suggestion that Northern Ireland was Irish.

However, BBC Northern Ireland was not simply a mouthpiece for the unionist government and made an effort to include some cultural programming that the nationalist community appreci-ated. Irish traditional music was occasionally featured in some programmes, much to the consternation of unionist officials. Still, the BBC in Northern Ireland remained focused on British institu-tions and culture and proved timid in addressing the interests of the Catholic minority. As McIntosh observes, 'While the station was not, therefore, a crude promoter of unionism and some attempts were made to represent the catholic community, equally it was not balanced in its representation of the communities in or the diversity of the state.'[19]

McIntosh identifies the BBC Northern Ireland radio service as moving through two distinct phases; 'pre-war ignoring the nature of the state, post-war becoming more regionalist and adopting aspects of local culture which controllers felt would not offend unionist sensibilities; aspects which would highlight only the positive features of the state and underplay the negative or conten-tious'.[20] This deference to the unionist establishment came under tremendous pressure when television took hold in the province, proving subversive in destabilising archaic political and social structures that failed to gain cross-community support.

The British government was initially reluctant to include Northern Ireland in its plans to extend television broadcasting throughout the UK, announcing in March 1951 that cutbacks would delay its arrival in the province. Andrew Stewart, Controller, BBC Northern Ireland, protested arguing that the plan to extend televi-sion coverage throughout Britain and not Northern Ireland was 'surely not equitable'.[21] A Television Action Committee, made up of retailers and representatives of the electrical trades, began a sus-tained lobbying campaign, putting pressure on Members of the Stormont and Westminster Parliaments to force the government to include Northern Ireland in the BBC's expansion plans.

When television arrived in Northern Ireland, it was primarily a relay station, transmitting programmes from London with very little home-produced material. Initial efforts by the Controller, R. D. Marriott, to develop programmes in the province for an audience in Northern Ireland were rebuffed as 'financially impracticable' by BBC London.[22] However, Marriott persisted, outlining a plan for a modest fortnightly magazine programme that would address life in the province intended for viewers in Northern Ireland. George Barnes, BBC director of television broadcasting in London, liked the idea of an inexpensive small film unit working in the province, seeing it as a 'useful example for what we may gradually have to do in other regions'.[23] The result was *Ulster Mirror*, a fifteen-minute fortnightly programme about life in the province that went on the air in 1955 just as a new high-power transmitter was coming online. John Hill addresses the political character of the programme in his study of cinema and Northern Ireland by noting that it always opened with the camera shot 'through opening gates of the processional avenue leading to Parliament House at Stormont. The same shot is used in all subsequent episodes and, given the symbolism involved, necessarily links the programme's outlook on "Ulster" with that of the unionist government.'[24]

Television programmes broadcast on the national network from London created a great deal of unease within Northern Ireland when addressing anything that could be defined as Irish. The Stormont government proved highly sensitive to any slight that it considered harmful to the people of Northern Ireland and was quick to complain. R. D. Marriott made this clear as early as August 1953 when he advised London that the BBC's difficulties in the province were 'accentuated by our peculiar political problems'.[25] He made reference to a feature broadcast on the day of the Ulster Grand Prix that covered the Kerry Fair in the Republic of Ireland, which had caused 'indignation'. 'I realise that material from [É]ire cannot be excluded, but could it be, at any rate so long as Northern Ireland has no television representation, be treated with considerable circumspection?'[26] London responded, noting that the staff in News had been reproved for 'their tactlessness', assuring Marriott that after being 'apprised of their imbecility' of including the offending feature that it would not happen again.[27]

In March 1954 the government protested on three separate occasions about BBC television programmes it regarded as problematic. Brookeborough complained about a tourist film broadcast on the BBC that referred to 'Ireland'; he was upset that it did not explain the reference was to the twenty-six counties of the Irish Republic and not Northern Ireland. He expressed anger at another programme broadcast on the same day, which was St Patrick's Day, which ended with the singing of *A Soldier's Song*. Later that same month, the Prime Minister wrote to the Director-General of the BBC, Sir Ian Jacob, to complain that the Catholic Bishop of Leeds, speaking on a religious programme, had referred to the intolerance towards the Catholic community in Northern Ireland. In December 1956 the BBC programme *Highlight* provoked more complaints when H. A. L. Craig denied that members of the IRA were terrorists and described Ireland as 'a mutilated country'.[28] That evening Henry McMullan, Head of the Northern Ireland Programme Department, was compelled to appear on television to refute the statement and 'give the facts about the I.R.A. campaign of violence'.[29] Later that week the Prime Minister himself appeared on the programme *Panorama* to explain the complexities of life in Northern Ireland. In one of the more bizarre incidents the government felt insulted when on 'September 23, 1957, Mr Gilbert Harding said on television that he thought Mr. George Bernard Shaw was handicapped by being an Ulsterman and a Protestant'.[30] As Shaw was a Dublin-born Protestant, this provoked the Government Chief Whip, Brian Faulkner to write to the BBC to protest.

When the American programme *Small World* was broadcast featuring an interview with Siobhan McKenna, controversy once again developed. The Belfast-born actress was interviewed by the renowned American journalist Edward Morrow and took the opportunity to denounce partition and describe the IRA as idealist, causing a furore once again. The BBC had decided to screen the programme despite McKenna's remarks after reviewing it carefully. When the broadcast took place in April 1958 the IRA's border campaign had caused the deaths of four policemen and the destruction of property within the province. An outraged Brian Faulkner, Chief Whip of the Unionist Party and future Prime Minister, resigned from his position on the BBC Northern Ireland Advisory Committee. The Northern Ireland Prime Minister, Lord Brookeborough, denounced the programme, as did Unionist MPs at Westminster. In the wake of the controversy a decision was made not to broadcast a second part of the series that included the rest of the McKenna interview.

One of the most famous controversies of the 'pre-Troubles' era concerned a series done by the highly acclaimed current affairs programme *Tonight*. Alan Whicker arrived in the province to report on life in Northern Ireland and in the course of his visit began developing material for eight ten-minute segments for the programme. Whicker remembers arriving in the province and completing three or four segments including one on the Giant's Causeway on the Antrim Coast.[31] The first of these features, transmitted throughout the UK in January 1959, focused on Belfast and the recently opened betting shops in the city. The programme regularly addressed changes or innovation in society and for Whicker and his crew a consideration of these enterprises made sense. Betting shops had recently been legalised in Northern Ireland and were about to be introduced to the rest of the United Kingdom. This first segment opened with a camera showing Belfast City Hall and the Stormont Parliament and then capturing sectarian graffiti on tenement walls. The film featured a close-up of a policeman's revolver while Whicker informed viewers, 'Northern Ireland, though intensely loyal, and the birthplace of most of Britain's best generals, had armed police but no conscription.'[32]

In his autobiography Whicker recalls watching the show in Northern Ireland where he was working on the other segments for *Tonight* with his director Barbara Vesey Brown. The two watched the programme in the lounge of a Londonderry hotel and he described the reaction the show caused. 'When the report ended there was silence in our hotel lounge. The man I had been drinking with turned to me: "You can't say that sort of thing." I was baffled. During the previous year I had reported in exactly the same straightforward way from 17 different countries without ever being told I could not get away with it. "Why ever not? Every word's true." "I know", he said, "but that doesn't matter. You just can't say that sort of thing."[33]

Although it did not provoke a stir in Britain it caused outrage in Northern Ireland where a BBC camera crew filming a football match were attacked. The *Northern Whig*, the *Belfast Telegraph* and the *Belfast Newsletter* all condemned the programme as a slanderous portrait of Northern Ireland. The *Northern Whig* described Whicker presenting a bleak portrait of Belfast, noting that cameras 'presented shots of dirty-looking streets and alley-ways, posters advertising cowboy films, and corner public houses. The greater part of the film dealt with the fact that betting had been legalized here and quite a number of punters were interviewed in bookmakers' premises. Most of those interviewed were unemployed, nearly all were regular punters, and each had his own views on the subject of betting.'[34] The *Belfast Newsletter* complained that Whicker arrived in the province looking for something unusual. He decided to focus on four subjects, 'that policeman carry revolvers; that offensive slogans such as "No Pope here" and "Vote Sinn Fein" are painted on walls in obscure streets; that betting shops are licenced and that public houses are open from 10 a.m. to 10 p.m. … there was no reference to the city's industries, to the general bearing of the citizens or to the fact that without the loyal help of Northern Ireland it is doubtful whether the Allies could have won the war against Hitler's Germany.'[35] Terence O'Neill and a number of other cabinet ministers were furious and drafted a statement that was delivered in the Northern Ireland Senate by Colonel Gordon expressing 'concern and indignation' at the 'offensive and unbalanced picture' the programme presented.[36]

Because of the uproar the BBC Northern Ireland Controller Robert McCall issued an extraordinary apology to the people of Northern Ireland. 'I am extremely sorry that viewers have found cause for distress and indignation over the film sequence in yesterday's edition of the programme "Tonight". I understand that reaction. The report was not prepared or edited by Northern Ireland staff. Our advice on programme content and treatment was sought and given. The result, regrettably did not accord with the advice … I am taking all possible steps to ensure that any future programmes will convey a balanced picture of life in Ulster.'[37]

A short time later McCall wrote to Grace Wyndham Goldie, BBC Assistant Head of Talks, Television, saying 'how much I hated having to decide that I should issue a press statement which implied a public chiding of my colleagues'.[38] He claimed that he had agonised over the decision but come to the conclusion 'that I should somehow reassure the public here that the BBC office in Northern Ireland had an interest in and [a] right to be interested in programming concerning the Province'. He complained of the 'tumult and shouting' the broadcast caused, reporting that there had been 'some hundreds of telephoned attacks on us', angry letters complaining of an 'inefficient and irresponsible Controller here' and 'slogans painted on the front of Broadcasting House … They said "Down with Whicker" – "Away with McCall"'. He also complained that his wife had received threatening phone calls at home: '"Your husband is Controller – Controller of what? You won't be here much longer. We'll see to that".' In the same correspondence McCall claimed that the BBC had been 'tremendously effective in liberalising the thinking of the Ulster communities. Obviously, there is a great deal to be done.'[39]

McCall's note illustrates a sense of frustration and perhaps some regret at having to apologise for the programme although he claimed 'I will fight like a cat, as always in the past, to protect the independence and the integrity of the BBC'.[40] Whicker for one was not impressed with the apology McCall had made to the people of Northern Ireland describing it as a 'craven statement grovelling at their "distress and indignation"'.[41] He maintains that the producer of *Tonight* Donald Baverstock and the BBC 'were thrown into a funk by this unexpected uprising of the massed ranks of hypocrisy. For the first time the new-look BBC TV service kowtowed to silly sound and fury. It was not a glorious moment for the Corporation.'[42]

Although neither one of them had seen the programme Dr Mitchell the Bishop of Down and Senator McGladdery flew to London to appear on the programme to address the controversy. After viewing the programme both found themselves in a difficult situation because they thought it was fair. The men were placed in the rather absurd position of attacking the programme anyway to satisfy critics back in Northern Ireland.[43] Despite the remarks made on television, Dr Mitchell was reported in the *Belfast Evening Telegraph* stating the programme 'had done … a good turn by exposing to the people of Ulster a situation which existed – the plight of the unemployed'.[44] Although press reports of the broadcast in Northern Ireland were for the most part wholly negative, there was some support for the programme. 'Ulsterwoman' wrote to the *Belfast Telegraph*, arguing that the slogans shown in the programme 'are something we should be ashamed of and do something about'. Another letter in the same paper signed 'Ex-Serviceman in County Down' congratulated Whicker on the programme, arguing 'we viewers do not want "cooked" TV pictures. Leave that to the Russians'.[45]

Terence O' Neill, acting as Prime Minister for Brookeborough, informed the Stormont Cabinet that a strongly worded letter of protest had been sent by the Northern Ireland Controller to the Director-General of the BBC. The Cabinet was told that the Northern Ireland representative on the Board of Governors, Ritchie McKee, 'would have an opportunity of seeing future films on the "Tonight" series on Northern Ireland before they were broadcast'.[46] McKee met the BBC Director-General to complain that the programme was 'offensive to the majority of viewers of Northern Ireland', claiming the programme harmed the tourist trade in the province and could damage the economy of Northern Ireland by 'giving a false picture to cross-channel industrialists'.[47] He also brought up the matter with the BBC Board of Governors where he claimed to have found 'a most sympathetic and attentive hearing'.[48]

The Cabinet was later advised that BBC headquarters in London had succumbed to pressure from Belfast and allowed a degree of censorship to be formalised. London made 'an important concession by agreeing that the Northern Ireland Head of Programmes should be given the opportunity of vetting future "Tonight" programmes dealing with Northern Ireland'.[49] At Stormont, Cabinet discussions addressed 'uneasiness regarding the anti-Ulster bias evinced by a number of well-known B.B.C. personalities'.[50] Given the controversy the broadcast provoked, the BBC decided that the other programmes Alan Whicker made about Northern Ireland should be withdrawn. They were never broadcast. The programme-makers did not return to Northern Ireland for another five years, having been effectively put off by the experience of trying to report on the realities of life in contemporary Northern Ireland.

The Director-General, Sir Ian Jacob, issued a formal directive in October 1959, maintaining that although Northern Ireland was part of the United Kingdom there were unique circumstances arising out of its relationship with the Republic of Ireland and the activities of the IRA. 'It is therefore most important that the controller Northern Ireland should be consulted about *any* programmes which deal with questions directly affecting Northern Ireland or relations between [É]ire and the United Kingdom.'[51] The BBC in London retreated from Northern Ireland after these incidents, and the province simply did not feature on the network except in rare news bulletins. Cathcart's study of the BBC concludes that the result of these controversies was dramatic. 'Effectively there was a Westminster rule in the BBC as there was in politics. Questions were not asked because they were the concern of another place. So the greater British public learnt little about what was going on in its own political backyard.'[52] The unionist government's success in pushing the BBC out of Northern Ireland, ultimately censoring its work, not only cut off the province from Britain but also gave a false sense of security to the political establishment. Television inevitably came back, asking awkward questions and ultimately undermining a political establishment that was unprepared for the challenges the medium provoked.

Television broadcasting in Northern Ireland underwent another significant change in 1959 with the establishment of an independent television franchise. The Independent Television Authority had been created by the Television Act of 1954 and was charged with awarding licences to qualified companies interested in commercial broadcasting. When the ITA announced it would accept bids for a commercial network in Northern Ireland the Prime Minister wanted to make sure a 'suitable' programme contractor could be found.[53] Brookeborough's previous experience with the ITA ensured he would be vigilant in trying to influence any decision concerning who might be granted a licence in Northern Ireland.

His government paid close attention to the ITA and tried to use its influence to discourage any programme that would address divisions within the province. The Deputy Director, B. C. Sendall was approached in the summer of 1955 and told of the Stormont government's opposition to news programmes that might give a platform to republicans 'who have only one aim in talking about Northern Ireland, to vilify it'.[54] One incident involving the ITA especially caused him great anxiety. In February 1957 the BBC Northern Ireland Controller, Andrew Stewart alerted him to an interview with the Chief of Staff of the IRA scheduled for broadcast on the programme *This Week*. A protest was quickly made to the Home Office in London and to the ITA and the broadcast was cancelled just as it was about to go on the air. In thanking Stewart the exasperated Prime Minister complained 'I can't for the life of me understand how the I.T.A. could ever have contemplated such a broadcast, which would not only have provided a boost for an illegal organization … but would have given heaven sent opportunity for misrepresentation and pernicious propaganda.'[55]

The Henderson family, owners of the *Belfast Newsletter*, made it known that they were interested in the franchise, much to the relief of the government which worked to ensure that the application was successful. This was one of the oldest newspapers in the UK and Ireland with a history of being staunchly unionist.[56] Another unionist newspaper group, the *Northern Whig* and the *Evening Telegraph*, also expressed an interest in winning the franchise. The chairman, James Cunningham, wrote to Brookeborough in October 1958 including a copy of his organisation's application. In writing to the Prime Minister, Cunningham maintained that he expected that others from within Northern Ireland and Britain would also apply but made the case that his application should ease concerns of his fellow unionists. 'As I believe the control of the station to be of importance to the Party I felt I should send you our application to keep you informed.'[57]

Throughout the application process Brookeborough was in constant touch with Colonel Arthur Chichester, an ally and member of the ITA Board. Chichester had been appointed with the Prime Minister's support, and both men were determined to see that the contractor chosen would be acceptable to the unionist government. As applications for the franchise came into the ITA, Chichester kept in close contact with Brookeborough, who knew the value of having Chichester on the board of the ITA but understood that the relationship had to be dealt with carefully. While the application process was ongoing, the Ulster Unionist Party Secretary in London wrote to his counterpart in Belfast expressing concern that when all the submissions were in, an application might appear from an organisation 'which might not be very acceptable to us'.[58] He asked the government to make private enquiries into the matter with Chichester 'to see whether he is laying the trail in Northern Ireland. I need hardly point out that this matter will require diplomatic handling as of course the Government is not directly involved and should not appear in the picture.'[59] Terence O'Neill, Minister for Finance (and future Prime Minister), also expressed concern about the contract falling into 'the wrong hands', inquiring what the Stormont government was doing to be sure this did not happen.[60] With an ailing and elderly Brookeborough detached from government, O'Neill wanted to be sure that Stormont was doing everything it could to be sure the franchise found a pair of safe unionist hands.

The two Northern Ireland applicants included a consortium headed by the Duke of Abercorn and the Henderson group headed by Lord Antrim. After reviewing the applications the ITA decided to award the contract to Lord Antrim's group. Brumwell Henderson became managing director of the commercial franchise, serving as Chief Executive of Ulster Television (UTV) from 1959 to 1983. His autobiography, *Brum – A Television Life*, published in 2003, recalls that before the two Northern Ireland consortiums completed their respective applications, he examined the make-up of each group and realised something was amiss. 'Along with one or two other members I noticed that both our consortium and the Duke of Abercorn's had a significant omission – no Catholics. Looking back from this distance in time it may seem incredible that this was not a priority from the outset but it is a measure of how different Northern Ireland was then that it was not.'[61] The Henderson group received a tip that may have made the difference. The Chair of the ITA Board, Sir Ivone Kirkpatrick, was a Catholic, and Henderson recalls that he was told the board was looking for a proposal that would be inclusive and have support from both communities within Northern Ireland. Although there was resistance, Henderson managed to convince his group of investors that they should identify suitable Catholic shareholders and invite them into the consortium.

Henderson believes that the inclusive nature of his group was the deciding factor in winning the contract. Although the *Belfast Newsletter* had a reputation as a staunch unionist publication with a history of using excited and inflammatory language, the paper had become more restrained under Brumwell Henderson.[62] Henderson regarded himself as a moderate unionist with 'a relatively apolitical view of Northern Ireland and though I supported the Union I was much less "Orange" than many people assumed. I disliked the parochialism and narrowness of much of Ulster life and believed that the future for everyone lay in a greater tolerance and a willingness to look forward and outward.'[63] He considered the ITA bid a business opportunity, and understood that if it was to become a profitable enterprise UTV needed to cultivate a large audience regardless of the political or religious make-up of its viewers.

As Managing Director of UTV, Henderson recalls that after the group's bid was successful there were difficulties in trying to overcome the sectarian prejudices that were woven into the fabric of society in Northern Ireland. When recruiting staff he ran into immediate difficulties with the chief accountant over application forms that required applicants to list their religion. Over eight thousand forms had been printed and the accountant refused to print new ones to omit the question that Henderson deemed objectionable. A solution was arrived at when the applications were simply guillotined, literally cutting out the offensive question, in the pressroom of the *Belfast Newsletter*.

Henderson ran into additional difficulties when a member of his board and the Stormont government objected to his hiring of Frank Brady, a Catholic from the Irish Republic, into a key position at the new station. As UTV was being established it became clear that identifying qualified staff within Northern Ireland could be problematic. The station therefore looked at applicants from outside the province and when Henderson wanted to hire Brady as Chief Engineer, a member of his own board objected. At the time, a working permit was required in Northern Ireland for the appointment of staff from outside the UK. Brady's religion and nationality became an issue not only for the UTV Board but also for the government of Northern Ireland, which debated hiring him on at least two occasions. After a lengthy discussion in the Cabinet, Henderson was summoned to Stormont to meet with the Minister for Labour to explain his desire to hire a Catholic born south of the border.

After meeting Henderson the minister reported to his Cabinet colleagues that he had been assured that the engineer in question 'would have no part in the initiation, preparation or presentation of programmes'.[64] Cabinet members found the appointment problematic because there might be 'criticism and even demands for the dismissal of this man if U.T.V. should present a programme deemed inimical to Northern Ireland'.[65] In the end the Minister for Labour was more worried that refusing to grant a work permit 'without valid reasons could give rise to damaging charges of discrimination which, if raised publicly at Westminster, or in other quarters, could not be fully and effectively dealt with'.[66] Minutes of the Cabinet meeting at Stormont indicate that after deliberations 'Ministers, albeit reluctantly, concluded that in all the circumstances they should approve the issue of the permit in this case.'[67] The fact that the entire Cabinet became involved in a decision about the hiring of a 'foreign-born' Catholic inside a private company illustrates the level of unease television caused within the Brookeborough Government and speaks to the deep-seated prejudice of the unionist establishment.

Ulster Television went on the air on October 31, 1959, and quickly became popular, posing a serious threat to BBC television. Financial constraints meant that in its formative years the new commercial station had no news programmes and very little home-produced material and simply relayed programmes from Britain. The one exception was *Roundabout*, a programme that successfully used a magazine format to appeal to a wide audience. This popular weekday programme looked at life throughout the province and helped liberalise television broadcasting in Northern Ireland. *Roundabout* certainly caught the attention of BBC

Northern Ireland, which looked to develop something similar to compete with the commercial upstart. UTV introduced a degree of competition to the market that quickly developed into a rivalry. Cathcart points to a positive development from the competition: 'each broadcasting organisation reached out in an ever more determined way into both the Northern Ireland communities for programme material and [each] sought to broaden the dialogue between them'.[68]

UTV targeted working-class viewers with popular programmes imported from the USA and Great Britain. For Henderson, building and holding an audience was essential for the venture to be financially viable. In 1959 there were approximately 50,000 television households in Northern Ireland, and he understood that it was critical that this number expand dramatically for the station to succeed. He organised an aggressive advertising campaign, telling his staff, 'the new channel would not only double the available programming but it would also offer more "popular" style and content … our aim was television for the Shankill and Falls Roads rather than for the Malone and Antrim Roads which, in my view, had the BBC to cater to them'.[69] The station opened with one of the company's shareholders, Sir Laurence Olivier, introducing the Governor of Northern Ireland, Lord Wakerhurst. This was followed by a short children's programme and a tour of Northern Ireland before tapping into ITV programmes from the mainland, including *The Adventures of Robin Hood*, *ITN News*, *77 Sunset Strip*, a Jimmy Jewel variety programme from London, wrestling and a Gary Cooper movie.[70] The opening evening concluded with Olivier reading Addison's poem *The Spacious Firmament*. With the exception of *Roundabout*, UTV simply fed its audience a steady diet of mostly American programmes such as *Highway Patrol*, *The Invisible Man*, *I Love Lucy* and *Rawhide*, all proving popular with viewers throughout the province.

BBC Northern Ireland resented the popularity of UTV, and its Controller Robert McCall and Brum Henderson clashed on a number of occasions but both grew increasingly concerned with the advent of a Dublin television service. Unionist politicians closely followed the debates that preceded the establishment of an Irish national television service and shared their anxiety. In

London the BBC was alarmed at some of the proposals submitted to the Irish government and worked closely with the Secretary of the Irish Department of Posts and Telegraphs, León Ó Broin, to discredit schemes it determined problematic. These included proposals calling for establishing commercial radio stations that would broadcast directly into the UK from Ireland in return for building a television service for the cash-strapped Irish government.[71]

The Stormont government and broadcasting officials became concerned that a Dublin station's signal would penetrate Northern Ireland. Overspill from transmitters in Belfast and the British mainland already enabled many residents of the Irish Republic access to British programmes. In fact, the political, cultural and economic consequences of this overspill had encouraged the Irish government to end years of debate and make a definitive decision to build a national service the same year that UTV went on the air.[72] When the Lemass Government announced its decision to establish a national television service, the Stormont government, worried about a Dublin service making its way across the border, contacted the Home Office in London expressing 'various misgivings about this plan'.[73] The Home Office was quick to assuage the concerns of Stormont, explaining that there should be 'no cause for alarm'.[74] Reference was made to the 1952 Stockholm Agreement that stipulated transmitters could only be powerful enough to serve the nation state, forbidding intentional broadcasting into another jurisdiction. The states that took part in the Stockholm Conference had agreed that any problems that might arise should be settled between the jurisdictions affected. The UK government was allowed two 50-kilowatt stations in Northern Ireland, one in Belfast and another in Derry. The Irish Republic was allowed five 50-kilowatt stations at Dublin, Kilkenny, Cork, Galway and Ballyshannon. Despite the fact that the constitution of the Irish Republic claimed jurisdiction over the thirty-two counties of Ireland, including the six counties that constituted the province of Northern Ireland, there was no effort made to develop an Irish service that would extend throughout the island of Ireland.[75]

In the late 1950s when the ITA was considering granting a licence to a station in Northern Ireland, London realised that these provisions had to be modified to accommodate any new commercial station and opened negotiations with the Irish Department of Posts and Telegraphs. These discussions resulted in the allocation of three stations in Northern Ireland with 100 kilowatts each, a transmitter for UTV and BBC Northern Ireland, and an additional transmitter for a future BBC station. The Irish Republic was allowed to increase to 100 kilowatts its transmitters in Dublin, Cork and Galway. Sligo was also allocated a 100-kilowatt transmitter, but this was specifically restricted from broadcasting in an easterly direction, towards Northern Ireland. During these negotiations the British urged the Irish government to accept the principle of not intentionally broadcasting into Northern Ireland, and Dublin acquiesced, accepting a low-power 10-kilowatt station for Cavan that would serve the border counties of the Irish Republic. In writing to the Stormont government, the Home Office in London explained that given these developments the overspill from transmitters in the Irish Republic into Northern Ireland would be negligible.

The British government was quite pleased with the results of their negotiations, boasting to Stormont, 'A comparison of the two sets of plans shows that the Irish republic has made extensive concessions to meet our requirements in Northern Ireland ... A very real concession was made in their agreeing to the power of the I.T.A. station at Belfast being raised from 50 kw to 100 kw, as this could be held to lessen the commercial value of any television service in Dublin.'[76] The Stormont government was assured that during these negotiations the British Post Office was sensitive to any efforts that might have been made to increase cross-border transmission into Northern Ireland 'with political or propaganda purposes in mind'.[77] British officials believed they had negotiated a good deal with Dublin, and communicated this explicitly to Stormont maintaining it was, 'their view that in these negotiations, which inevitably involved a certain amount of give and take, the United Kingdom took more than it gave'.[78]

The Home Office told Stormont that even though an Irish service had yet to begin broadcasting in the Irish Republic, thousands of people south of the border were able to view the BBC and soon would be watching UTV. 'This fact must obviously have some adverse effect on the chances of successful establishment of a television service in the republic and is, we believe, a matter of some concern to the republican authorities.'[79] London made it clear that it did not want to reopen negotiations with Dublin in an attempt to block incidental overspill into Northern Ireland. It clearly felt this was an impossible task. London assured the unionist government that there would be no attempt from Dublin to transmit propaganda into the province, explaining it had 'done a good job of work for Northern Ireland, for which they deserve the gratitude of those in Northern Ireland who will benefit'.[80] Nevertheless, Stormont remained anxious about overspill and continued to contact the Home Office when press reports suggested that it would be more substantial than expected.[81]

Once the fears of Stormont were eased regarding the dangers of overspill, the issue of television relay companies distributing programmes from the Irish Republic exercised considerable anxiety within the government. These companies were interested in enabling viewers in Northern Ireland to receive, via cable, television signals from Telefís Éireann. Once again the unionist government was worried about political and religious propaganda being transmitted from the Irish Republic, stirring up difficulties in the province while shareholders and management of UTV were concerned about competition from an Irish service. Cabling required a transfer company first to obtain permission from local authorities before formally applying for licences from the Post Office to relay signals to subscribers. When pressed for information about relays, the Home Office in London tried to reassure nervous Stormont officials that the terms of licences precluded the transmission of political or religious propaganda. The Home Office declined a request from Belfast that British Post Office officials notify the government of Northern Ireland each and every time it received an application for a relay licence. There was a palatable sense of fear about what might be transmitted from a Dublin station, not only from an older generation of unionist leaders but younger more moderate politicians including the future Prime Minister Terence O'Neill. He was convinced that uncensored transmissions from Dublin 'could be expected to arouse adverse comment if indeed not hostile reaction or even violence'.[82]

Stormont was not only worried about programmes from south of the border upsetting the province but also concerned about 'the moral "tone" of broadcasts from London'. This was especially true of a number of plays and programmes taken by UTV from programme companies in Great Britain. Brian Faulkner, Minister for Home Affairs, raised this directly with the ITA in Belfast complaining of immoral programmes coming into homes in Northern Ireland. An ITA official, William Wilson, replied that the ITA was 'greatly concerned' and were trying to get programme companies to deliver programmes with 'more healthy standards'.[83] When Brian Faulkner met Wilson and officials from the ITA to address the issue, discussions turned to the 'threat' a Dublin television station might pose. ITA officials took the opportunity to complain to the minister that a successful commercial station broadcasting from Dublin might undercut advertising rates from UTV and take away paying customers. Perhaps understanding that Faulkner was not all that concerned with the profit margin of UTV, Wilson played the political card, warning the minister 'the Government should also be concerned in view of the possibility of propaganda programmes being carried by a relay system'.[84]

Understanding that no licence could be issued without the support of local authorities, the government's Publicity Committee, which Brian Faulkner chaired, asked the Minister of Health and Local Government to inform the government each and every time an application was being made. Writing on behalf of the Publicity Committee, the cabinet secretary A. J. Kelly explained, 'If information about applications can be obtained it would enable consideration to be given to the taking, if necessary, of appropriate action. You will understand that political considerations come into this and Ministers, I think, would be anxious to guard against the wholesale propagation by relay companies of programmes originating from the Republic.'[85] It is clear the government was concerned with the prospect of the nationalist minority receiving programmes broadcast from Dublin. Health and Local Government replied to Kelly, pointing out that trying to work out informal agreements with 'suitable' (i.e., Protestant) local authorities would be 'preaching to the converted while approaching "unsuitable" local authorities would be bad publicity and would achieve precisely the opposite result to that wished for by the Cabinet Publicity Committee'.[86]

A short time later Post Office Headquarters in Northern Ireland wrote to the government explaining that a request had been received from the Larne Television Relay Company Ltd seeking a licence to 'pipe' programmes from the Dublin station once it went on the air. The government was told that 'The answer would normally be "Yes" provided the terms of the licence are observed' [but the Post Office wanted to] 'avoid giving a reply … which might subsequently cause embarrassment.'[87] The Post Office asked if the government had any view as to how the query might be answered. The matter was left to drop, but this changed once the Dublin station began broadcasting.

When Telefís Éireann began broadcasting in 1961 the Northern Ireland Post Office informed the government that it expected applications from companies interested in bringing these broadcasts to customers throughout the province. It made it clear that if Stormont objected to any applications it had to specify 'if these were mainly on political grounds or to protect U.T.V.'[88] Although there was some support for reciprocal programming between Dublin and Belfast, Brian Faulkner, Minister for Home Affairs, strenuously objected. He argued that, 'inevitably some Irish programmes would offend Ulster opinion and the Government should not put itself in the position of having facilitated their reception in Northern Ireland'.[89] The issue was allowed to drift until the Cabinet was forced to make a decision in May 1964. In response to recommendations made by the Pilkington Committee the British Home Office was drawing up new licences. London wanted to know if the position of the Northern Ireland government towards licencing had changed. UTV made it clear once again that they were 'totally opposed', concerned that they could lose revenue to Telefís Éireann especially since it 'was not bound by the British I.T.A. limitation on foreign (particularly American) material'.[90] The Prime Minister and the Cabinet made it clear to London that the 'relay of Telefís Éireann programmes into Northern Ireland should be totally resisted (bearing in mind both the possibility of undesirable programmes from the political and constitutional viewpoints, and the strong views of U.T.V.)'.[91]

This prohibition on relaying RTÉ programmes into Northern Ireland was a factor in Dublin considering contravening existing bilateral and international agreements seven years later. In the summer of 1970, when the Irish Government was considering building a high-power transmitter at Clermont Carn in County Louth, a joint RTÉ–Department of Posts and Telegraphs report pointed to the fact that 'relay systems in the Six Counties are expressly precluded from relaying our programmes'.[92]

The nationalist community in Northern Ireland expected Telefís Éireann would be made available throughout the island of Ireland once the new television service went on the air. However an article appearing in the *Sunday Independent* stating that Dublin had decided to institute 'picture partition' created tremendous unease telling readers: 'As a result of decisions announced very quietly, more than a million viewers are going to be placed outside the ken of the new Irish television service.'[93] This article led to questions in the Dáil about the intentions of the new broadcasting service. The government denied that it would prevent viewers in Northern Ireland from receiving broadcasts and later when queried answered with assurances that viewers in Northern Ireland would be able to receive broadcasts though the quality of reception could not be guaranteed.[94] The files of the Departments of the Taoiseach and Posts and Telegraphs contain dozens of letters from residents of the province asking when they would receive programmes from south of the border. Many of these letters were answered with vague promises of renewed efforts to improve or upgrade transmitters but the truth is that when the Irish television service was being established, in spite of Fianna Fáil's anti-partitionist rhetoric and the claims of the 1937 Irish Constitution, 'the border defined the nation'.[95] This was due to a number of factors, especially international treaties the Dublin government was party to that regulated the allocation of wavelengths and the location of transmitters. At the time the most recent, the Stockholm Agreement signed in June of 1961, regulated the power of transmitters needed to serve the jurisdiction of the signatories. As noted the Irish and British Post Offices had also worked out a bilateral agreement in January 1959.

As early as March 1961 the Ulster Branch of the Gaelic Athletic Association (GAA) wrote to Seán Lemass demanding that all of Ulster be able to receive the broadcasts of the new television station. A resolution adopted unanimously by the Ulster GAA strongly protested the failure of the Irish government to provide for the residents of Ulster.

> Customs barriers make no difference to the allegiance shown to the Irish nation by the Gaels of the Six Counties, and they are entitled to demand that no cultural barrier be set up between them and the rest of the country. Children in the counties mentioned are subject to demoralising and denationalising influences arising from the present Television Services. If they are to be denied the good influences that it is hoped the new Irish service will exercise, then it could rightly be said that they are being deliberately cast off and ostracised from their own nation.[96]

When the GAA held its congress in the Gresham Hotel a month later the issue was raised once again. Patrick Flynn, the chairman of the Ulster Council of the GAA told the congress that there was 'great resentment and disappointment that there would be no booster station to give a service in the North from Radio [É]ireann TV. The reason given was because of some international agreement. There was, however, a BBC transmitter three miles from the Donegal border and, that being so, it was difficult to see where subserviency ended and diplomacy began.'[97] The GAA demanded a meeting with the Taoiseach to make their concerns known. Michael Hilliard met with a GAA delegation and carefully explained the government's predicament, indicating that international agreements limited the ability of the new television service to broadcast directly into Northern Ireland. He noted that the government were anxious that the new service would be available in Northern Ireland but that this would have to be from 'overflow' from transmitters south of the border.[98]

Eddie McAteer M.P., the leader of the Nationalist Party in Northern Ireland met with Lemass and asked about the stories circulating in the press that Telefís Éireann would not be received north of the border. Lemass assured him that 'so far as I know, these reports are not correct and that arrangements for the service would enable Six-County viewers to receive programmes'.[99] He promised

McAteer that he would send him a private letter to confirm this and wrote to the Minister for Posts and Telegraphs, Michael Hilliard asking for advice. Hilliard suggested McAteer be told that viewers in Northern Ireland would receive the signals from the new service 'but the quality of reception will naturally vary with distance from the transmitters and other factors. In general, reception should be much the same as the quality of British television transmissions received in the northern half of the state.'[100] Hilliard avoided stating explicitly that the new service would not have a transmitter dedicated to viewers in Northern Ireland although he maintained 'we are of course, anxious to give the best possible coverage of the Six Counties from our transmitters but requests for public assurances that we will do so only help to create difficulties'.[101] When Lemass wrote to McAteer he assured him 'viewers in the Six Counties will receive the proposed programmes' but cautioned that until the service was operational it would be 'difficult to be precise about the quality of reception.'[102]

Viewers in Northern Ireland remained disappointed once Telefís Éireann commenced broadcasting, as reception remained problematic. Individuals and organisations in Northern Ireland continued to complain that there was no reception in the province. In January 1964 the Nationalist Party wrote directly to Kevin McCourt, the director-general complaining that 'the present coverage is scanty and altogether inadequate to the need and demand'.[103] The Nationalist Party also requested the Irish television and radio service open an office in Belfast to 'show the flag' and to 'serve as a focus for news and features'.[104] McCourt replied a short time later indicating that plans to build a number of smaller transmitters to augment the existing five national transmitters might improve reception in Northern Ireland but that to extend full coverage into the province high-power transmitters would have to be built along the border, maintaining: 'I am very much afraid that such a project raised questions of policy and international frequency allocations, to say nothing of finance, which would not be wholly for Radio [É]ireann to decide.'[105] He also rejected a request from the Nationalist Party for Telefís Éireann to open an office in Belfast noting that Radio Éireann had a reporter dedicated to Northern Ireland and that opening an office and adding staff would be 'beyond our economic or true needs'.[106] The Irish national television service paid little attention to life in the province until the start of the civil rights campaign in 1968.

With the outbreak of violence in Northern Ireland Dublin began to revisit the question of broadcasting television directly into the province. In the summer of 1970 a joint RTÉ–Posts and Telegraphs committee reported to the government that only 14 per cent of the population in Northern Ireland could receive RTÉ television broadcasts but that if a UHF transmitter was built at Clermont Carn in County Louth the figure would rise to over 60 per cent after five years.[107] The joint committee concluded that interference with other radio or television stations would not be an issue and that viewers in Northern Ireland would only need a simple and inexpensive outdoor aerial for reception. In researching the legal question of international regulations it was pointed out that the 1961 Stockholm Agreement required Ireland to give notice of its intentions to the International Frequency Registration Board (IFRB) and await reactions from other jurisdictions before beginning construction of a transmitter. The committee made it clear that the British would oppose the establishment of a transmitter on the border aimed into Northern Ireland and that if a decision was made to proceed regardless of this opposition 'we would be the first Signatory to break the Stockholm Agreement. We would have to renege on international Radio Regulations which we are a party. And for all this it is highly probable that we would achieve nothing, as the British could still, if they wished, block our signals and render the new station ineffective in the Six Counties.'[108]

The Dublin government knew that the transmitter would upset the British government but by the summer of 1972 Irish government policy was evolving amidst increasing political instability and growing violence in Northern Ireland. A detailed memorandum addressing the issue reveals that the Irish government was vacillating. The document rejected a confidential communication received from the British government in July of 1971 opposing the plan, defining London's objections as 'either slight or unfounded'.[109]

The fact of the matter is that Britain is publicly committed to handing over Northern Ireland if a majority in that part of Ireland so desire. Britain's claim to sovereignty is, therefore, conditional. It is perfectly proper for us to seek through the media of radio and television to beam to the disputed territory our hopes and proposals for the unification of our people and territory in peace and justice. We could thus provide a powerful voice for the forces of moderation.[110]

The document noted that the British Prime Minister, Edward Heath had written to the Taoiseach, Jack Lynch, in May 1971 complaining that 'direct transmission by R.T.E. into N.I. might increase rather than lessen tension'.[111] However these concerns were now dismissed as unwarranted: 'In this respect we have been more scrupulous than the British in seeing that the men of violence do not find a platform on our national networks'.[112] There was speculation that the British might initially object to the transmitter but 'tacitly acquiesce' because in 'any public discussion of the matter, the flimsiness of the British counter-argument would show up against the Government's strong moral and common-sense case'.[113] It was also pointed out that since the Stormont government had been prorogued 'a possible source of protest may have been silenced'.[114]

There were security concerns addressed in the document, as it was understood that a transmitter on the border might be a focus 'for Orange attack'. However the issue that created the most concern was that residents in Northern Ireland with distinctive aerials might be at risk. 'This could become a distinctive badge of affiliation to the South and, to marauding Orange extremists, especially in minority areas, could offer a target for attack'.[115] In the end the government approved the proposal by Posts and Telegraphs to notify the International Frequency Registration Board of the proposed establishment of a high power UHF transmitter at Clermont Carn, County Louth. The project faced a number of obstacles but the transmitter became operational in 1981.

Throughout the 1960s the Stormont government remained sensitive to programmes that were made about the province, and the controversy that had developed concerning the programme

Tonight in 1959 was brought up once again when Alan Whicker returned to the province in January 1964. The *Sunday Independent* reported that Whicker and the *Tonight* team had returned to Northern Ireland to film a programme about discrimination in Derry and Enniskillen, but these plans were mysteriously changed. The nationalist MP for Foyle and leader of the nationalist Party, Eddie McAteer, reported he had been approached by the BBC about the programme but feared that Stormont had learned of the project and stepped in to thwart it. He explained that he had been surprised to learn that the BBC was in Derry accompanied by a government press official and were now 'more interested in visiting a fairy rath near the city and said they wanted light material not discrimination'.[116]

During the visit Whicker addressed the 1959 controversy, defining Stormont's reaction to the programme as extraordinary. He complained that the unionist government had pressured the BBC into withdrawing a number of programmes the *Tonight* team had made about life in the province. When asked about trying again to develop current affairs programmes, Whicker accused the government of bullying and censorship: 'No government deserves the Government you have here. This is the only place in the world where you can't report honestly without silly people kicking up a storm about what is the truth.'[117] He reminded his interviewer that the programme broadcast was the first in a more extensive series intended to address events in the province. 'We have another nine stories on N.I. which have been set aside following the kick-up when the first one was transmitted.'[118]

The *Belfast Telegraph* interviewed Trevor Philpott, a colleague of Whicker, who explained that people knew very little about Northern Ireland, largely because the province received very little publicity in Great Britain. He described himself as amazed that the Whicker reports had been 'thrown in the waste paper basket after only one had been shown ... we know so little about the province – and by banning films the man across the water will never get to know anything'.[119] He added that the entire episode had damaged the image of Northern Ireland with current affairs programmes in Britain and doubted that reporters would be interested in returning a second time. A few days later at Stormont the

Prime Minister refused to be drawn into a debate with nationalists about the government's efforts to censor BBC programmes. An internal memorandum prepared for the Prime Minister denied that the government practiced any form of censorship and maintained that the questions from the opposition were provoked by Whicker 'having said rude things about the Northern Ireland Government'.[120]

On occasion UTV could also create problems for the Stormont government, an example being the broadcast of an episode of *This Week* in December 1965. The programme probed the 'modernisation process' in the province that the government of Terence O'Neill was keen to promote; the programme has been described as 'probably the first to cast a genuinely critical eye across Northern Ireland'.[121] It featured an aggressive interview of Brian Faulkner, Minister for Home Affairs, who was asked about discrimination and gerrymandering. But this was unusual, and critical programmes about the province were rare. In fact, the next *This Week* programme that addressed Northern Ireland, with a feature about Ian Paisley, was not broadcast in the province after the local ITA office concluded it could lead to public disorder.

In the years leading up to the outbreak of 'the Troubles' the unionist government remained keenly aware that television could undermine the image of Stormont throughout the UK. When journalists visited from the 'mainland' there was a concerted effort to explain to reporters and film crews that they had to understand the unique situation in Northern Ireland, but always through a distinctive unionist perspective. BBC Northern Ireland controller Robert McCall made this point in a memorandum to the BBC director-general, explaining it was imperative that on arrival visiting producers and journalists enter into the fullest liaison with his staff in Belfast. 'The peculiarities of life, politics and religion in this region are such that local advice is essential if unnecessary "blobs" are to be avoided.'[122]

In February 1967 the Northern Ireland Civil Rights Association was established and after a period of relative inactivity began a series of marches in the spring of 1968 that were influenced by the strategies of Martin Luther King, Jr., in the US. The leaders of the civil rights campaign understood the power of television and hoped to use it to force London to intervene to redress many long held grievances of the Catholic community. In June 1968 a young articulate Stormont MP, Austin Currie, occupied a house in the village of Caledon on the Tyrone, Armagh, Monaghan border to call attention to discrimination in the allocation of public housing by the unionist-controlled Dunganon Rural District Council. The house he chose to occupy had been given to a 19-year-old single Protestant woman in spite of the fact that there were many Catholic families on a waiting list living in dire conditions. The print and electronic media had been following protests at the small housing estate and calls were made to make sure television cameras would be on hand for the inevitable eviction. The subsequent television coverage proved compelling and succeeded in highlighting the discrimination that existed in the province. Currie recalls that he returned home that evening and 'I sat in my own front room and watched myself being interviewed on the news from London. It was the first time, as far as I knew, that any interview had ever taken place on British national television on the subject of discrimination against the minority in Northern Ireland.'[123] Calls from supporters came into the Currie home offering congratulations including one from the Labour MP, Paul Rose, who was Chairman of the Campaign for Democracy in Ulster, a group of Westminster MPs who supported the cause of civil rights in Northern Ireland. According to Currie, Rose told him, '"the message is at long last getting through to those the Unionists fear – British politicians and British public opinion. Keep it up"'.[124]

That autumn one particular civil rights march gained the civil rights campaign international attention and sympathy while profoundly damaging the image of the Stormont government. On October 5, 1968, civil rights leaders announced they would march in Derry, ignoring a ban issued by the hard-line Minister of Home Affairs, William Craig. During the demonstration the Royal Ulster Constabulary attacked the demonstrators, viciously beating helpless marchers with batons. Gerry Fitt MP from West Belfast, and three other Labour MPs who had travelled from England for the march, experienced the police violence firsthand. A bloodied Gerry Fitt had to be transported to the hospital in an

16   Royal Ulster Constabulary in Derry, October 5, 1968.

ambulance for medical treatment. What made the event extraordinary was the fact that an RTÉ cameraman, Gay O'Brien, and sound technician, Eamon Hays, captured the violence on film as it unfolded. This sensational footage made its way into the BBC programme *Twenty-Four Hours*, causing uproar. After the incident O'Neill's Government issued a statement 'supporting in a firm way the decisions of the Minister (William Craig) and the actions of the police in Londonderry'.[125] The juxtaposition of truncheon-wielding policemen attacking unarmed civil rights marchers and the statement of the government heavily damaged its credibility. In London, the British government grew increasingly alarmed and embarrassed at developments in the province and began to put pressure on Stormont to speed up long-overdue reforms. In his history of the BBC in Northern Ireland, Jonathan Bardon argues that the images captured by RTÉ destabilised the province and 'changed the course of Northern Ireland's history'.[126]

RTÉ's footage of the October 5, 1968 disturbances was picked up by international news organisations and broadcast around the world. The cause of the civil rights campaign in Northern Ireland and reaction of the Royal Ulster Constabulary quickly became front-page international news. Neil Hickey, a correspondent and member of the editorial board of *TV Guide* addressed American television coverage of these events in the widely circulated television magazine pointing out that this march was seen in the context of the struggles that confronted the American civil rights movement. He argues that these images

> dramatized for millions of horrified TV watchers in Britain and around the world – many for the first time – the fact that something was very wrong in Northern Ireland. The now famous TV film shows members of the Royal Ulster Constabulary – then totally unsophisticated about the presence of TV cameras – charging into the midst of peaceful marchers, cracking skulls with their batons, dragging some demonstrators roughly to police vans, battering others with high-powered water cannon. Unbeknownst to the constables, the whole world was watching.[127]

A week after the Derry mêlée, O'Neill wrote a long, insightful memorandum for his Cabinet addressing the crisis that was threatening the stability of the province. He argued that it was critical that members of the government understand that difficult decisions had to be made about reform. He clearly understood that television and press coverage of the Derry disturbances had changed the situation dramatically. The Prime Minister told his colleagues that his government was already under tremendous pressure from London to initiate substantial reforms in the province. According to O'Neill the unflattering publicity meant left-wing sources were demanding that British Prime Minister Harold Wilson intervene:

> Up to now he has fobbed off these pressures from our point of view very well. With his many other headaches, our affairs have not been high up on his agenda. With Northern Ireland calm, and a general feeling that slow but steady progress was underway, he could contain the situation by references to our talks – though not without a veiled threat on occasions. I would be failing in my duty if I did not make it clear to you that, in my view, Londonderry has dramatically altered this situation to our great disadvantage. Whether the press and T.V. coverage was fair is immaterial. We have now become a focus of world opinion; indeed we know through official channels that the Embassy

and B.I.S. in America have been under intense pressure from the American press.[128]

O'Neill made it clear that these events were transformative not because of the actions of the RUC but because they were filmed and transmitted on television screens around the world. In the House of Commons at Westminster shortly after the disturbances, Captain Orr, leader of the Unionist Party, objected to a question about the upcoming meeting between the British Prime Minister Harold Wilson and the Prime Minister of Northern Ireland, defining it as mischievous. Wilson responded to Orr, 'Up to now we have perhaps had to rely on the statements of himself and others on these matters. Since then we have had British television.'[129]

In Belfast O'Neill pleaded with his Cabinet to understand the reality of the situation, arguing that reforms had to be introduced and dismissing excited talk of a unilateral declaration of independence for Northern Ireland as absurd. He was convinced that unless the Cabinet was willing to make substantial changes the constitutional position of Northern Ireland would be in danger. He understood that the Northern Ireland Parliament would be suspended and direct rule from Westminster established if his government failed to act. O'Neill explained that when the expected summons from London arrived, it was imperative that he be able to promise Wilson his government was committed to substantial reforms. He understood how hard it would be to initiate reforms in the aftermath of the disturbances in Derry but again he stressed that difficult choices had to be made:

> Of course there are anti-partition agitators prominently at work, but can any of us truthfully say in the confines of this room that the minority has no grievance calling for remedy? Believe me, I realise the appalling political difficulties we face. The first reaction of our own people to the antics of Fitt and Curry and the abuse of the world's press is to retreat into old hard-line attitudes. But if this is *all* we can offer, we face a period when we govern Ulster by police power alone, against a background of mounting disorder. Are we ready, and would this be wise, to face up to this?[130]

For O'Neill the 1920 Government of Ireland Act that had created Northern Ireland and its parliament was at stake. Although he accepted that selling concessions to 'our people' would be difficult, he argued 'Things like the multiple vote at local government elections and the position of the Mater Hospital are not essential to maintain our position.' He went so far as to say, 'we may even in time have to make a bitter choice between losing Londonderry and losing Ulster'.[131] When the Cabinet met and discussed the Prime Minister's memorandum it was agreed that in making concessions the 'multiple vote in local government should not be regarded as sacrosanct' and the government should try to reach accommodation with the Mater Hospital.[132]

As expected when he met with Harold Wilson, Terence O'Neill came under intense pressure to initiate significant reforms to address the most egregious grievances articulated by the civil rights campaign. Tension in O'Neill's Cabinet remained high as the uncompromising William Craig jockeyed for position in the hopes of replacing the prime minister. Responding to a November 16th civil rights march that had once again defied the government ban, the Cabinet considered whether it should issue a statement about enforcing all future bans. Along with other colleagues in the Cabinet, William Craig had been lobbying for a harder line against the civil rights marches that were taking place, especially in Derry. He wanted the infamous B-Specials mobilised and told his Cabinet colleagues that police morale was at a disturbingly low ebb as they had been prevented by their superiors from 'dealing effectively with militants'.[133] Others in the cabinet also called for 'using all necessary force' to enforce the ban on marchers while the Attorney General argued that the ban should not be amended in any way and that a 'firm statement would be desirable to boost police morale, restore public confidence and allay concern of the Parliamentary Party'.[134]

As tensions ran high throughout the province a beleaguered O'Neill announced a set of sweeping reforms on November 22 designed to mollify both the British Prime Minister and moderates in the civil rights organisation. As tension grew and hard-liners within his own party worked to undermine his policies he decided to address the province on television, appearing both on the BBC and UTV. O'Neill's famous 'Ulster at the crossroads' speech told civil rights leaders 'your voice has been heard, and clearly heard. Your duty now is to take the heat out of the situation.' He also tried to reassure supporters of his own Ulster Unionist Party while denouncing as 'lunatics' hard-liners who advocated independence from Britain.[135] He was able to bring calm to the province for the month of December and gain enough support to dismiss the uncompromising William Craig from the Cabinet. It was perhaps the only time the unionist government at Stormont had taken advantage of television successfully. It would be the last. Although many moderate leaders of the civil rights movement heeded O'Neill's call to give his reforms a chance, a more confrontational group, People's Democracy, decided to embark on a contentious march from Belfast to Derry on New Year's Day 1969. Once again television played a critical role, capturing the ensuing violence, including a vicious attack on the marchers by loyalists at Burntollet Bridge. These images were broadcast internationally as 'television footage vividly recorded history in the making and not only vied with reports about the Vietnam War but also played its part in giving Northern Ireland a sharp push towards the precipice'.[136]

In his study of Irish-America and the Northern Ireland crisis, historian Andrew Wilson notes that many of these events were broadcast on the three main US television networks. The film from RTÉ and British sources showed the 'RUC wading into peaceful civil rights protesters, cracking heads with their batons and blasting others with high-powered water cannon'.[137] As demonstrations continued the mainstream American press compared events in Northern Ireland with the campaign for civil rights in the American South. At that time, the three national networks – CBS, NBC and ABC – were an influential source of news and information for the American public. One of the iconic network 'anchormen' of the period, Chet Huntley, closed an evening's news broadcast in August 1969 drawing this parallel for his audience: 'The Catholics in Ulster are the same as the Blacks in the United States; they've been deprived of their rights, harried into slums, and denied jobs, hurt and slashed, ever since the Battle of the Boyne. And like Blacks they've revolted; and like Blacks they've burned down the very ghettoes that were built to contain them; and like Blacks they've been shot down.'[138] In the American press unionists were compared to bigoted Southern whites, while the Orange Order was matched up to the Ku Klux Klan. Although

17 Bernadette Devlin is filmed by RTÉ cameraman Bestick Williams, April 25, 1969. Devlin was interviewed for *Féach*, in her uncle's house in Cookstown, County Tyrone.

these simplistic comparisons failed to address the complexities of events in Northern Ireland or the USA, they resonated within mainstream America, and especially the Irish diaspora.

These news reports were a cause of tremendous concern for the British government, embarrassed by the hostile reaction these televised events provoked. The leaders of the Northern Ireland Civil Rights Association understood the power of the television images. Bernadette Devlin, who was elected to Westminster in April 1969 became what historian Joe Lee describes as a 'media star' and an 'accomplished public performer'.[139] She told one interviewer: 'In retrospect, I realised the police had actually done us a great favour'.[140] In London that spring BBC Director-General

Charles Curren once again reminded staff that it was critical all programmes dealing with Northern Ireland or Ireland be made in close consultation with the controller in Northern Ireland. 'Everything possible must be done to ensure that our output does not exacerbate the situation.'[141] Curran ordered that any 'observations or objections by the C.N.I. [Controller Northern Ireland] … must be carefully considered by the head of the department concerned, and I should expect them normally to be accepted'.[142] In these circumstances Waldo Maguire, the controller of BBC Northern Ireland, held a great degree of influence over the coverage of events that spiralled out of control in the ensuing months.

Unable to unite an increasingly fractious Unionist Party, Terence O'Neill resigned on April 28, 1969, and was replaced by James Chichester-Clark. When viewing O'Neill's resignation today, which was broadcast on television, the sense of missed opportunity is remarkable. That summer proved to be one of the most difficult for the province and after intense rioting in Derry, culminating in the 'Battle of the Bogside', Chichester-Clark mobilised the B-Specials, the auxiliary police force despised by the Catholic community who regarded it a sectarian vigilante force. The Minister of Home Affairs told the Cabinet that the B-Specials would 'guard threatened Roman Catholic houses in Protestant areas (with Protestant houses in Roman Catholic areas being protected by the R.U.C.). This would help to relieve regular police and demonstrate that the USC existed to help preserve law and order in the interests of all sections of the community.'[143] The Inspector General of the RUC and the Deputy Inspector attended the Cabinet meeting that decided against instituting a curfew and against a ban on the traditional Orange parades.[144] The mobilising of the B-Specials and their placement within Catholic communities and near Catholic homes in Protestant areas was not seen as a gesture of goodwill by the Catholic community, but rather a deliberate provocation meant to intimidate the minority community.

Once again, television cameras transmitted images of disorder and seeming anarchy, causing alarm in Belfast, London and Dublin. The 'Battle of the Bogside' witnessed Catholics in Derry defending their neighbourhood from the RUC with stones and

Molotov Cocktails. Images of the stand-off that developed again made their way into homes throughout the UK, Ireland, and much of the world, creating acute embarrassment for the British government. The chaos that engulfed Derry spread to Belfast and in the midst of burnings and violence three thousand Catholics and five hundred Protestants were forced to flee from their homes. Images of burning streets and fleeing refugees were transmitted internationally as were reports that members of the security forces participated in the mayhem. The violence forced London to send in the army on August 15, 1969. Television cameras filmed the arrival of British soldiers and the reception they received in the streets of Belfast as Catholic women brought tea to welcome them and the protection they offered their besieged communities.

Writing about the events of that summer, Rex Cathcart addresses the dilemma that confronted the BBC especially on the nights of August 14 and 15 when five people were killed, hundreds injured, and many homes and buildings burned. Should the BBC report accurately on events and risk inflaming the situation or produce a sanitised, censored version that would simply report on the lawlessness convulsing the province? It chose the second option and transmitted material 'that was carefully "sanitised" to ensure emotional outbursts, inflammatory and violent accusations were not screened'.[145] The BBC Controller for Northern Ireland, Waldo Maguire, explained his position to the Northern Ireland Advisory Council, maintaining that it was imperative the BBC understand that residents of Northern Ireland experiencing the violence firsthand were watching these broadcasts:

> In the present atmosphere of hatred and fear, we have to recognise that the broadcasting of violently opposed views, passionately and offensively expressed, could have direct and immediate consequences on the streets of Belfast and Londonderry. This then is the dilemma. While taking account of the fact that the network news bulletins and programmes are being seen and heard in Northern Ireland, the BBC must not fail in its duty to the rest of the United Kingdom, to present news fully and fairly, to explain the background to the violence, to provide a platform for the expression of all significant opinion.[146]

McGuire identified two options, the first that the BBC could treat Northern Ireland as a foreign country and produce 'the same kind of uninhibited programme which would be made if the shooting, rioting, looting and arson were taking place in a foreign country: and then ensure it is not carried on Northern Ireland transmitters'. However an alternative was chosen to 'modify to some extent the presentation ... in a way designed to avoid extreme provocation'.[147] The censorship in place from the outbreak of rioting in Belfast until the arrival of British troops meant that the BBC failed to accurately report these events. The veteran reporter Martin Bell, who spent a good deal of time covering Northern Ireland, many years later reflected on this policy:

> We made a mistake ... in 1969, in August of that year when Catholics were burned out of their homes in the Falls by Protestants who attacked them from the Shankill. The BBC reports then gave no indication of who these refugees were. They just spoke of refugees. The public was not to know whether they were Catholic or Protestant or who was attacking whom. That has been seen as a grave mistake, and in eight years of reporting this thing, on and off, that was probably the only time when I was stopped from the powers above from saying what I wanted to say.[148]

When the Stormont Cabinet met to review the security situation in the province a few days later there was alarm at the manner with which events had been portrayed on television, even if the BBC reporting was 'sanitised'. Cabinet conclusions reported:

> Ministers commented on the press and television presentation of the situation in Northern Ireland and expressed concern that the Government's policies and actions were being inaccurately or misleadingly reported; that any suggestion of involvement by subversive organisations was discounted; and that the public were being subjected to much comment and speculation on the consequences of the situation. It was the general view of the ministers that an urgent press conference should be held, at which the Prime Minister and several of his colleagues could explain the Government's views on the wider issues involved.[149]

At the same Cabinet meeting ministers were informed that Chichester-Clarke had been summoned to London for a meeting with the British Prime Minister and that London wanted the B-Specials withdrawn from front-line positions.

A short time later Chichester-Clark took issue with a BBC

programme *Scene Around Six* because it contained a menacing interview with a member of the Ulster Volunteer Force. The Prime Minister protested to Lord Dunleath who represented Northern Ireland on the BBC Board of Governors. Lord Dunleath responded to the Prime Minister's protest explaining that he had seen the programme and was shocked, not because there was any indiscretion in the transmission 'but because of the ominous significance of its content'.[150] Lord Dunleath explained that the BBC was doing its best to provide balanced reporting on the growing violence in the province, pointing out that it was being constantly criticised by all sides. 'It has been interesting to note how even individual programmes have evoked volumes of abuse in equal proportions from either side but from diametrically opposed standpoints. One can only hope that, if the level of criticism is the same from each quarter, it means one is approximating to a middle course.'[151] Chichester-Clark was told that all of the output was 'subject to the closest possible scrutiny not only in the Northern Ireland Region but also in the top echelon of the BBC News Service in London'.[152] He pointed out that other news media had carried the story and that if the BBC had not it 'would have left themselves open to valid criticism had they suppressed it'.[153]

Chichester-Clark was not impressed by the reply, complaining that he felt it was wrong for the BBC to be 'countenancing an organisation which is proscribed'.[154] He made it clear that he believed the BBC had not considered the consequences of its broadcast, arguing that it was 'overlooking the greater effect which T.V. has on people's minds, and the fact that T.V. seems to have a great gift of inflaming people'.[155] The Prime Minister was deeply concerned that television was complicating his political life and adding to an already tense situation in the province. Lord Dunleath later reported that he had discussed the Prime Minister's complaints at length with senior staff at the BBC news and current affairs department in London and all agreed that the broadcast of the UVF interview was correct. He once again assured the Prime Minister that the BBC took their responsibilities 'extremely seriously in all matters connected with the Northern Ireland situation'.[156]

Interest in Northern Ireland grew within Great Britain as the deployed British troops became increasingly engaged in confrontation with the Catholic community and eventually the Provisional IRA. BBC news teams became more interested in trying to report on incidents by going beyond official reports released by the British Army or the Information Office at Stormont. In trying to produce balanced reports and look at both sides of complicated issues, BBC reporters created tremendous difficulties for their superiors and the governments in Belfast and London. The Northern Ireland government complained incessantly about television coverage of 'the Troubles,' reacting to any slight that was detected with letters of protest to Charles Curran, the Director-General of the BBC.

For instance in February 1971 security forces carried out a disruptive house-to-house search in New Lodge, a Catholic section of Belfast. The BBC news report maintained that the honeymoon between the Catholic community and the British Army was over because heavy-handed army tactics were alienating moderate Catholic opinion. BBC correspondent John Bierman reported, 'There are growing doubts about the Army's impartiality among moderate middle class Catholics desperately anxious to hold their co-religionists back from extremism.'[157] A local businessman was interviewed who explained that the Catholic community increasingly regarded the army as supplanting the RUC, pointing out it was conducting aggressive house-to-house searches exclusively in Catholic areas. Although the reporter quoted General Erskine Crum as arguing the army was impartial, the audience was told that 'in the dismal back streets the Catholics are more and more looking to one or the other wing of the IRA ... In Ardoyne for instance, where they peppered this Army observation post with machine gun fire, the Provos ... have the almost total backing of the local population'.[158] The Joint Security Committee, representing both the British Army and the Royal Ulster Constabulary, was outraged at the report and issued a statement denying that there was a growing sense of Catholic alienation:

> The programme in question implied that respectable, moderate, middle-class Roman Catholic opinion had growing doubts about the Army's impartiality and asserted that in certain areas the IRA have 'the almost total backing of the local population'. The judgement of this Committee is that any sway which subversive organisations assert

is largely based on intimidation. It has been made abundantly clear by both Governments and by the Army and police commanders that the searches and other forms of security activity are directed not against any section of the population but against any organisations which for any motive sets itself against the law.[159]

While the security committee might have been oblivious to the growing alienation of the Catholic community, they understood quite clearly that negative news reports questioning security policy could adversely affect public opinion throughout the UK. The report upset the Stormont government, which was convinced that the BBC was undermining the forces of law and order in the province. Responding to the programme, Thomas M. Roberts, Deputy Director, Government Information Services at Stormont, captured the essence of the complaints many unionists had with the BBC:

> One of the main problems of the BBC is that it does not give, nor want to appear to give, authority or backing to the state. In a recent discussion with Mr. Waldo Maguire, indeed he made this very point to me, that the BBC was holding the balance between one side and the other. It seems quite monstrous that a public corporation should not take the side of the lawful authority but want to give equal support to those who by unconstitutional means are attempting to bring the State down.[160]

Roberts indicated that the Northern Ireland Prime Minister had complained to the BBC director-general about the 'general attitude to Ulster and particularly the attitude of programmes like "Panorama", "24 Hours", "The World at One" and "The World this Weekend"'.[161] The government was upset that 'some Roman Catholics with access to the news media are attempting to turn the spotlight from the IRA to the security forces with allegations of partiality and rough handling'.[162] Roberts wanted BBC reporters to follow in the footsteps of their ITA counterparts and, on arrival in the province, come to Stormont Castle for debriefings by his staff 'to get up to date facts on the Northern Ireland situation. We know there would be BBC News Division resistance to this. But it seems to me to be perfectly legitimate and no ITN reporters come to Belfast without checking in with us first. We could fairly claim that they are often more factually accurate than their opposite numbers in the BBC.'[163]

Another programme broadcast that winter, *Twenty-Four Hours*, further added to growing tensions, featuring an interview with two members of the Provisional IRA. The programme caused predictable outrage from Unionist and Conservative politicians and was condemned in the Westminster House of Commons where Home Secretary Reginald Maudling promised an investigation. The correspondent Bernard Faulk had not followed procedure and consulted with the controller in Northern Ireland, Waldo Maguire. Faulk soon found himself under investigation by the Royal Ulster Constabulary who may have been looking for an opportunity to make an example of the so-called 'firemen' reporting on events in the province for London-based programmes. Appearing in a Belfast court, Faulk refused to identify the men he interviewed, citing promises he had made to the men and journalistic code. He was sentenced to four days in jail which he served for refusing to identify the men he interviewed. The Faulk affair was covered widely in the press and proved a turning point in the BBC's coverage of 'the Troubles', sending an ominous message to journalists reporting from Northern Ireland. The BBC took the matter seriously, issuing a directive stating that no member of the Provisional IRA could be interviewed without the explicit permission of the director-general.

In March 1971 the ineffective Chichester-Clark was replaced by Brian Faulkner as Prime Minister; Faulkner would be the last Prime Minister of Northern Ireland.[164] Amid a relentless campaign of violence by the Provisional IRA, Faulkner introduced the highly controversial policy of internment in August 1971. When the Cabinet met to review the policy at the end of the first week of internment there was disquiet within the government on a number of fronts. The Prime Minister rejected a complaint by the Minister of Community Relations who 'was worried about the one-sided nature of the operation and about the divisive effect it could have on political opinion in Britain'.[165] Faulkner defended the policy, stating that it would be applied to anyone regardless of religious or political affiliation. He explained that 'at present he was advised there was no case to justify the detention of Protestants'.[166] The Attorney General, who attended the Cabinet meeting supported the Prime Minister and 'confirmed that the Police had been genuinely unable to furnish him with any information suggesting that a subversive organisation existed in the Protestant community'.[167] All chose to ignore the existence of the Ulster Volunteer Force, a lethal sectarian paramilitary organisation established in June of 1966. As noted above, the UVF was the subject of a controversial interview that provoked a vociferous protest to the BBC from Chichester-Clark.

Less than a week after the introduction of internment the British Army held a major press conference to declare the policy a success, claiming the IRA had been dealt a stunning defeat. According to a spokesman the army had 'killed twenty or thirty gunmen and wounded as many more ... The leadership of the IRA had been lifted ... and their ranks decimated, with three hundred suspects interned'.[168] While the British Army was addressing the print and electronic media the Provisional IRA held a rival press conference at Saint Peter's School in nearby Whiterock. The event was arranged by Patrick Kennedy, a Stormont MP for Republican Labour, and featured Joe Cahill, a leading republican defiantly mocking Faulkner and the British Army. Cahill claimed that the IRA knew internment was coming and that in the fighting that took place two IRA members had been shot and only thirty interned. The fact that a leading figure in the Provisional IRA was able to hold a news conference in broad daylight outraged the Stormont government. Faulkner informed his Cabinet a short time later that the police were investigating the event and would issue a report concerning what 'action would be taken' against those who organised or participated in it.[169]

Internment proved a disaster for the unionist government and London and was followed by a relentless wave of bombings and killings. Prior to the introduction of internment there were thirty-four deaths in Northern Ireland due to political violence; between the time of its introduction and the end of 1971 there were 139.[170] The heavy-handed tactics of the security forces and reports of abuse of internees further discredited the Stormont and Westminster governments and led to the increased alienation of the nationalist minority and in some quarters growing support for the Provisional IRA.

As these events unfolded unionists became increasingly concerned with what actions the British government would take to try to come to terms with a crisis that appeared intractable. Faulkner had been warned that if internment failed the result would be the suspension of the Stormont government and the introduction of direct rule from London.[171] Later that year, the Labour Party added to the sense of foreboding for unionists by adopting a resolution accepting that Ireland should be reunited. Once again a BBC television programme underscored the dire situation confronting the unionist government. The leader of the party, Harold Wilson, was interviewed by the current affairs programme *Twenty Four Hours* and explained his party's decision.[172] The interview was transcribed for stunned government ministers at Stormont who found the remarks of the leader of the opposition at Westminster unsettling. Wilson maintained that internment had:

> alienated the Catholic population totally, ... the British Army that we put in two years ago ... were cheered by the Catholics when they went in. There were almost festivities on the streets and now they are spitting on them and the political effects of internment I think are devastating and that is why whatever might have provided a basis of the political solution we must have along side of a military solution. ... now because the Catholic population has [become] alienated, driven more into supporting the gunmen more than they want to be and that is why I think we have to have a much more fundamental solution. Hence my proposals for the dream of a united Ireland.[173]

In the same interview, again transcribed for the Northern Ireland Cabinet, Wilson called for the transfer of security to Westminster, in effect stripping the Stormont government of the responsibility for supervising the work of the security forces.

A short time later Brian Faulkner felt compelled to issue a formal statement denying reports by the BBC that the Heath Government had transferred the responsibility for security from Belfast to London. Although a BBC report indicated the Home Secretary had made such an announcement in London, Faulkner was quick to dismiss the report as erroneous. 'For the BBC to have carried such a misleading report is in itself regrettable, but not to have checked either with the Home Office or with the Northern Ireland government on a point of such major importance is scarcely excusable.'[174] In fact, the report was four months premature.[175]

With British soldiers on the ground in Northern Ireland, the source of criticism of television coverage shifted. No longer was the critique emanating only from the Stormont government; now it came from London, especially from the Conservative Members of Parliament. When Edward Heath became Prime Minister, the critique of BBC reporters questioning British army tactics, policies, reports and strategy infuriated many government members. Rex Cathcart points to an incident that occurred in Catholic West Belfast in October 1971 as an important turning point. On that evening troops were involved in a house-to-house search looking for arms when they fired on a car that they reported later had fired on them. Two women were killed in the incident and a BBC television crew quickly learned that the army's version of events differed sharply from that of the driver and local people who witnessed the killings. The report of Keith Graves from the street in West Belfast where the incident happened highlighted these discrepancies although he gave the last word to the officer in charge of the soldiers who had killed the women.[176]

The story provoked outrage in Westminster as Unionist and Conservative MPs denounced the BBC. Eighty Unionist and Conservative MPs met with the Home Secretary Reginald Maudling, urging him to persuade both the BBC and ITA to avoid any reporting that would undermine the very difficult work of the army. Maudling later met with the Chairman of the BBC Board of Governors, Lord Hill, to complain. Lord Hill defended the work of the BBC and responded to the criticism, arguing that the BBC took its responsibilities concerning Northern Ireland seriously. He also argued that much of the criticism was unfair and that there was a misunderstanding of what the BBC was trying to do in the province:

> We see it as our over-riding responsibility to report the scene as it is in all its tragedy to all people of the United Kingdom. We do not side with Catholics or Protestants. The BBC and its staff abhor the terrorism of the IRA and report their campaign of murder with revulsion. Broadly the charges are that the BBC reporters and editors snipe at the army, and are 'soft' towards the IRA. These charges are untrue,

and deeply resented by our staff, many of whom do their work at great risk to themselves.[177]

The protest by unionist and conservative Members of Parliament in the autumn of 1971 impacted subsequent BBC coverage of events in the province. Editorial control was tightened once again and any story about Northern Ireland now had to be cleared in London. With the British army on the streets the Conservative Government became increasingly sensitive to news reports that challenged official reports and statements about events in a region that had long been ignored by London. Some BBC staff members grew increasingly concerned with an atmosphere of self-censorship developing within the broadcasting organisation. Desmond Taylor, Editor of News and Current Affairs, denied censorship was an issue, maintaining that the only changes made required reporters to seek permission any time an interview with the IRA was being planned.

However, BBC current affairs programming continued to create problems for the Heath and Faulkner Governments. In this highly charged atmosphere a programme titled *The Question of Ulster* created anger from Conservative and Unionist MPs, and again Home Secretary Reginald Maudling intervened to try to suppress the project. Unionists and Tories were incensed that the BBC would allow Bernadette Devlin and former Fianna Fáil TD Neil Blaney to participate in the programme that brought together a range of viewpoints on the crisis. Efforts at suppressing the broadcast were resisted by the BBC's Chairman Lord Hill who defended the programme. *The Question of Ulster* was successfully broadcast to a large audience and well received in Northern Ireland, Great Britain and the Republic of Ireland. However as 'the Troubles' continued, coverage of events in the province offered by the BBC and ITA programmes remained controversial, resulting in more overt forms of censorship that lasted well into the 1990s.

South of the border, RTÉ was caught off guard by the outbreak of violence in Northern Ireland. With a few notable exceptions, before 1968 there had been very little attention paid to life in the province.[178] The producer of *Seven Days* who filmed a programme about gerrymandering in Derry before the outbreak of violence recalls that there was little known about Northern Ireland in the Irish Republic and little interest in addressing life in the province within RTÉ.[179] This was also true of the print media: the only national newspaper to provide comprehensive coverage of events in Northern Ireland before the outbreak of violence was the the *Irish Times*.[180] RTÉ did not have a correspondent dedicated to Belfast until February 1968 when an office was opened and Martin Wallace was named full-time correspondent for Northern Ireland. Technical and logistical problems made it difficult for film to be made available for the evening news, meaning that in the critical early days of the civil rights movement little actual film made it on to the television news. Initially radio coverage offered better and more immediate reporting of events leading up to the outbreak of violence in the summer of 1969. This failure to address life in the province prior to 1968 was compounded by the relative inexperience of RTÉ staff in Northern Ireland and the unwillingness of some to work there. This put pressure on senior producers who ended up spending a great deal of time in Belfast as demonstrations began to destabilise Northern Ireland.[181]

The relationship between the Fianna Fáil Government and the national broadcasting service was already strained when 'the Troubles' erupted in the summer of 1969. A week before the 'Battle of the Bogside', and the subsequent arrival of British troops, the Taoiseach met with editors of the national press, the director-general and the head of news at RTÉ to address what was described as a new phase in the activities of the IRA. Referring to arson attacks that had taken place earlier that summer in Meath and Louth, Lynch predicted that more were to be expected. In these circumstances he asked for media support to ensure the IRA was not glamorised by using 'such phrases as "expert job", "commando-type raid" [that] had a bad effect on immature minds'.[182] The Taoiseach explained that the government would take a 'more active line' against the IRA, which he described as fragmented and numbering approximately 1,200 members, many of whom were strongly influenced by socialism. He was unsure how the IRA might react to the introduction of British troops into Northern Ireland although he mentioned 'if the initial emotional reaction could be overcome, the use of British troops in the North would be to our advantage because it would provide evidence that the Stormont government could no longer control the situation'.[183]

When he met with the same group of media executives a month later, British troops were on the ground in Northern Ireland and the situation had changed dramatically. He made it clear that the situation was very dangerous, that Catholics 'in the Falls Road had got more arms and felt they could now defend themselves. In addition, there were now people inside the barricades who wanted to create trouble. For their part, Protestants were also scared. They saw a threat to their way of life and security.'[184] In these circumstances he explained that 'the desire for the unity of the whole country be pressed carefully' and that Protestants had to understand that they 'had nothing to fear from us'.[185]

Once the Provisional IRA was formed and embarked upon its 'armed struggle', the Lynch Government grew increasingly anxious with coverage of events, especially the exposure given to members of Sinn Féin and both the Official and Provisional wings of the IRA.[186] This eventually led to the Minister for Posts and Telegraphs Gerard Collins dismissing the RTÉ Authority in November 1972. Before sacking the authority, Collins carefully addressed what he determined was a history of reckless behaviour on the part of the national broadcasting service, laying out the reasons the RTÉ Authority should be dismissed. He recounted that in June 1971 his government refused to participate in a radio programme featuring people he defined as subversive. At the time Mike Burns, host of *This Week,* contacted the Minister of Justice, inviting him onto the programme that featured representatives of both the Official and Provisional IRA. The Minister declined, and when the Taoiseach, Jack Lynch, was informed of the programme he told RTÉ that the broadcast 'was contrary to the national interest', maintaining that 'subversive elements should not be given RTÉ facilities as a platform for their publicity'.[187] The director-general decided to go ahead with the programme even though he was told that the government was seriously considering intervening and issuing an order under Section 31 of the Broadcasting Act.

Later that year Collins learned RTÉ intended to broadcast

a programme featuring interviews with Sean MacStiofáin and Cathal Goulding, two leading members of the IRA. Collins told his Cabinet colleagues that he 'urged very strongly on the Chairman of the Authority the undesirability of going ahead with this project but to no avail'.[188] This prompted Collins to issue a written directive under Section 31 (1) of the Broadcasting Act in October 1971 ordering the station to 'refrain from broadcasting any matter that could be calculated to promote the aims and activities of any organisation which engages in, promotes, encourages or advocates the attainment of any particular objective by violent means'.[189] The directive was issued during a period of ferocious violence in Northern Ireland that was exacerbated by the introduction of internment without trial aimed exclusively at republican paramilitaries. By the time the directive was issued 135 people had been killed since violence erupted in Northern Ireland in July 1969.[190]

The RTÉ Authority complained about the order, arguing that it was written in terms that were unclear and imprecise but issued a statement promising 'a balanced comprehensive broadcasting service which would be authentic in itself and fully responsive to the needs of the whole community within the added constraints of the direction'.[191] The Chairman of the RTÉ Authority, Dónall Ó Móráin, wrote to Collins asking for clarification of the order and later sent the minister a detailed memorandum explaining the Authority's interpretation of the directive. The Authority complained that the order presented 'great difficulties of interpretation starting with the phrase "any matter that could be calculated to promote ..." Indeed the Authority thinks that the terms of the direction generally are so imprecise as to be unsatisfactory in principle and to place an unfair burden onto the Authority.'[192] Collins was not impressed and refused to respond, believing the order was clear and direct. After the directive under Section 31 of the Broadcasting Act was issued, Collins maintained that initially there was less cause to complain, although tension between the government and RTÉ remained high. Collins reported that 'several individual programmes seriously trespassed against the spirit, if not the letter of this direction'.[193]

Despite the order Collins issued, RTÉ coverage of the violence in Northern Ireland continued to be controversial and caused increasing acrimony and bitter complaints from political leaders of all parties. Less than a year after it was issued Fine Gael Deputy Gerard L'Estrange launched a scathing attack on RTÉ in the Dáil maintaining that the government's directive had been 'flouted by slick operators in that organisation. Certain men in that organisation have built up and glorified men of violence'.[194] Collins responded noting that he too remained concerned with the performance of RTÉ and its coverage of the violence in Northern Ireland, explaining that although it was not his intention to act as a censor he had found it necessary to issue a directive under Section 31 of the Broadcasting Act. He told the Dáil that he had 'no doubt whatever that the Authority will take note of the views expressed here' and promised to convey his views to the RTÉ Authority shortly.[195]

The matter finally came to a head on Sunday November 19, 1972. A lunchtime radio programme included the summary of an interview of the IRA Chief of Staff, Seán Mac Stiofáin, who was quoted by correspondent Kevin O'Kelly as defending what the IRA leader referred to as the 'armed struggle', stating that in spite of a lull in bombing 'we can escalate at will'. Mac Stiofáin discussed the killing of Protestants while offering assurances that their rights would be protected in a unified Ireland, noting 'any Protestants that have been killed by the I.R.A. have been killed because they have been serving in one or other of the British occupation forces'.[196]

The government reacted swiftly after this broadcast, approving a letter from Collins to Dónall Ó Móráin, ominously protesting that the broadcast 'was in contravention of the direction issued to Radio Telefís Éireann on 1st October, 1971 under Section 31 of the Broadcasting Authority Act, 1960'.[197] Collins directed the chairman to call a meeting of the Authority 'as a matter of immediate urgency', demanding to know how it was going to respond to what the minister believed was a clear violation of the order. The Authority met and prepared a four-page letter defending the impartiality of the national broadcaster and arguing that it had been diligent to ensure that the minister's directive, as interpreted by RTÉ, would not be violated. It accepted that in the specific radio programme cited by the minister 'editorial decisions taken showed defective judgement' and promised that this conclusion would be conveyed to all staff.[198]

The government met two days later to consider its options and to review the response of the Authority. Before meeting Collins prepared a lengthy report, stating 'For a long time, RTÉ has been broadcasting programmes tending to encourage subversive elements in the community.'[199] The report chronicled the tension building between the state and RTÉ, arguing that the Authority had failed to abide by the directive issued under Section 31 of the Broadcasting Act issued October 1, 1971. The Lynch Government examined the Authority's response, defined it as inadequate and sacked the RTÉ Authority on November 24.[200] Members learned of their dismissal via a short note signed by a civil servant in Posts and Telegraphs just as the government was announcing the composition of a new RTÉ Authority.[201]

Dónall Ó Móráin issued a statement to the press which included copies of the correspondence between Collins and the Authority. This included the original Section 31 directive, which he once again defined as 'vague', complaining 'we have been asked to do an impossible task not knowing who was to be either judge or jury of our performance and without the right of appeal which other citizens have the privilege of enjoying'.[202] Years later, Ó Móráin argued that the vast majority of Irish politicians had no knowledge of Northern Ireland and 'what they wanted least was a day-by-day coverage by RTÉ of violence' claiming they were not 'capable of coping intellectually, emotionally or physically' with the outbreak of the Troubles.[203] In a letter to the editor of the *Irish Times*, T. W. Moody, undoubtedly the most influential intellectual to serve both the radio and television service, he argued: 'A democratic society needs to face disagreeable truths, and the best service the communications media can render at a time of grave crisis may well be to help it to do so.'[204]

Ironically the decision of Collins to dismiss the RTÉ Authority was attacked in the Dáil by Conor Cruise-O'Brien, who accused the government of 'using a big stick to come down not on the IRA but on RTÉ because they refer to the existence of the IRA. RTÉ have a duty to cover news of evil – an evil the Government have not been anxious to deal with. The government want to stop the RTÉ coverage but they have shown little anxiety to stop the evil itself.'[205] Section 31 of the Broadcasting Act was later amended when Conor Cruise-O'Brien was Minister for Posts and Telegraphs in a coalition Fine Gael–Labour government. The strict regime of political censorship put in place proved tremendously controversial and lasted until January 1994, when it was suspended during the peace process in the lead-up to an IRA cease-fire. The firing of the RTÉ Authority was an extraordinary measure that illustrated the Lynch Government was not only tremendously concerned about the IRA having access to the airwaves but also worried that the violence consuming Northern Ireland could spill into the Irish Republic, creating serious political instability. Lynch had absolutely no reservations about the decision to sack the public authority responsible for television and radio broadcasting in the state. On being told that many would conclude the decision reflected poorly on his commitment to freedom of speech, he replied 'Fuck them.'[206]

In Northern Ireland the introduction of television helped to undermine a state that had governed without consensus since its establishment in 1920. Television reports from London in the 1950s that were critical of policies and practices in the province created tremendous unease for a unionist-controlled government that ignored fundamental problems in a deeply divided society. Initially the government at Stormont succeeded in suppressing reports that it found problematic, but this became an impossible task when the Northern Irish Civil Rights Association began a series of marches to protest discrimination in the state. When awkward, heavy-handed attempts were made to suppress the civil rights campaign in the autumn of 1968, cameras were there to capture images of police brutality that were transmitted throughout the world, forcing the British government to pressure Stormont to initiate substantial reforms that were deeply unpopular with many unionists. These reforms failed to calm the unrest buffeting Northern Ireland and continued protests led to more unrest and the introduction of the British Army. Once the Provisional IRA began its campaign of violence, republicans came to understand the power of the medium and grew increasingly adept at using it. Political elites in Belfast and London, like their counterparts in Dublin, resented the power of the medium and aggressive questioning from reporters who grew increasingly sceptical of government decisions and policies. South of the border the coverage afforded the IRA and Sinn Féin alarmed the government, resulting in the implementation of a strict regime of censorship.

Television proved a complicated modernising force on both sides of the border as 'the Troubles' gained momentum, unnerving political establishments in Dublin, Belfast, and London. While 'the Troubles' have ended, debates concerning political censorship remain as relevant today as they were when censorship in broadcasting became a reality in both the Irish Republic and the United Kingdom of Great Britain and Northern Ireland.

Notes

1 See Robert Savage, *Irish Television: The Political and Social Origins* (Cork University Press, Cork, 1996), 46–7.

2 The programme *Pattern of Ulster* was transmitted on May 26, 1953, and local BBC staff offered advice on the thirty-minute documentary. An episode in the BBC documentary series *About Britain* focusing on Northern Ireland was broadcast the following year, July 30, 1954. Both were filtered through BBC officials in the province to ensure no controversial issues would be addressed that might embarrass the unionist government. See John Hill, *Cinema and Northern Ireland* (British Film Institute, London, 2006), 152–3.

3 Rex Cathcart, *The Most Contrary Region, the BBC in Northern Ireland 1924–1984* (Blackstaff Press, Belfast, 1984), 174.

4 Ibid., 164.

5 For an insightful consideration of the early development of broadcasting in Ireland, see Martin McLoone, 'The Construction of a Partitionist Mentality: Early Broadcasting in Ireland', in *Broadcasting in a Divided Community, Seventy Years of the BBC in Northern Ireland* (ed.) Martin McLoon (Institute of Irish Studies, Belfast, 1996).

6 Cathcart, *Most Contrary Region,* 165.

7 Public Records Office of Northern Ireland [hereafter PRONI], Cab/875/3, *Memorandum by the Minister of Home Affairs on the BBC in Northern,* May 19, 1952.

8 Ibid.

9 Ibid.

10 Ibid.

11 PRONI, Cab 4/875/5, Cabinet Meeting Minutes, May 22, 1952.

12 Martin McLoone, *Film, Media and Popular Culture in Ireland* (Irish Academic Press, Dublin, 2008), 193.

13 *Sunday Independent,* May 18, 1952, quoted in Cathcart, *Most Contrary Region,* 166. Glengall Street in Belfast was the address of Ulster Unionist Party headquarters.

14 Cathcart, *Most Contrary Region,* 167.

15 Ibid.

16 Gillian McIntosh, *The Force of Culture: Unionist Identities in Twentieth-Century Ireland* (Cork University Press, Cork, 1999), 94.

17 Ibid., 80.

18 Ibid., 81–2.

19 Ibid., 83.

20 Ibid., 95.

21 BBC Written Archives, Caversham, T16/222/1, Stewart to Director-General, March 20, 1951.

22 Ibid. BBC Director of Television Service George Barnes to controller, BBC Northern Ireland, R. D. Marriott, August 4, 1953.

23 Ibid., memorandum of Barnes to Head of Films BBC, London, September 29, 1953.

24 John Hill, *Cinema and Northern Ireland* (British Film Institute, London, 2006), 153.

25 BBC Written Archives, Caversham, T16/222/1, Marriott to Barnes, August 25, 1953.

26 Ibid.

27 Ibid., Barnes to Marriott, September 4, 1953.

28 PRONI, Cab 9F/165/12/2, Cabinet memorandum, May 7, 1959.

29 Ibid.

30 Ibid.

31 Author's interview with Alan Whicker, who spoke to me about these events from his home in Jersey, UK, June 10, 2009.

32 Alan Whicker, *Within Wicker's World* (Elm Tree Books, London, 1982). See also Liz Curtis, *Ireland and the Propaganda War* (Pluto Press, London, 1984).

33 Ibid., 154–5.

34 *Northern Whig,* quoted in Cathcart, *Most Contrary Region,* 190.

35 *Belfast Newsletter,* January 12, 1959.

36 PRONI, CAB 9F/165/12/2, correspondence and statement dated January 12, 1959.

37 PRO, CAB 9F/165/12/2, *Belfast Newsletter,* January 12, 1959.

38 BBC Written Archives, Caversham, T16/591 TV Policy Programme policy 'Tonight' and Northern Ireland 1959–1964. Robert McCall to

Grace Wyndham Goldie, January 14, 1959. Also quoted in Cathcart, *Most Contrary Region*, 192–3.

39 Ibid.

40 Ibid.

41 Whicker, *Within Wicker's World*, 155. Whicker made it clear that there was no effort made by BBC Northern Ireland to influence or shape his work and if there had been he 'would not stand for it'. (Author's interview with Alan Whicker, June 10, 2009).

42 Ibid., 155–6.

43 Cathcart, *Most Contrary Region* 193.

44 BBC Written Archive, Caversham, T16/591, TV policy, Programme Policy, Tonight and Northern Ireland, 1959–1964. Press clipping of the *Belfast Evening Telegraph*, January 14, 1959. The newspaper carried a summary of eight letters it had received both for and against the programme.

45 *Belfast Telegraph*, January 13, 1959

46 PRONI, Cab/41080, minutes of Cabinet Meeting, January 14, 1959.

47 PRONI, Cab 9F/165/12/2, memorandum from McKee to the government.

48 Ibid.

49 PRONI, Cab 4/1081, 3

50 Ibid., 4

51 BBC Written Archives, Caversham, R34/1.627/1 policy [É]ire, 1949–1976, document from the Director-General titled, *Northern Ireland and [É]ire*, October 20, 1959. This directive replaced an earlier version that addressed radio programming issued July 26, 1949. This stipulated that the controller in Northern Ireland be consulted about any programmes developed by the BBC concerning Éire. Added emphasis.

52 Cathcart, *Most Contrary Region*, 193.

53 PRONI, Cab 9F/165/11, Brookeborough to Chichester, December 3, 1957.

54 Ibid., Ewart Northwoll to Eric Mongomery, Press Officer Stormont, August 22, 1955.

55 Ibid., Brookeborough to Stewart, February 4, 1957.

56 John Horgan, *Irish Media: A Critical History since 1922* (Routledge, London, 2001), 23.

57 PRONI Cab 9F/165/11, Cunningham to Brookeborough, October 8, 1958.

58 Ibid., Gransden to Kelly, November 26, 1957.

59 Ibid.

60 PRONI Cab 9F/165/11, Government memorandum from O'Neill, September 9, 1959.

61 Brumwell Henderson, *Brum – A Television Life* (Appletree Press,

Belfast, 2003), 50.

62 Horgan, *Irish Media*, 23. During the War of Independence, the paper ran an editorial that declared, 'It is the bigotry of the [Catholic Church], and its constant efforts, open and secret, to increase its power, which have brought a large part of Ireland to the lawlessness which is disgracing it today.'

63 Henderson, *Brum – A Television Life*, 51.

64 PRONI, Cab 4/1094, Conclusions of a Cabinet meeting, June 10, 1959.

65 Ibid.

66 Ibid.

67 Ibid.

68 Cathcart, *Most Contrary Region*, 186–7.

69 Henderson, *Brum – A Television Life*, 66.

70 Ibid., 69

71 See Savage, *Irish Television*, Chapter 6.

72 Ibid., Chapter 1.

73 PRONI, Miscellaneous Cabinet papers, letter from L. C. Green, Home Office, Whitehall to Stormont Cabinet Secretary, A. J. Kelly, January 27, 1959. (CIM.812/1/13)

74 Ibid.

75 See Savage, *Irish Television*, 134–5.

76 PRONI, Miscellaneous Cabinet papers, letter from L. C. Green, Home Office, Whitehall to Stormont Cabinet Secretary, A. J. Kelly, January 27, 1959. (CIM.812/1/13)

77 Ibid.

78 Ibid.

79 Ibid.

80 Ibid.

81 Ibid. Ironically, when it came to overspill of British programming into the Irish Republic, there was some debate within the Home Office and the ITA if it should be measured and quantified for commercial purposes. After some discussion it was agreed not to take into commercial account viewers in the Irish Republic. The Home Office's advice was accepted, stipulating that 'nothing should, at this stage, be said to the republic to make them aware that we were at all sensitive on this question. In other words we should keep our own hands clean, thus putting ourselves in a good position to make a protest should the television authority in the republic make any unilateral claims for cross-border audience.'

82 Ibid. Extracts from Cabinet Conclusions, May 4, 1960.

83 Ibid.

84 Ibid.

85 Ibid., Kelly to R. F. Green, Ministry of Health and Local Government,

June 30, 1960.

86 Ibid., Green to Kelly, July 6, 1960.

87 Ibid., de Jong to Dunbar, July 21, 1960.

88 PRONI, Cab/4/1188/7, Memorandum from the Secretary of the Government, February 19, 1962.

89 PRONI, Cab 4/1188/10, Cabinet Minutes, February 22, 1962.

90 PRONI, Cabinet Memorandum by H. Black, April 27, 1965.

91 Ibid.

92 National Archive of Ireland (NAI), 2001/78/17, *Report of the Committee to Consider the Question of Getting RTÉ Television Signals into the Six Counties*, July, 3, 1970, 2.

93 NAI, 2001/78/27, *Sunday Independent*, October 30, 1960, 4.

94 NAI, 2001/78/16, the *Sunday Independent* article forced the Department of Posts and Telegraphs to consider how these questions might be answered. In November 1960 the answer was simply that the government had not taken a decision to prevent the transmission of television signals to Northern Ireland.

95 See Savage, *Irish Television*, 135.

96 NAI, Department of the Taoiseach, S14996 E/61. Letter to Seán Lemass from the Secretary of the Ulster Branch of the GAA, March 9, 1961.

97 Ibid., *Irish Times*, April 3, 1961.

98 Ibid., transcript of the meeting May 19, 1961.

99 Ibid., Lemass to Minister for Posts and Telegraphs Michael Hilliard, April 14, 1961.

100 Ibid., Hilliard to Lemass, April 20, 1961.

101 Ibid.

102 NAI, 2001/78/16, Lemass to McAteer, April 20, 1961.

103 NAI, 2001/78/77, Letter from Patrick McGill, Nationalist Parliamentary Party Secretary to Kevin McCourt, January 22, 1964.

104 Ibid.

105 Ibid., McCourt to McGill, Nationalist Parliamentry Party, February 24, 1964.

106 Ibid.

107 NAI, 2001/78/17, *Report of the Committee to Consider the Question of Getting RTE Television Signals into the Six Counties*, July 3, 1970, 2. It was pointed out that the earliest a station could become operational was 1974. As has been noted in Chapter 1 the research completed by the Irish Department of Posts and Telegraphs estimated that in 1957 approximately 40 per cent of the Irish population could recive television broadcasts from transmitters in Northern Ireland.

108 Ibid., 5.

109 NAI, 2003/16/436, Department of the Taoiseach Memorandum,

June, 13, 1972.

110 Ibid.

111 Ibid.

112 Ibid.

113 Ibid.

114 Ibid.

115 Ibid., 2

116 PRONI, Cab 9F/165/12/2, *Sunday Independent*, article by James Kelly, January 26, 1964, 5.

117 Ibid.

118 Ibid. *Belfast Telegraph* article by Robin Walsh.

119 Ibid.

120 PRONI, Cab/9F/165/12/2, supplementary memorandum prepared for the Prime Minister. This document was prepared for O'Neill who was asked about the government's suppression of the *Tonight* programmes in the Northern Ireland House of Commons January 29, 1964. (*Northern Ireland Hansard* vol. 56, no. 5, January 29, 1964).

121 Hill, *Cinema and Northern Ireland*, 156–9.

122 BBC Written Archives, Caversham, T16/222/3 TV Policy, Television Development Northern Ireland file 3, 1960–1967, McCall, Controller BBC Northern Ireland to BBC director-general, January 13, 1964.

123 Currie, Austin, *All Hell Will Break Loose* (O'Brien Press, Dublin, 2004), 98.

124 Ibid.

125 PRONI, Cab/4/1406, memorandum by the Prime Minister, October 14, 1968.

126 Jonathan Bardon, *Beyond the Studio: A History of BBC Northern Ireland* (Blackstaff Press, Belfast, 2000), 29.

127 Neil Hickey, 'The Battle for Northern Ireland: How TV Tips The Balance', *TV Guide*, September 26, 1981. The article is quoted from an unpublished paper presented to the American Conference for Irish Studies, Dublin, 1987 by K. Michelle Howard, Kassian A. Kovalcheck, and Joseph and Beverly O'Rourke. Hickey was writing during the 1981 hunger strikes looking back to American media coverage of Northern Ireland since 1968.

128 PRONI, Cab/4/1406, memorandum by the Prime Minister, October 14, 1968. (B.I.S. is the British Information Service).

129 Cathcart, *Most Contrary Region*, 166

130 PRONI, Cab/4/1406, memorandum by the Prime Minister, October 14, 1968.

131 Ibid.

132 Ibid. Conclusions of a Meeting of the Cabinet Held at Stormont Castle, October 14, 1968. The funding of the Roman Catholic Mater

Hospital remained a contentious issue as it was denied state funding by Stormont. See Marianne Elliott, *The Catholics of Ulster* (Penguin Press, London, 2000), 407.

133 PRONI, Cab/4/1417, Cabinet Conclusions, November 19, 1968.

134 Ibid.

135 Terence O'Neill, *Ulster at the Crossroads* (Faber and Faber, London, 1969), 140–6. For an informed account of O'Neill's tenure as Prime Minister of Northern Ireland, see Marc Mulholland, *Northern Ireland at the Crossroads, Ulster Unionism in the O'Neill Years* (Basingstoke, London, 2000).

136 Bardon, *Beyond the Studio*, 29–30.

137 Andrew Wilson, *Irish America and the Ulster Conflict 1968–1995* (Catholic University Press, Washington D.C., 1995), 21.

138 Ibid.

139 Joseph Lee, *Ireland 1912–1985, Politics and Society* (Cambridge University Press, Cambridge, 1989), 424.

140 Wilson, *Irish America and the Ulster Conflict 1968–1995*, 20.

141 BBC Written Archives, Caversham, R108/37, Northern Ireland-policy Guidance 1969–1973, notice from Charles Curran, April 25, 1969.

142 Ibid.

143 PRONI, Cab/4/1457.

144 Ibid.

145 Cathcart, *Most Contrary Region*, 211.

146 Ibid., 210.

147 Ibid.

148 Ibid.

149 PRONI, Cab/4/1462, Cabinet meeting August 16, 1969.

150 PRONI, Cab/9F/165/12/2, Lord Dunleath to Chichester-Clark, September 5, 1969.

151 Ibid.

152 Ibid.

153 Ibid.

154 Ibid., Chichester-Clark to Dunleath, September 8, 1969.

155 Ibid.

156 Ibid., Dunleath to O'Neill, September 16, 1969.

157 Ibid., Transcription of BBC News, Wednesday, February 17, 1971.

158 Ibid.

159 Ibid., press release from the Joint Security Committee, February 18, 1971.

160 Ibid., Roberts to Brook, February 10, 1971.

161 Ibid.

162 Ibid.

163 Ibid.

164 Before he was replaced, the BBC current affairs programme *Twenty-Four Hours* filmed a programme predicting his demise. This programme was not broadcast due to the protests of Maguire. See Cathcart, *Most Contrary Region*, 218–19.

165 PRONI, CAB/4/1609 Cabinet Meeting, August 17, 1971.

166 Ibid.

167 Ibid.

168 J. Boyer Bell, *The Irish Troubles: A Generation of Violence 1967–1992* (St Martin's Press, New York, 1993), 222.

169 PRONI, CAB/4/1609 Cabinet Meeting, August 17, 1971.

170 Paul Bew, *Ireland, the Politics of Enmity, 1789–2006* (Oxford University Press, Oxford, 2007), 503.

171 Ibid.

172 Harold Wilson and the Labour Party were defeated in national elections held June 18, 1970, and a Conservative government headed by Edward Heath came to power. The policy shift of Labour took place in November 1971.

173 PRONI, Cab/9F/165/12/2, transcript of *Twenty-Four Hours*, interview with Harold Wilson, November 25, 1971.

174 Ibid., press release from the Northern Ireland Information Service, December 3, 1971.

175 Stormont was prorogued and direct rule introduced in March 1972, a short time after 'Bloody Sunday' when British soldiers shot and killed thirteen civil rights demonstrators in Derry.

176 The incident is addressed in David McKittrick, Seamus Kelters, Brian Feeney and Chris Thornton, *Lost Lives: The Stories of the Men, Women and Children who Died as a Result of the Northern Ireland Troubles* (Mainstream Publishing Company, 1999, Edinburgh), 107–8.

177 Cathcart, *Most Contrary Region, 224*

178 *Radharc* made a film about Derry in 1965 that was held back by RTÉ during a thaw in relations between Dublin and Belfast at the time of the Lemass–O'Neill meetings.

179 Author's interview with Lelia Doolan, November 20, 2008, Dublin. The *7 Days* programme was made in July 1968.

180 See Rex Cathcart with Michael Muldoon, 'The Mass Media in Twentieth-century Ireland', in *New History of Ireland, Vol. VII, Ireland 1921–1984* (ed) J. R. Hill (Oxford University Press, Oxford, 2004), 704.

181 For a disturbing but compelling account of reporting on the violence in the early years of 'the Troubles' see Kevin Myers, *Watching the Door, A Memoir 1971–1978* (Lilliput Press, Dublin, 2006).

182 RTÉ Authority Archives, Minutes of the Authority, 'Note of a meeting with An Taoiseach on Wednesday, 6 August 1969', submitted to the

RTÉ Authority by Thomas Hardiman.

183 Ibid.

184 Ibid., meeting between Lynch and editors of the national dailies, head of news and director-general, September 4, 1969, submitted to the RTÉ Authority by Thomas Hardiman.

185 Ibid. Lynch believed that the arrival of troops in the province and recent visit by Home Secretary James Callaghan signalled that the constitutional position of the Northern Ireland government had changed and that the Irish government should respond, although he admitted that if pressed to explain about what interim steps might be taken 'he could not do so'.

186 RTÉ Authority Archive, Minutes of the Authority, September 13, 1961. The Radio Éireann Authority had decided, after taking advice from the Lemass Government in August 1961, not to allow Sinn Féin to partake in political broadcasts when running for office in the Irish Republic. This was of course not Provisional Sinn Féin but nevertheless the party was informed 'that Radio Éireann could not entertain its request for inclusion in broadcasts, as the elected representatives of Sinn Féin had not taken their seats in the sixteenth Dáil, and that Radio Éireann had no evidence that Sinn Féin recognises and accepts the authority of the Oireachtas, under which Radio Éireann itself functions'.

187 NAI, 203/16/278, Memorandum for the government from the Minister of Posts and Telegraphs, November 24, 1972.

188 Ibid.

189 Ibid.

190 McKittrick et al., *Lost Lives*, 103.

191 RTÉ Authority Archives, Ó Moráin to Collins, October 15, 1971.

192 Ibid.

193 NAI, 203/16/278, Memorandum for the government from the Minister of Posts and Telegraphs, November 24, 1972.

194 RTÉ Authority Archive, 13 June 1972, L'Estrange speech, 1. The deputy's speech was copied for senior members of RTÉ, and a detailed rebuttal was written to dispute the allegations made by L'Estrange.

195 Ibid., 8.

196 NAI, 203/16/278, Memorandum for the Government, November 21, 1972, submitted by Posts and Telegraphs, Annex D. Script of broadcast, Sunday, November 19, 1972.

197 RTÉ Written Archives, John Irvine papers, Collins to Ó Moráin, November 21, 1972.

198 RTÉ Authority Archives, Ó Moráin to Collins, 22 November 1972.

199 NAI 203/16/278, Memorandum for the government, 24 November 1972.

200 Ibid. This file contains the decision of the government on 24 November

1972 to remove the existing members of the RTÉ Authority and appoint seven new members, chaired by Joseph Scanell.

201 RTÉ Written Archives, John Irvine papers, Statement of Dónal Ó Moráin, November 24, 1972.

202 Ibid.

203 *Irish Broadcasting Review*, 10, Spring 1981, 19.

204 *Irish Times*, November 27, 1972, quoted in Kieran Woodman, *Media Control in Ireland 1923–1983* (Southern Illinois University Press, Carbondale, IL, 1985), 180.

205 *Irish Broadcasting Review*, 10, Spring 1981, 19.

206 T. Ryle Dwyer, *Nice Fellow: A Biography of Jack Lynch* (Mercier Press,Cork, 2001), 295.

Conclusion

Television was a critical component in the transformation that altered Irish society throughout the 1960s and into the 1970s. During this period television was *not* a passive actor, but an active agent often aggressively testing the limits of the medium and the patience of governments. Indeed television not only presented news but often created news and controversy.

In Northern Ireland the relative tranquility of the 1960s was shattered by the outbreak of political violence at the end of the decade. Although broadcasters in Dublin and London had made forays into Northern Ireland, most paid little attention to the province. This changed dramatically in 1968 with the beginning of the campaign for civil rights as protesters succeeded in using television to take their case for reform outside the province to a wider and more sympathetic audience. Many protesters were strongly influenced by the tactics, strategies and rhetoric of the American civil rights campaign, which came to their homes via television news. Cameras from London and Dublin chronicled growing protest by addressing in simple yet dramatic terms the inequality that had long been part of life in the province. Images of young men and women marching while chanting 'one man one vote' and singing 'we shall overcome' resonated with international audiences.

Subsequent television coverage of police misconduct transmitted worldwide played a direct role in undermining the authority, and ultimately the legitimacy of the northern state. As unrest and violence spread throughout the province television chronicled Northern Ireland's harrowing descent into decades of turmoil and violence. RTÉ, BBC and ITA reporting of the crisis proved tremendously controversial throughout the long years of 'the Troubles'. The social, political, and cultural implications of this coverage and, critically, its management remain a tremendously complex subject. War, censorship and the politics of shaping or 'spinning' news and information remains a critical part of contemporary life as relevant today as during the period covered by this book.

In the Irish Republic some viewers had already been able to receive British programmes before Telefís Éireann went on the air on New Year's Eve 1961. However by 1972 television was ubiquitous, the vast majority of citizens had access to television and a wide range of domestic and foreign programming. Throughout this period the ranks of the new television service were filled with young, ambitious, university-educated men and women who were determined to use the medium to hold institutions accountable. Many were idealists hoping to exploit the public service remit of Irish television to pose difficult questions about the past and present in an effort to improve the future. As the decade progressed viewers were exposed to increasingly sophisticated indigenous broadcasts providing greater access to information concerning social, political and cultural issues. This enhanced a growing sense of openness in Irish society and a gradual trend towards secularisation as the medium began to undermine the influence of the government, churches and a host of cultural and political organisations.

That television in the Irish Republic was established as a hybrid, a commercial public service; that is, expected to pay its own way while informing, educating and entertaining viewers – profoundly affected its development throughout the 1960s and into the 1970s. This is critical to understanding the dilemma that confronted RTÉ. From the outset, officials responsible for broadcasting understood that the new television and radio service had to sustain itself financially if it was to remain free of direct government control. This burden compromised the medium's public service role, and was a tremendous source of frustration to many who wanted to use the medium to inform, educate and entertain viewers. This anxiety continues to challenge RTÉ today, undermining its efforts as a national public service broadcaster.

Bibliography

Archives and libraries

BBC Written Archives, Caversham
Boston College, O'Neill Library
Cashel Diocesan Archives
Dublin Diocesan Archives
Galway Diocesan Archives
National Archives of Ireland
National Library of Ireland, Manuscripts Collection
Public Record Office, Belfast
Public Records Office, Kew
Representative Church Body Archive, Dublin
RTÉ Authority Archives
RTÉ Library
RTÉ Stills Library
RTÉ Written Archives
Trinity College Dublin Archives
University College Dublin Archives
University of Notre Dame Archives
University of Texas, Austin Archives
University of Wisconsin Archives

Publications

Adams, Michael, *Censorship: The Irish Experience* (University of Alabama Press, Tuscaloosa, AL, 1968).
Andrews, C. S., *Man of No Property* (Lilliput Press, Dublin, 2001).
Arnold, Bruce, *Jack Lynch, Hero in Crisis* (Merlin, Dublin, 2001).
Barton, Ruth (ed.), *Screening Irish-America: Representing Irish-America in Film and Television* (Irish Academic Press, Dublin, 2009).

Bell, J. Boyer, *The Irish Troubles: A Generation of Violence 1967–1992* (St Martin's Press, New York, 1993).

Bew, Paul, *Ireland: The Politics of Enmity, 1789–2006* (Oxford University Press, Oxford, 2007).

Bew, Paul and Henry Patterson, *Sean Lemass and the Making of Modern Ireland* (Gill and Macmillan, Dublin, 1982).

Bloomfield, Ken, *Stormont in Crisis: A Memoir* (The Blackstaff Press, Belfast, 1994).

Brown, Terence, *Ireland: A Social and Cultural History, 1922 to the Present* (Cornell University Press, Ithaca, NY, 1985).

Browne, Vincent (ed.), *Magill Book of Irish Politics* (Magill Publications, Dublin, 1981).

Bunreacht na hÉireann, Constitution of Ireland (Stationery Office, Dublin, 2003).

Byrne, Gay with Deirdre Purcell, *The Time of My Life* (Gill and Macmillan, Dublin, 1989).

Carty, Francis Xavier, *Hold Firm: John Charles McQuaid and the Second Vatican Council* (Columba Press, Dublin, 2007).

Cathcart, Rex, *The Most Contrary Region: The BBC in Northern Ireland 1924–1984* (Blackstaff Press, Belfast, 1984).

Cathcart, Rex with Michael Muldoon, 'The Mass Media in twentieth-century Ireland', in *New History of Ireland, Vol. VII, Ireland 1921–1984* (ed.) J. R. Hill (Oxford University Press, Oxford, 2004).

Chubb, Basil, *The Government and Politics of Ireland* (Longman, New York, 1992).

Connolly, Linda, *The Irish Women's Movement: From Revolution to Devolution* (Macmillan, Basingstoke, 2002).

Connolly, Sean, *The Oxford Companion to Irish History* (Oxford University Press, Oxford, 1998).

Cooney, John, *John Charles McQuaid, Ruler of Catholic Ireland: The Man and the Mask* (O'Brien Press, Dublin, 1999).

Corcoran, Mary and Mark O'Brien (eds), *Political Censorship and the Democratic State: The Irish Broadcasting Ban* (Four Courts Press, Dublin, 2005).

Crowley, Tony, *War of Words: The Politics of Language 1537–2004* (Oxford University Press, Oxford, 2004).

Currie, Austin, *All Hell Will Break Loose* (O'Brien Press, Dublin, 2004).

Curtis, Liz, *Ireland and the Propaganda War* (Pluto Press, London, 1984).

Daley, Mary and Margaret O'Callaghan, *1916 in 1966: Commemorating the Easter Rising* (Royal Irish Academy, Dublin, 2007).

Delaney, Enda, 'Emigration, Political Culture, and Post-war Irish Society', in *The Lemass Era, Politics and Society in the Ireland of Sean Lemass* (eds) Brian Girvin and Gary Murphy (University College Dublin Press,

Dublin, 2005).

Delap, Breandán, 'Irish and the Media', in *A New View of the Irish Language* (eds) Caoilfhionn Nic Pháidín and Sean Ó Cearnaigh (Cois Life, Dublin, 2008).

Devlin, Paddy, *Straight Left: An Autobiography* (Blackstaff Press, Belfast, 1993).

Doolan, Lelia, Jack Dowling and Bob Jack Quinn, *Sit Down and Be Counted: The Cultural Evolution of a Television Station* (Dublin, Wellington Publishers, 1969).

Doyle, John, *A Great Feast of Light: Growing Up Irish in the Television Age* (Aurum Press, London, 2005).

Dunn, Joseph, *No Tigers in Africa* (Columba Press, Dublin, 1986).

—— *No Lions in the Hierarchy* (Columba Press, Dublin, 1994).

—— *No Vipers in the Vatican* (Columba Press, Dublin, 1996).

Dwyer, T. Ryle, *Nice Fellow: A Biography of Jack Lynch* (Mercier Press, Cork, 2001).

Earls, Maurice, 'The Late Late Show, Controversy and Context in Television and Irish Society', in *21 Years of Irish Television* (eds) Martin McLoone and John MacMahon (Irish Film Institute, Dublin 1984).

Elliott, Marianne, *The Catholics of Ulster* (Penguin Press, London, 2000).

English, Richard, *Armed Struggle: The History of the IRA* (Oxford University Press, Oxford, 2003).

Fallon, Brian, *An Age of Innocence: Irish Culture 1930–1960* (Gill and Macmillan, Dublin, 1998).

Fanning, Ronan, *Independent Ireland* (Helicon, Dublin, 1983).

Ferriter, Diarmaid, *The Transformation of Ireland, 1900–2000* (Profile Books, London, 2004).

—— *Judging Dev* (Royal Irish Academy, Dublin, 2008).

Fisher, Desmond, *Broadcasting in Ireland* (Routledge and Kegan Paul, London, 1978).

FitzGerald, Garret, *All in a Life: An Autobiography* (Gill and Macmillan, Dublin, 1991).

Foster, R.F., *Modern Ireland 1600–1972* (Penguin, New York, 1988).

—— *Luck and the Irish: A Brief History of Change from 1970* (Oxford University Press, Oxford, 2008).

Fuller, Louise, *Irish Catholicism since 1950: The Undoing of a Culture* (Gill and Macmillan, Dublin, 2002).

Garvin, Tom, *Preventing the Future: Why was Ireland so Poor for so Long?* (Gill and Macmillan, Dublin, 2004).

—— *Judging Lemass: The Measure of the Man* (Royal Irish Academy, Dublin, 2009).

Gibbons, Luke, *Transformations in Irish Culture* (Cork University Press, Cork, 1996).

Girvin, Brian, *From Union to Union: Nationalism, Democracy and Religion in Ireland* (Gill and Macmillan, Dublin, 2002).

Girvin, Brian and Gary Murphy (eds), *The Lemass Era: Politics and Society in the Ireland of Sean Lemass* (University College Dublin Press, Dublin, 2005).

Goan, Cathal, 'Teilifís na Gaeilge: Ten Years A-Growing', in *New Hibernia Review*, 11:2 (2007).

Gorham, Maurice, *Forty Years of Irish Broadcasting* (Talbot Press, Dublin, 1967).

Harmon, Maurice, *Sean O'Faolain: A Life* (Constable, London, 1994).

Henderson, Brumwell, *Brum – A Television Life* (Appletree Press, Belfast, 2003).

Hickey, Neil, 'The Battle for Northern Ireland : How TV Tips The Balance', *TV Guide*, September 26, 1981.

Higgins, Roisín, '"I am the narrator over-and-above- … The Caller of the Dead": Pageant and Drama in 1916', in *1916 in 1966 Commemorating the Easter Rising* (eds) Mary Daly and Margaret Callaghan (Royal Irish Academy, Dublin, 2007).

Hill, John, *Cinema and Northern Ireland* (British Film Institute, London, 2006).

Hill, Myrtle, *Women in Ireland: A Century of Change* (Blackstaff Press, Belfast, 2003).

Horgan, John, *Sean Lemass: The Enigmatic Patriot* (Gill and Macmillan, Dublin, 1997).

—— *Irish Media: A Critical History* (Routledge, London, 2001).

—— *Broadcasting and Public Life* (Four Courts Press, Dublin, 2004).

Howard, Michelle, Kassian A. Kovalcheck, and Joseph and Beverly O'Rourke, 'Images of Ireland in Times of Crisis: US Television Evening News Coverage of Northern Ireland' (Unpublished paper presented to the American Conference for Irish Studies, Dublin, 1987).

Irwin, John, *My Time is My Own: An Irishman at the BBC* (Max Parrish and Co Ltd, London, 1955).

Jackson, Alvin, *Ireland 1798–1998* (Blackwell, Oxford, 1999).

Kelly, Adrian, *Compulsory Irish: Language and Education in Ireland 1870s–1970s* (Irish Academic Press, Dublin, 2002).

Kelly, Peter V. 'Africa in Radharc Documentaries 1966 to 1993' (Unpublished MA Film and Television Studies, Dublin City University, Dublin, 2004).

Kenny, Mary, *Goodbye to Catholic Ireland* (Sinclair-Stevenson, London, 1997).

Keogh, Dermot, *Jack Lynch: A Biography* (Gill and Macmillan, Dublin, 2008).

—— *Twentieth Century Ireland, Nation and State* (Gill and Macmillan, Dublin, 1994).

Kiberd, Declan, *Inventing Ireland: The Literature of the Modern Nation* (Jonathan Cape, London, 1995).

Lee, Joseph, *Ireland 1912–1985* (Cambridge University Press, Cambridge, 1989).

Lynch, Brian, 'Steering Clear: Broadcasting and the Church, 1926–1951', *New Hibernia Review*, 4:2 (Summer 2000).

Mac Con Iomaire, Liam, *Breandán Ó hEithir, Iomramh Aonair* (Cló Iar-Chonnachta, Indreabhán, Conamara, 2000).

McIntosh, Gillian, *The Force of Culture: Unionist Identities in Twentieth-Century Ireland* (Cork University Press, Cork, 1999).

McKittrick, David, Seamus Kellers, Brian Feeney and Chris Thornton, *Lost Lives, the Stories of the Men, Women and Children who Died as a Result of the Northern Ireland Troubles* (Mainstream Publishing Company, Edinburgh, 1999).

McLoone, Martin, 'The Construction of a Partitionist Mentality: Early Broadcasting in Ireland', in *Broadcasting in a Divided Community, Seventy Years of the BBC in Northern Ireland* (ed.) Martin McLoone (Institute of Irish Studies, Belfast, 1996).

—— *Film, Media and Popular Culture in Ireland* (Irish Academic Press, Dublin, 2008).

McLoone, Martin and John McMahon, *Television and Irish Society: 21 Years of Irish Television* (Radio Telefís Éireann, Dublin, 1984).

Mulholland, Marc, *Northern Ireland at the Crossroads: Ulster Unionism in the O'Neill Years*, 1960–9 (Macmillan, London, 2000).

Myers, Kevin, *Watching the Door: A Memoir 1971–1978* (Lilliput Press, Dublin, 2006).

Nic Shuibhne, Niamh, 'The Constitution, the Courts and the Irish Language', in *Ireland's Evolving Constitution 1937–1997* (eds) Tom Murphy and Patrick Twomey (Hart Publishing, Oxford, 1998).

O'Brien, Connor Cruise, *Memoir: My Life and Themes* (Cooper Square Press, New York, 2000).

O'Brien, Harvey, *The Real Ireland: The Evolution of Ireland in Documentary Film* (Manchester University Press, Manchester, 2004).

Ó Broin, León, *Just Like Yesterday* (Gill and Macmillan, Dublin, 1985).

Ó Dochartaigh, Niall, *From Civil Rights to Armalites: Derry and the Birth of the Irish Troubles* (Cork University Press, Cork, 1997).

O'Donnell, Kenneth P. and David Powers with Joe McCarthy, *'Johnny, We Hardly Knew Ye'* (Little, Brown & Company, Boston, 1970).

Ó Grianna, Séamus, *The Lights of Heaven* (ed.) Nollaig Mac Congáil (Galway, Arlen House, 2006).

O'Halpin, Eunan, *Defending Ireland: The Irish State and its Enemies since 1922* (Oxford University Press, Oxford, 1999).

O'Hehir, Michael, *My Life and Times* (Dublin, Blackwater Press, 1996).

O'Leary, Philip, *Gaelic Prose in the Irish Free State 1922–1939* (University College Dublin Press, Dublin, 2004).

—— *Writing Beyond the Revival: Facing the Future in Gaelic Prose 1940–1951* (University College Dublin Press, Dublin, forthcoming).

O'Neill, Terence, *Ulster at the Crossroads* (Faber and Faber, London, 1969).

Ó Murchú, Liam, A *Time to Love?* (Gill and Macmillan, Dublin, 1986).

Ó Raigáin, Pádraig, *Language Policy and Social Reproduction, Ireland 1893–1993* (Clarendon Press, Oxford, 1997).

Ó Tauthaigh, Gearóid, 'Language, Literature and Culture in Ireland Since the War', in *Ireland 1945–1970* (ed.) Joseph Lee (Gill and Macmillan, Dublin, 1979).

—— 'The State and the Language: An Historical Perspective', in *A New View of the Irish Language* (eds) Caoilfhionn Nic Pháidín and Seán Ó Cearnaigh (Cois Life, Dublin, 2008).

Parliamentary Debates, Dáil Éireann, Official Report' (Stationery Office, Dublin, 1919–).

Patterson, Henry, *Ireland Since 1939: The Persistence of Conflict* (Penguin, New York, 2007).

Pine, Richard, *2RN and the Origins of Irish Radio* (Four Courts Press, Dublin, 2002).

Pettitt, Lance, *Screening Ireland: Film and Television Representation* (Manchester University Press, Manchester, 2000).

Quinn, Bob, *Maverick: A Dissident View of Broadcasting Today* (Dingle, Brandon Books, 2001).

Rockett, Kevin, *Irish Film Censorship* (Four Courts Press, Dublin, 2004).

Rolston, Bill and David Miller (eds) *War and Words: The Northern Ireland Media Reader* (Beyond the Pale Publications, Belfast, 1996).

Rose, Peter, *How The Troubles Came to Northern Ireland* (Palgrave, London, 2000).

Savage, Robert J., *Irish Television: The Political and Social Origins* (Cork University Press, Cork, 1996).

—— *Sean Lemass* (Historical Association of Ireland, Dublin, 1999).

—— 'Constructing/deconstructing the image of Sean Lemass's Ireland', in *Ireland in the New Century, Politics, Culture and Identity* (ed.) Robert J. Savage (Four Courts Press, Dublin, 2003).

—— 'Introducing television in the Age of Sean Lemass', in *The Lemass Era, Politics and Society in the Ireland of Sean Lemass* (eds) Brian Girvin and Gary Murphy (University College Dublin Press, Dublin, 2005).

Thornley, Yseult, *Unquiet Spirit: Essays in Memory of David Thornley* (Liberties Press, Dublin, 2008).

Tobin, Fergal, *The Best of Decades* (Gill and Macmillan, Dublin, 1984).

Walsh, Dick, *The Party: Inside Fianna Fáil* (Gill and Macmillan, Dublin, 1986).

Watson, Iarfhlaith, *Broadcasting in Irish* (Four Courts Press, Dublin, 2003).

Whelan, Gerard with Carolyn Swift, *Spiked: Church–State Intrigue and the Rose Tattoo* (New Island, Dublin, 2002).

Whyte, J. H., *Church and State in Modern Ireland, 1923–1970* (Gill and Macmillan, Dublin, 1971).

Whicker, Alan, *Within Wicker's World* (Elm Tree Books, London, 1982).

Wilson, Andrew, *Irish America and the Ulster Conflict 1968–1995* (Catholic University Press, Washington D.C., 1995).

Woodman, Kieran, *Media Control in Ireland 1923–1983* (Southern Illinois University Press, Carbondale, IL, 1985)

Newspapers

Anderson Indiana Bulletin
Belfast Newsletter
Belfast Telegraph
Broadcasting
Catholic Herald
Church of Ireland Gazette
Cork Examiner
The Corkman
Daily Mail
Derry Journal
Evansville Indiana Courier
Evening Herald
Evening Mail
Evening Press
Galway Observer
Hibernia
Inniu
Irish Broadcasting Review
Irish Independent
Irish News
Irish Press
The Irish Tatler and Sketch
Irish Times
Limerick Leader
Northern Whig
Sunday Express
Sunday Independent
Sunday Press
Television Mail

Index

CPSIA information can be obtained
at www.ICGtesting.com
Printed in the USA
FFOW01n0518260116
20675FF